UQ HOLDER!

KEN AKAMATSU

vol.4

CHARACTERS

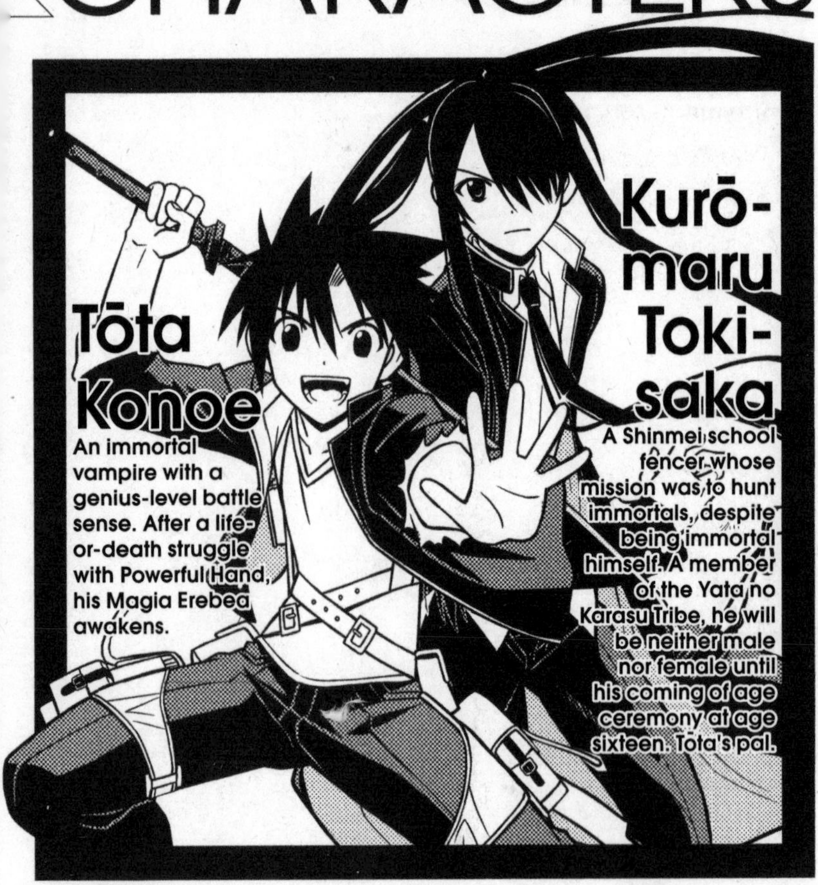
Tōta Konoe
An immortal vampire with a genius-level battle sense. After a life-or-death struggle with Powerful Hand, his Magia Erebea awakens.
Kurō-maru Toki-saka
A Shinmei school fencer whose mission was to hunt immortals, despite being immortal himself. A member of the Yata no Karasu Tribe, he will be neither male nor female until his coming of age ceremony at age sixteen. Tota's pal.

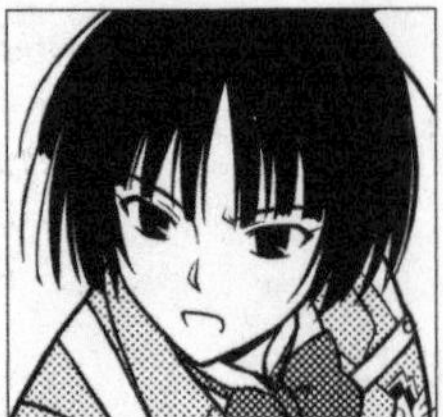

UQ HOLDER NO. 4

Karin

Cool-headed and ruthless. Her immortality is S-class. Also known as the Saintess of Steel.

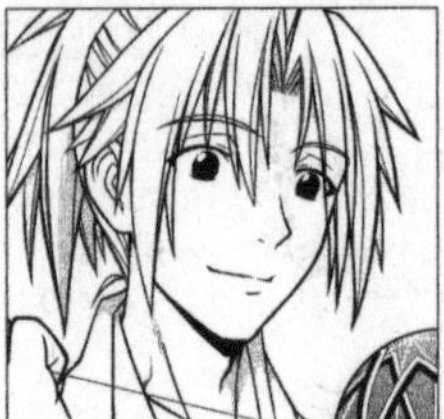

UQ HOLDER NO. 10

Ameya Ikkū

Very good with his hands.

UQ HOLDER!

■■■ Ken Akamatsu Presents

PMSCS
Private Military & Security Company "POWERFUL HAND"

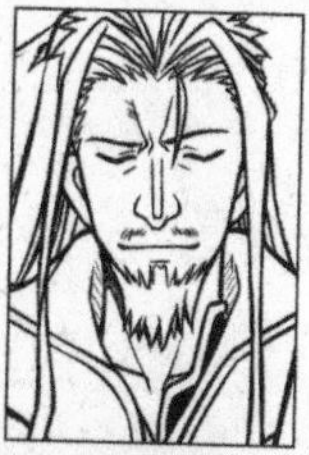

Nagumo
The blind immortal hunter.

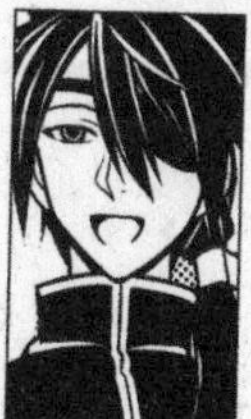

Chao Xinxâi
A wizard who manipulates shadow spirits. Attribute: super creeper. Defeated by Karin.

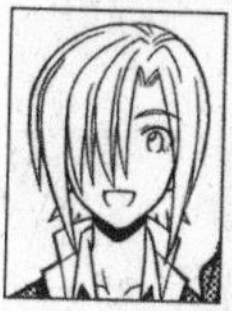

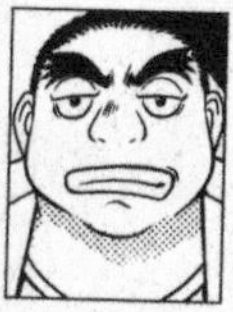

Tōta's pals from the countryside.

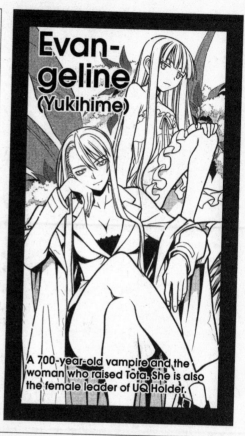

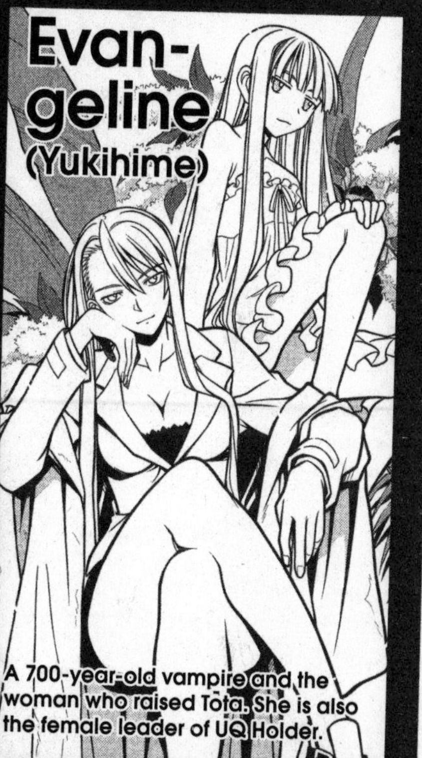
Evan-
geline
(Yukihime)
A 700-year-old vampire and the woman who raised Tōta. She is also the female leader of UQ Holder.

"UQ Holder Numbers"

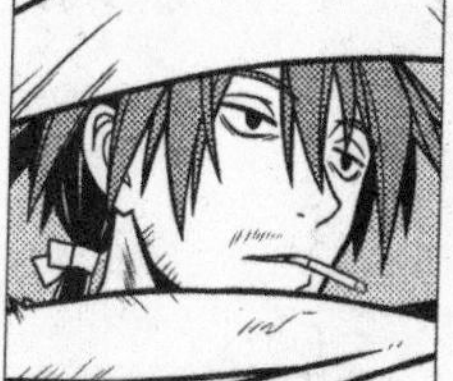

UQ HOLDER NO.2

Jinbei Shishido
Leader of UQ Holder. An immortal who has been alive for 1,400 years.

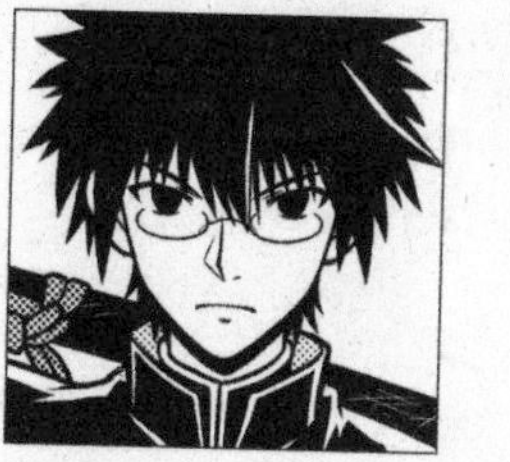

UQ HOLDER NO. 6

Gengorō Makabe
Runs the family.

THE STORY SO FAR

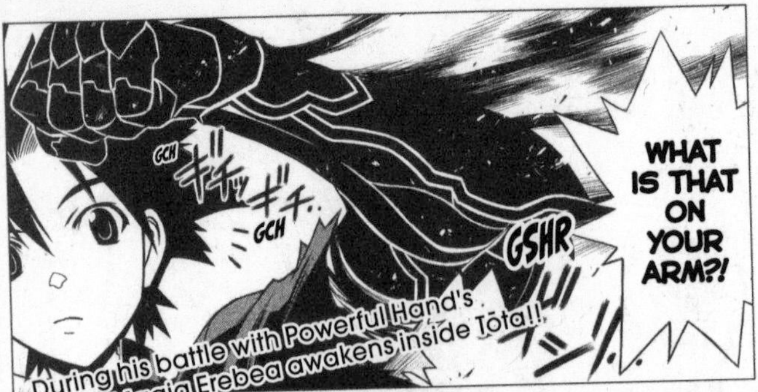
WHAT IS THAT ON YOUR ARM?!
GSHR
GCH
GCH
During his battle with Powerful Hand's Kaito, Magia Erebea awakens inside Tota!!

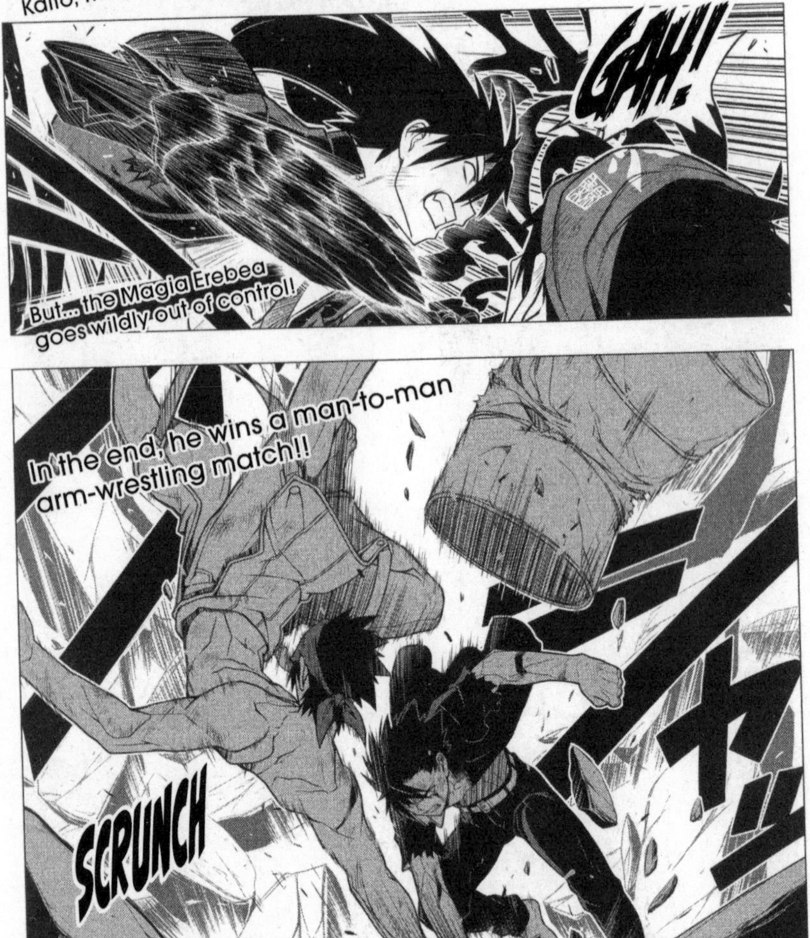
GAH!!
But... the Magia Erebea goes wildly out of control!!
In the end, he wins a man-to-man arm-wrestling match!!
SCRUNCH

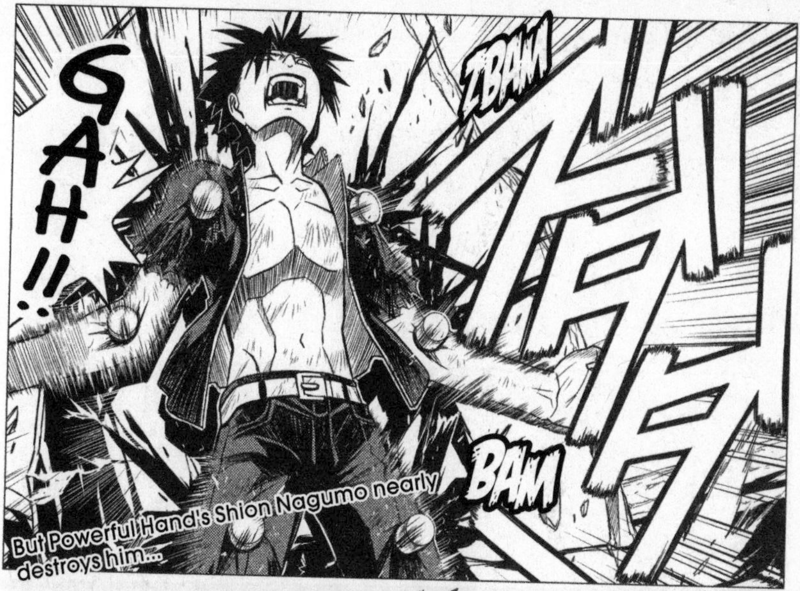
ZBAM
GAH!!!
BAM
But Powerful Hand's Shion Nagumo nearly destroys him...

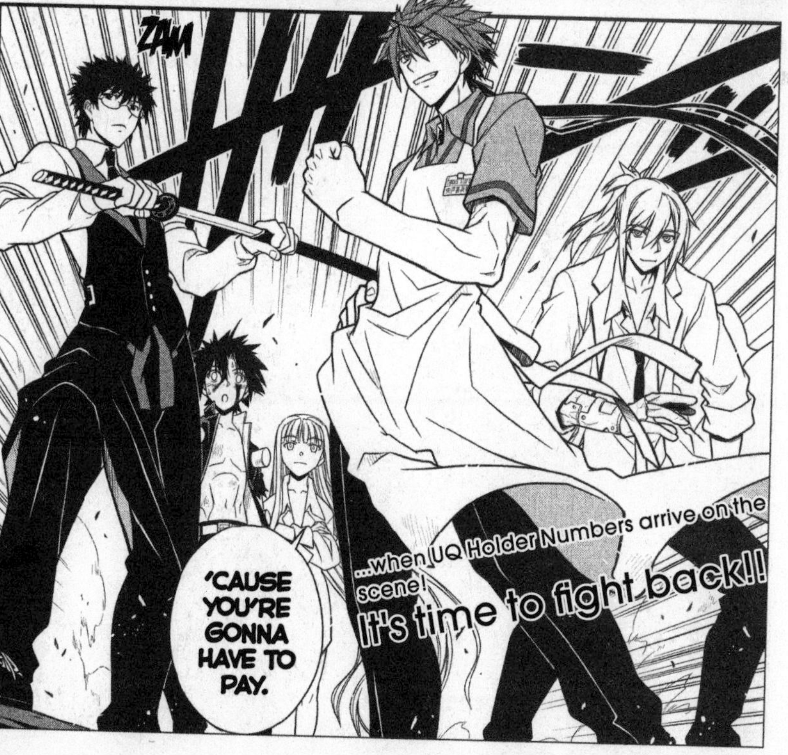
ZAM
...when UQ Holder Numbers arrive on the scene!
It's time to fight back!!
'CAUSE YOU'RE GONNA HAVE TO PAY.

CONTENTS

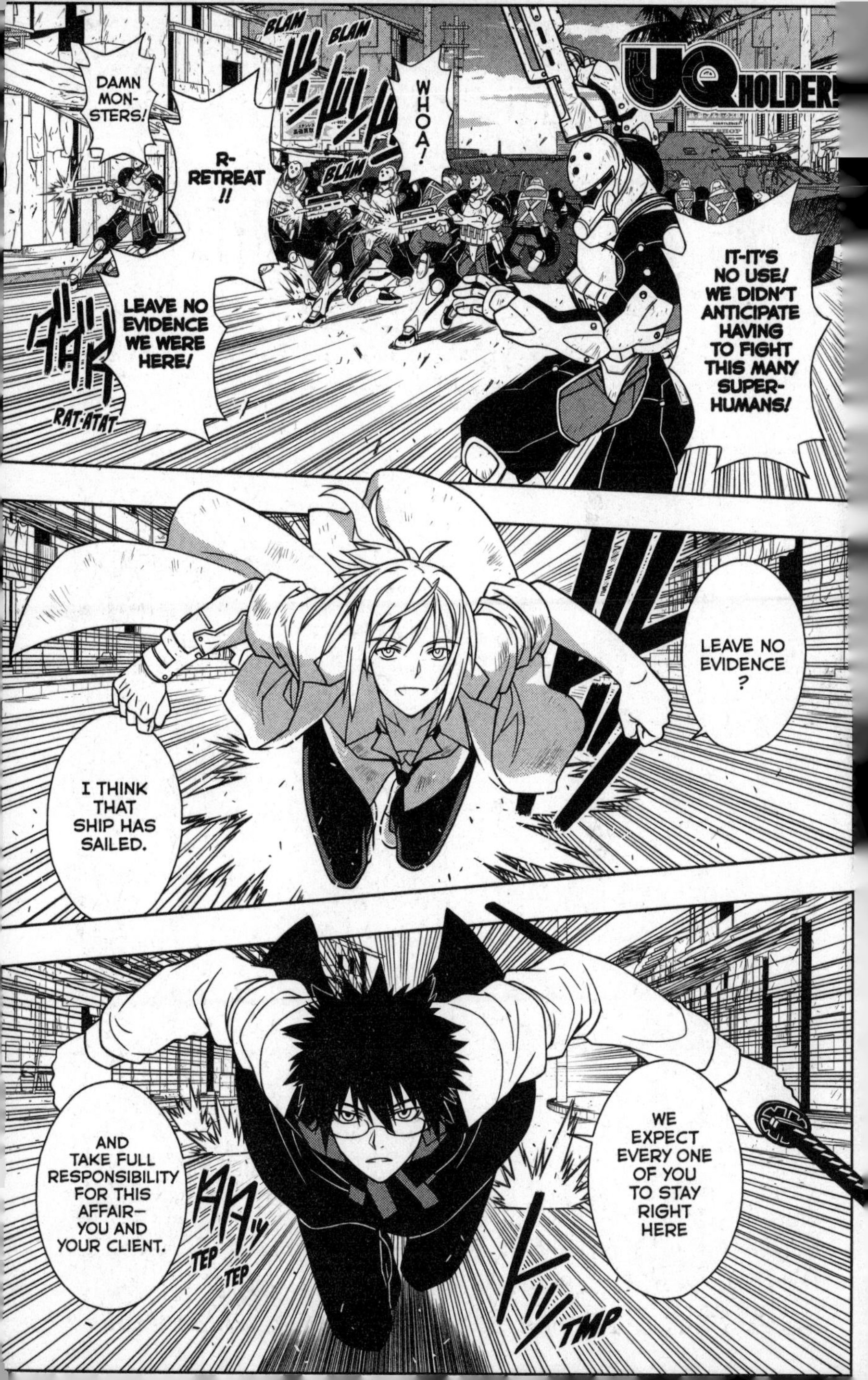
UQ HOLDER!
BLAM BLAM
WHOA!
BLAM
IT-IT'S NO USE! WE DIDN'T ANTICIPATE HAVING TO FIGHT THIS MANY SUPER-HUMANS!
R-RETREAT!!
DAMN MON-STERS!
LEAVE NO EVIDENCE WE WERE HERE!
RAT-ATAT
LEAVE NO EVIDENCE?
I THINK THAT SHIP HAS SAILED.
WE EXPECT EVERY ONE OF YOU TO STAY RIGHT HERE
TMP
AND TAKE FULL RESPONSIBILITY FOR THIS AFFAIR—YOU AND YOUR CLIENT.
TEP TEP

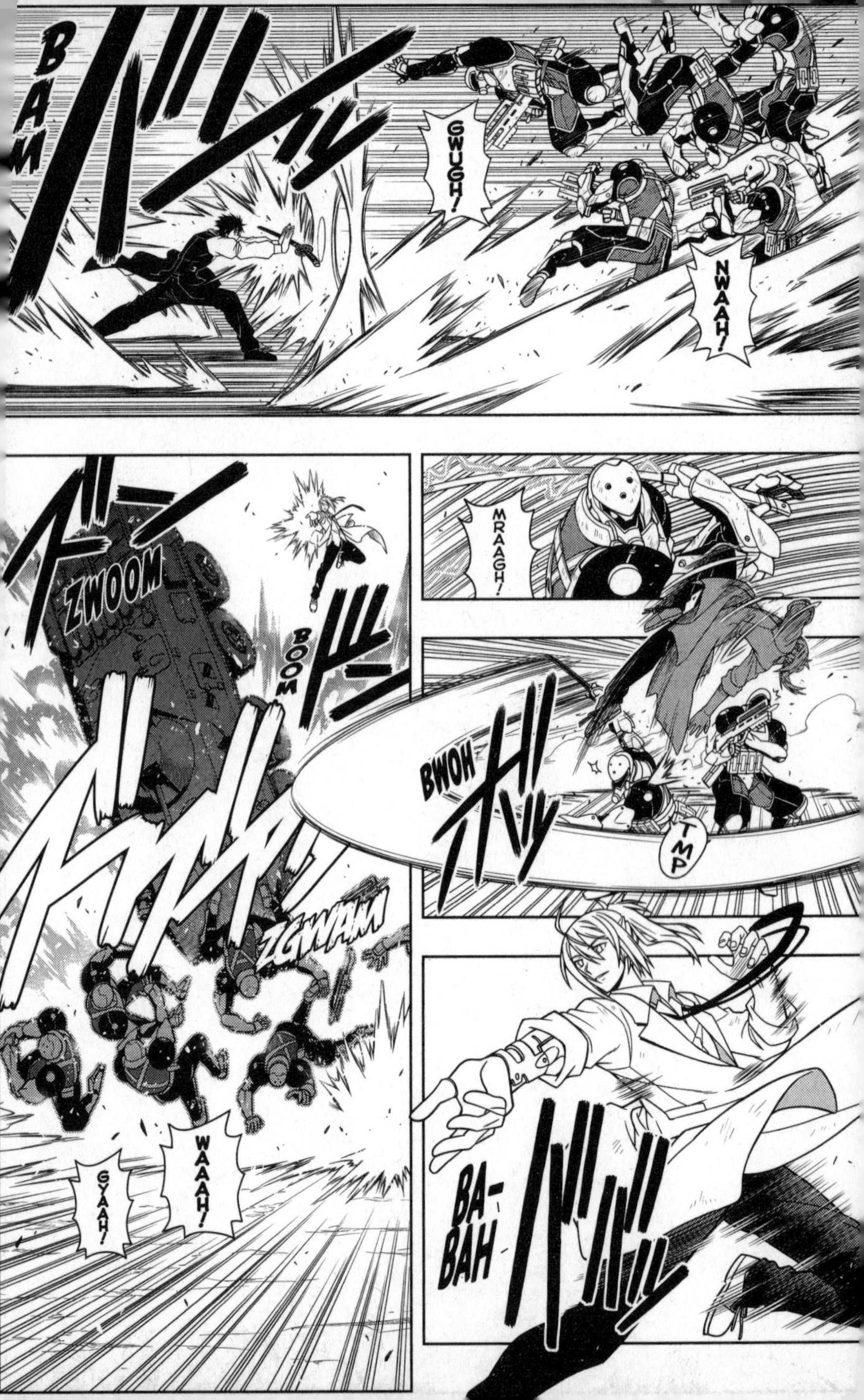
GWUGH!
NWAAH!
BAM
MRAAGH!
BWOH
TMP
BA-BAH
ZWOOM
BOOM
ZGWAM
WAAAH!
GYAAH!

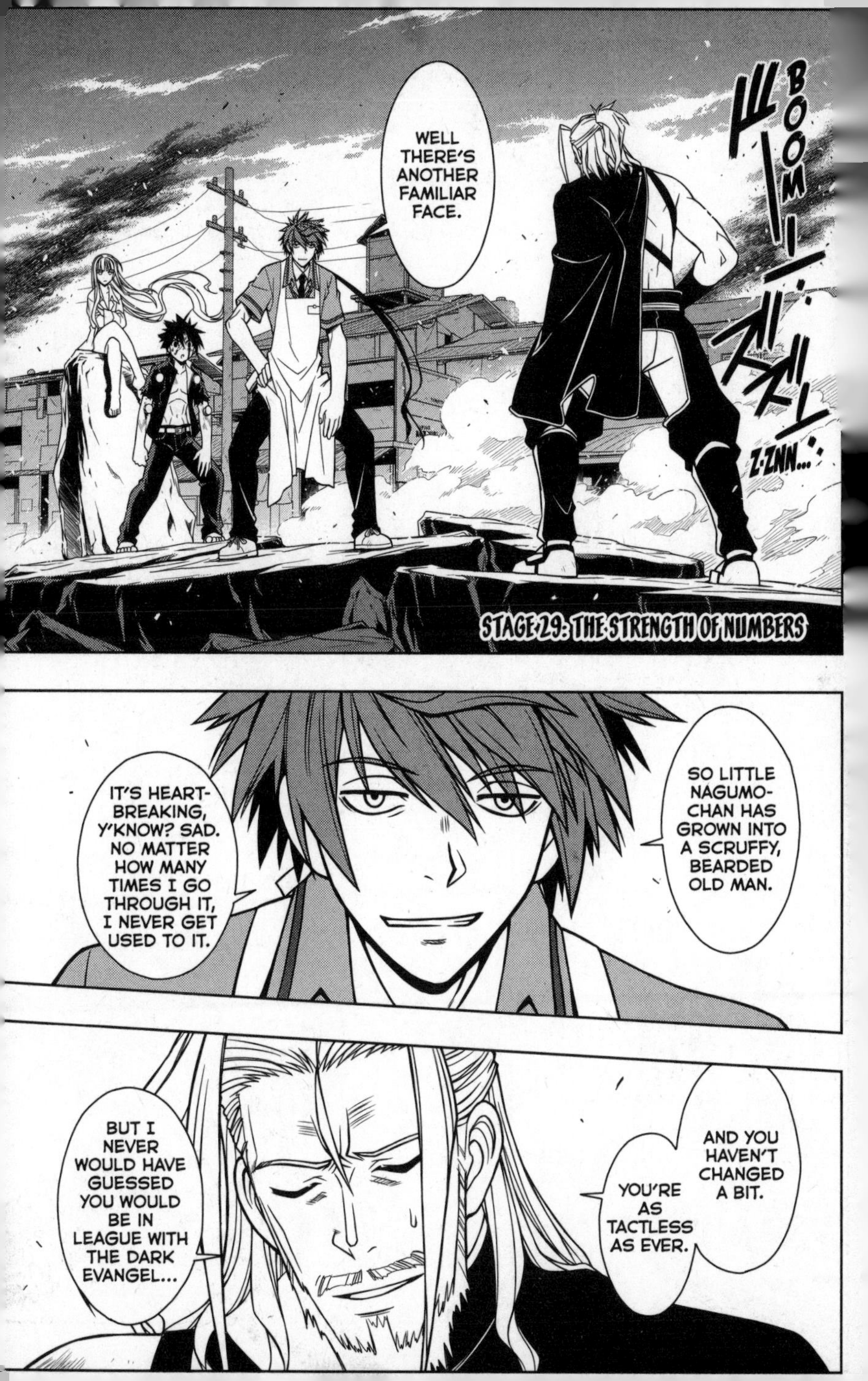
BOOM!
Z-ZNN...
WELL THERE'S ANOTHER FAMILIAR FACE.
STAGE 29: THE STRENGTH OF NUMBERS
SO LITTLE NAGUMO-CHAN HAS GROWN INTO A SCRUFFY, BEARDED OLD MAN.
IT'S HEART-BREAKING, Y'KNOW? SAD. NO MATTER HOW MANY TIMES I GO THROUGH IT, I NEVER GET USED TO IT.
AND YOU HAVEN'T CHANGED A BIT.
YOU'RE AS TACTLESS AS EVER.
BUT I NEVER WOULD HAVE GUESSED YOU WOULD BE IN LEAGUE WITH THE DARK EVANGEL...

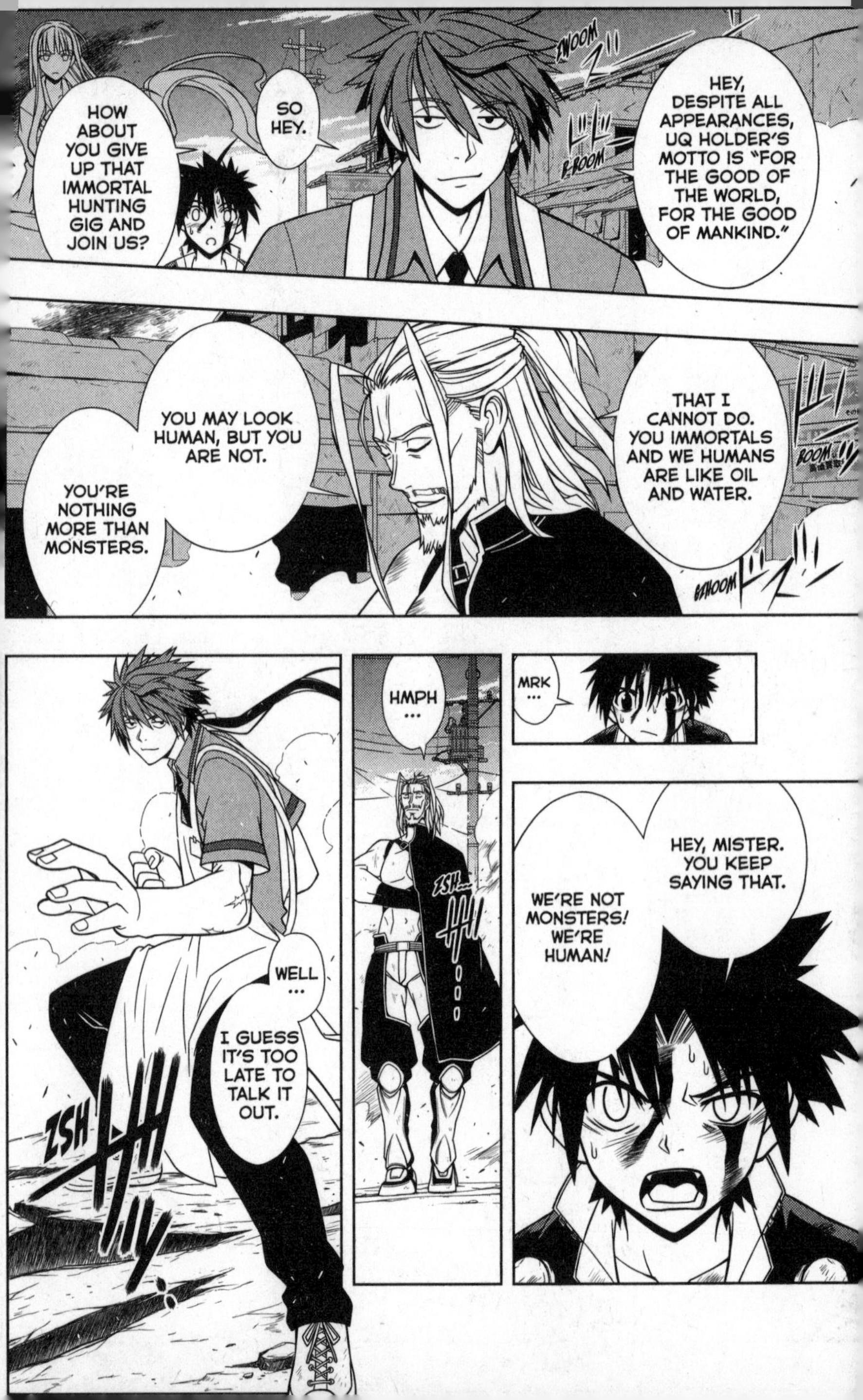
ZWOOM
HEY, DESPITE ALL APPEARANCES, UQ HOLDER'S MOTTO IS "FOR THE GOOD OF THE WORLD, FOR THE GOOD OF MANKIND."
B-BOOM
SO HEY.
HOW ABOUT YOU GIVE UP THAT IMMORTAL HUNTING GIG AND JOIN US?
BOOM
THAT I CANNOT DO. YOU IMMORTALS AND WE HUMANS ARE LIKE OIL AND WATER.
WHOOM
YOU MAY LOOK HUMAN, BUT YOU ARE NOT.
YOU'RE NOTHING MORE THAN MONSTERS.
MRK ...
HEY, MISTER. YOU KEEP SAYING THAT.
WE'RE NOT MONSTERS! WE'RE HUMAN!
HMPH ...
ZSH...
WELL ...
I GUESS IT'S TOO LATE TO TALK IT OUT.
ZSH

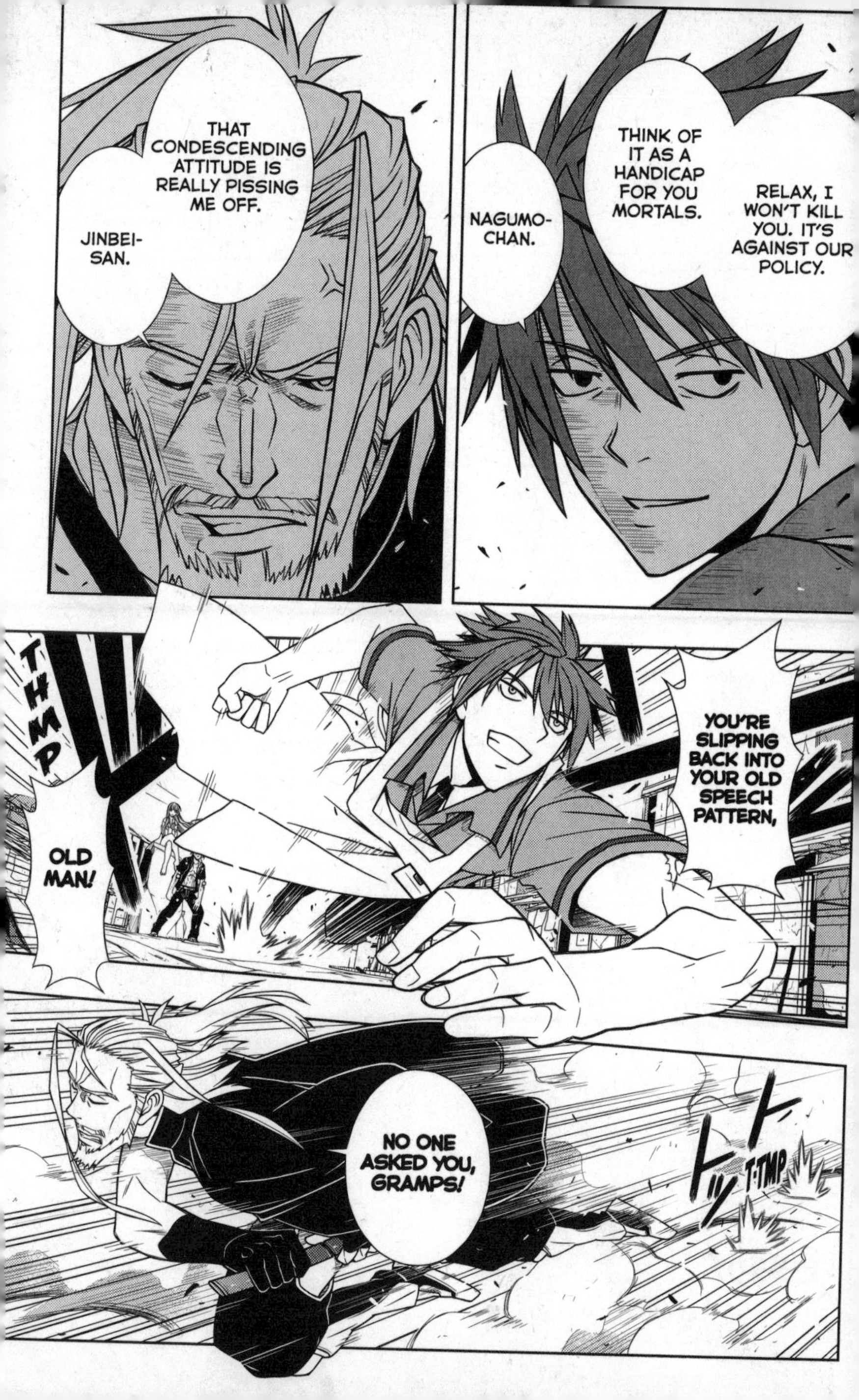
RELAX, I WON'T KILL YOU. IT'S AGAINST OUR POLICY.
THINK OF IT AS A HANDICAP FOR YOU MORTALS.
NAGUMO-CHAN.
THAT CONDESCENDING ATTITUDE IS REALLY PISSING ME OFF.
JINBEI-SAN.
YOU'RE SLIPPING BACK INTO YOUR OLD SPEECH PATTERN,
THMP
OLD MAN!
T-TMP
NO ONE ASKED YOU, GRAMPS!

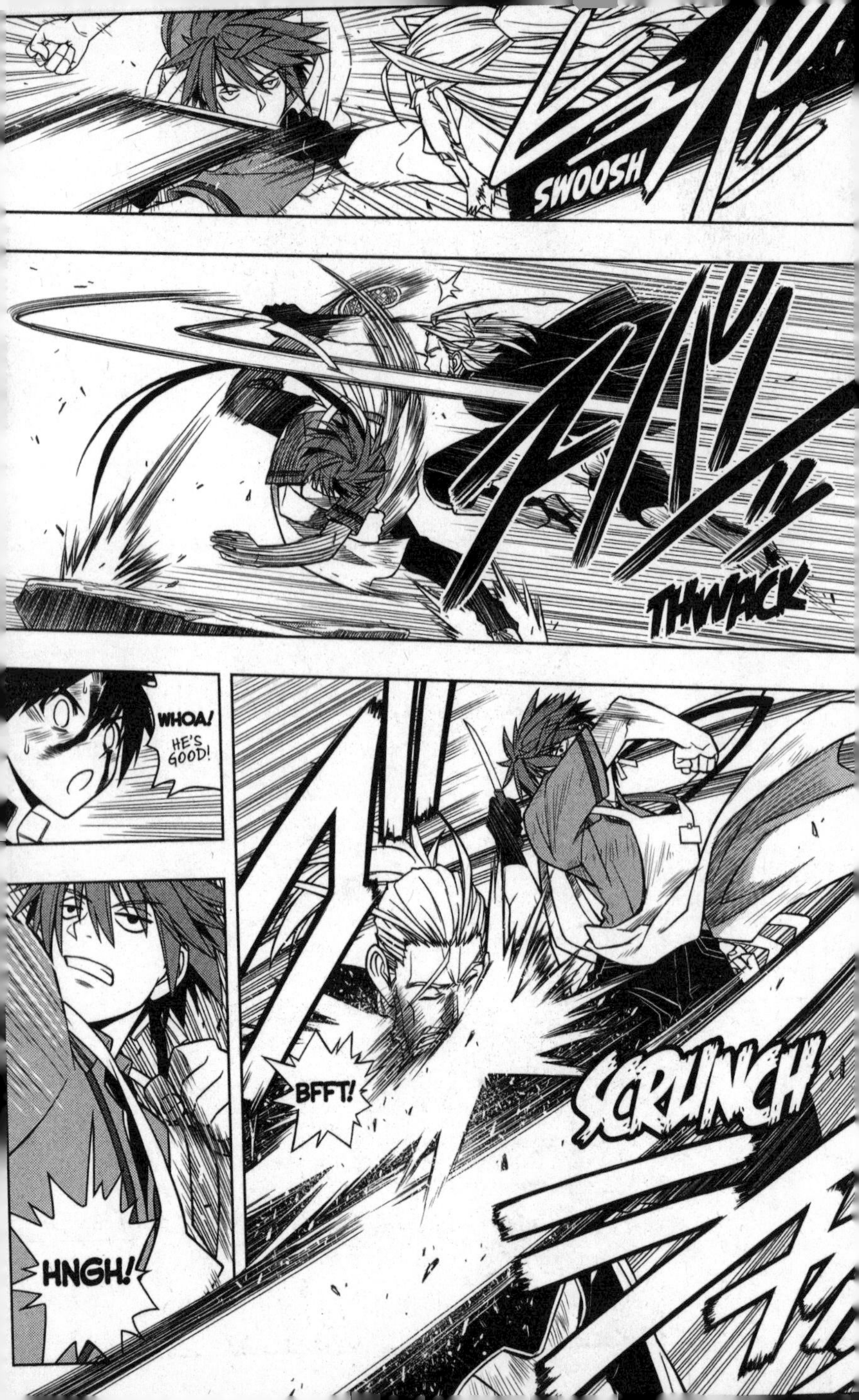
SWOOSH
THWACK
SCRUNCH
BFFT!
WHOA!
HE'S GOOD!
HNGH!

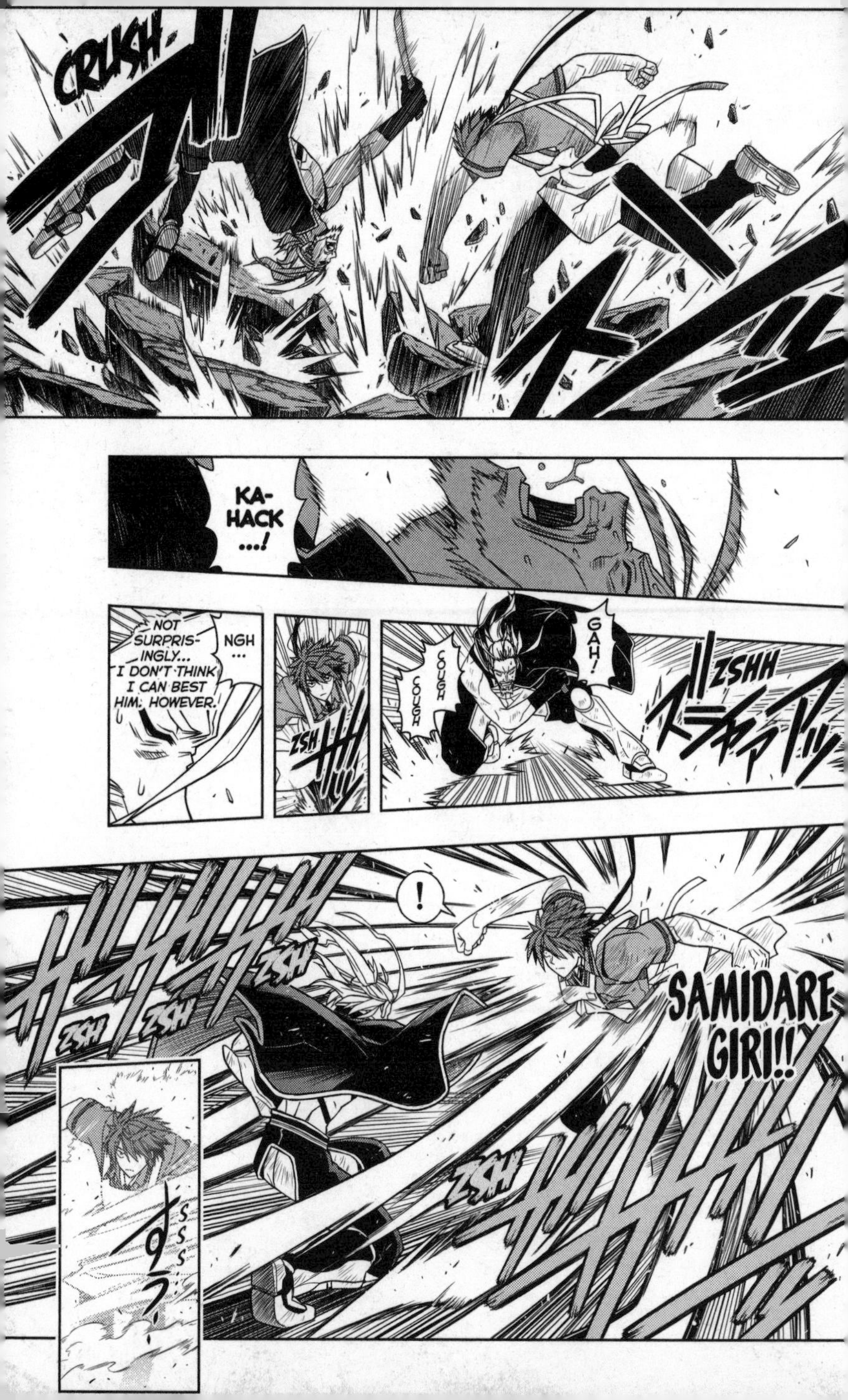
CRUSH
KA-HACK...!
ZSHH
GAH!
COUGH COUGH
ZSH
NGH...
NOT SURPRIS-INGLY... I DON'T THINK I CAN BEST HIM. HOWEVER.
!
SAMIDARE GIRI!!
ZSH
ZSH
ZSH
ZSH
SSS

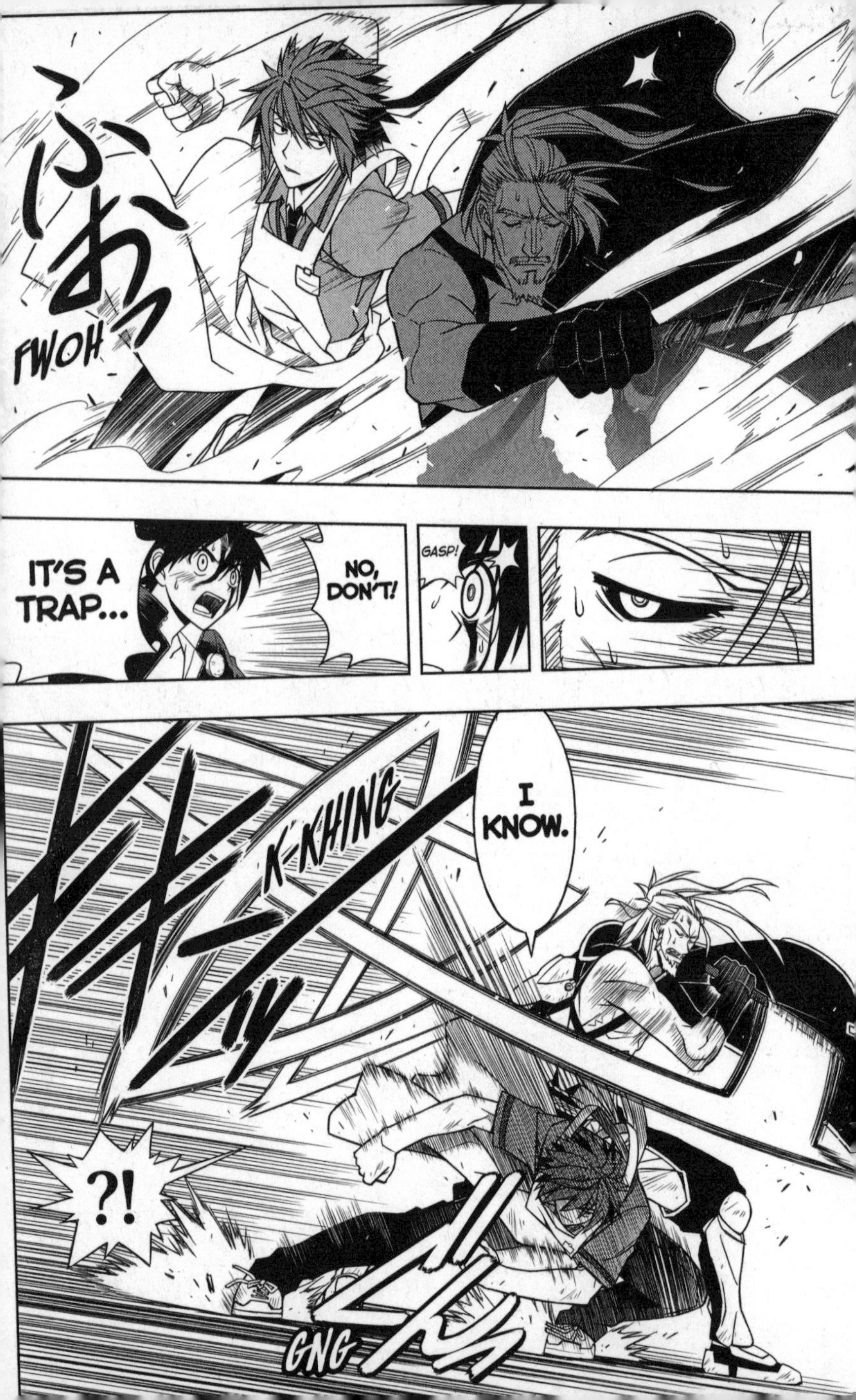
ふぉっ
FWOH
GASP!
NO, DON'T!
IT'S A TRAP...
I KNOW.
K-KHING
?!
GNG

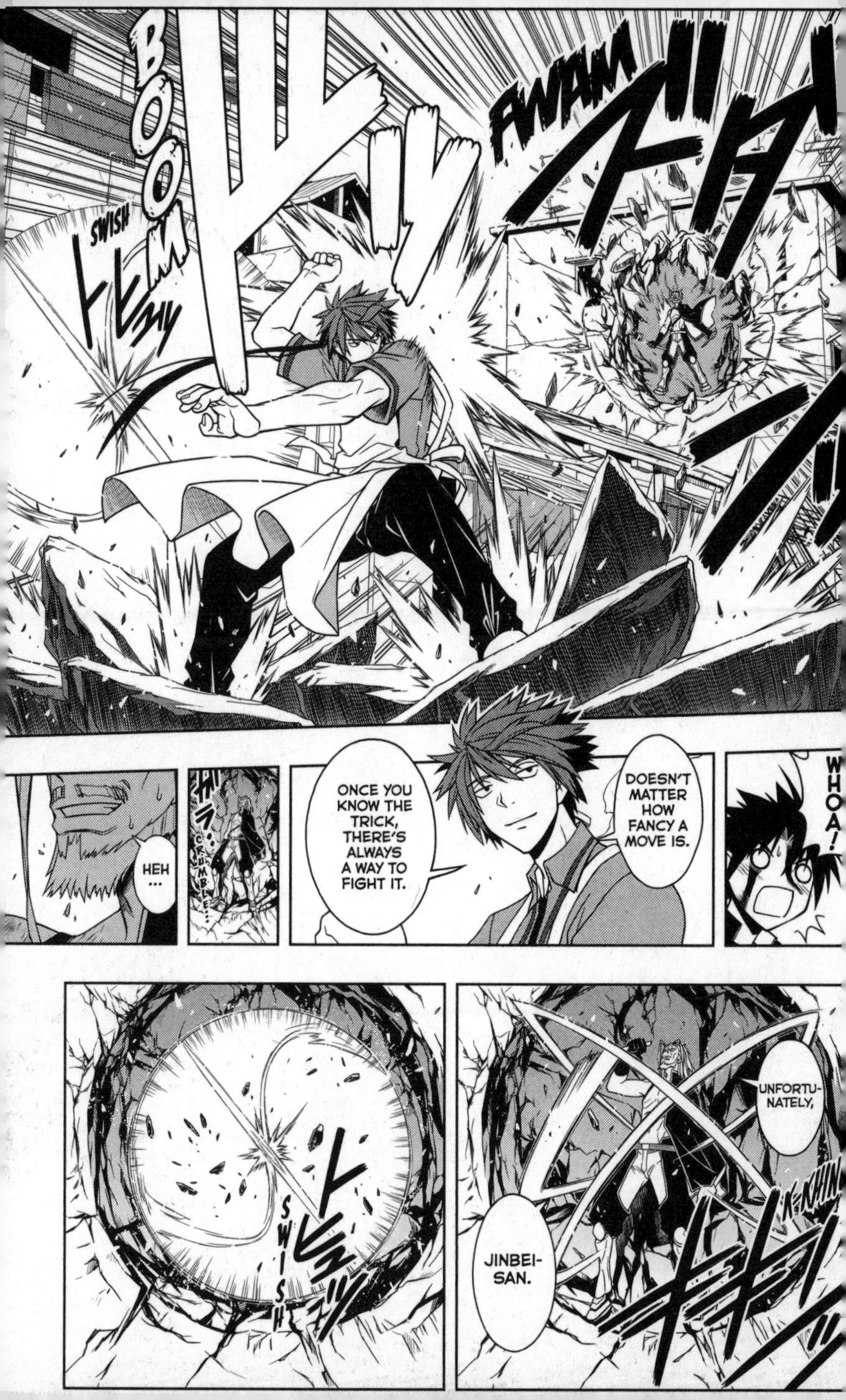
FWAM
BOOM
SWISH
WHOA!
DOESN'T MATTER HOW FANCY A MOVE IS.
ONCE YOU KNOW THE TRICK, THERE'S ALWAYS A WAY TO FIGHT IT.
CRUMBLE...
HEH...
UNFORTU-NATELY,
JINBEI-SAN.
K-KHIN
SWISH

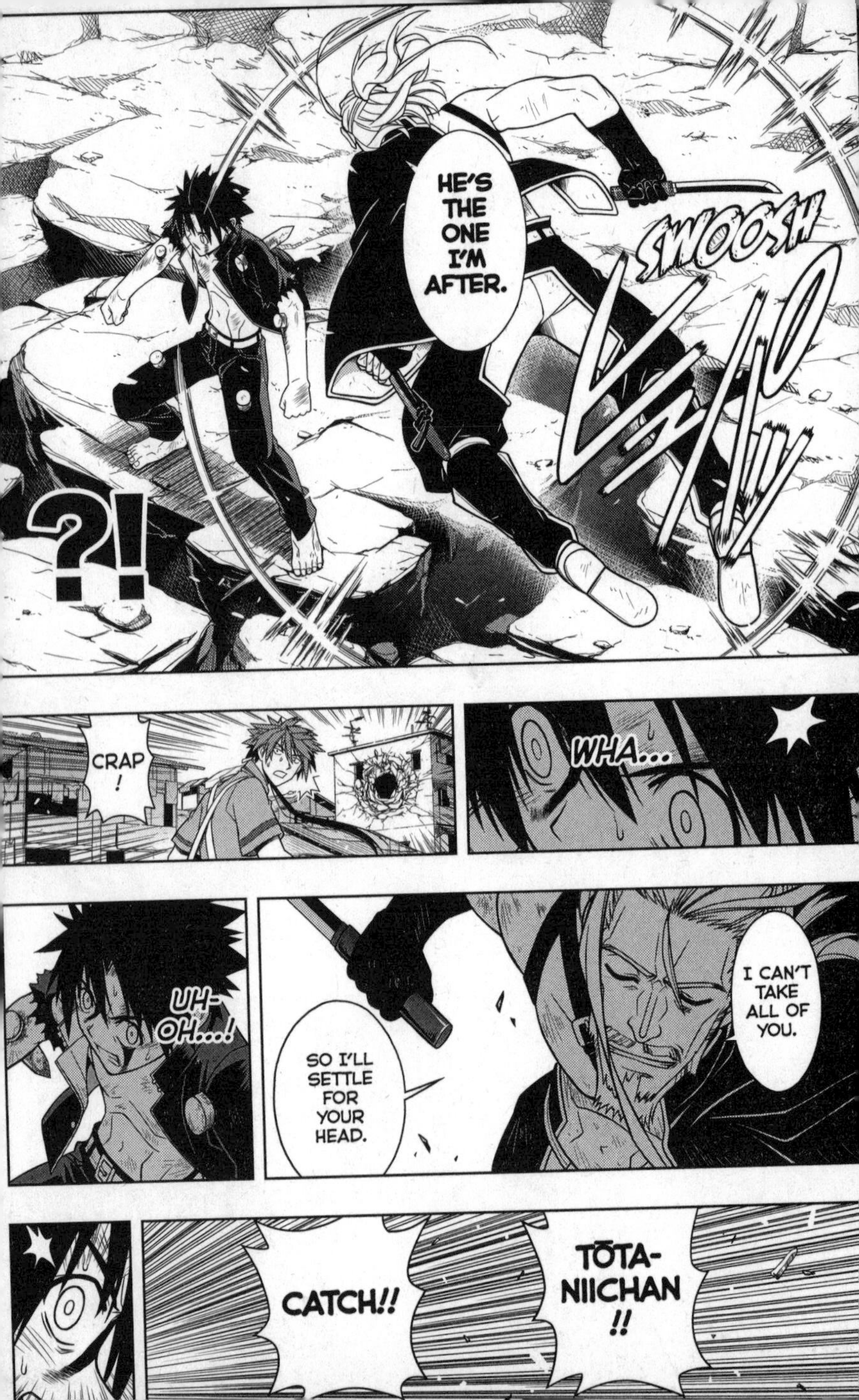
SWOOSH
HE'S THE ONE I'M AFTER.
?!
WHA...
CRAP!
I CAN'T TAKE ALL OF YOU.
SO I'LL SETTLE FOR YOUR HEAD.
UH-OH...!
TŌTA-NIICHAN!!
CATCH!!

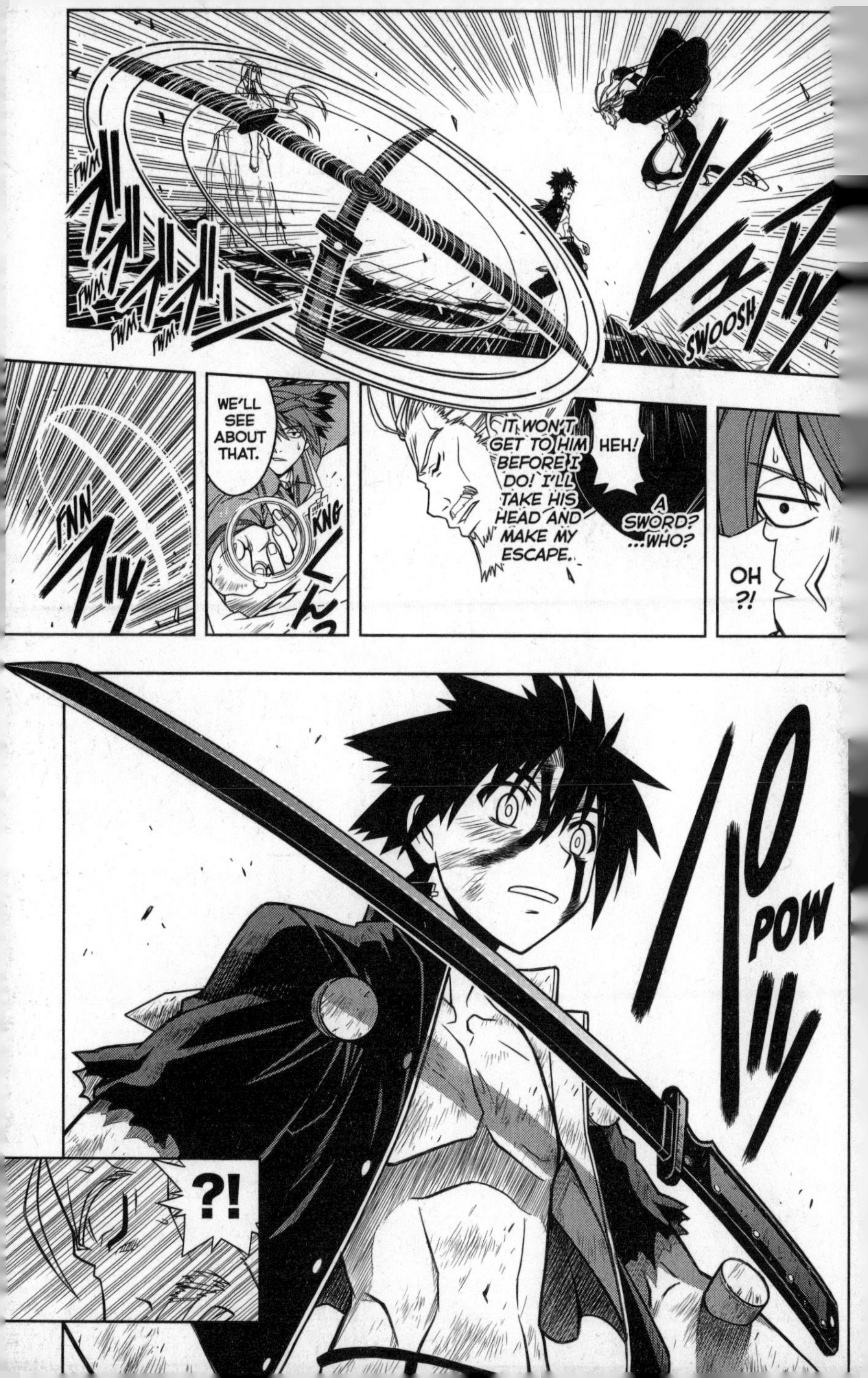
SWOOSH
FWM
FWM
FWM
FWM
FWM
OH ?!
HEH!
A SWORD? ...WHO?
IT WON'T GET TO HIM BEFORE I DO! I'LL TAKE HIS HEAD AND MAKE MY ESCAPE..
KNG
WE'LL SEE ABOUT THAT.
FNN
POW
?!

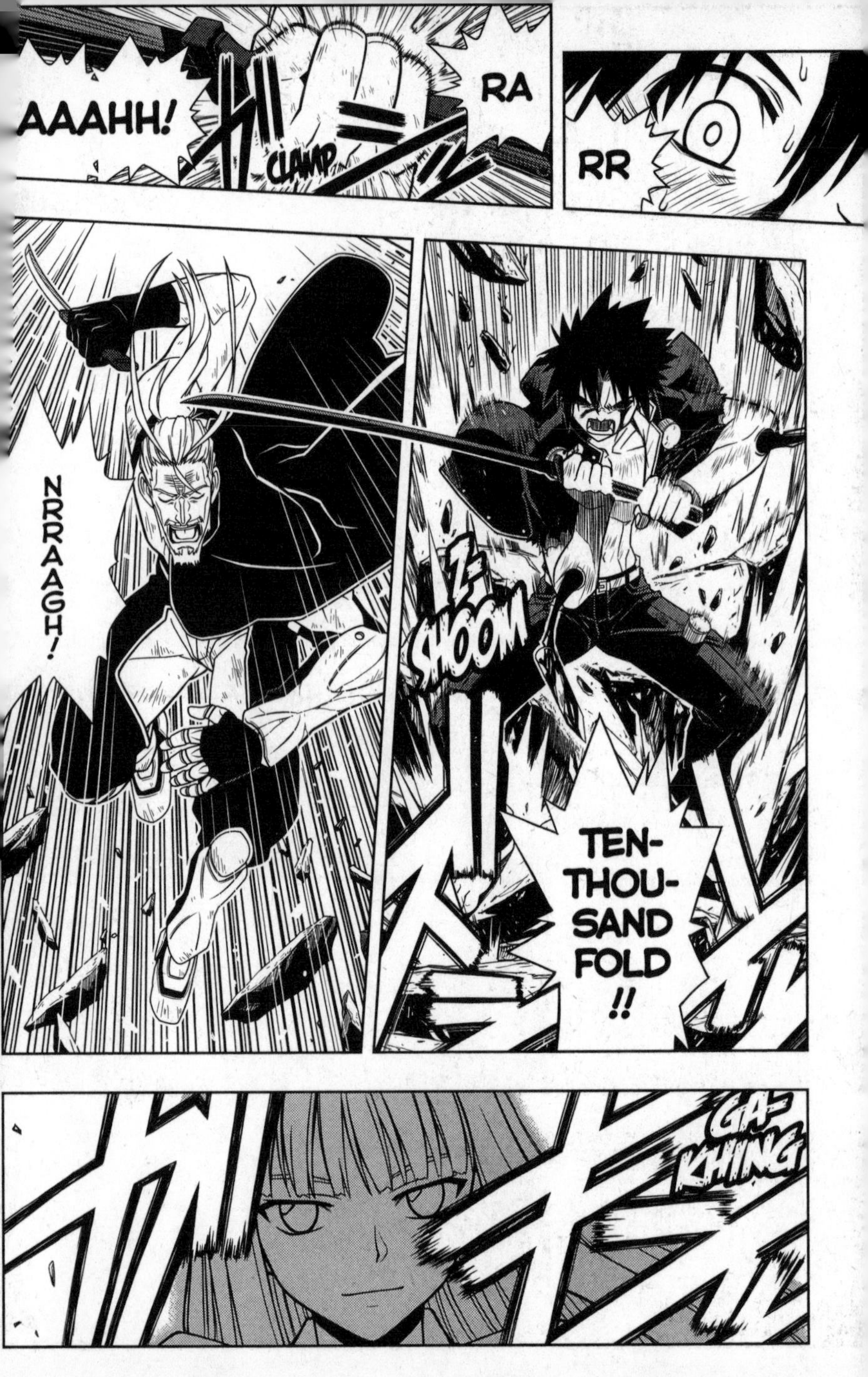
RR
RA
CLAMP
AAAHH!
Z-SHOOM
TEN-THOUSAND FOLD!!
NRRAAGH!
GA-KHING

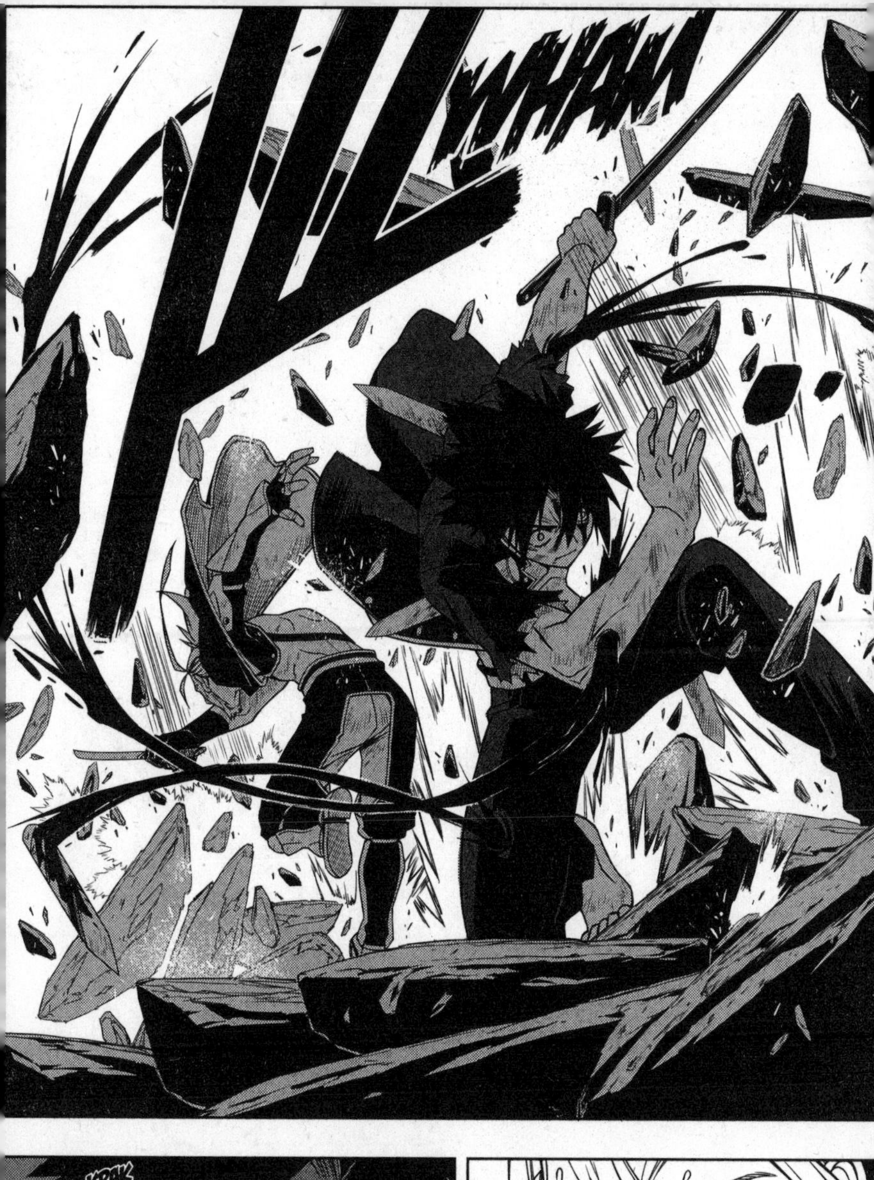

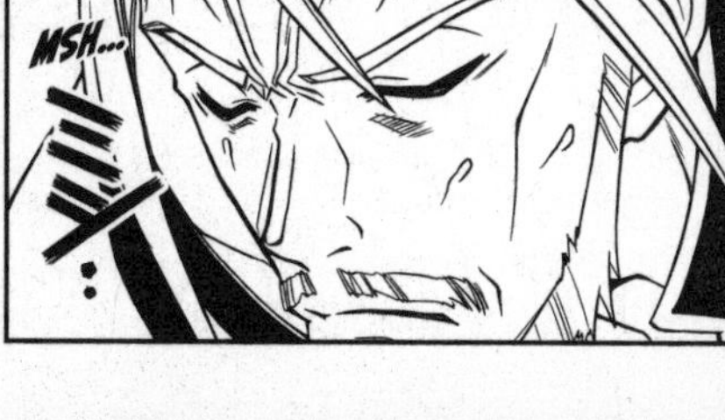
MSH...
ミシ…

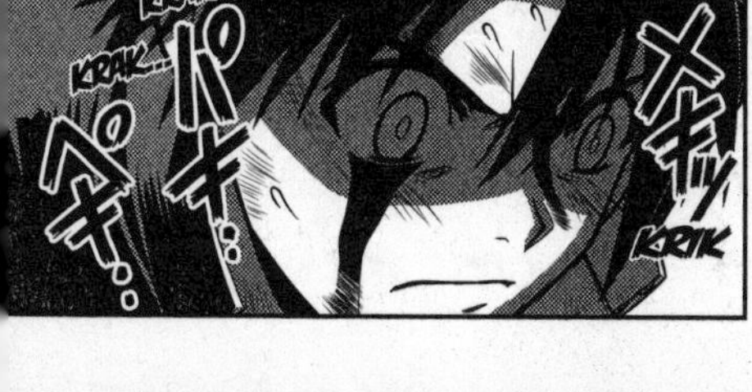
メキッ
KRIK
パキ…
ペキ…
KRAK
KRAK...

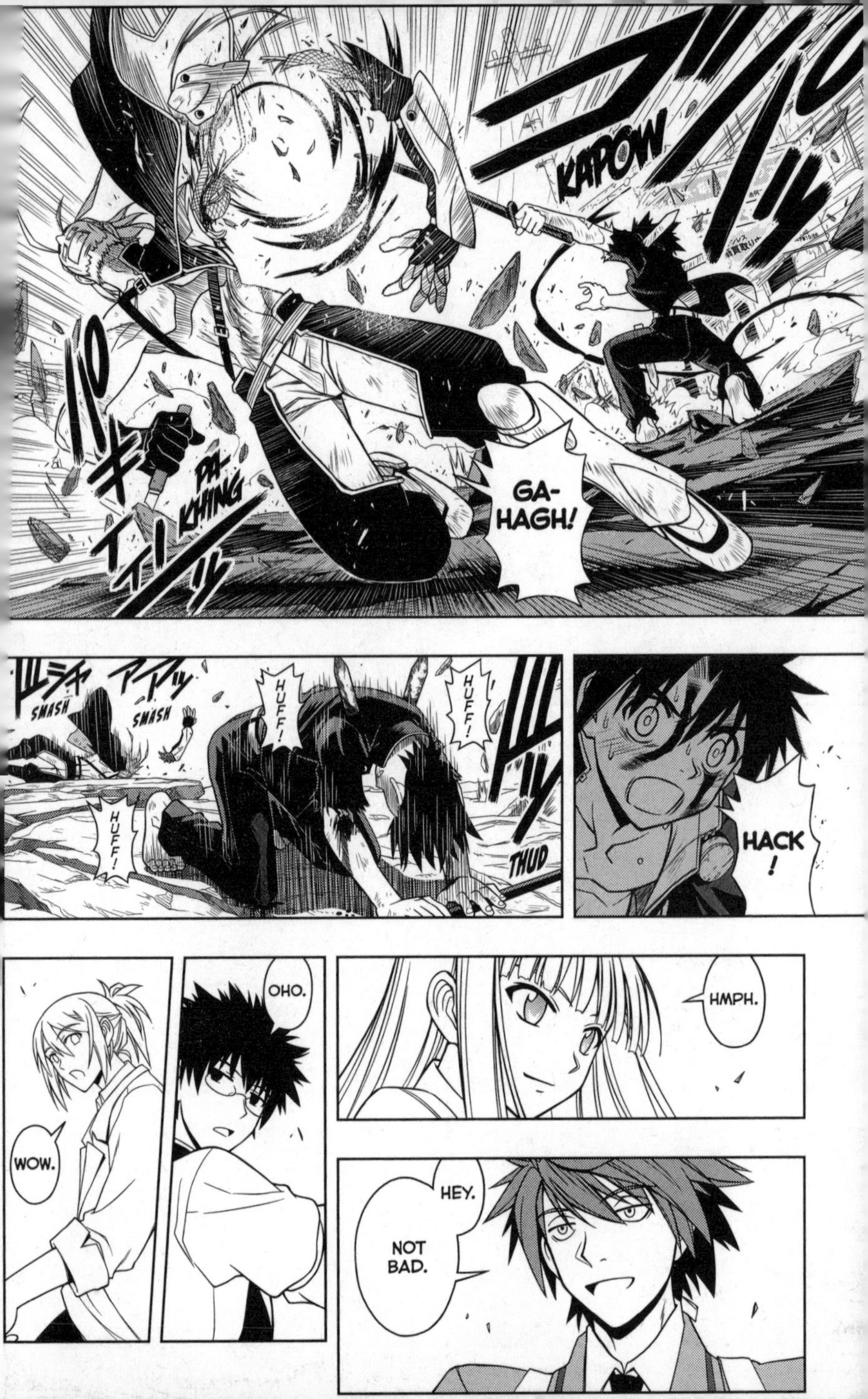
KAPOW
GA-HAGH!
PA-KHING
HACK!
THUD
HUFF! HUFF!
HUFF!
SMASH
SMASH
HUFF!
HMPH.
HEY.
NOT BAD.
OHO.
WOW.

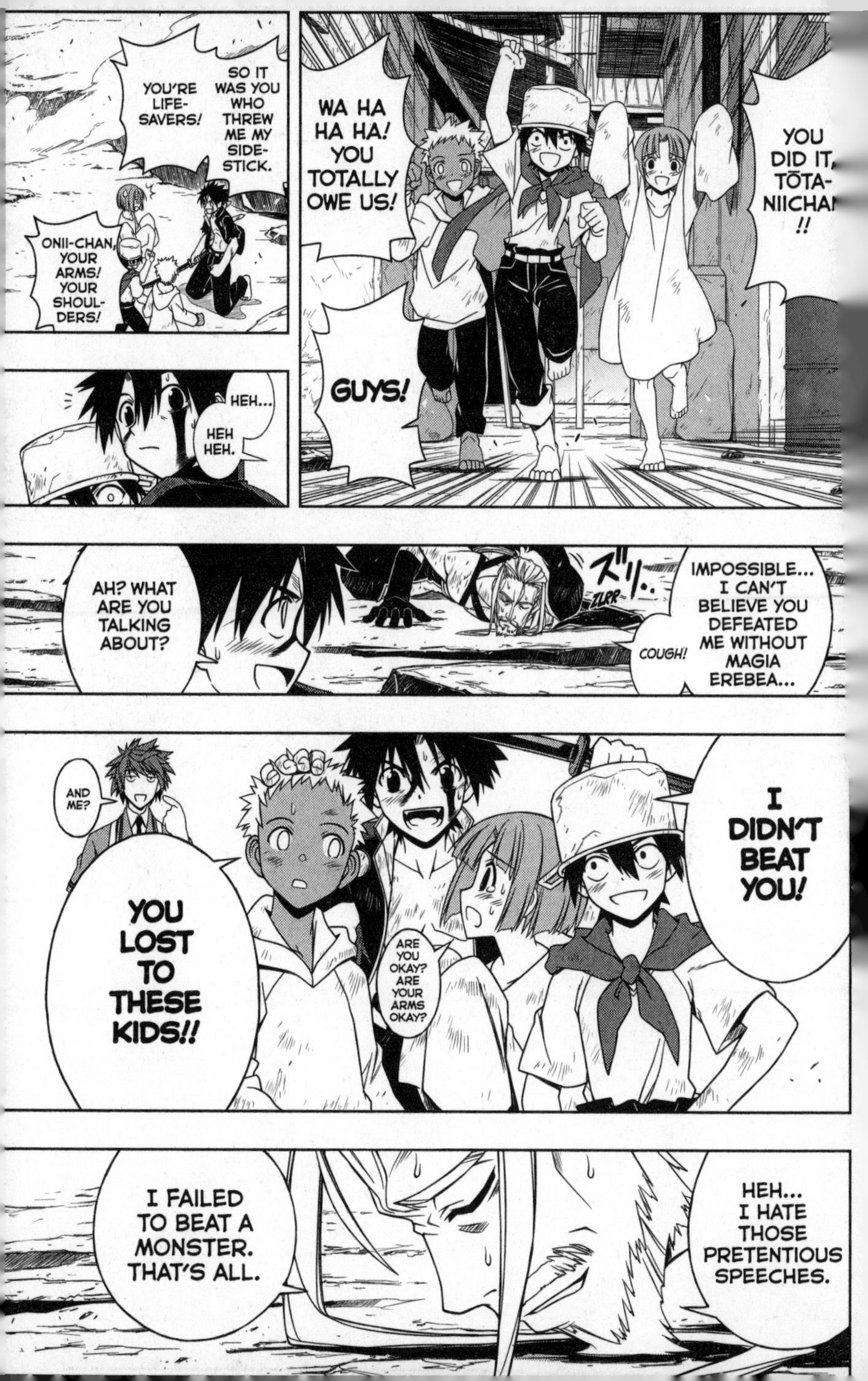

YOU DID IT, TŌTA-NIICHA !!
WA HA HA HA! YOU TOTALLY OWE US!
GUYS!
SO IT WAS YOU WHO THREW ME MY SIDE-STICK.
YOU'RE LIFE-SAVERS!
ONII-CHAN, YOUR ARMS! YOUR SHOUL-DERS!
HEH...
HEH HEH.
IMPOSSIBLE... I CAN'T BELIEVE YOU DEFEATED ME WITHOUT MAGIA EREBEA...
COUGH!
ズリ..
ZLRR
AH? WHAT ARE YOU TALKING ABOUT?
I DIDN'T BEAT YOU!
ARE YOU OKAY? ARE YOUR ARMS OKAY?
YOU LOST TO THESE KIDS!!
AND ME?
HEH... I HATE THOSE PRETENTIOUS SPEECHES.
I FAILED TO BEAT A MONSTER. THAT'S ALL.

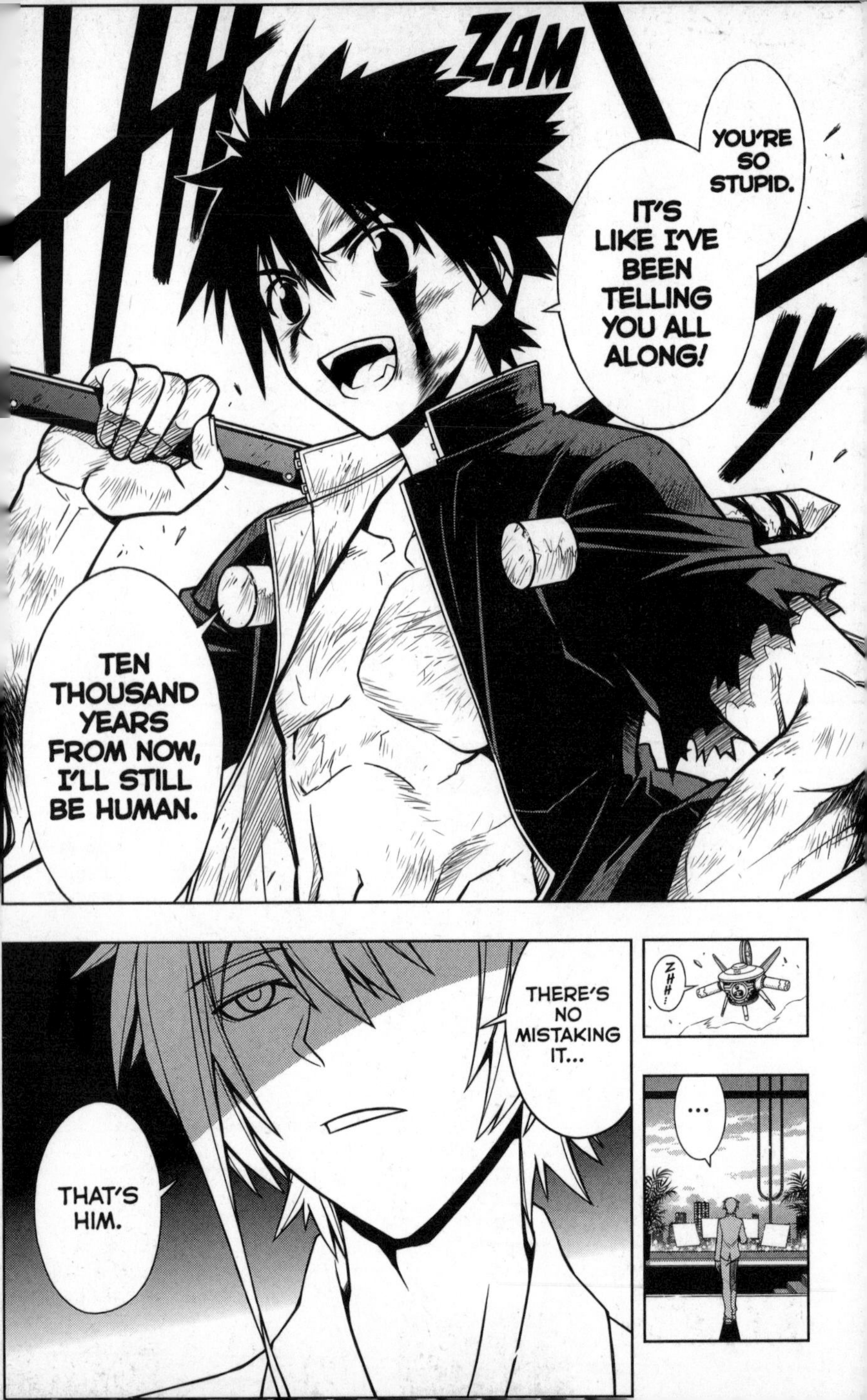
ZAM
YOU'RE SO STUPID.
IT'S LIKE I'VE BEEN TELLING YOU ALL ALONG!
TEN THOUSAND YEARS FROM NOW, I'LL STILL BE HUMAN.
ZHH...
...
THERE'S NO MISTAKING IT...
THAT'S HIM.

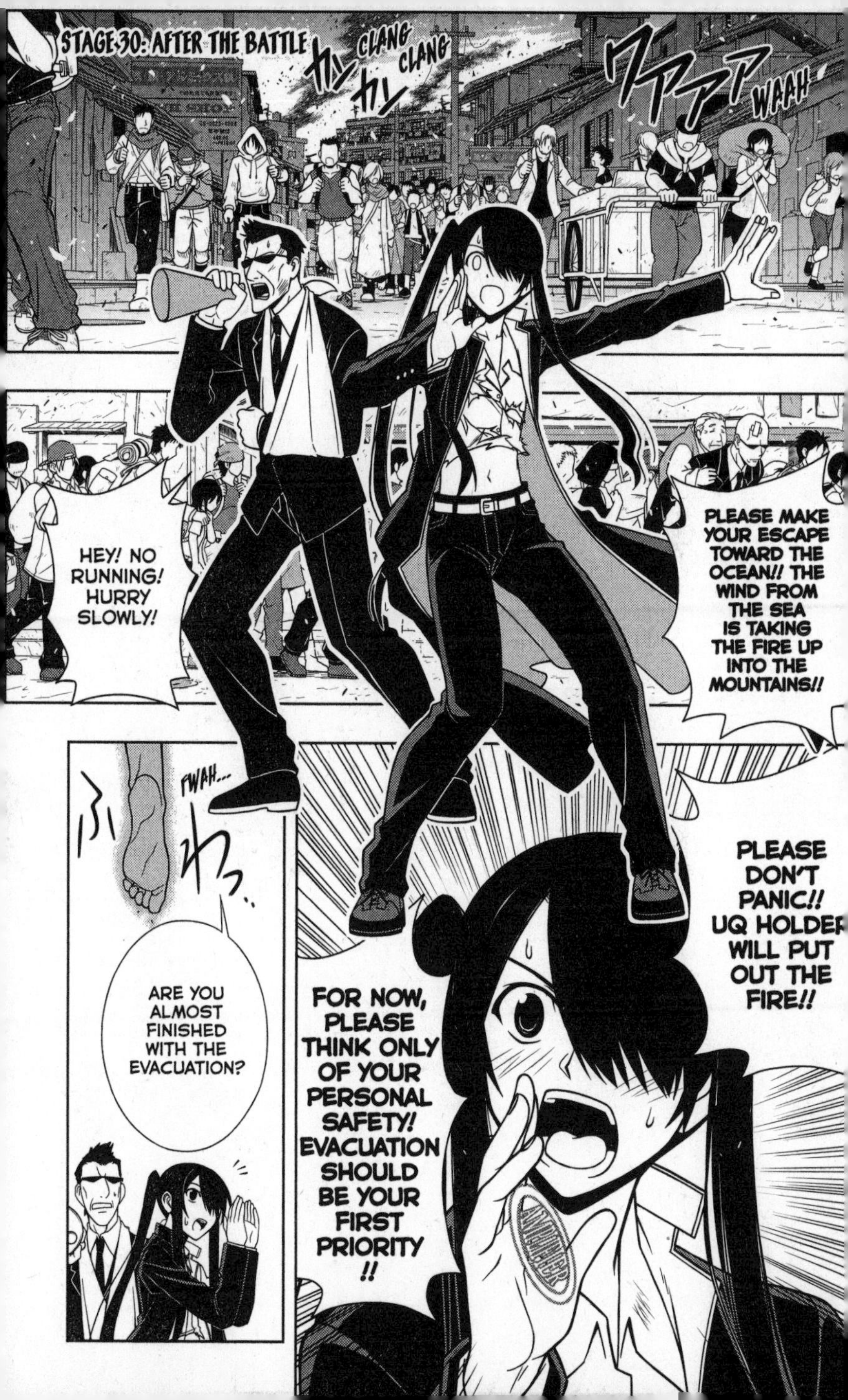
STAGE 30: AFTER THE BATTLE
ワァァァ WAAH
カン CLANG
カン CLANG
PLEASE MAKE YOUR ESCAPE TOWARD THE OCEAN!! THE WIND FROM THE SEA IS TAKING THE FIRE UP INTO THE MOUNTAINS!!
HEY! NO RUNNING! HURRY SLOWLY!
PLEASE DON'T PANIC!! UQ HOLDER WILL PUT OUT THE FIRE!!
FOR NOW, PLEASE THINK ONLY OF YOUR PERSONAL SAFETY! EVACUATION SHOULD BE YOUR FIRST PRIORITY!!
ふわっ FWAH...
ARE YOU ALMOST FINISHED WITH THE EVACUATION?

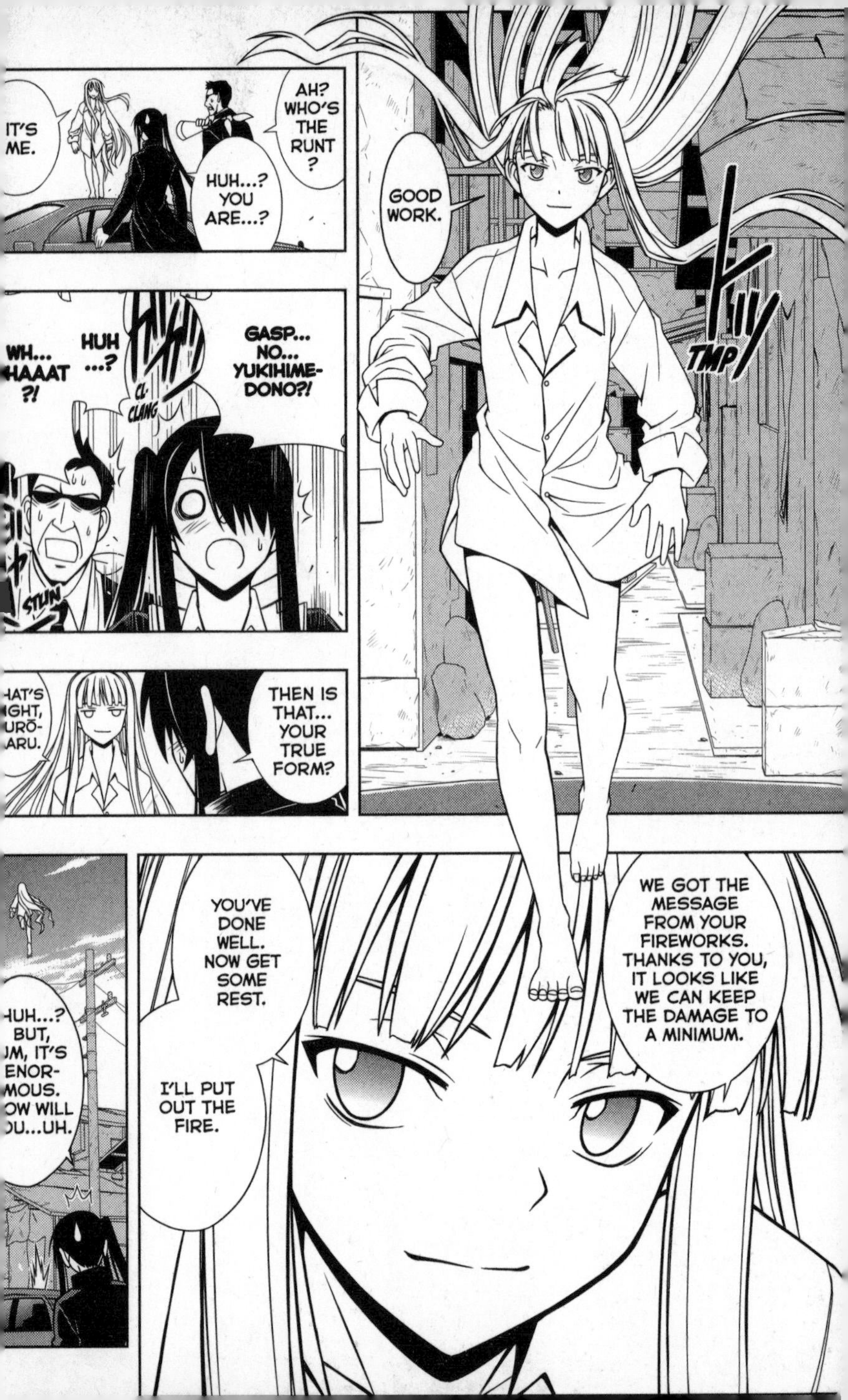
GOOD WORK.
TMP
AH? WHO'S THE RUNT?
HUH...? YOU ARE...?
IT'S ME.
GASP... NO... YUKIHIME-DONO?!
CL-CLANG
HUH ...?
WH... HAAAT ?!
STUN
THEN IS THAT... YOUR TRUE FORM?
HAT'S IGHT, URŌ-ARU.
WE GOT THE MESSAGE FROM YOUR FIREWORKS. THANKS TO YOU, IT LOOKS LIKE WE CAN KEEP THE DAMAGE TO A MINIMUM.
YOU'VE DONE WELL. NOW GET SOME REST.
I'LL PUT OUT THE FIRE.
HUH...? BUT, UM, IT'S ENOR-MOUS. OW WILL OU...UH.

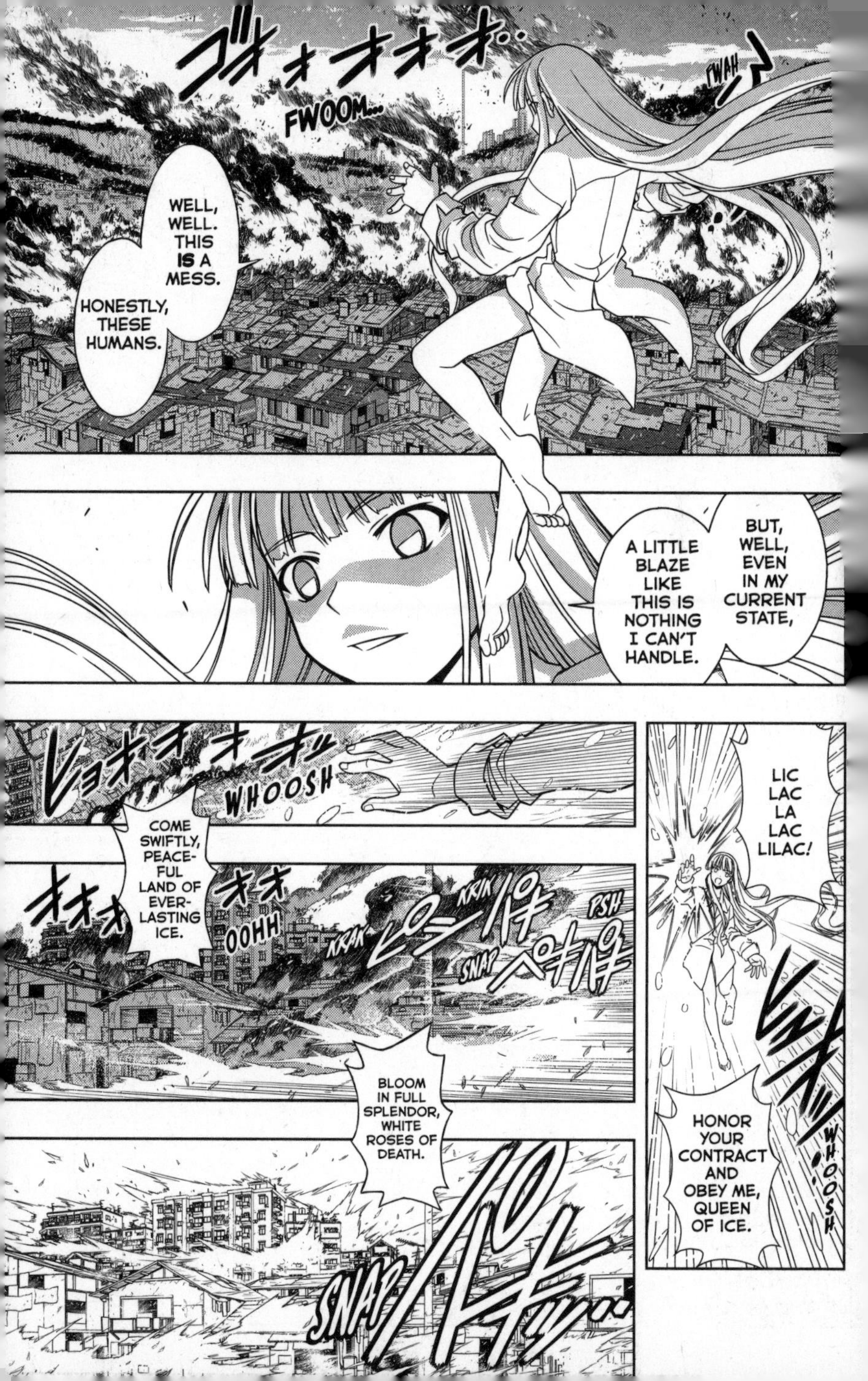
FWAH
FWOOM...
WELL, WELL. THIS IS A MESS.
HONESTLY, THESE HUMANS.
BUT, WELL, EVEN IN MY CURRENT STATE,
A LITTLE BLAZE LIKE THIS IS NOTHING I CAN'T HANDLE.
LIC LAC LA LAC LILAC!
HONOR YOUR CONTRACT AND OBEY ME, QUEEN OF ICE.
WHOOSH
WHOOSH
COME SWIFTLY, PEACE-FUL LAND OF EVER-LASTING ICE.
OOHH
KRAK
KRIK
PSH
SNAP
BLOOM IN FULL SPLENDOR, WHITE ROSES OF DEATH.
SNAP

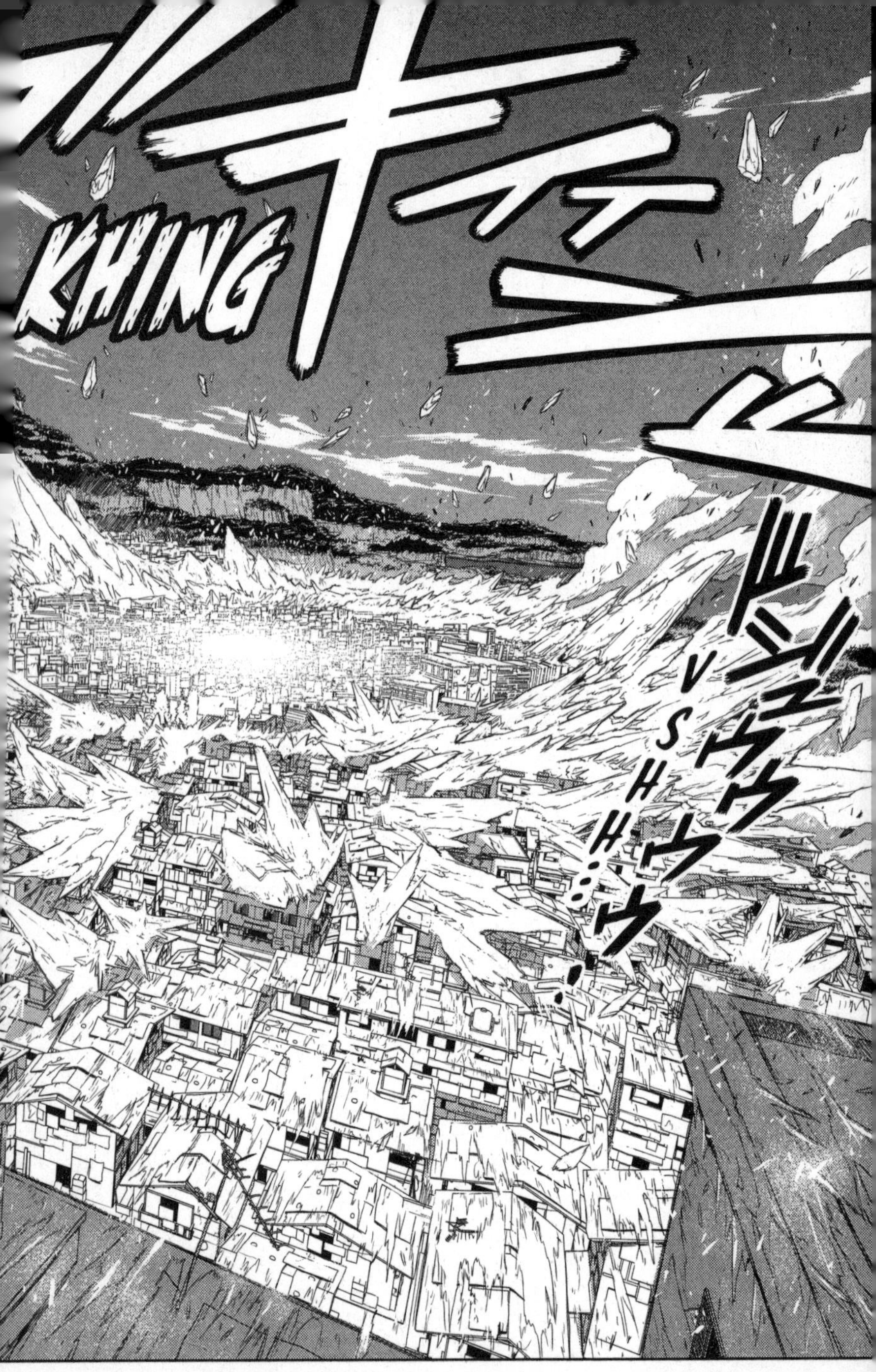
KHING
VSHHH...!!

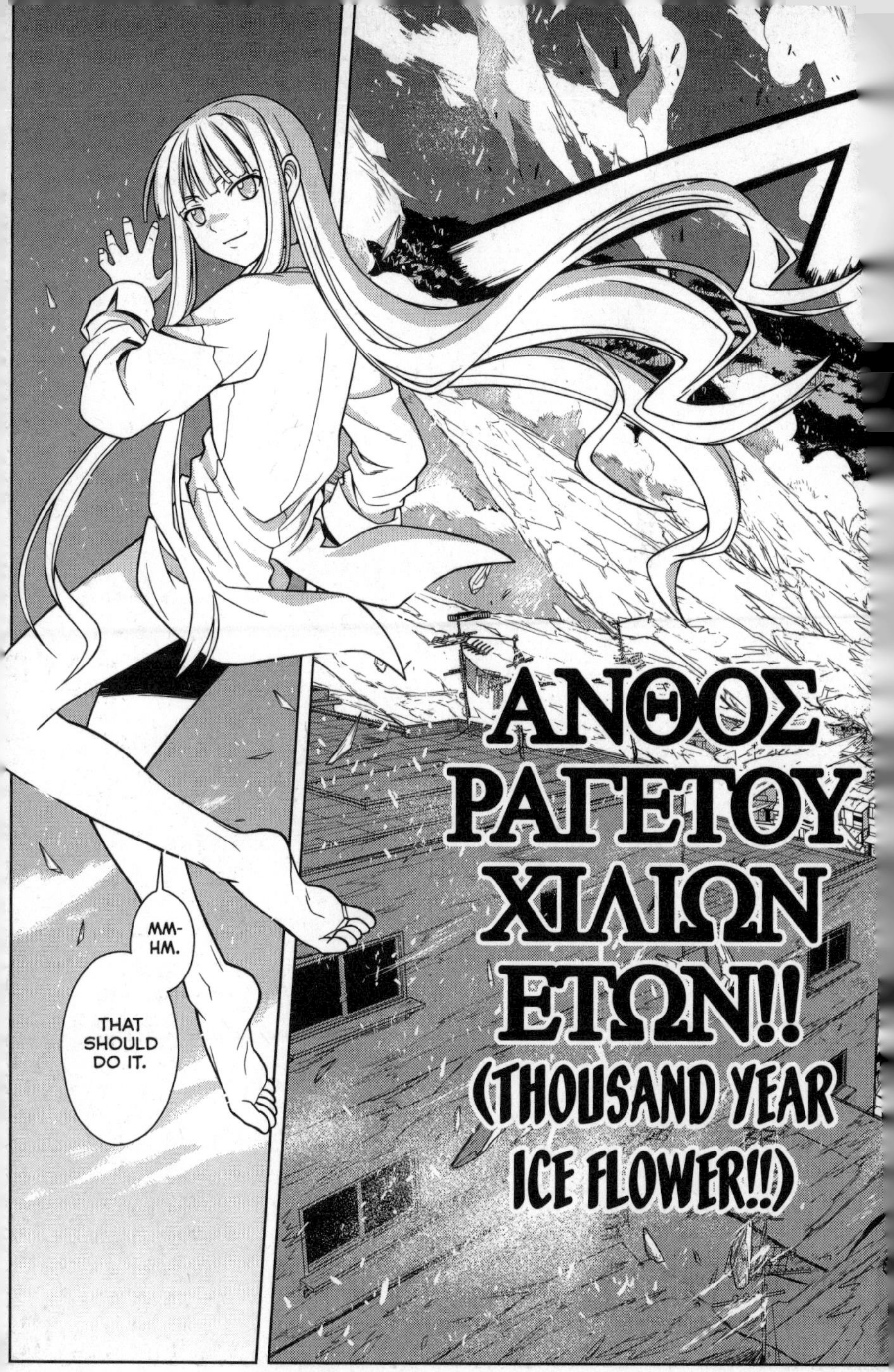
ΑΝΘΟΣ ΡΑΓΕΤΟΥ ΧΙΛΙΩΝ ΕΤΩΝ!!
(THOUSAND YEAR ICE FLOWER!!)
MM-HM.
THAT SHOULD DO IT.

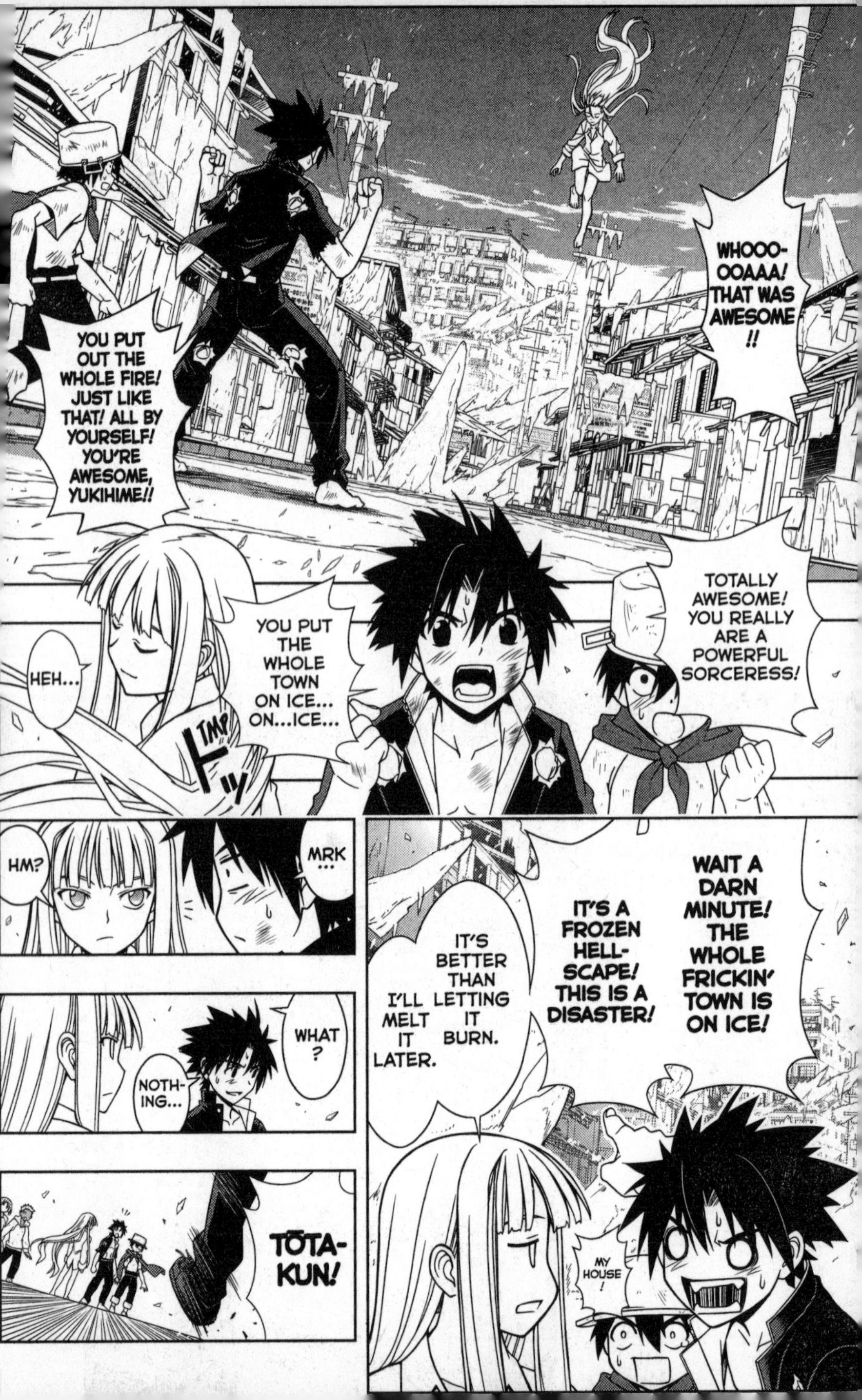
WHOOO-OOAAA! THAT WAS AWESOME!!
YOU PUT OUT THE WHOLE FIRE! JUST LIKE THAT! ALL BY YOURSELF! YOU'RE AWESOME, YUKIHIME!!
TOTALLY AWESOME! YOU REALLY ARE A POWERFUL SORCERESS!
YOU PUT THE WHOLE TOWN ON ICE... ON...ICE...
HEH...
TMP
WAIT A DARN MINUTE! THE WHOLE FRICKIN' TOWN IS ON ICE!
IT'S A FROZEN HELL-SCAPE! THIS IS A DISASTER!
IT'S BETTER THAN LETTING IT BURN.
I'LL MELT IT LATER.
MY HOUSE!
MRK...
HM?
WHAT?
NOTH-ING...
TŌTA-KUN!

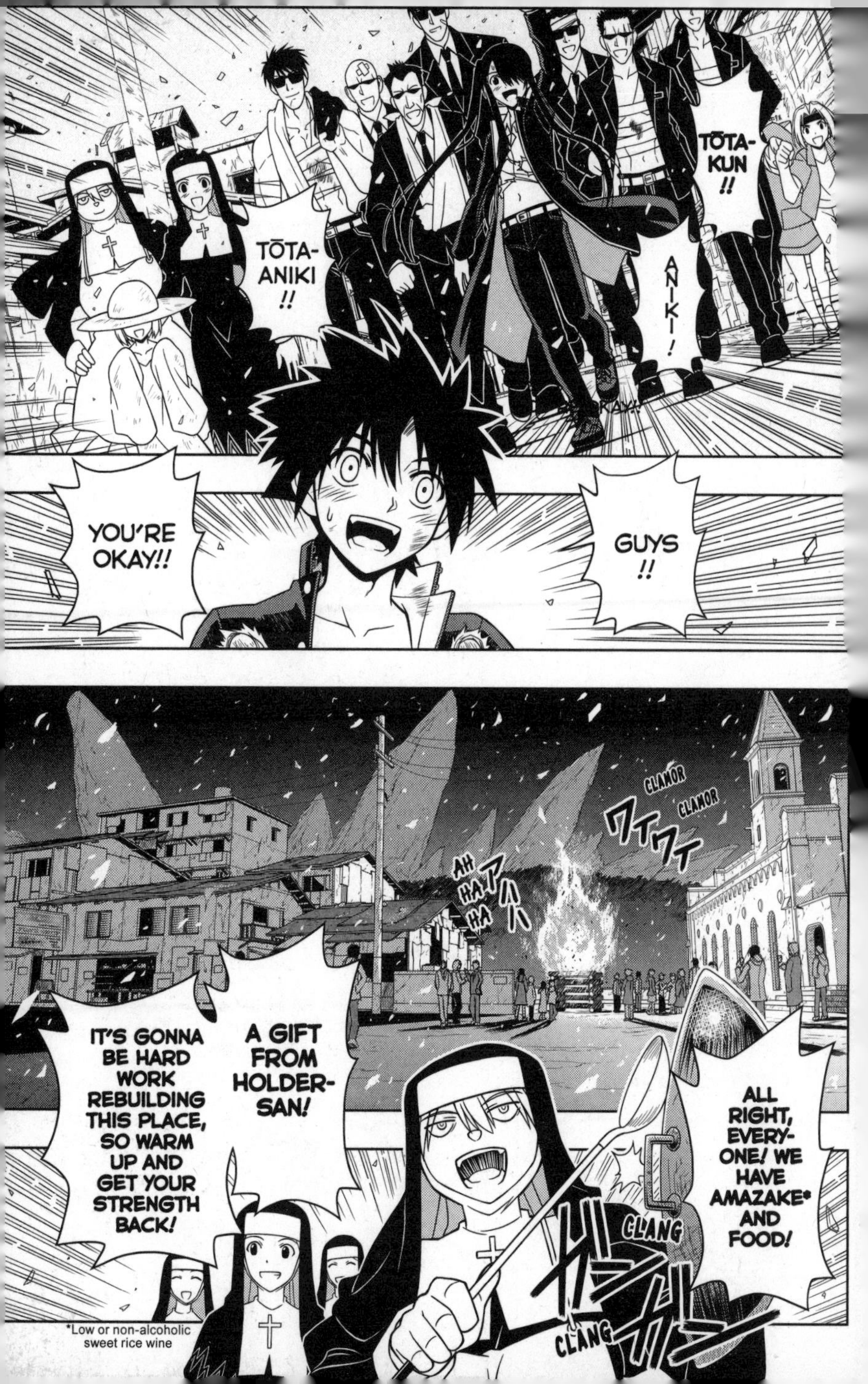
TŌTA-KUN!!
ANIKI!
TŌTA-ANIKI!!
GUYS!!
YOU'RE OKAY!!
CLAMOR CLAMOR
AH HA HA
ALL RIGHT, EVERYONE! WE HAVE AMAZAKE* AND FOOD!
A GIFT FROM HOLDER-SAN!
IT'S GONNA BE HARD WORK REBUILDING THIS PLACE, SO WARM UP AND GET YOUR STRENGTH BACK!
CLANG
CLANG

*Low or non-alcoholic sweet rice wine

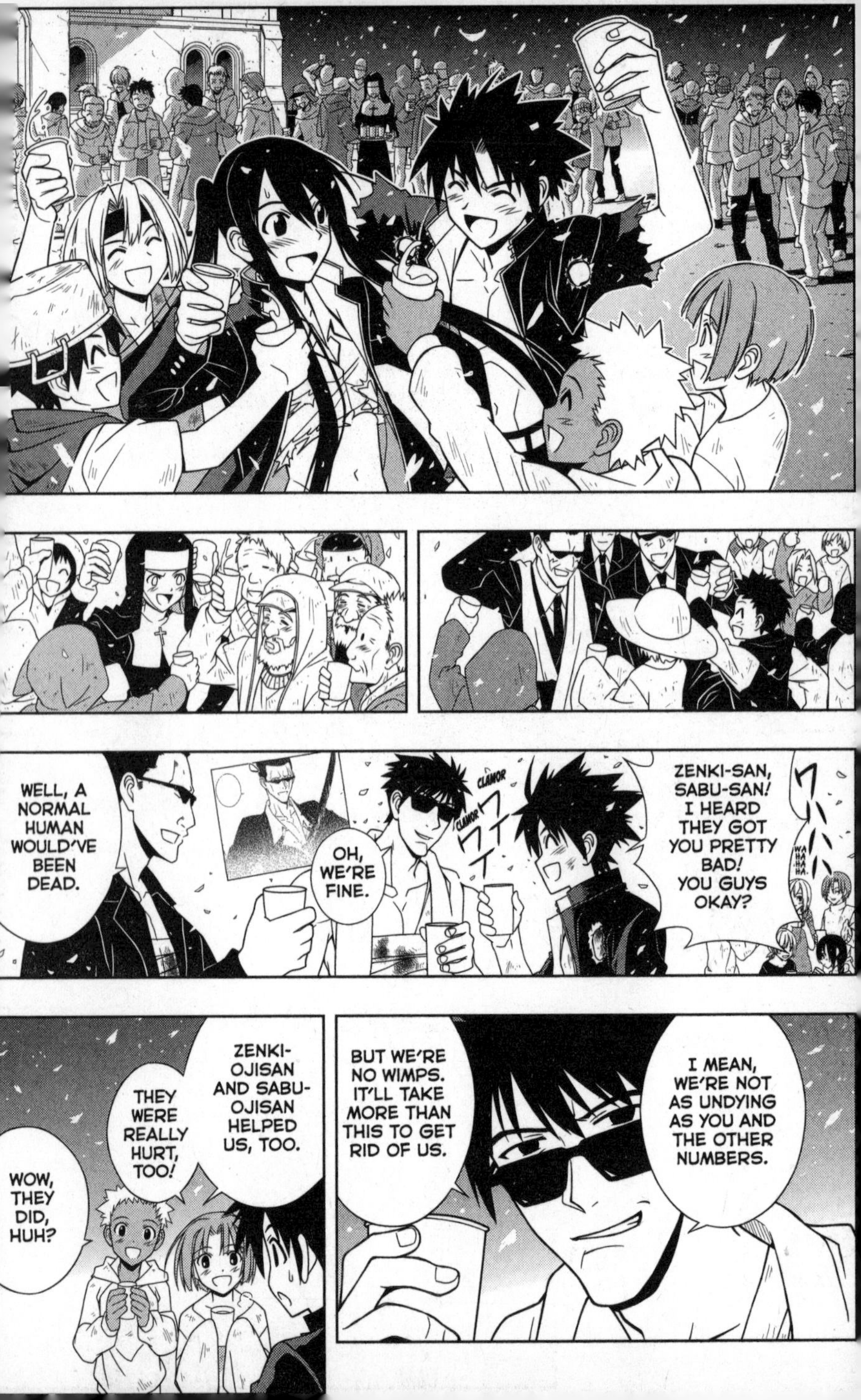
ZENKI-SAN, SABU-SAN! I HEARD THEY GOT YOU PRETTY BAD! YOU GUYS OKAY?
WAHAHAHA
CLAMOR
CLAMOR
OH, WE'RE FINE.
WELL, A NORMAL HUMAN WOULD'VE BEEN DEAD.
I MEAN, WE'RE NOT AS UNDYING AS YOU AND THE OTHER NUMBERS.
BUT WE'RE NO WIMPS. IT'LL TAKE MORE THAN THIS TO GET RID OF US.
ZENKI-OJISAN AND SABU-OJISAN HELPED US, TOO.
THEY WERE REALLY HURT, TOO!
WOW, THEY DID, HUH?

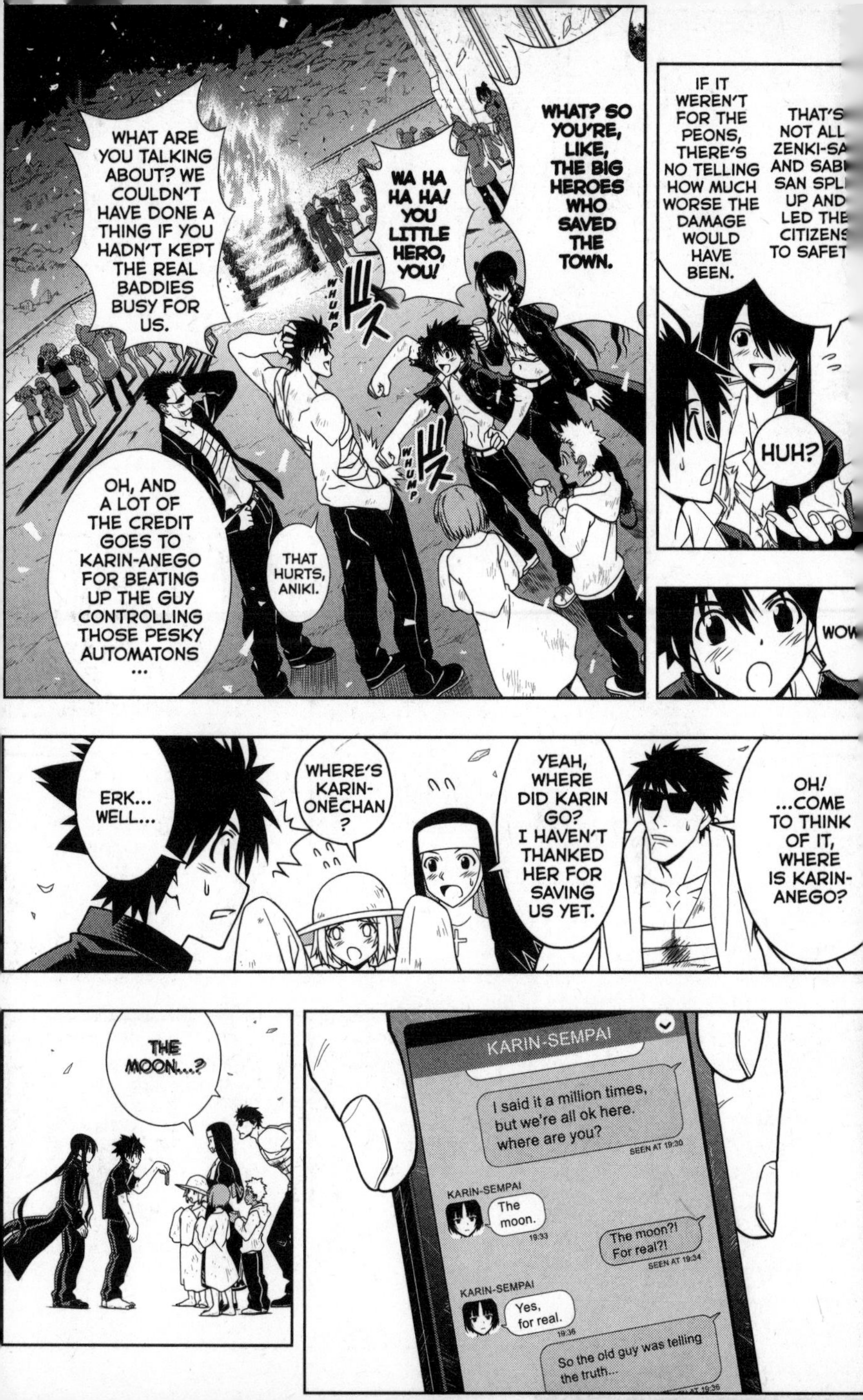
THAT'S NOT ALL ZENKI-SA AND SABI SAN SPL UP AND LED THE CITIZENS TO SAFET
IF IT WEREN'T FOR THE PEONS, THERE'S NO TELLING HOW MUCH WORSE THE DAMAGE WOULD HAVE BEEN.
HUH?
WOW
WHAT? SO YOU'RE, LIKE, THE BIG HEROES WHO SAVED THE TOWN.
WA HA HA HA! YOU LITTLE HERO, YOU!
WHAT ARE YOU TALKING ABOUT? WE COULDN'T HAVE DONE A THING IF YOU HADN'T KEPT THE REAL BADDIES BUSY FOR US.
WHUMP
WHUMP
THAT HURTS, ANIKI.
OH, AND A LOT OF THE CREDIT GOES TO KARIN-ANEGO FOR BEATING UP THE GUY CONTROLLING THOSE PESKY AUTOMATONS ...
OH! ...COME TO THINK OF IT, WHERE IS KARIN-ANEGO?
YEAH, WHERE DID KARIN GO? I HAVEN'T THANKED HER FOR SAVING US YET.
WHERE'S KARIN-ONĒCHAN?
ERK... WELL...
KARIN-SEMPAI
I said it a million times, but we're all ok here. where are you?
SEEN AT 19:30
KARIN-SEMPAI
The moon.
19:33
The moon?! For real?!
SEEN AT 19:34
KARIN-SEMPAI
Yes, for real.
19:36
So the old guy was telling the truth...
THE MOON...?

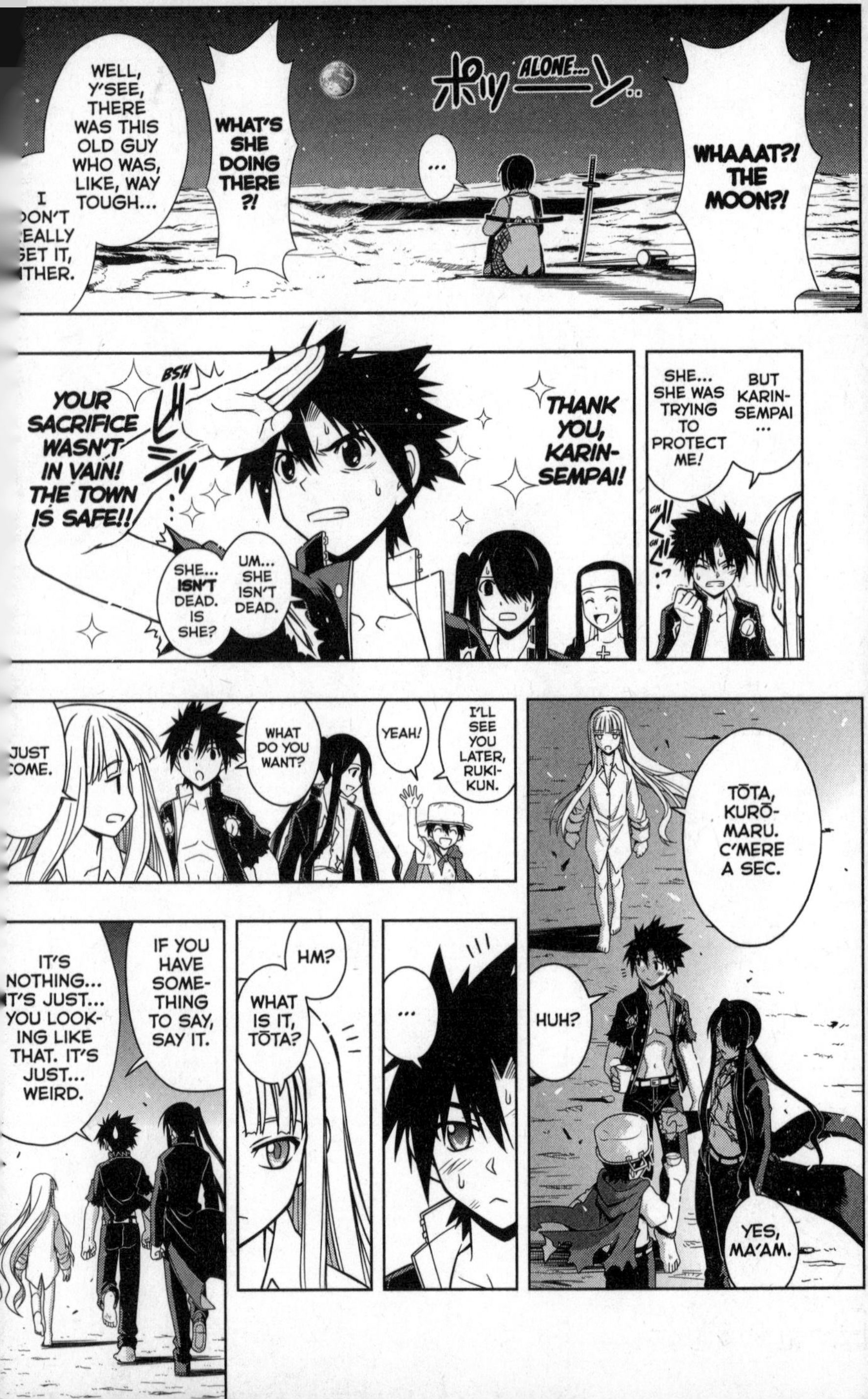
WHAAAT?! THE MOON?!
ポツ ALONE... ン
...
WHAT'S SHE DOING THERE?!
WELL, Y'SEE, THERE WAS THIS OLD GUY WHO WAS, LIKE, WAY TOUGH...
I ON'T EALLY ET IT, THER.
BUT KARIN-SEMPAI...
SHE... SHE WAS TRYING TO PROTECT ME!
GH GH
THANK YOU, KARIN-SEMPAI!
BSH
YOUR SACRIFICE WASN'T IN VAIN! THE TOWN IS SAFE!!
UM... SHE ISN'T DEAD.
SHE... ISN'T DEAD. IS SHE?
TŌTA, KURŌ-MARU. C'MERE A SEC.
HUH?
YES, MA'AM.
I'LL SEE YOU LATER, RUKI-KUN.
YEAH!
WHAT DO YOU WANT?
JUST OME.
...
HM?
WHAT IS IT, TŌTA?
IF YOU HAVE SOME-THING TO SAY, SAY IT.
IT'S NOTHING... T'S JUST... YOU LOOK-ING LIKE THAT. IT'S JUST... WEIRD.

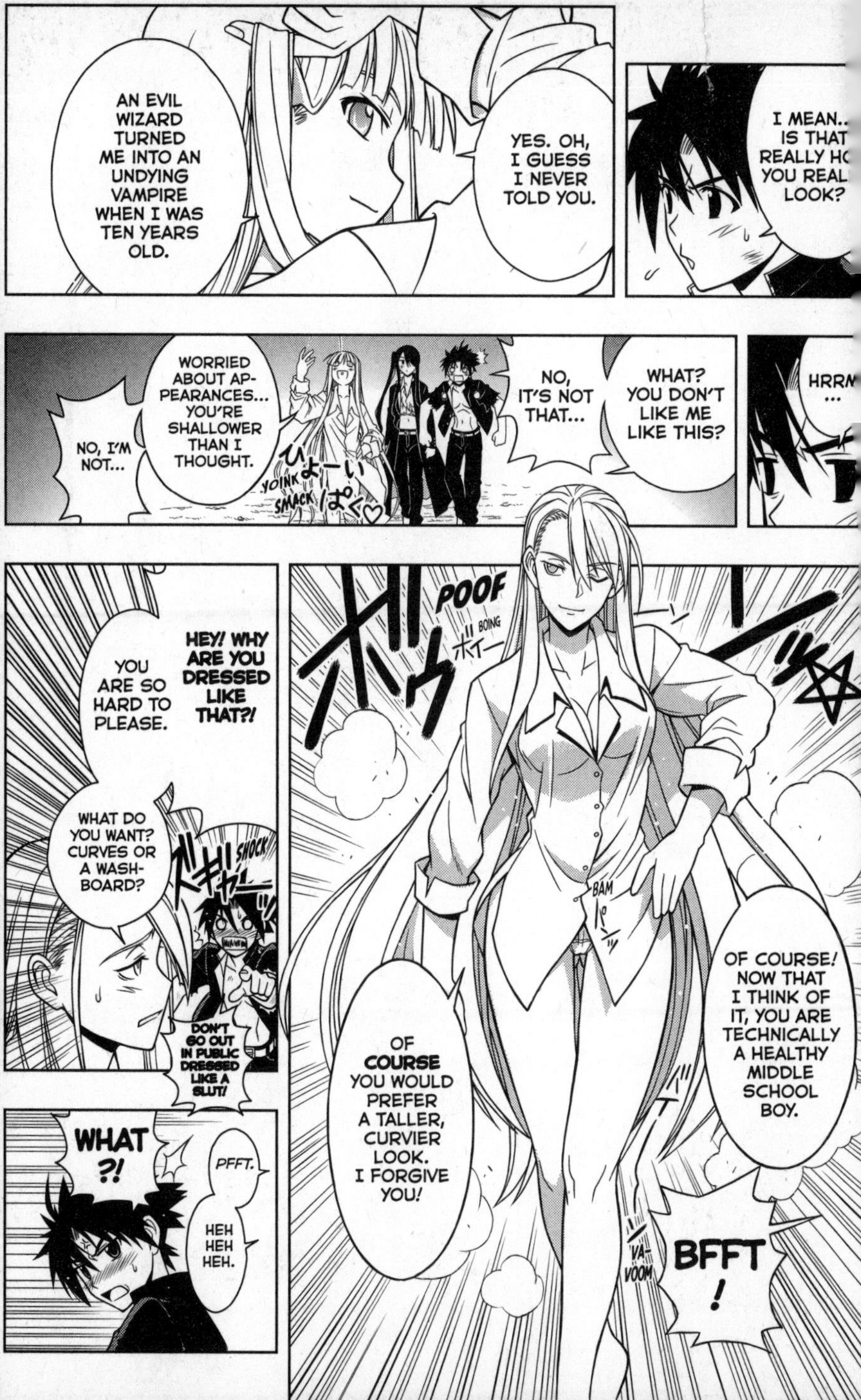
I MEAN..
IS THAT
REALLY HO
YOU REAL
LOOK?
YES. OH, I GUESS I NEVER TOLD YOU.
AN EVIL WIZARD TURNED ME INTO AN UNDYING VAMPIRE WHEN I WAS TEN YEARS OLD.
HRRM ...
WHAT? YOU DON'T LIKE ME LIKE THIS?
NO, IT'S NOT THAT...
WORRIED ABOUT AP-PEARANCES... YOU'RE SHALLOWER THAN I THOUGHT.
YOINK ひょーい
SMACK ぱく♡
NO, I'M NOT...
POOF
BOING
OF COURSE! NOW THAT I THINK OF IT, YOU ARE TECHNICALLY A HEALTHY MIDDLE SCHOOL BOY.
BAM
OF COURSE YOU WOULD PREFER A TALLER, CURVIER LOOK. I FORGIVE YOU!
VA-VOOM
BFFT !
HEY! WHY ARE YOU DRESSED LIKE THAT?!
YOU ARE SO HARD TO PLEASE.
WHAT DO YOU WANT? CURVES OR A WASH-BOARD?
SHOCK
DON'T GO OUT IN PUBLIC DRESSED LIKE A SLUT!
PFFT.
WHAT ?!
HEH HEH HEH.

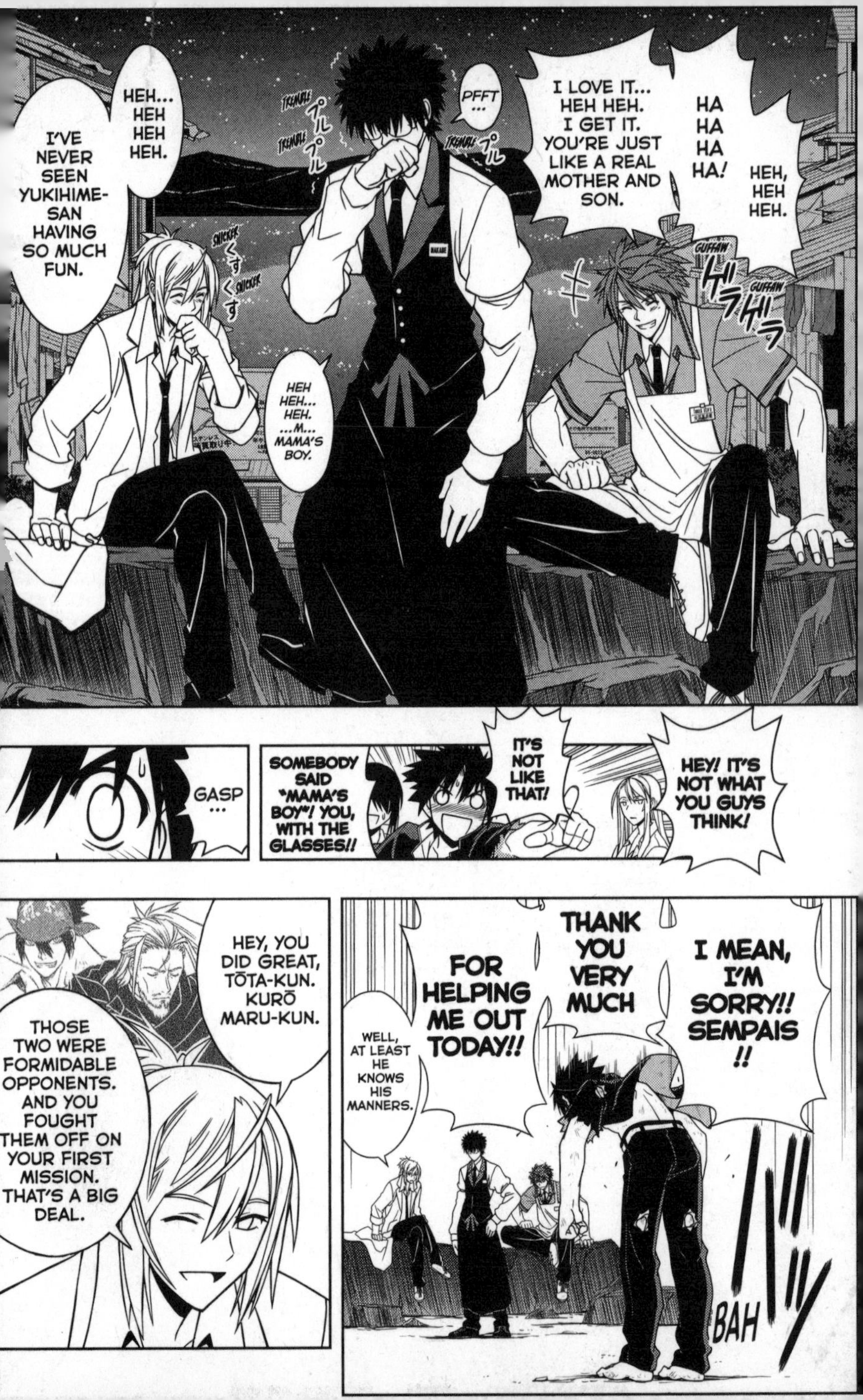
I LOVE IT... HEH HEH. I GET IT. YOU'RE JUST LIKE A REAL MOTHER AND SON.
HA HA HA HA!
HEH, HEH HEH.
GUFFAW
GUFFAW
PFFT ...
TREMBLE
TREMBLE
TREMBLE
HEH... HEH HEH HEH.
I'VE NEVER SEEN YUKIHIME-SAN HAVING SO MUCH FUN.
SNICKER
SNICKER
HEH HEH... HEH. ...M... MAMA'S BOY.
HEY! IT'S NOT WHAT YOU GUYS THINK!
IT'S NOT LIKE THAT!
SOMEBODY SAID "MAMA'S BOY"! YOU, WITH THE GLASSES!!
GASP ...
I MEAN, I'M SORRY!! SEMPAIS !!
THANK YOU VERY MUCH
FOR HELPING ME OUT TODAY!!
WELL, AT LEAST HE KNOWS HIS MANNERS.
BAH
HEY, YOU DID GREAT, TŌTA-KUN. KURŌ MARU-KUN.
THOSE TWO WERE FORMIDABLE OPPONENTS. AND YOU FOUGHT THEM OFF ON YOUR FIRST MISSION. THAT'S A BIG DEAL.

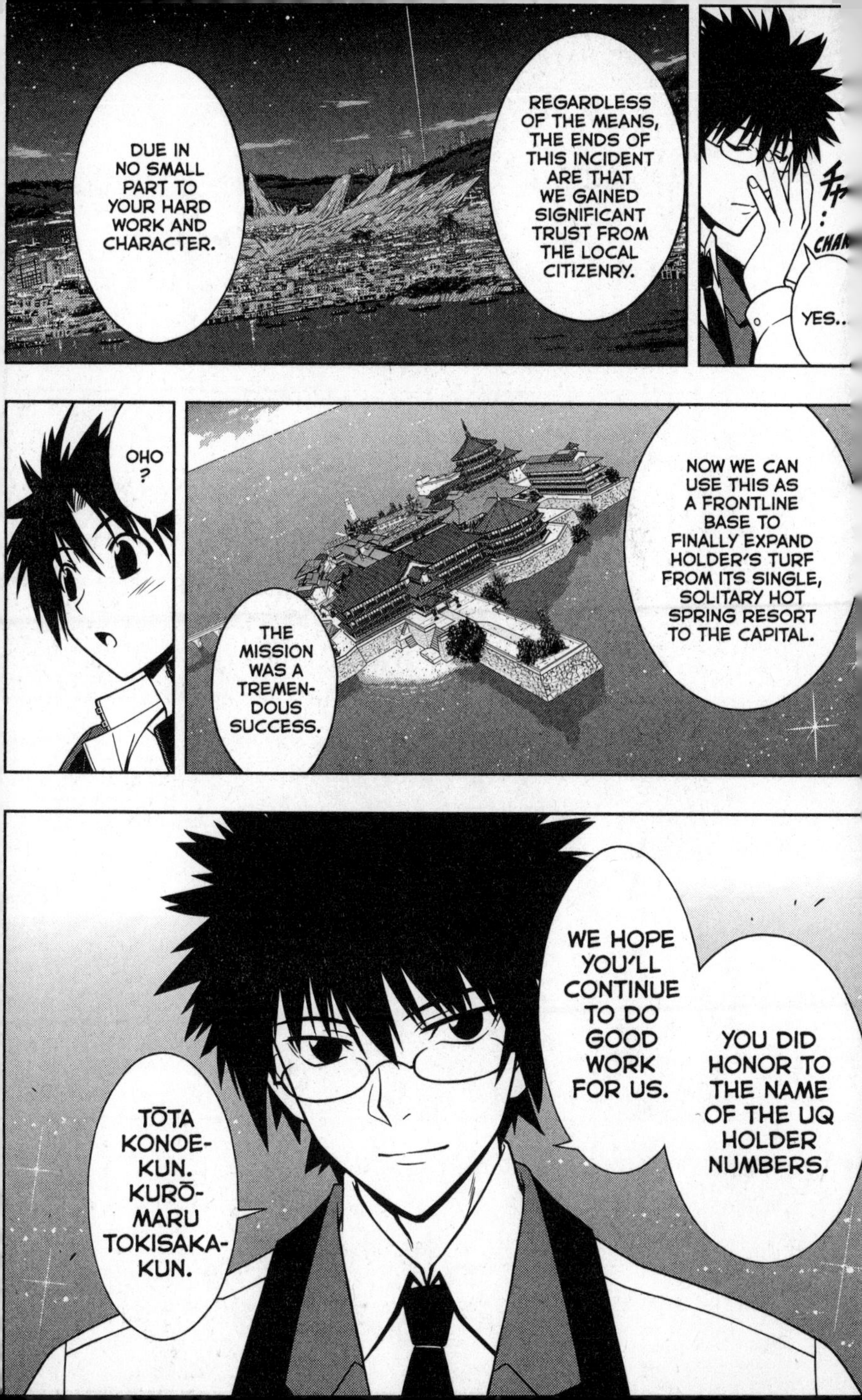
CHA
YES...
REGARDLESS OF THE MEANS, THE ENDS OF THIS INCIDENT ARE THAT WE GAINED SIGNIFICANT TRUST FROM THE LOCAL CITIZENRY.
DUE IN NO SMALL PART TO YOUR HARD WORK AND CHARACTER.
NOW WE CAN USE THIS AS A FRONTLINE BASE TO FINALLY EXPAND HOLDER'S TURF FROM ITS SINGLE, SOLITARY HOT SPRING RESORT TO THE CAPITAL.
THE MISSION WAS A TREMENDOUS SUCCESS.
OHO ?
YOU DID HONOR TO THE NAME OF THE UQ HOLDER NUMBERS.
WE HOPE YOU'LL CONTINUE TO DO GOOD WORK FOR US.
TŌTA KONOE-KUN. KURŌMARU TOKISAKA-KUN.

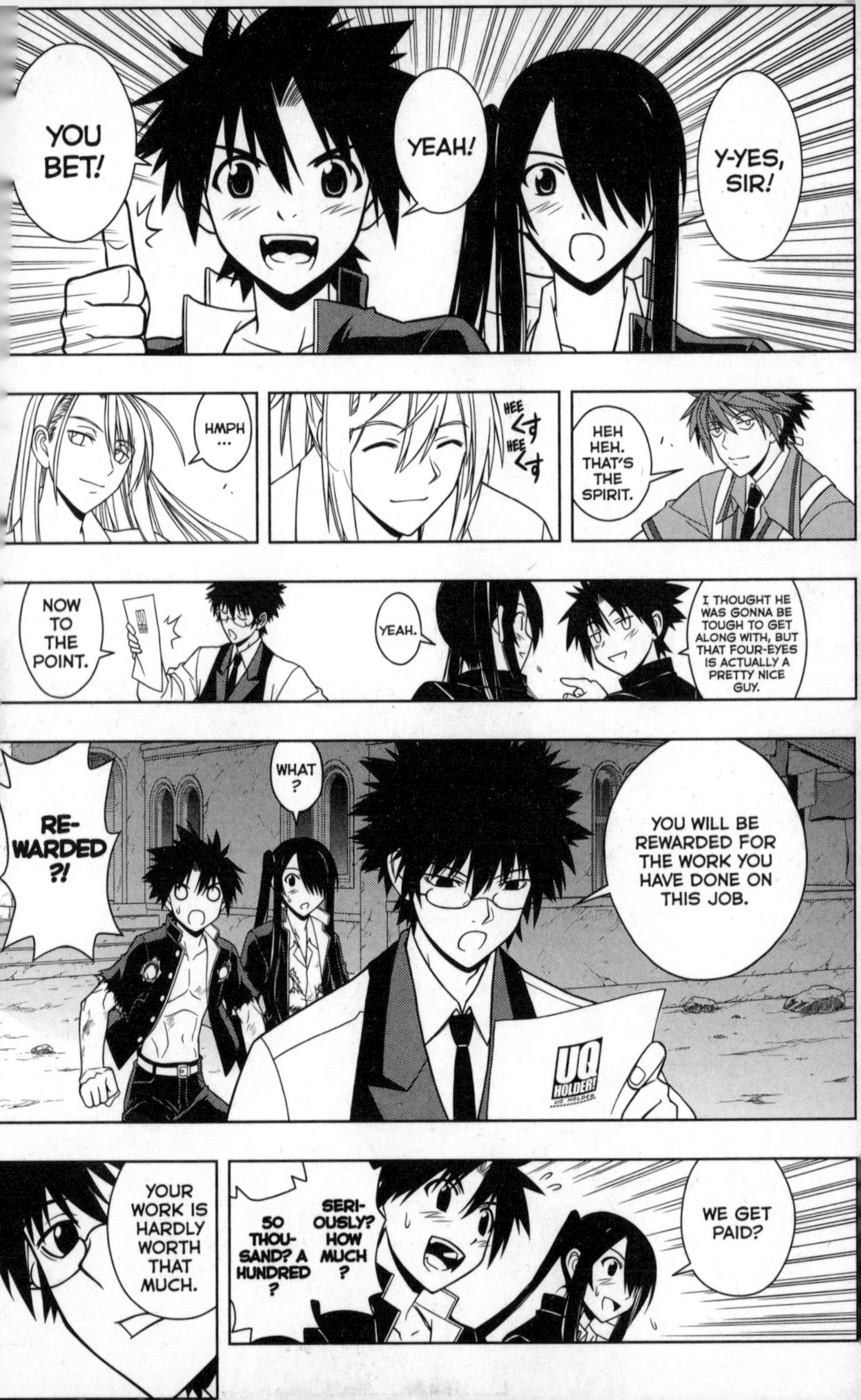

Y-YES, SIR!
YEAH!
YOU BET!
HEH HEH. THAT'S THE SPIRIT.
HEE くす HEE くす
HMPH ...
I THOUGHT HE WAS GONNA BE TOUGH TO GET ALONG WITH, BUT THAT FOUR-EYES IS ACTUALLY A PRETTY NICE GUY.
YEAH.
NOW TO THE POINT.
YOU WILL BE REWARDED FOR THE WORK YOU HAVE DONE ON THIS JOB.
WHAT?
RE-WARDED?!
WE GET PAID?
SERI-OUSLY? HOW MUCH?
SO THOU-SAND? A HUNDRED?
YOUR WORK IS HARDLY WORTH THAT MUCH.

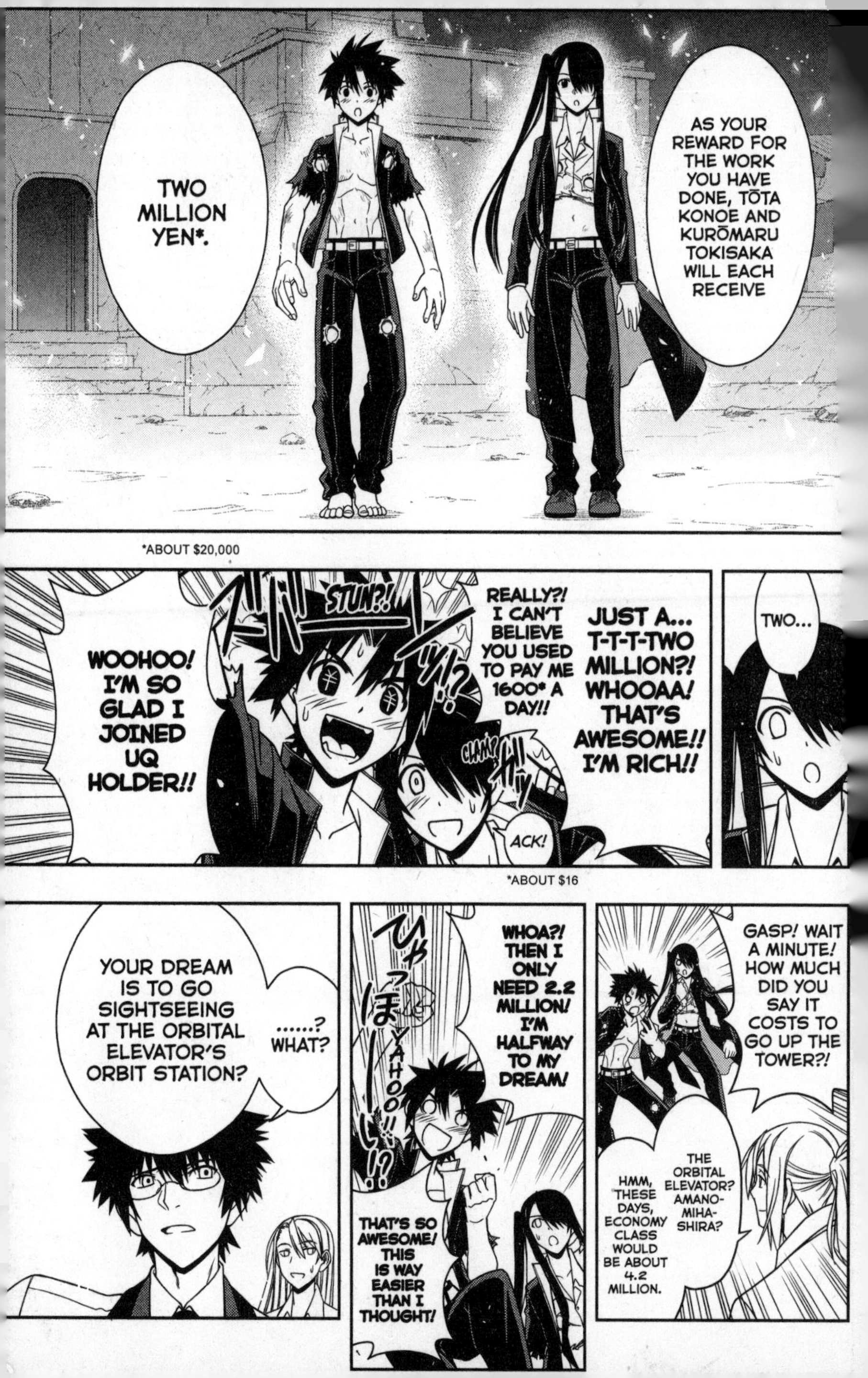
AS YOUR REWARD FOR THE WORK YOU HAVE DONE, TŌTA KONOE AND KURŌMARU TOKISAKA WILL EACH RECEIVE
TWO MILLION YEN*.
*ABOUT $20,000
TWO...
JUST A... T-T-T-TWO MILLION?! WHOOAA! THAT'S AWESOME!! I'M RICH!!
REALLY?! I CAN'T BELIEVE YOU USED TO PAY ME 1600* A DAY!!
STUN?!
ACK!
WOOHOO! I'M SO GLAD I JOINED UQ HOLDER!!
*ABOUT $16
GASP! WAIT A MINUTE! HOW MUCH DID YOU SAY IT COSTS TO GO UP THE TOWER?!
THE ORBITAL ELEVATOR? AMANO-MIHASHIRA?
HMM, THESE DAYS, ECONOMY CLASS WOULD BE ABOUT 4.2 MILLION.
WHOA?! THEN I ONLY NEED 2.2 MILLION! I'M HALFWAY TO MY DREAM!
YAHOO!!
THAT'S SO AWESOME! THIS IS WAY EASIER THAN I THOUGHT!
YOUR DREAM IS TO GO SIGHTSEEING AT THE ORBITAL ELEVATOR'S ORBIT STATION?
......? WHAT?

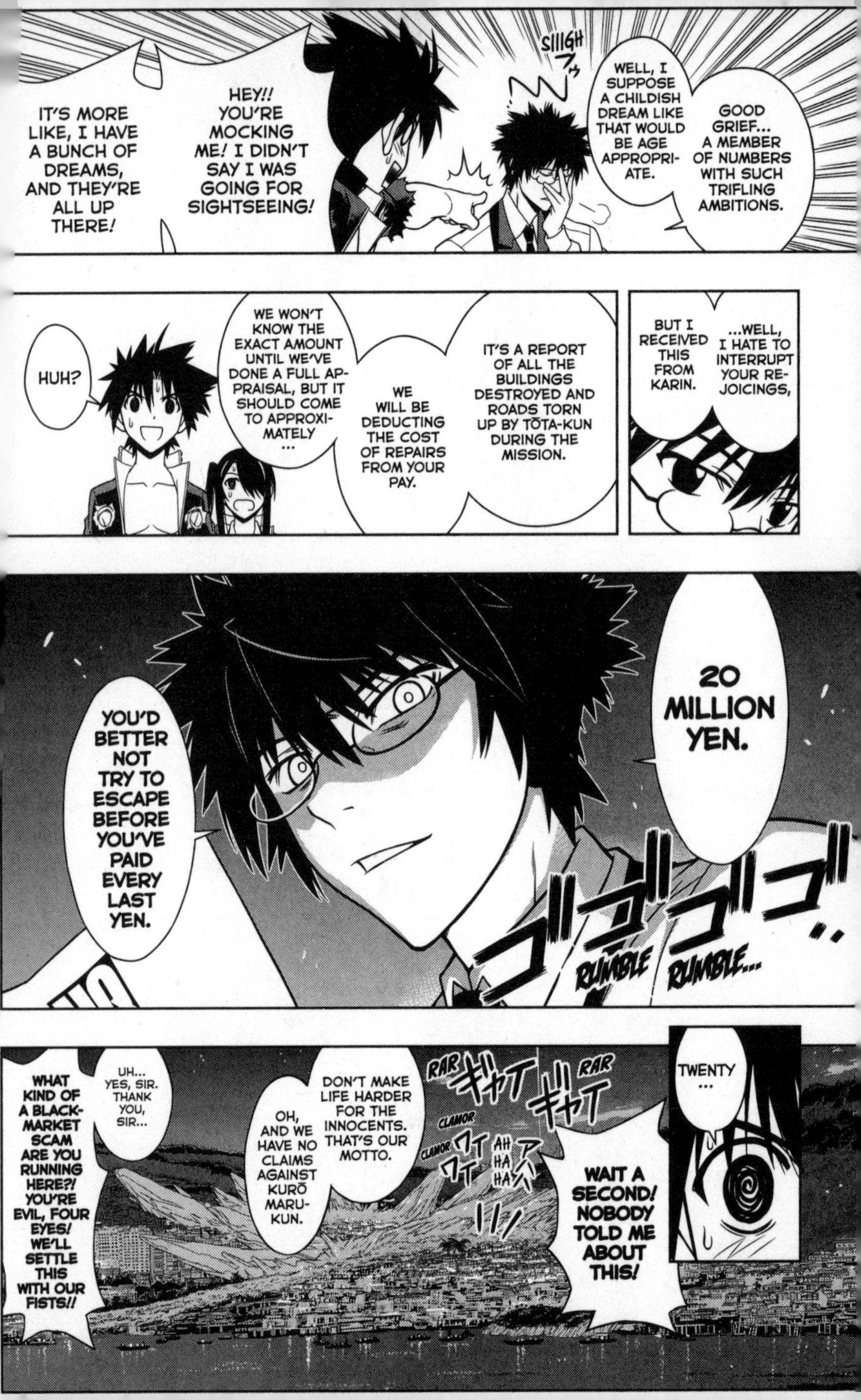
GOOD GRIEF... A MEMBER OF NUMBERS WITH SUCH TRIFLING AMBITIONS.
WELL, I SUPPOSE A CHILDISH DREAM LIKE THAT WOULD BE AGE APPROPRI-ATE.
SIIIGH
HEY!! YOU'RE MOCKING ME! I DIDN'T SAY I WAS GOING FOR SIGHTSEEING!
IT'S MORE LIKE, I HAVE A BUNCH OF DREAMS, AND THEY'RE ALL UP THERE!
...WELL, I HATE TO INTERRUPT YOUR RE-JOICINGS,
BUT I RECEIVED THIS FROM KARIN.
IT'S A REPORT OF ALL THE BUILDINGS DESTROYED AND ROADS TORN UP BY TŌTA-KUN DURING THE MISSION.
WE WILL BE DEDUCTING THE COST OF REPAIRS FROM YOUR PAY.
WE WON'T KNOW THE EXACT AMOUNT UNTIL WE'VE DONE A FULL AP-PRAISAL, BUT IT SHOULD COME TO APPROXI-MATELY ...
HUH?
20 MILLION YEN.
YOU'D BETTER NOT TRY TO ESCAPE BEFORE YOU'VE PAID EVERY LAST YEN.
RUMBLE RUMBLE...
TWENTY ...
WAIT A SECOND! NOBODY TOLD ME ABOUT THIS!
RAR RAR
CLAMOR CLAMOR
AH HA HA
DON'T MAKE LIFE HARDER FOR THE INNOCENTS. THAT'S OUR MOTTO.
OH, AND WE HAVE NO CLAIMS AGAINST KURŌ MARU-KUN.
UH... YES, SIR. THANK YOU, SIR...
WHAT KIND OF A BLACK-MARKET SCAM ARE YOU RUNNING HERE?! YOU'RE EVIL, FOUR EYES! WE'LL SETTLE THIS WITH OUR FISTS!!

UQ HOLDER!

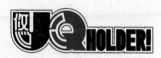

UQ HOLDER!

ユーキューホルダー!

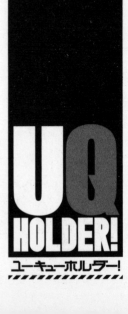

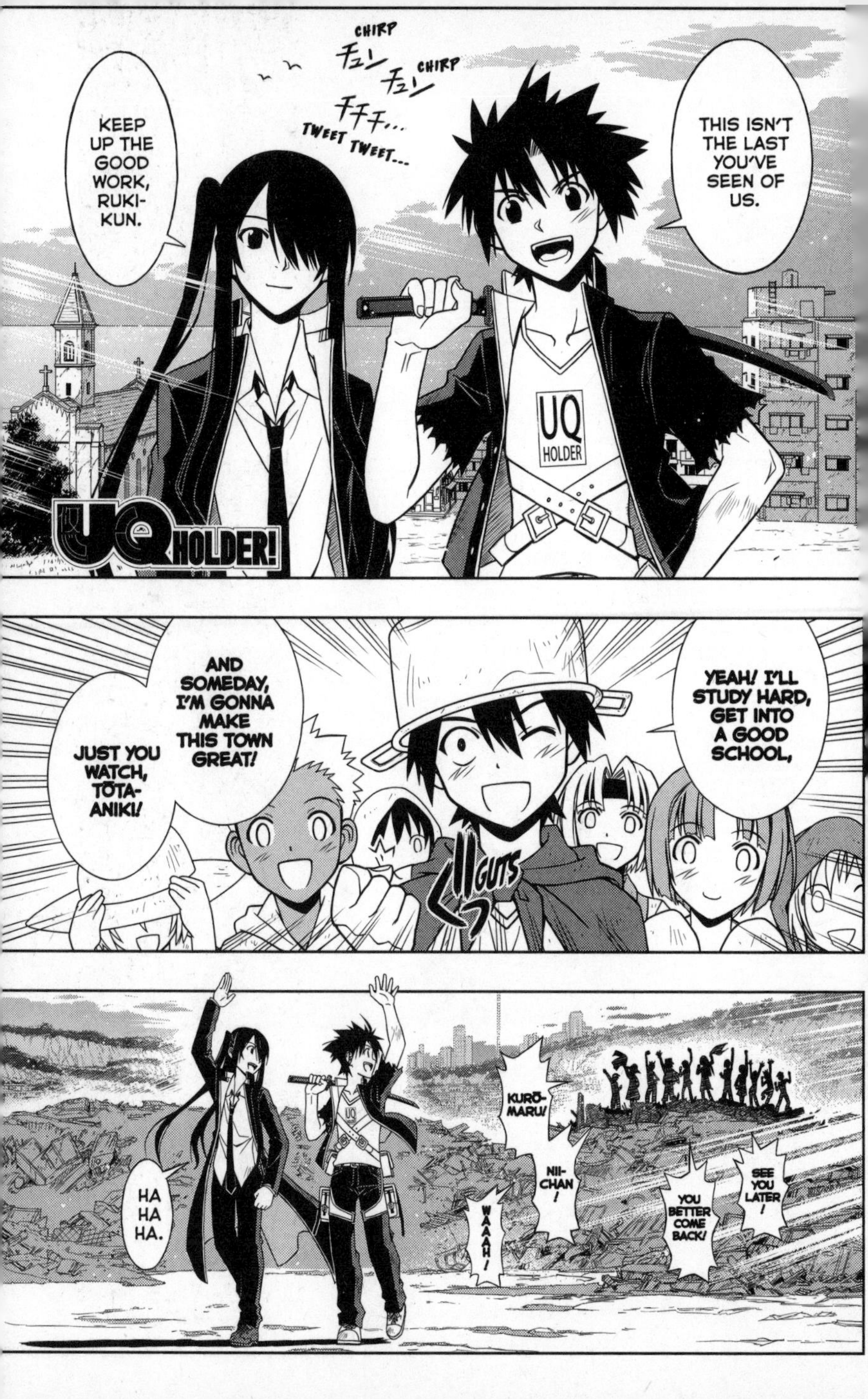
THIS ISN'T THE LAST YOU'VE SEEN OF US.
チュン CHIRP
チュン CHIRP
チチチ... TWEET TWEET...
KEEP UP THE GOOD WORK, RUKI-KUN.
YEAH! I'LL STUDY HARD, GET INTO A GOOD SCHOOL,
AND SOMEDAY, I'M GONNA MAKE THIS TOWN GREAT!
JUST YOU WATCH, TŌTA-ANIKI!
GUTS
SEE YOU LATER!
YOU BETTER COME BACK!
NII-CHAN!
KURŌ-MARU!
WAAAH!
HA HA HA.

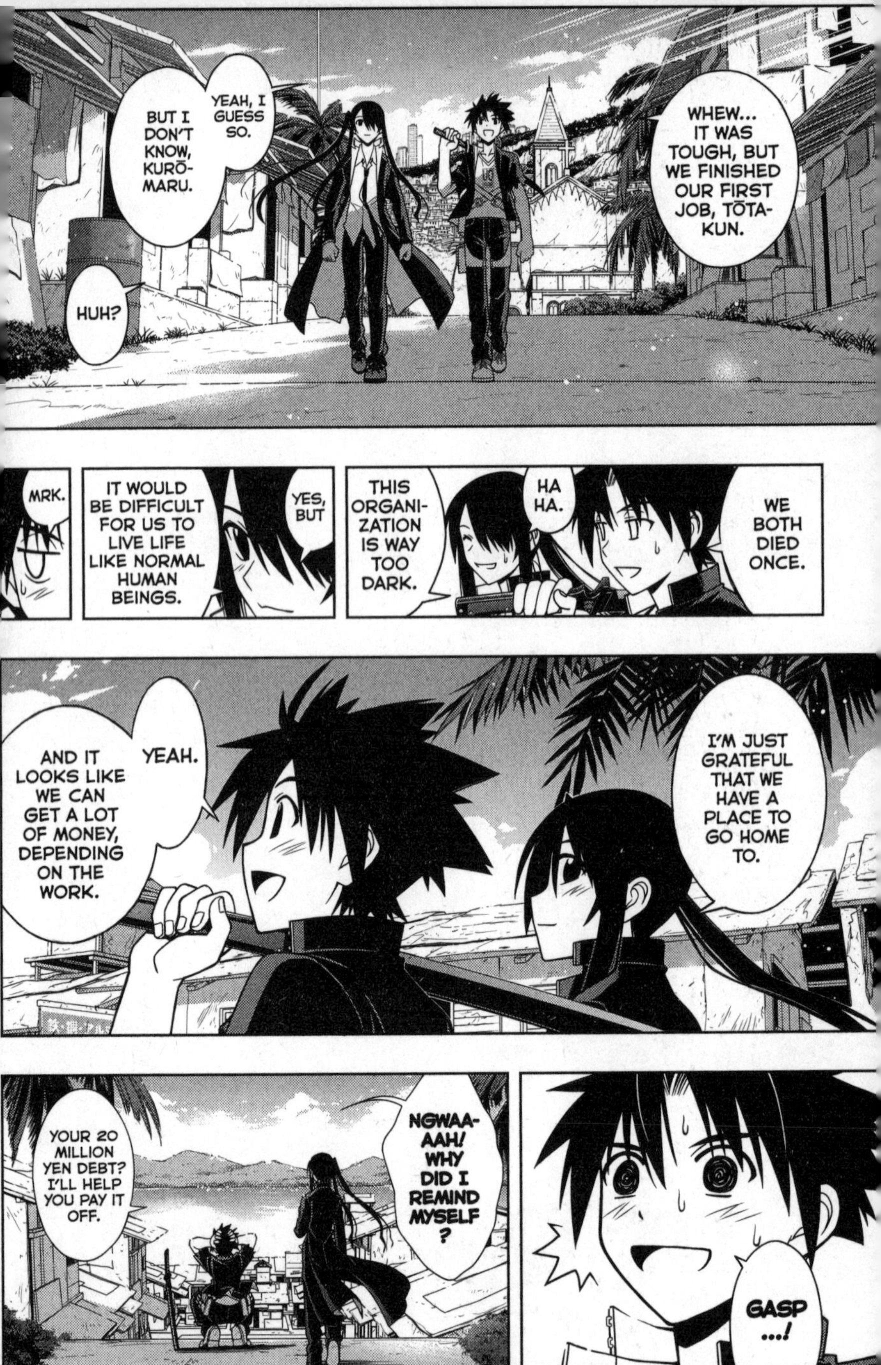
WHEW... IT WAS TOUGH, BUT WE FINISHED OUR FIRST JOB, TŌTA-KUN.
YEAH, I GUESS SO.
BUT I DON'T KNOW, KURŌMARU.
HUH?
WE BOTH DIED ONCE.
HA HA.
THIS ORGANIZATION IS WAY TOO DARK.
YES, BUT
IT WOULD BE DIFFICULT FOR US TO LIVE LIFE LIKE NORMAL HUMAN BEINGS.
MRK.
I'M JUST GRATEFUL THAT WE HAVE A PLACE TO GO HOME TO.
YEAH.
AND IT LOOKS LIKE WE CAN GET A LOT OF MONEY, DEPENDING ON THE WORK.
GASP ...!
YOUR 20 MILLION YEN DEBT? I'LL HELP YOU PAY IT OFF.
NGWAAAAH! WHY DID I REMIND MYSELF?

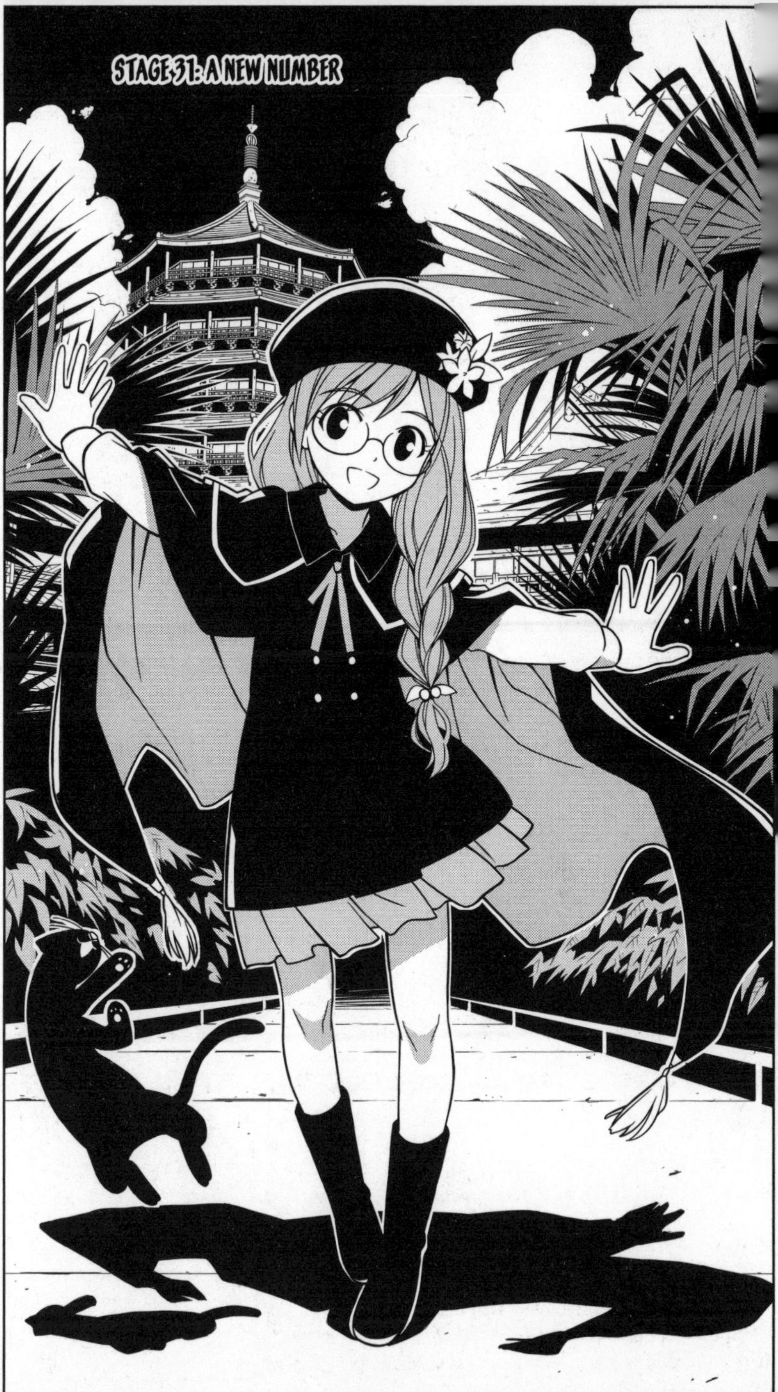
STAGE 31: A NEW NUMBER

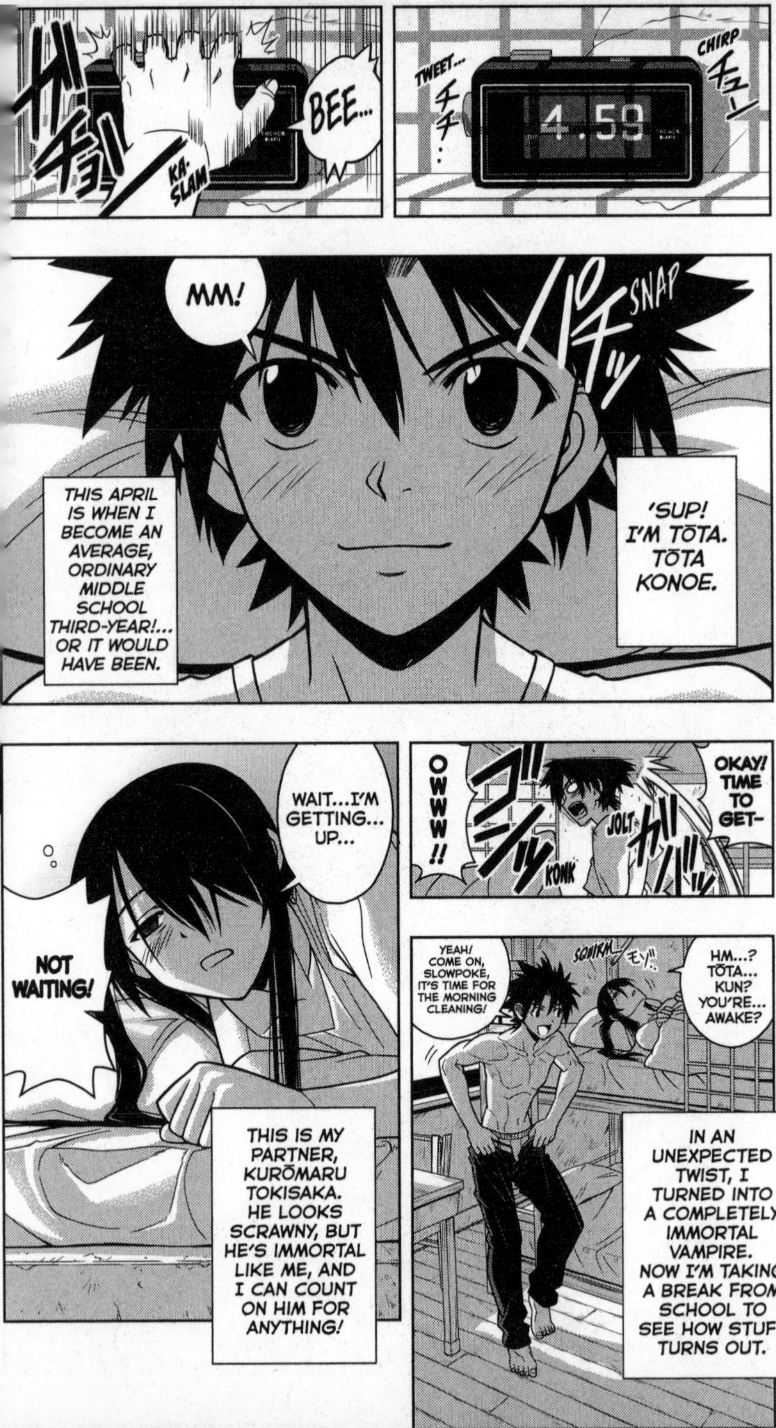

CHIRP
チュン
TWEET...
チチ...
4.59
BEE...
KA-SLAM
MM!
SNAP
パチッ
'SUP! I'M TŌTA. TŌTA KONOE.
THIS APRIL IS WHEN I BECOME AN AVERAGE, ORDINARY MIDDLE SCHOOL THIRD-YEAR!... OR IT WOULD HAVE BEEN.
OKAY! TIME TO GET-
JOLT
ガバッ
KONK
ゴンッ
OWWW!!
HM...? TŌTA... KUN? YOU'RE... AWAKE?
SQUIRM
モゾ
YEAH! COME ON, SLOWPOKE, IT'S TIME FOR THE MORNING CLEANING!
IN AN UNEXPECTED TWIST, I TURNED INTO A COMPLETELY IMMORTAL VAMPIRE. NOW I'M TAKING A BREAK FROM SCHOOL TO SEE HOW STUFF TURNS OUT.
WAIT...I'M GETTING... UP...
NOT WAITING!
THIS IS MY PARTNER, KURŌMARU TOKISAKA. HE LOOKS SCRAWNY, BUT HE'S IMMORTAL LIKE ME, AND I CAN COUNT ON HIM FOR ANYTHING!

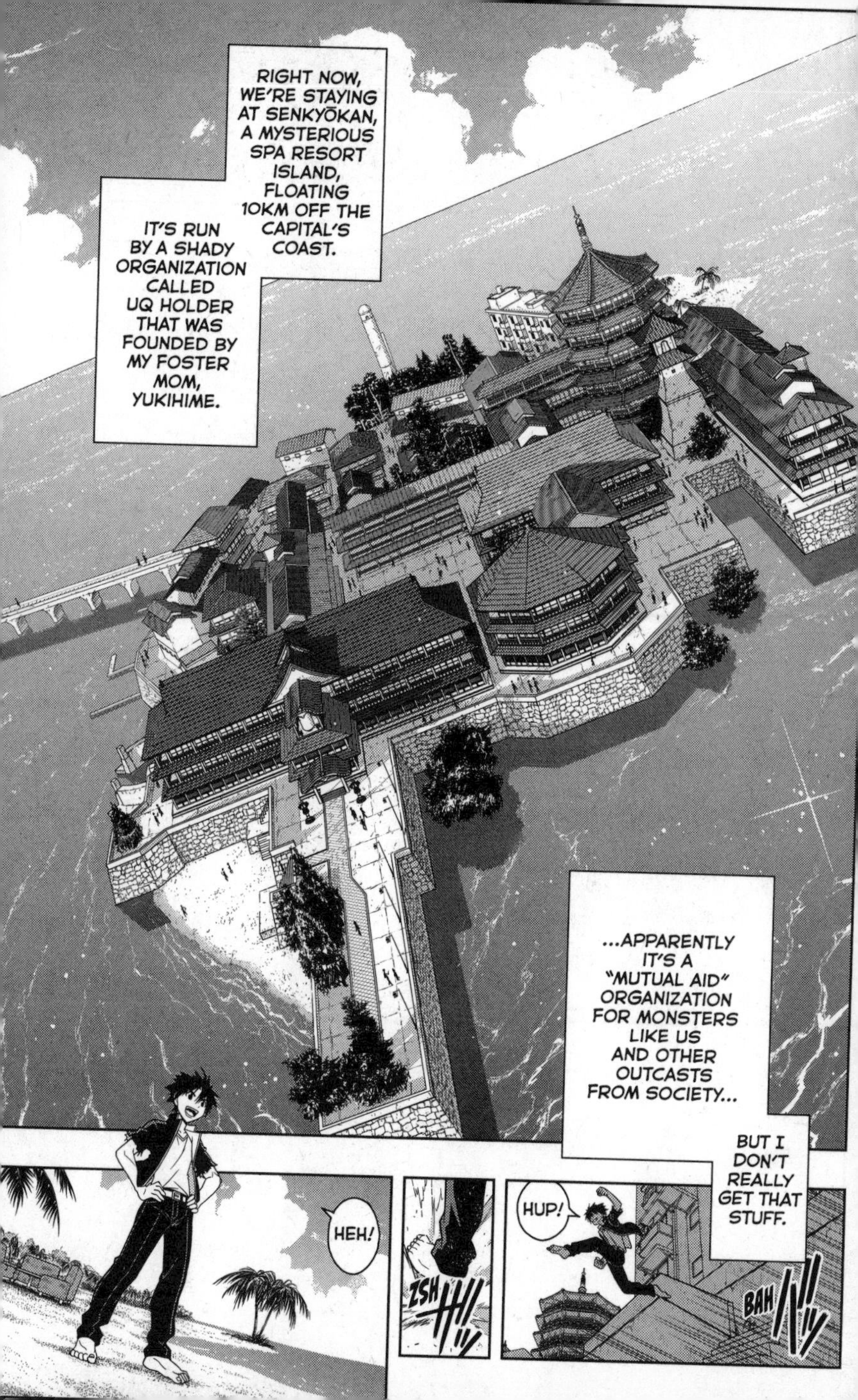
RIGHT NOW, WE'RE STAYING AT SENKYŌKAN, A MYSTERIOUS SPA RESORT ISLAND, FLOATING 10KM OFF THE CAPITAL'S COAST.
IT'S RUN BY A SHADY ORGANIZATION CALLED UQ HOLDER THAT WAS FOUNDED BY MY FOSTER MOM, YUKIHIME.
...APPARENTLY IT'S A "MUTUAL AID" ORGANIZATION FOR MONSTERS LIKE US AND OTHER OUTCASTS FROM SOCIETY...
BUT I DON'T REALLY GET THAT STUFF.
HUP!
BAH
ZSH
HEH!

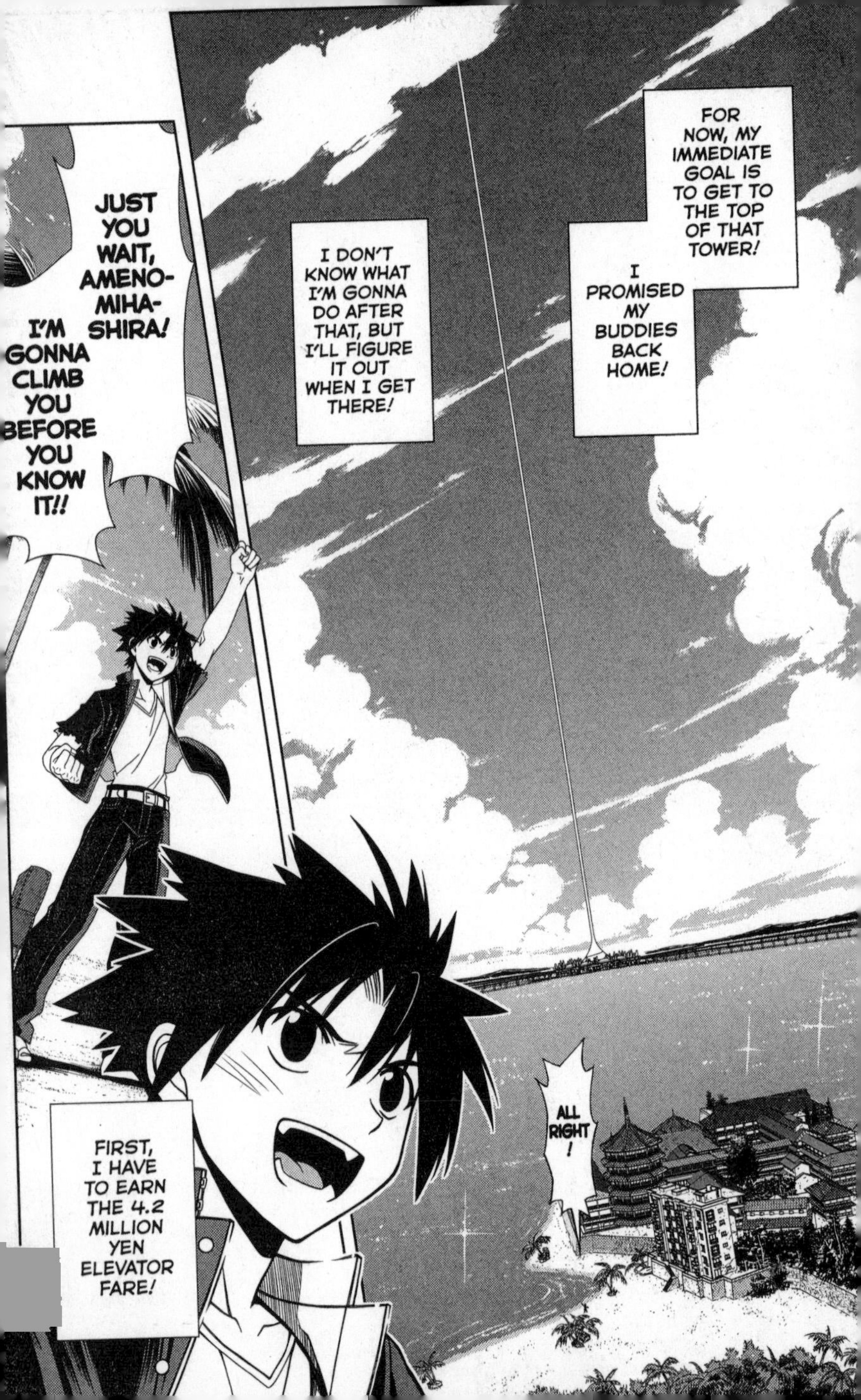
FOR NOW, MY IMMEDIATE GOAL IS TO GET TO THE TOP OF THAT TOWER!
I PROMISED MY BUDDIES BACK HOME!
I DON'T KNOW WHAT I'M GONNA DO AFTER THAT, BUT I'LL FIGURE IT OUT WHEN I GET THERE!
ALL RIGHT!
FIRST, I HAVE TO EARN THE 4.2 MILLION YEN ELEVATOR FARE!
JUST YOU WAIT, AMENO-MIHA-SHIRA!
I'M GONNA CLIMB YOU BEFORE YOU KNOW IT!!

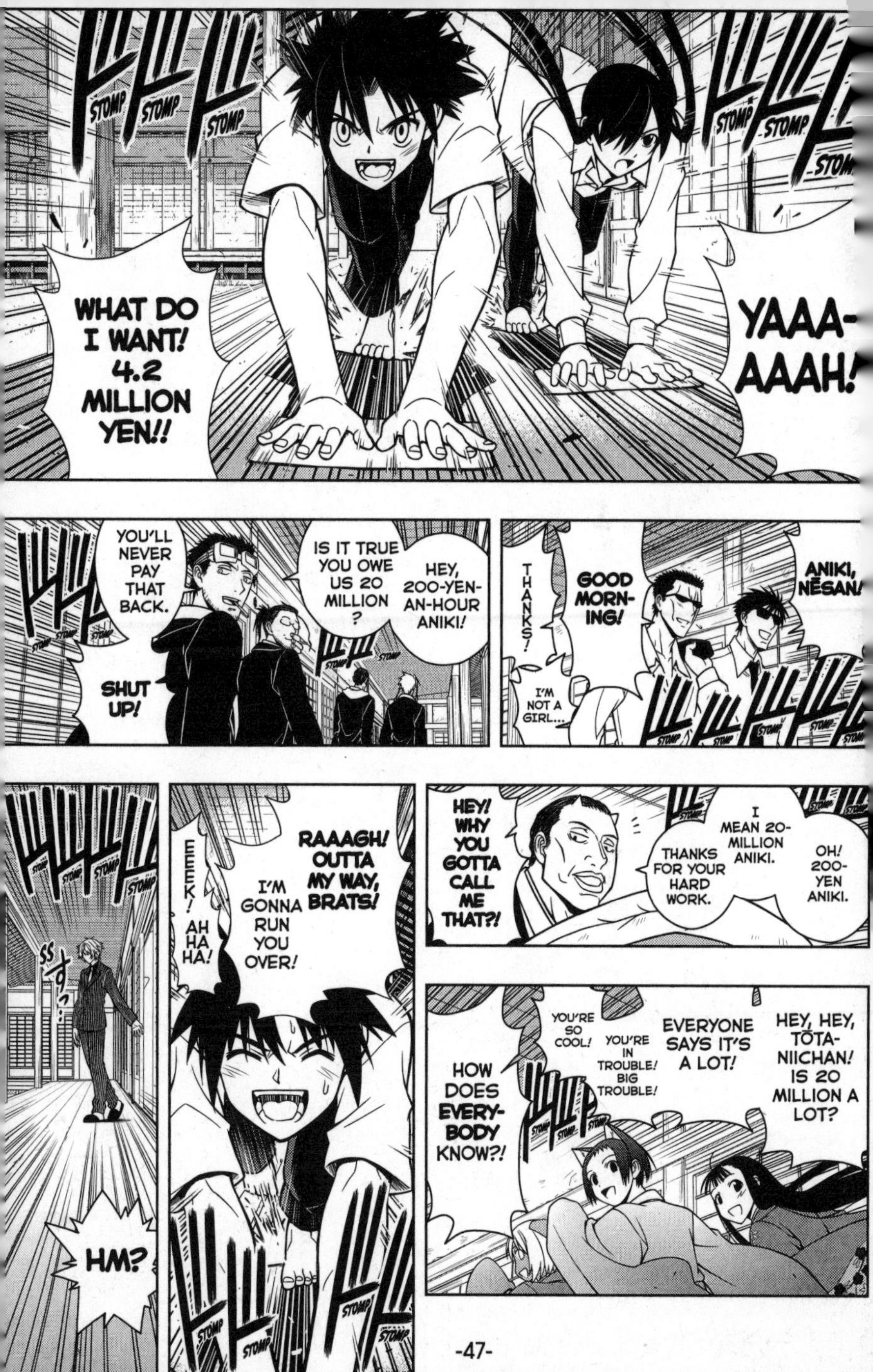
STOMP STOMP STOMP
YAAAA-AAAH!
STOMP STOMP STOMP
WHAT DO I WANT! 4.2 MILLION YEN!!
ANIKI, NĒSAN!
GOOD MORNING!
THANKS!
I'M NOT A GIRL...
STOMP STOMP STOMP
HEY, 200-YEN-AN-HOUR ANIKI!
IS IT TRUE YOU OWE US 20 MILLION?
YOU'LL NEVER PAY THAT BACK.
SHUT UP!
STOMP STOMP
OH! 200-YEN ANIKI.
I MEAN 20-MILLION ANIKI.
THANKS FOR YOUR HARD WORK.
HEY! WHY YOU GOTTA CALL ME THAT?!
HEY, HEY, TŌTA-NIICHAN! IS 20 MILLION A LOT?
EVERYONE SAYS IT'S A LOT!
YOU'RE IN TROUBLE! BIG TROUBLE!
YOU'RE SO COOL!
HOW DOES EVERYBODY KNOW?!
STOMP STOMP STOMP
RAAAGH! OUTTA MY WAY, BRATS!
I'M GONNA RUN YOU OVER!
EEEK!
AH HA HA!
STOMP STOMP STOMP
STOMP STOMP STOMP STOMP
SS すっ
HM?

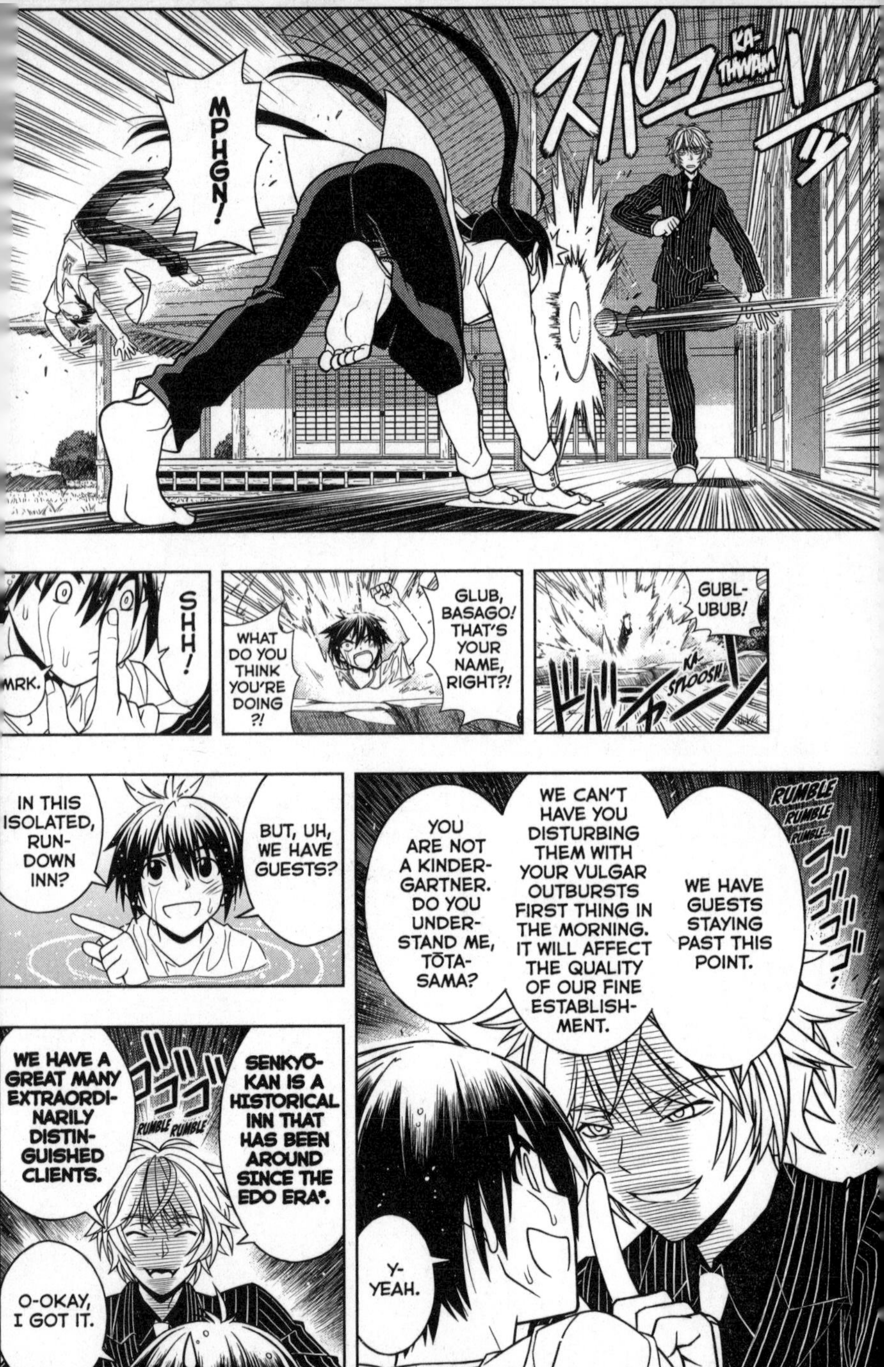
KA-THWAM
MPHGN!
GUBL-UBUB!
KA-SPLOOSH
GLUB, BASAGO! THAT'S YOUR NAME, RIGHT?!
WHAT DO YOU THINK YOU'RE DOING?!
SHH!
MRK.
RUMBLE RUMBLE RUMBLE...
WE HAVE GUESTS STAYING PAST THIS POINT.
WE CAN'T HAVE YOU DISTURBING THEM WITH YOUR VULGAR OUTBURSTS FIRST THING IN THE MORNING. IT WILL AFFECT THE QUALITY OF OUR FINE ESTABLISHMENT.
YOU ARE NOT A KINDERGARTNER. DO YOU UNDERSTAND ME, TŌTA-SAMA?
Y-YEAH.
BUT, UH, WE HAVE GUESTS?
IN THIS ISOLATED, RUN-DOWN INN?
SENKYŌ-KAN IS A HISTORICAL INN THAT HAS BEEN AROUND SINCE THE EDO ERA*.
RUMBLE RUMBLE
WE HAVE A GREAT MANY EXTRAORDINARILY DISTINGUISHED CLIENTS.
O-OKAY, I GOT IT.

*1603-1868

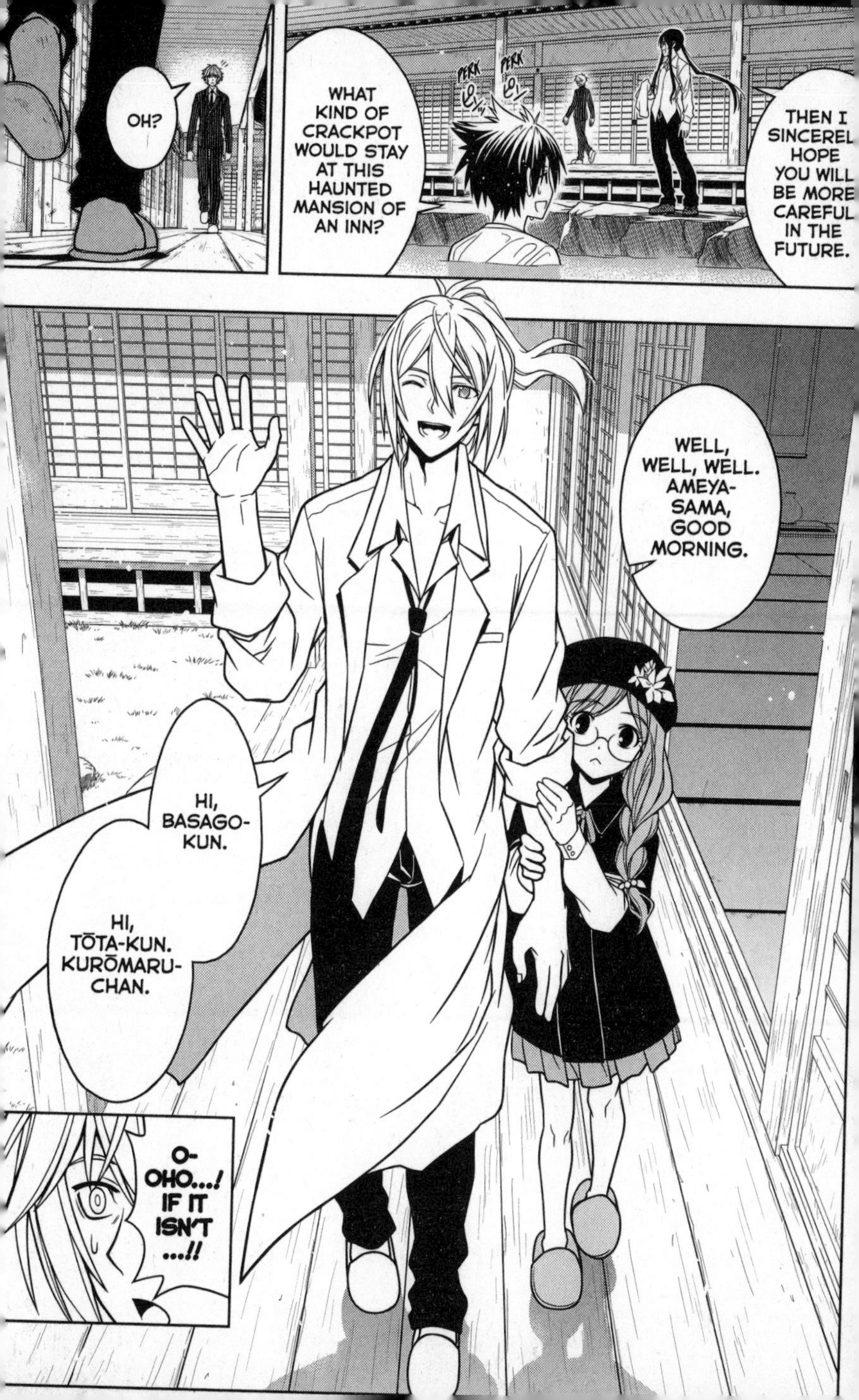
THEN I SINCEREL HOPE YOU WILL BE MORE CAREFUL IN THE FUTURE.
PERK PERK
WHAT KIND OF CRACKPOT WOULD STAY AT THIS HAUNTED MANSION OF AN INN?
OH?
WELL, WELL, WELL. AMEYA-SAMA, GOOD MORNING.
HI, BASAGO-KUN.
HI, TŌTA-KUN. KURŌMARU-CHAN.
O-OHO...! IF IT ISN'T ...!!

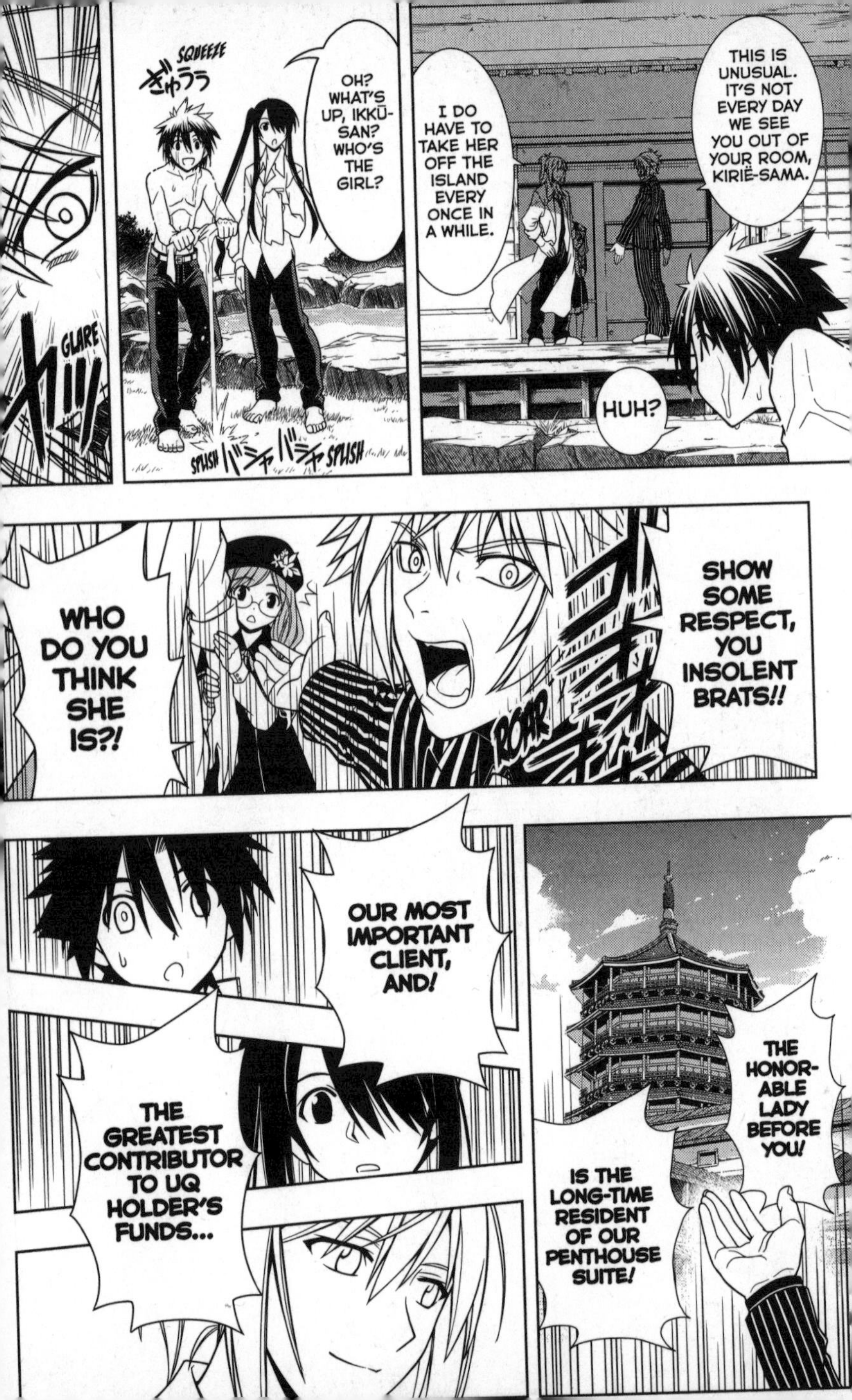

THIS IS UNUSUAL. IT'S NOT EVERY DAY WE SEE YOU OUT OF YOUR ROOM, KIRIË-SAMA.
I DO HAVE TO TAKE HER OFF THE ISLAND EVERY ONCE IN A WHILE.
HUH?
OH? WHAT'S UP, IKKŪ-SAN? WHO'S THE GIRL?
SQUEEZE
ぎゅうう
SPLISH
バシャバシャ
SPLISH
GLARE
カッ!!
SHOW SOME RESPECT, YOU INSOLENT BRATS!!
ROAR
WHO DO YOU THINK SHE IS?!
THE HONORABLE LADY BEFORE YOU!
IS THE LONG-TIME RESIDENT OF OUR PENTHOUSE SUITE!
OUR MOST IMPORTANT CLIENT, AND!
THE GREATEST CONTRIBUTOR TO UQ HOLDER'S FUNDS...

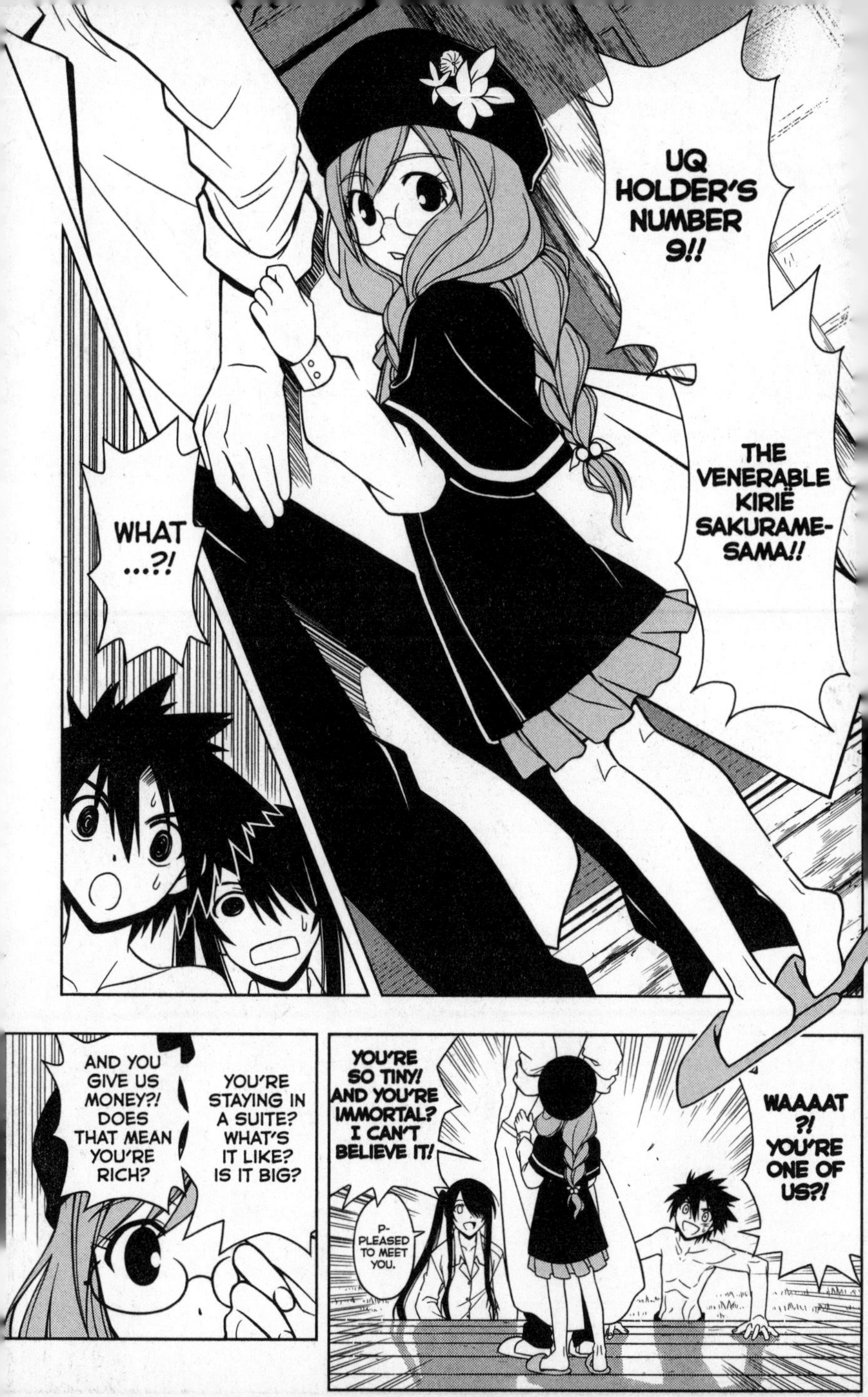
UQ HOLDER'S NUMBER 9!!
THE VENERABLE KIRIË SAKURAME-SAMA!!
WHAT...?!
WAAAAT?! YOU'RE ONE OF US?!
YOU'RE SO TINY! AND YOU'RE IMMORTAL? I CAN'T BELIEVE IT!
P-PLEASED TO MEET YOU.
YOU'RE STAYING IN A SUITE? WHAT'S IT LIKE? IS IT BIG?
AND YOU GIVE US MONEY?! DOES THAT MEAN YOU'RE RICH?

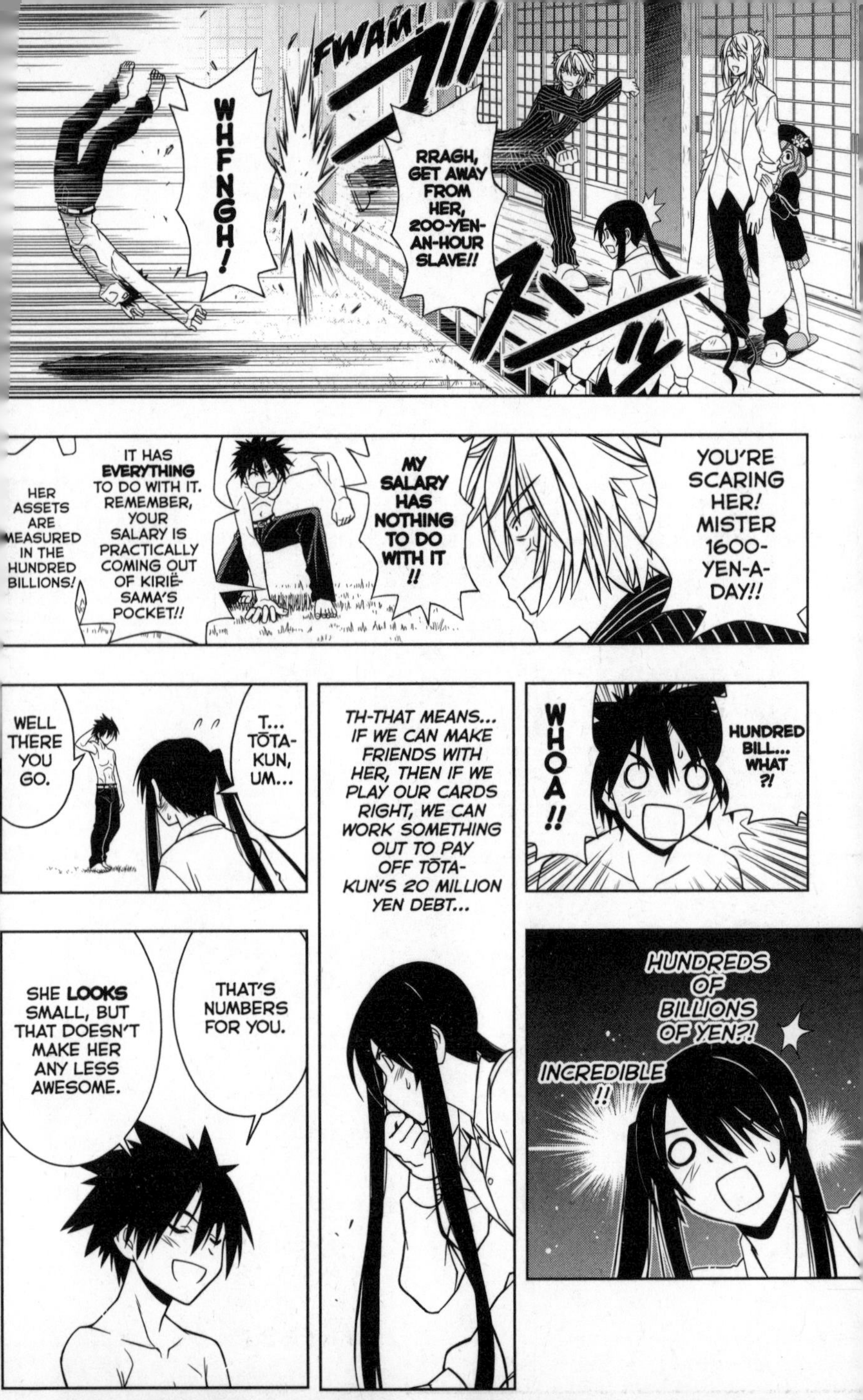
FWAM!
RRAGH, GET AWAY FROM HER, 200-YEN-AN-HOUR SLAVE!!
WHFNGH!
YOU'RE SCARING HER! MISTER 1600-YEN-A-DAY!!
MY SALARY HAS NOTHING TO DO WITH IT!!
IT HAS EVERYTHING TO DO WITH IT. REMEMBER, YOUR SALARY IS PRACTICALLY COMING OUT OF KIRIË-SAMA'S POCKET!!
HER ASSETS ARE MEASURED IN THE HUNDRED BILLIONS!
HUNDRED BILL... WHAT?!
WHOA!!
HUNDREDS OF BILLIONS OF YEN?!
INCREDIBLE!!
TH-THAT MEANS... IF WE CAN MAKE FRIENDS WITH HER, THEN IF WE PLAY OUR CARDS RIGHT, WE CAN WORK SOMETHING OUT TO PAY OFF TŌTA-KUN'S 20 MILLION YEN DEBT...
T... TŌTA-KUN, UM...
WELL THERE YOU GO.
THAT'S NUMBERS FOR YOU.
SHE LOOKS SMALL, BUT THAT DOESN'T MAKE HER ANY LESS AWESOME.

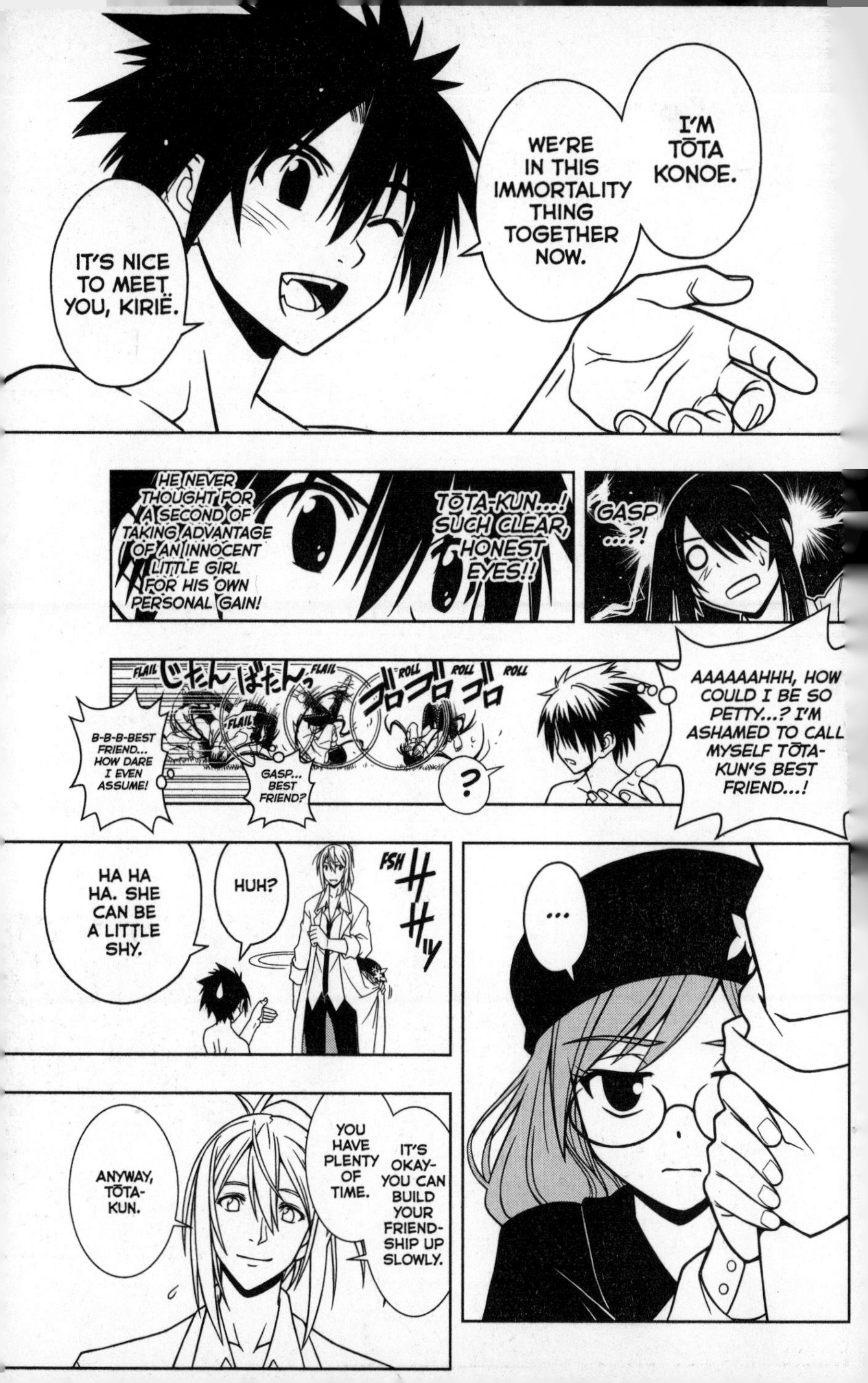
I'M TŌTA KONOE.
WE'RE IN THIS IMMORTALITY THING TOGETHER NOW.
IT'S NICE TO MEET YOU, KIRIË.
GASP ...?!
TŌTA-KUN...! SUCH CLEAR, HONEST EYES!!
HE NEVER THOUGHT FOR A SECOND OF TAKING ADVANTAGE OF AN INNOCENT LITTLE GIRL FOR HIS OWN PERSONAL GAIN!
AAAAAAHHH, HOW COULD I BE SO PETTY...? I'M ASHAMED TO CALL MYSELF TŌTA-KUN'S BEST FRIEND...!
?
ROLL ROLL ROLL
FLAIL FLAIL FLAIL
GASP... BEST FRIEND?
B-B-B-BEST FRIEND... HOW DARE I EVEN ASSUME!
...
FSH
HUH?
HA HA HA. SHE CAN BE A LITTLE SHY.
IT'S OKAY- YOU CAN BUILD YOUR FRIEND-SHIP UP SLOWLY.
YOU HAVE PLENTY OF TIME.
ANYWAY, TŌTA-KUN.

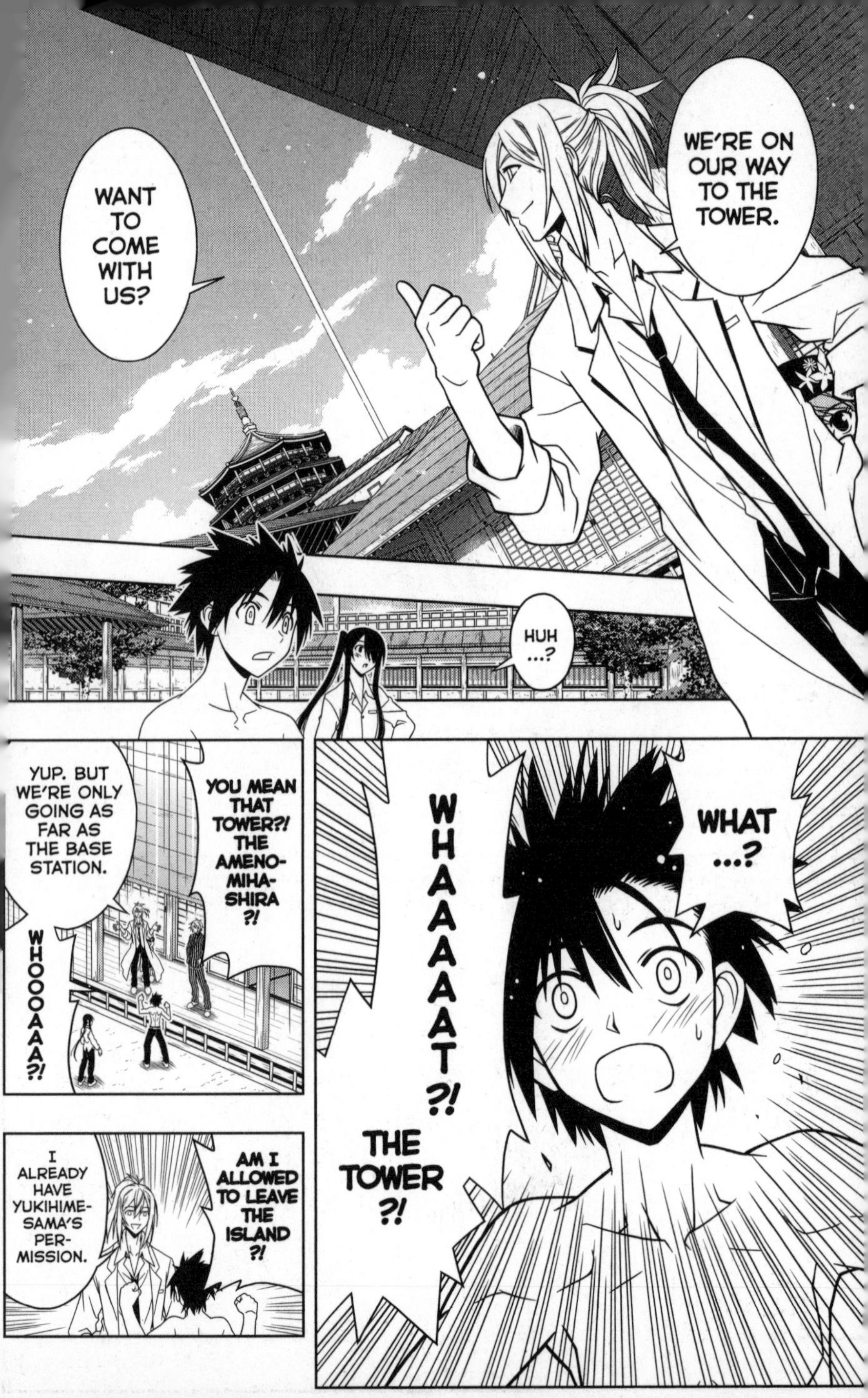
WE'RE ON OUR WAY TO THE TOWER.
WANT TO COME WITH US?
HUH ...?
WHAT ...?
WHAAAAAT?!
THE TOWER?!
YOU MEAN THAT TOWER?! THE AMENO-MIHA-SHIRA?!
YUP. BUT WE'RE ONLY GOING AS FAR AS THE BASE STATION.
WHOOOAAA?!
AM I ALLOWED TO LEAVE THE ISLAND?!
I ALREADY HAVE YUKIHIME-SAMA'S PER-MISSION.

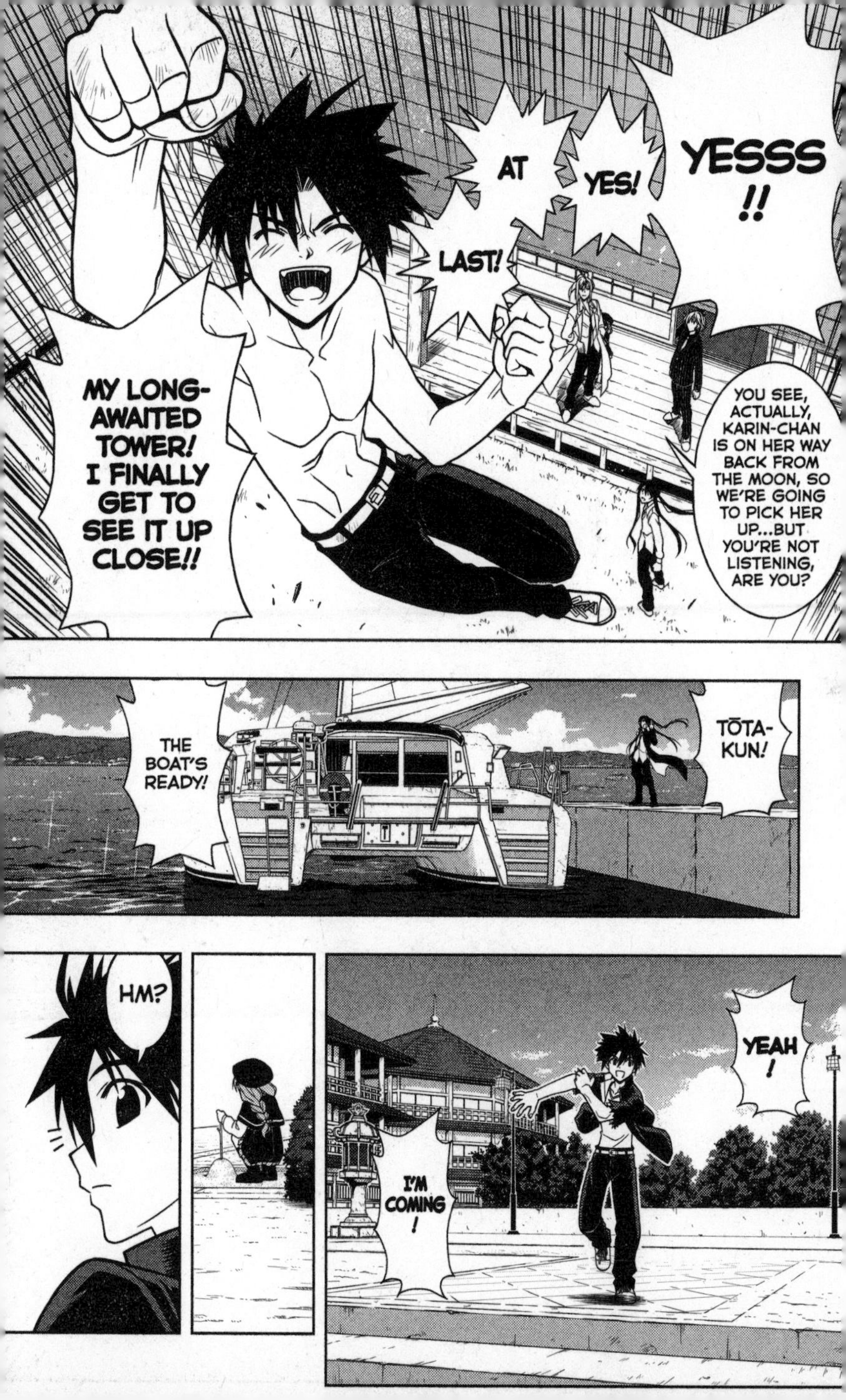
YESSS !!
YES!
AT
LAST!
YOU SEE, ACTUALLY, KARIN-CHAN IS ON HER WAY BACK FROM THE MOON, SO WE'RE GOING TO PICK HER UP...BUT YOU'RE NOT LISTENING, ARE YOU?
MY LONG-AWAITED TOWER! I FINALLY GET TO SEE IT UP CLOSE!!
TŌTA-KUN!
THE BOAT'S READY!
YEAH !
I'M COMING !
HM?

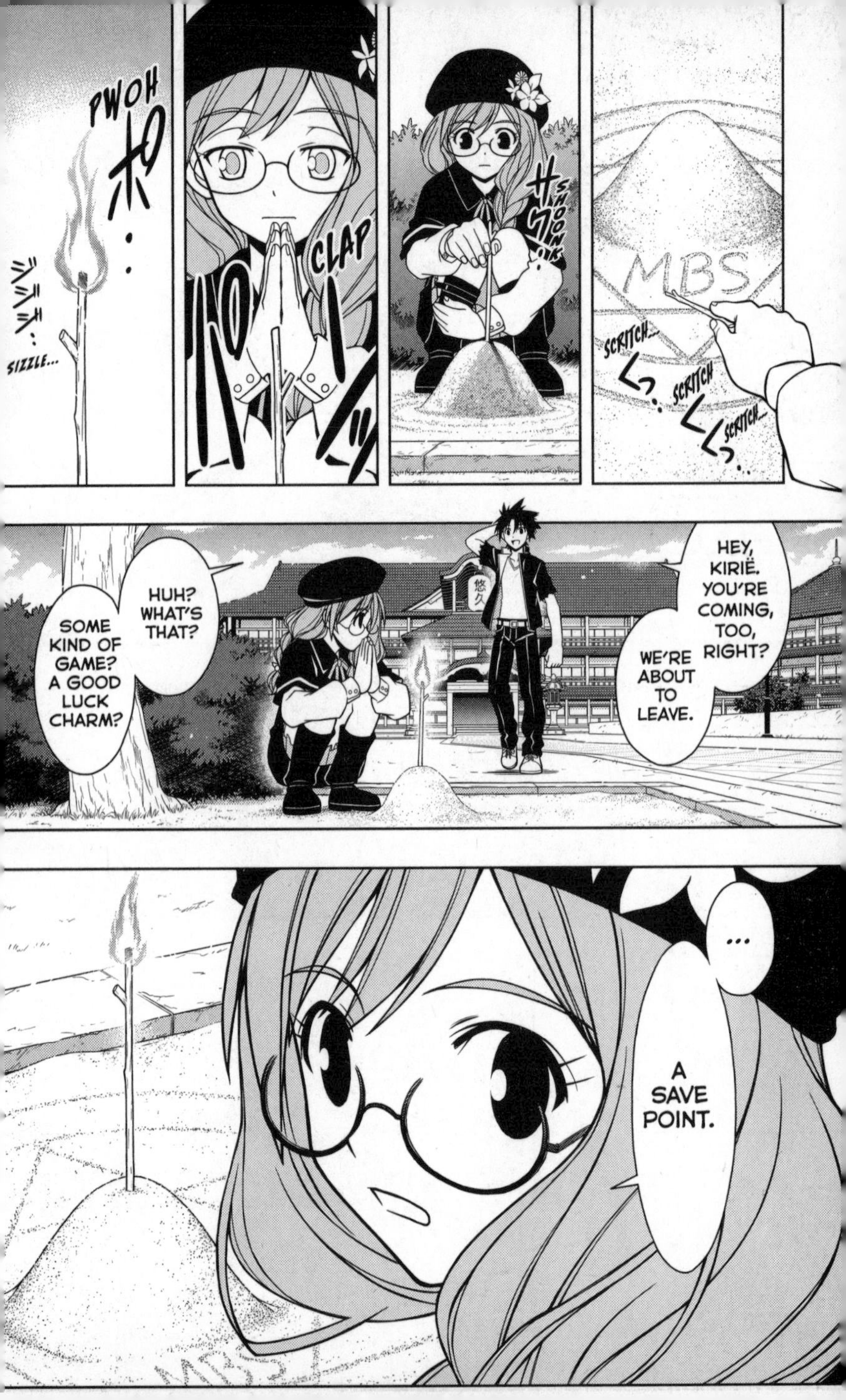
SCRITCH...
SCRITCH
SCRITCH...
SHOONK
CLAP
PWOH
SIZZLE...
HEY, KIRIË. YOU'RE COMING, TOO, RIGHT?
WE'RE ABOUT TO LEAVE.
悠久
HUH? WHAT'S THAT?
SOME KIND OF GAME? A GOOD LUCK CHARM?
...
A SAVE POINT.

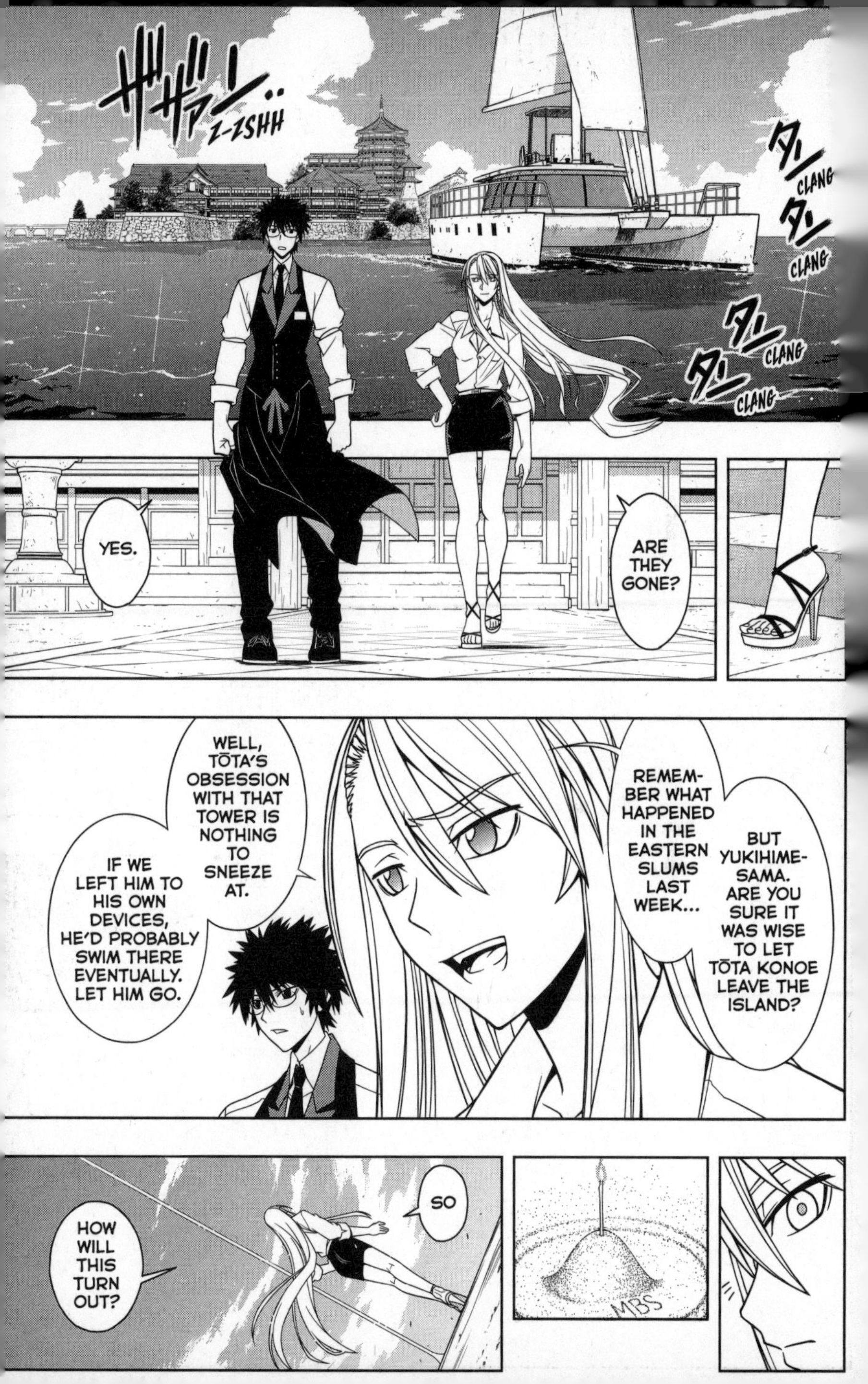
Z-ZSHH
CLANG
CLANG
CLANG
CLANG
ARE THEY GONE?
YES.
BUT YUKIHIME-SAMA. ARE YOU SURE IT WAS WISE TO LET TŌTA KONOE LEAVE THE ISLAND?
REMEM-BER WHAT HAPPENED IN THE EASTERN SLUMS LAST WEEK...
WELL, TŌTA'S OBSESSION WITH THAT TOWER IS NOTHING TO SNEEZE AT.
IF WE LEFT HIM TO HIS OWN DEVICES, HE'D PROBABLY SWIM THERE EVENTUALLY. LET HIM GO.
MBS
SO
HOW WILL THIS TURN OUT?

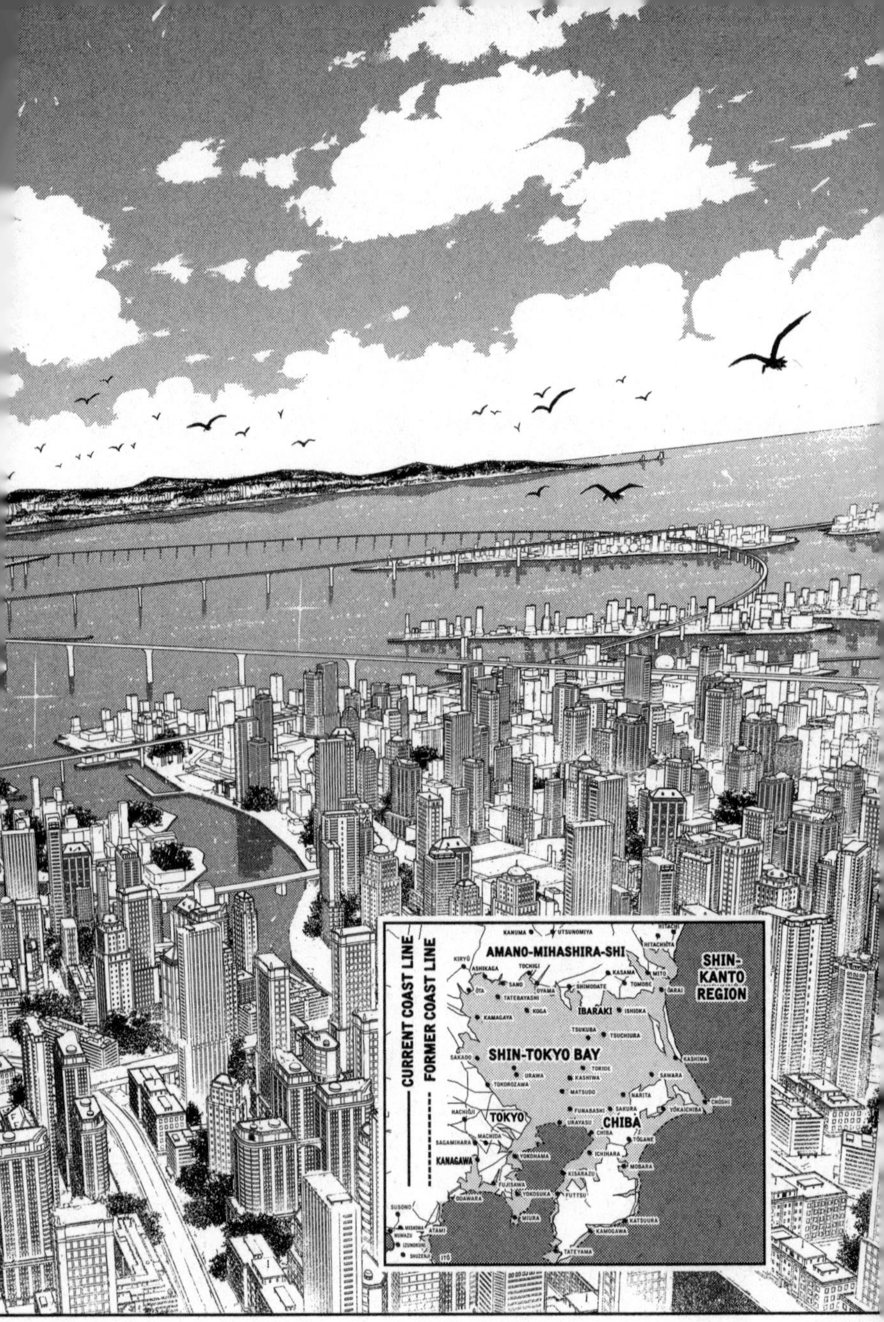
CURRENT COAST LINE
FORMER COAST LINE
SHIN-KANTO REGION
AMANO-MIHASHIRA-SHI
SHIN-TOKYO BAY
IBARAKI
TOKYO
CHIBA
KANAGAWA
KANUMA
UTSUNOMIYA
HITACHI
HITACHIŌTA
KIRYŪ
ASHIKAGA
TOCHIGI
KASAMA
MITO
SANO
OYAMA
SHIMODATE
TOMOBE
ŌTA
ŌARAI
TATEBAYASHI
KOGA
ISHIOKA
KAMAGAYA
TSUKUBA
TSUCHIURA
SAKADO
KASHIMA
TORIDE
URAWA
KASHIWA
SAWARA
TOKOROZAWA
MATSUDO
NARITA
CHŌSHI
HACHIŌJI
FUNABASHI
SAKURA
YŌKAICHIBA
URAYASU
CHIBA
MACHIDA
TŌGANE
SAGAMIHARA
ICHIHARA
YOKOHAMA
MOBARA
KISARAZU
FUJISAWA
YOKOSUKA
FUTTSU
ODAWARA
SUSONO
MIURA
KATSUURA
MISHIMA
ATAMI
NUMAZU
KAMOGAWA
IZUNOKUNI
SHUZENJI
ITŌ
TATEYAMA

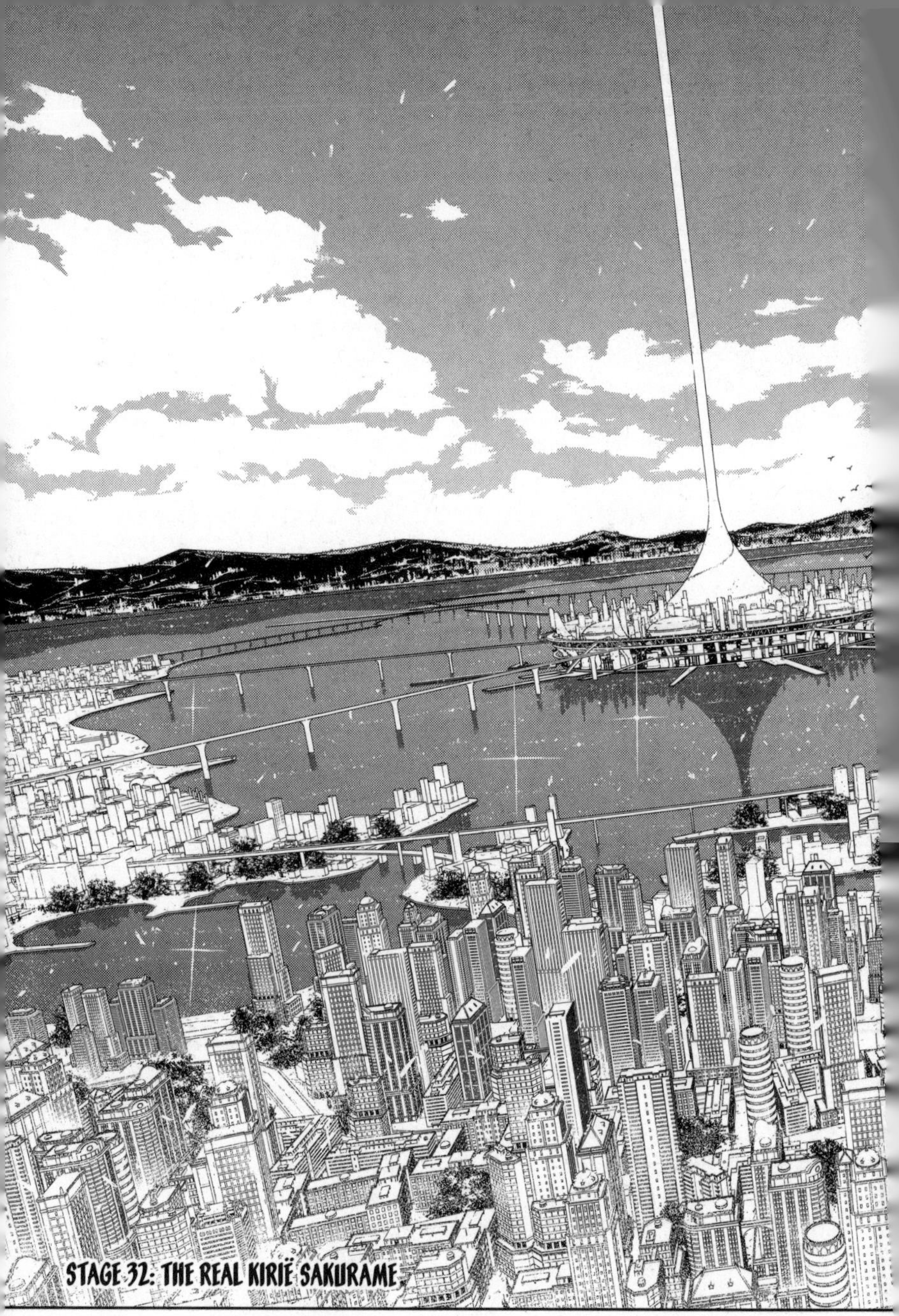
STAGE 32: THE REAL KIRIË SAKURAME

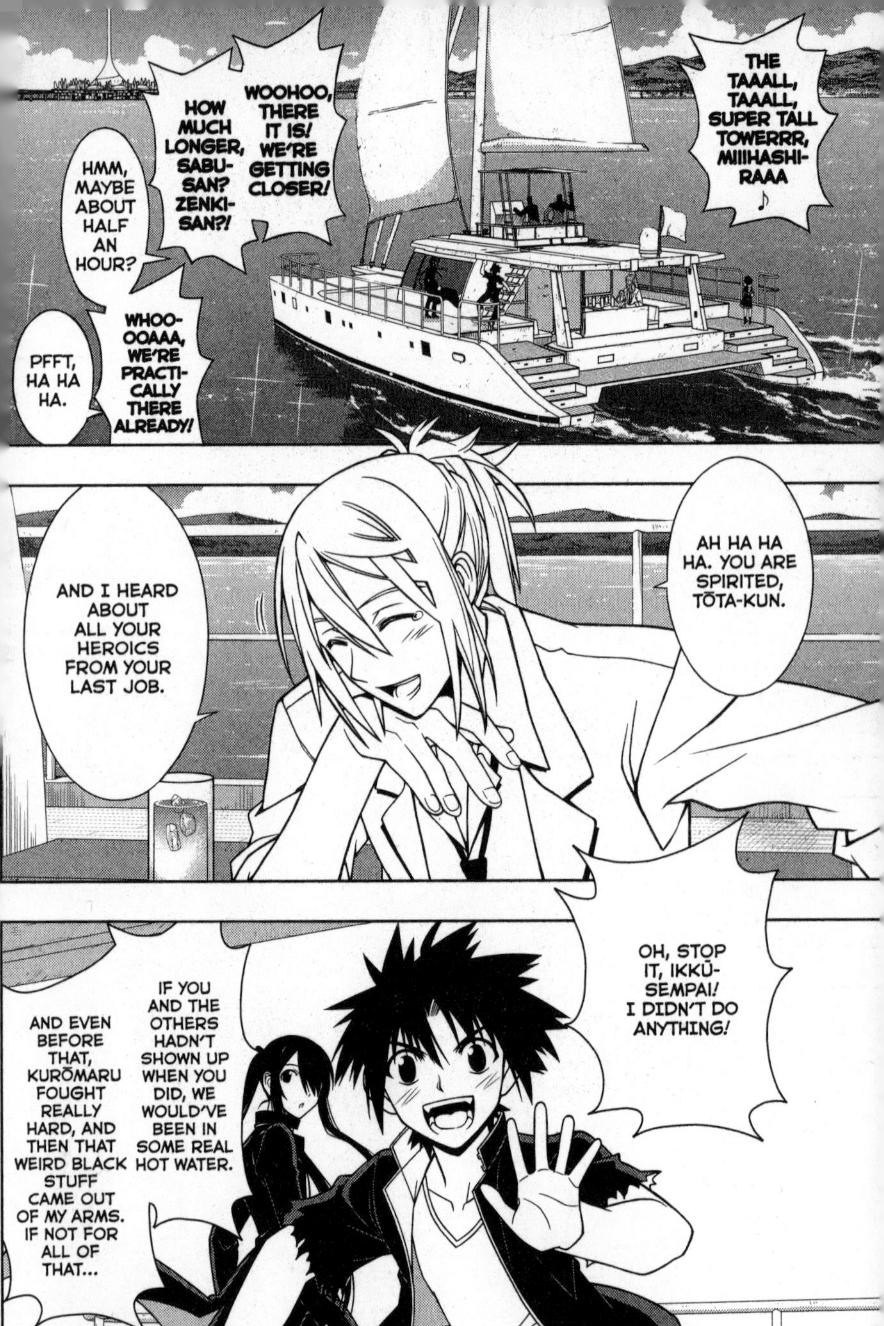
THE TAAALL, TAAALL, SUPER TALL TOWERRR, MIIIHASHI-RAAA ♪
WOOHOO, THERE IT IS! WE'RE GETTING CLOSER!
HOW MUCH LONGER, SABU-SAN? ZENKI-SAN?!
HMM, MAYBE ABOUT HALF AN HOUR?
WHOO-OOAAA, WE'RE PRACTI-CALLY THERE ALREADY!!
PFFT, HA HA HA.
AH HA HA HA. YOU ARE SPIRITED, TŌTA-KUN.
AND I HEARD ABOUT ALL YOUR HEROICS FROM YOUR LAST JOB.
OH, STOP IT, IKKŪ-SEMPAI! I DIDN'T DO ANYTHING!
IF YOU AND THE OTHERS HADN'T SHOWN UP WHEN YOU DID, WE WOULD'VE BEEN IN SOME REAL HOT WATER.
AND EVEN BEFORE THAT, KURŌMARU FOUGHT REALLY HARD, AND THEN THAT WEIRD BLACK STUFF CAME OUT OF MY ARMS. IF NOT FOR ALL OF THAT...

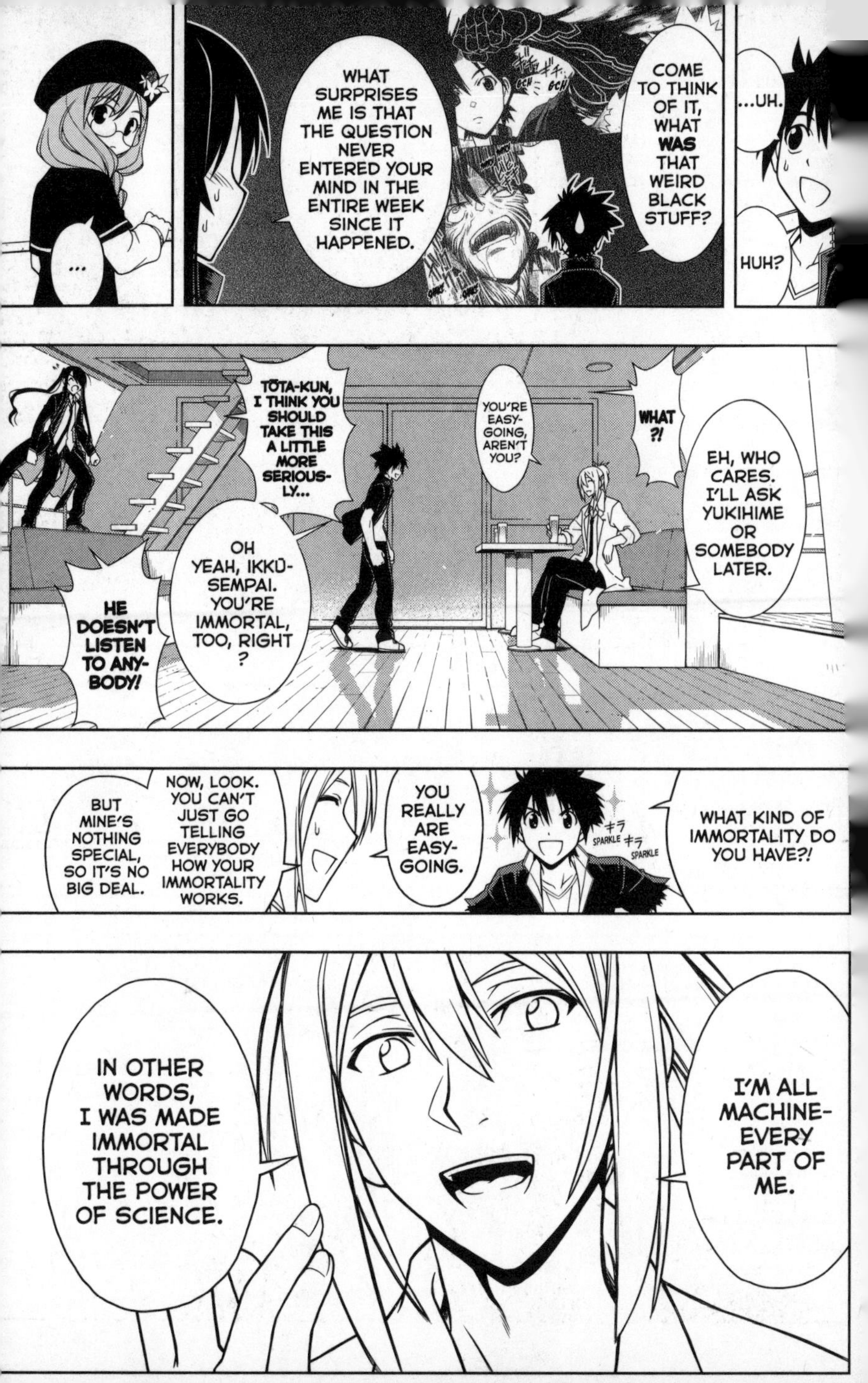
...UH.
HUH?
COME TO THINK OF IT, WHAT **WAS** THAT WEIRD BLACK STUFF?
GCH GCH
WHAT SURPRISES ME IS THAT THE QUESTION NEVER ENTERED YOUR MIND IN THE ENTIRE WEEK SINCE IT HAPPENED.
...
EH, WHO CARES. I'LL ASK YUKIHIME OR SOMEBODY LATER.
WHAT?!
YOU'RE EASY-GOING, AREN'T YOU?
TŌTA-KUN, I THINK YOU SHOULD TAKE THIS A LITTLE MORE SERIOUSLY...
OH YEAH, IKKŪ-SEMPAI. YOU'RE IMMORTAL, TOO, RIGHT?
HE DOESN'T LISTEN TO ANYBODY!
WHAT KIND OF IMMORTALITY DO YOU HAVE?!
キラ SPARKLE キラ SPARKLE
YOU REALLY ARE EASY-GOING.
NOW, LOOK. YOU CAN'T JUST GO TELLING EVERYBODY HOW YOUR IMMORTALITY WORKS.
BUT MINE'S NOTHING SPECIAL, SO IT'S NO BIG DEAL.
I'M ALL MACHINE-EVERY PART OF ME.
IN OTHER WORDS, I WAS MADE IMMORTAL THROUGH THE POWER OF SCIENCE.

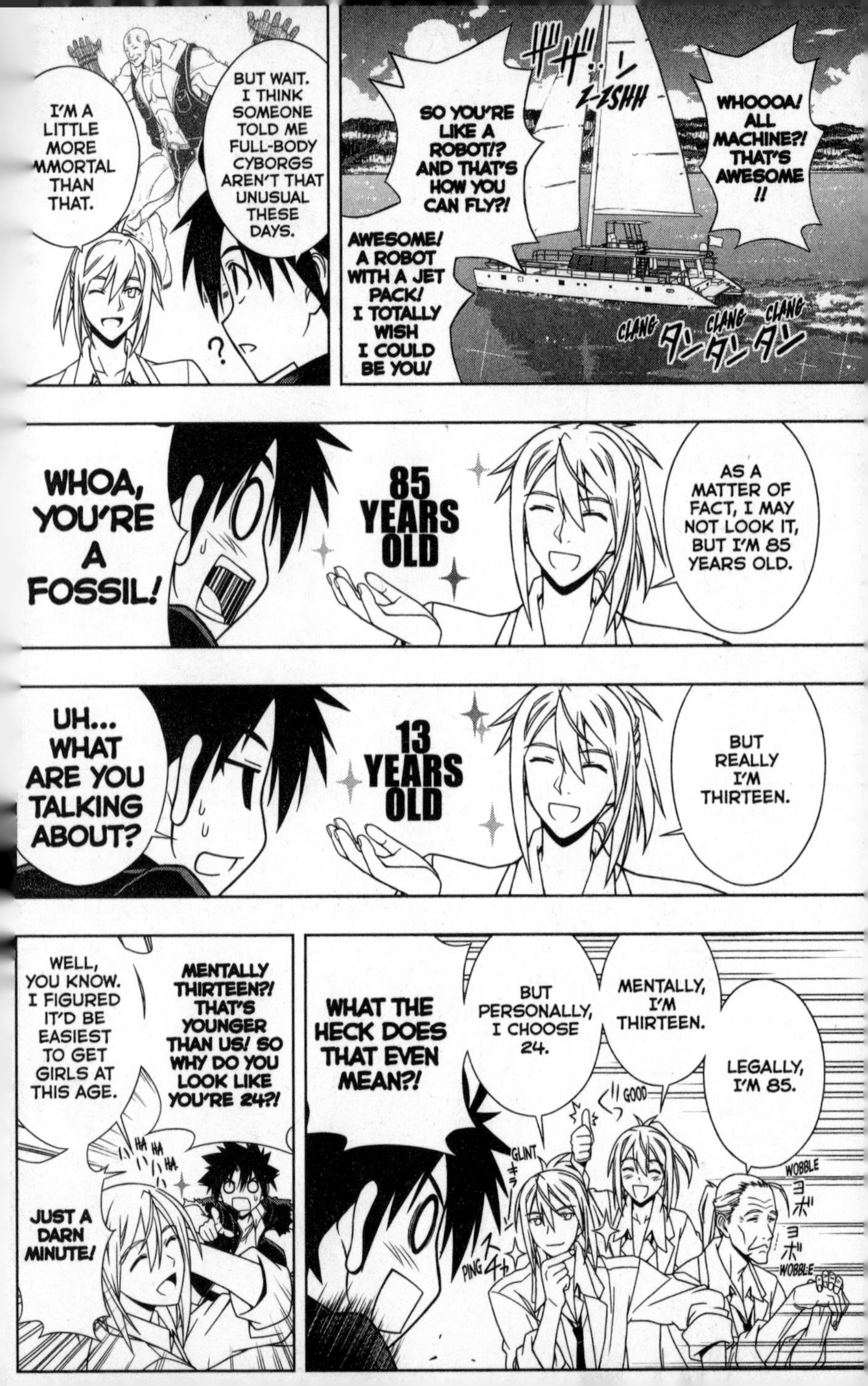

WHOOOA! ALL MACHINE?! THAT'S AWESOME!!
Z-ZSHH
SO YOU'RE LIKE A ROBOT!? AND THAT'S HOW YOU CAN FLY?!
AWESOME! A ROBOT WITH A JET PACK! I TOTALLY WISH I COULD BE YOU!
CLANG CLANG CLANG
BUT WAIT. I THINK SOMEONE TOLD ME FULL-BODY CYBORGS AREN'T THAT UNUSUAL THESE DAYS.
I'M A LITTLE MORE MMORTAL THAN THAT.
AS A MATTER OF FACT, I MAY NOT LOOK IT, BUT I'M 85 YEARS OLD.
85 YEARS OLD
WHOA, YOU'RE A FOSSIL!
BUT REALLY I'M THIRTEEN.
13 YEARS OLD
UH... WHAT ARE YOU TALKING ABOUT?
LEGALLY, I'M 85.
MENTALLY, I'M THIRTEEN.
BUT PERSONALLY, I CHOOSE 24.
GOOD
GLINT
WOBBLE
WOBBLE
PING
WHAT THE HECK DOES THAT EVEN MEAN?!
MENTALLY THIRTEEN?! THAT'S YOUNGER THAN US! SO WHY DO YOU LOOK LIKE YOU'RE 24?!
WELL, YOU KNOW. I FIGURED IT'D BE EASIEST TO GET GIRLS AT THIS AGE.
HA HA HA
JUST A DARN MINUTE!

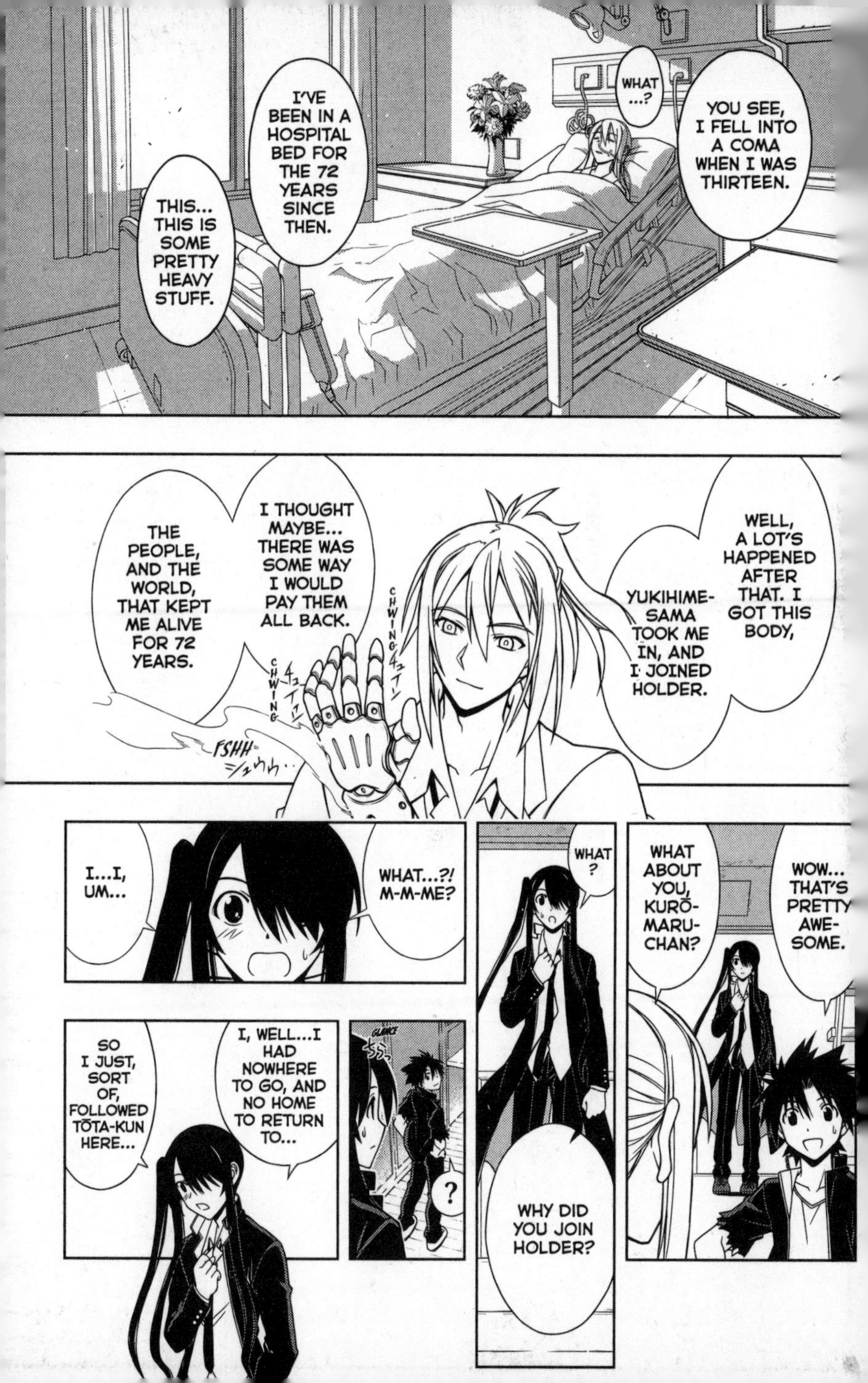
YOU SEE, I FELL INTO A COMA WHEN I WAS THIRTEEN.
WHAT ...?
I'VE BEEN IN A HOSPITAL BED FOR THE 72 YEARS SINCE THEN.
THIS... THIS IS SOME PRETTY HEAVY STUFF.
WELL, A LOT'S HAPPENED AFTER THAT. I GOT THIS BODY,
YUKIHIME-SAMA TOOK ME IN, AND I JOINED HOLDER.
CHWING
CHWING
I THOUGHT MAYBE... THERE WAS SOME WAY I WOULD PAY THEM ALL BACK.
THE PEOPLE, AND THE WORLD, THAT KEPT ME ALIVE FOR 72 YEARS.
FSHH
WOW... THAT'S PRETTY AWE-SOME.
WHAT ABOUT YOU, KURŌ-MARU-CHAN?
WHAT ?
WHY DID YOU JOIN HOLDER?
WHAT...?! M-M-ME?
I...I, UM...
GLANCE
?
I, WELL...I HAD NOWHERE TO GO, AND NO HOME TO RETURN TO...
SO I JUST, SORT OF, FOLLOWED TŌTA-KUN HERE...

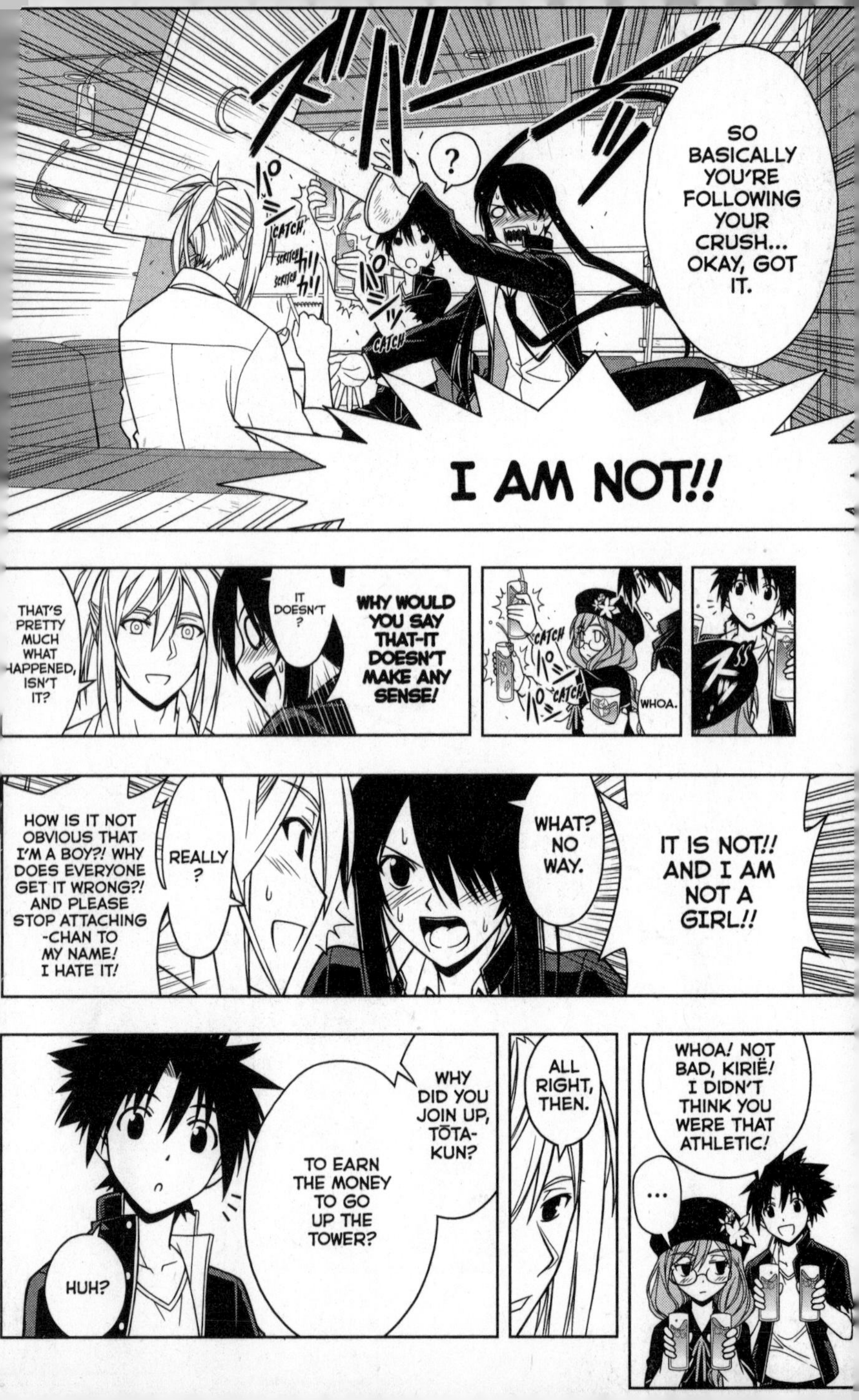
SO BASICALLY YOU'RE FOLLOWING YOUR CRUSH... OKAY, GOT IT.
?
CATCH
SCRITCH
SCRITCH
CATCH
I AM NOT!!
CATCH
CATCH
WHOA.
WHY WOULD YOU SAY THAT-IT DOESN'T MAKE ANY SENSE!
IT DOESN'T?
THAT'S PRETTY MUCH WHAT HAPPENED, ISN'T IT?
IT IS NOT!! AND I AM NOT A GIRL!!
WHAT? NO WAY.
REALLY?
HOW IS IT NOT OBVIOUS THAT I'M A BOY?! WHY DOES EVERYONE GET IT WRONG?! AND PLEASE STOP ATTACHING -CHAN TO MY NAME! I HATE IT!
WHOA! NOT BAD, KIRIË! I DIDN'T THINK YOU WERE THAT ATHLETIC!
...
ALL RIGHT, THEN.
WHY DID YOU JOIN UP, TŌTA-KUN?
TO EARN THE MONEY TO GO UP THE TOWER?
HUH?

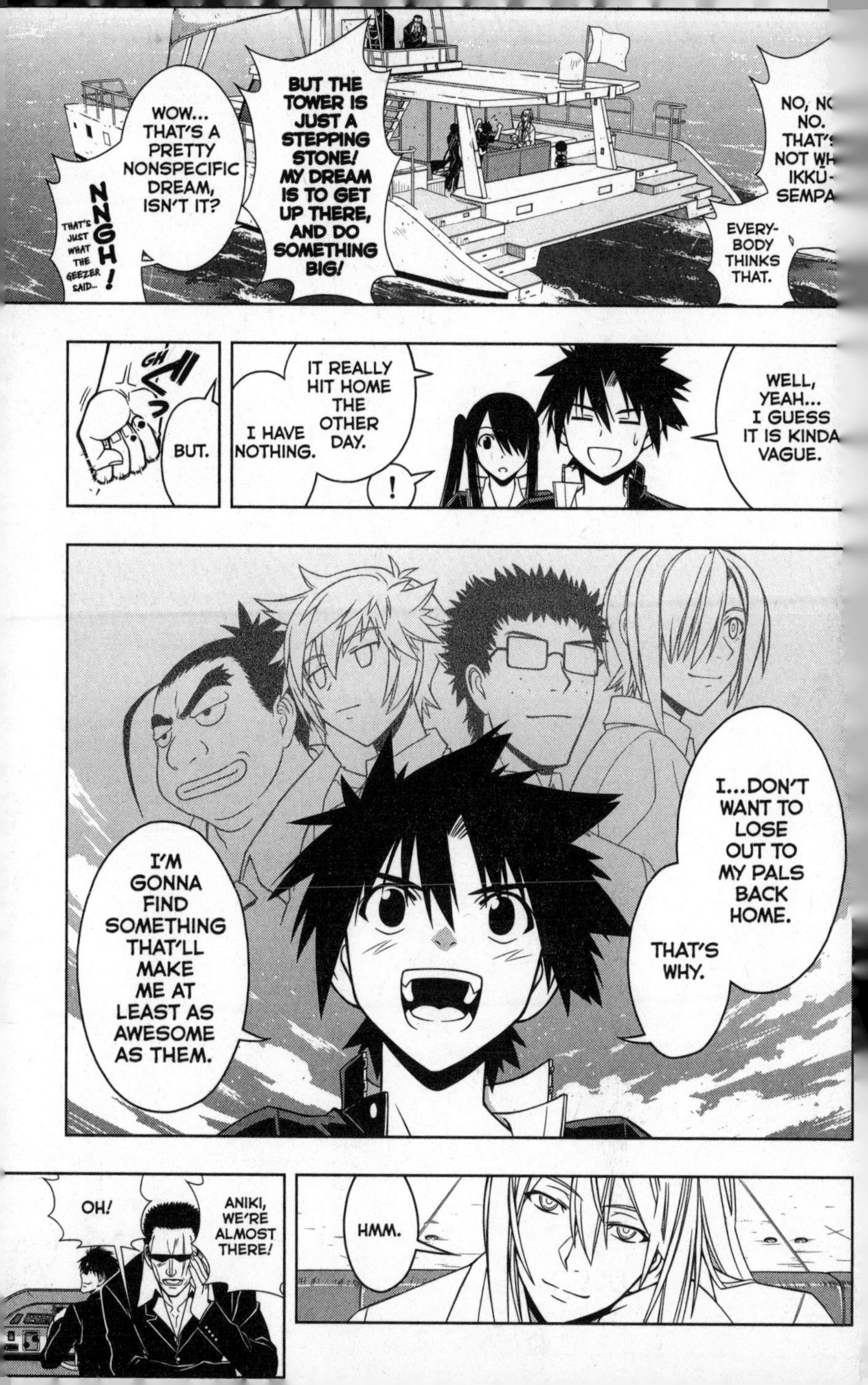
NO, NO NO. THAT'S NOT WH IKKŪ-SEMPA
EVERYBODY THINKS THAT.
BUT THE TOWER IS JUST A STEPPING STONE! MY DREAM IS TO GET UP THERE, AND DO SOMETHING BIG!
WOW... THAT'S A PRETTY NONSPECIFIC DREAM, ISN'T IT?
NNGH!
THAT'S JUST WHAT THE GEEZER SAID...
WELL, YEAH... I GUESS IT IS KINDA VAGUE.
!
IT REALLY HIT HOME THE OTHER DAY.
I HAVE NOTHING.
GH
BUT.
I...DON'T WANT TO LOSE OUT TO MY PALS BACK HOME.
THAT'S WHY.
I'M GONNA FIND SOMETHING THAT'LL MAKE ME AT LEAST AS AWESOME AS THEM.
HMM.
ANIKI, WE'RE ALMOST THERE!
OH!

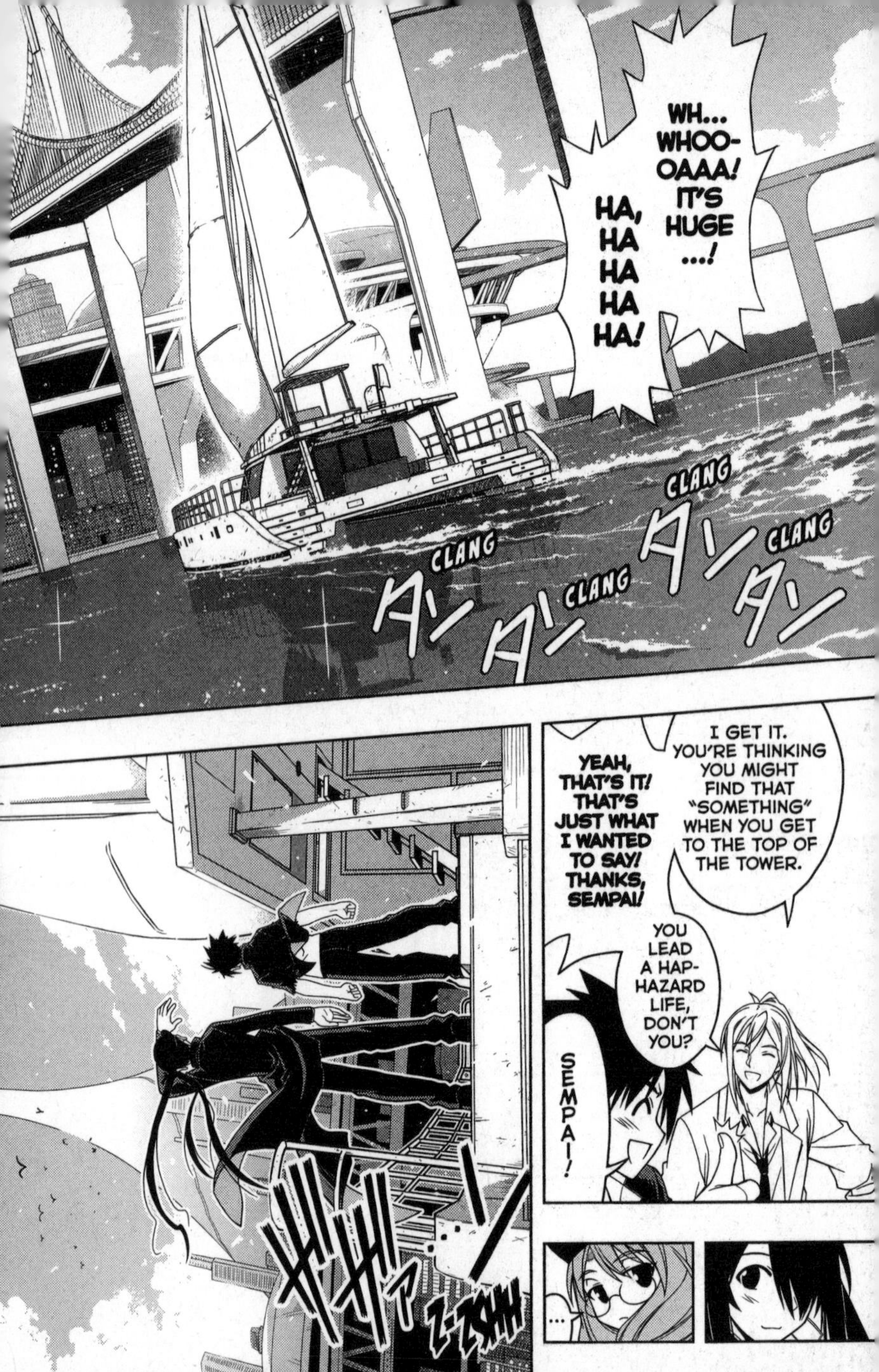
WH... WHOOOAAA! IT'S HUGE ...!
HA, HA HA HA HA!
CLANG
タン
CLANG
タン
CLANG
ダン
CLANG
タン
I GET IT. YOU'RE THINKING YOU MIGHT FIND THAT "SOMETHING" WHEN YOU GET TO THE TOP OF THE TOWER.
YEAH, THAT'S IT! THAT'S JUST WHAT I WANTED TO SAY! THANKS, SEMPAI!
YOU LEAD A HAP-HAZARD LIFE, DON'T YOU?
SEMPAI!
...
Z-ZSHHH

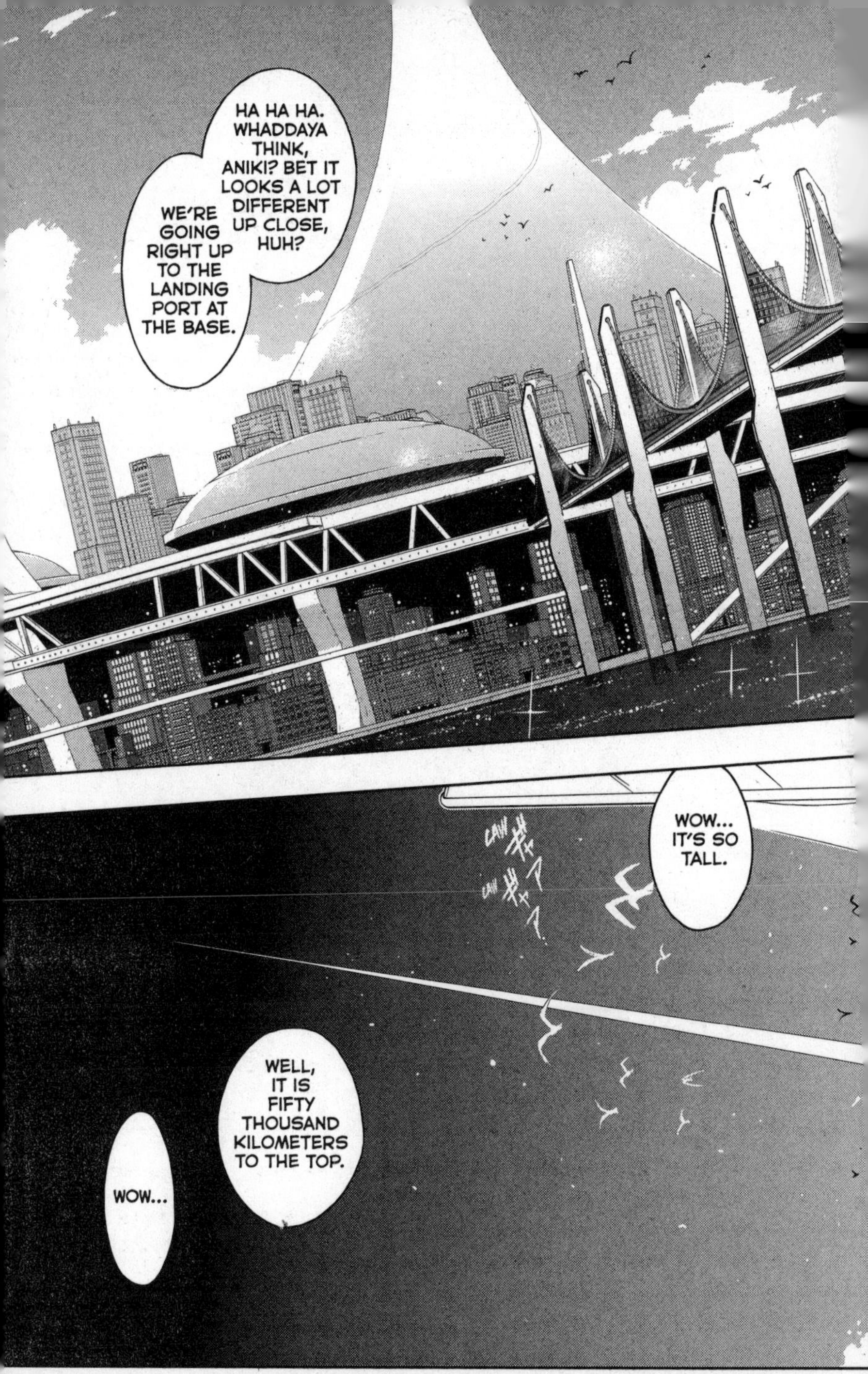
HA HA HA. WHADDAYA THINK, ANIKI? BET IT LOOKS A LOT DIFFERENT UP CLOSE, HUH?
WE'RE GOING RIGHT UP TO THE LANDING PORT AT THE BASE.
WOW... IT'S SO TALL.
CAW
CAW
WELL, IT IS FIFTY THOUSAND KILOMETERS TO THE TOP.
WOW...

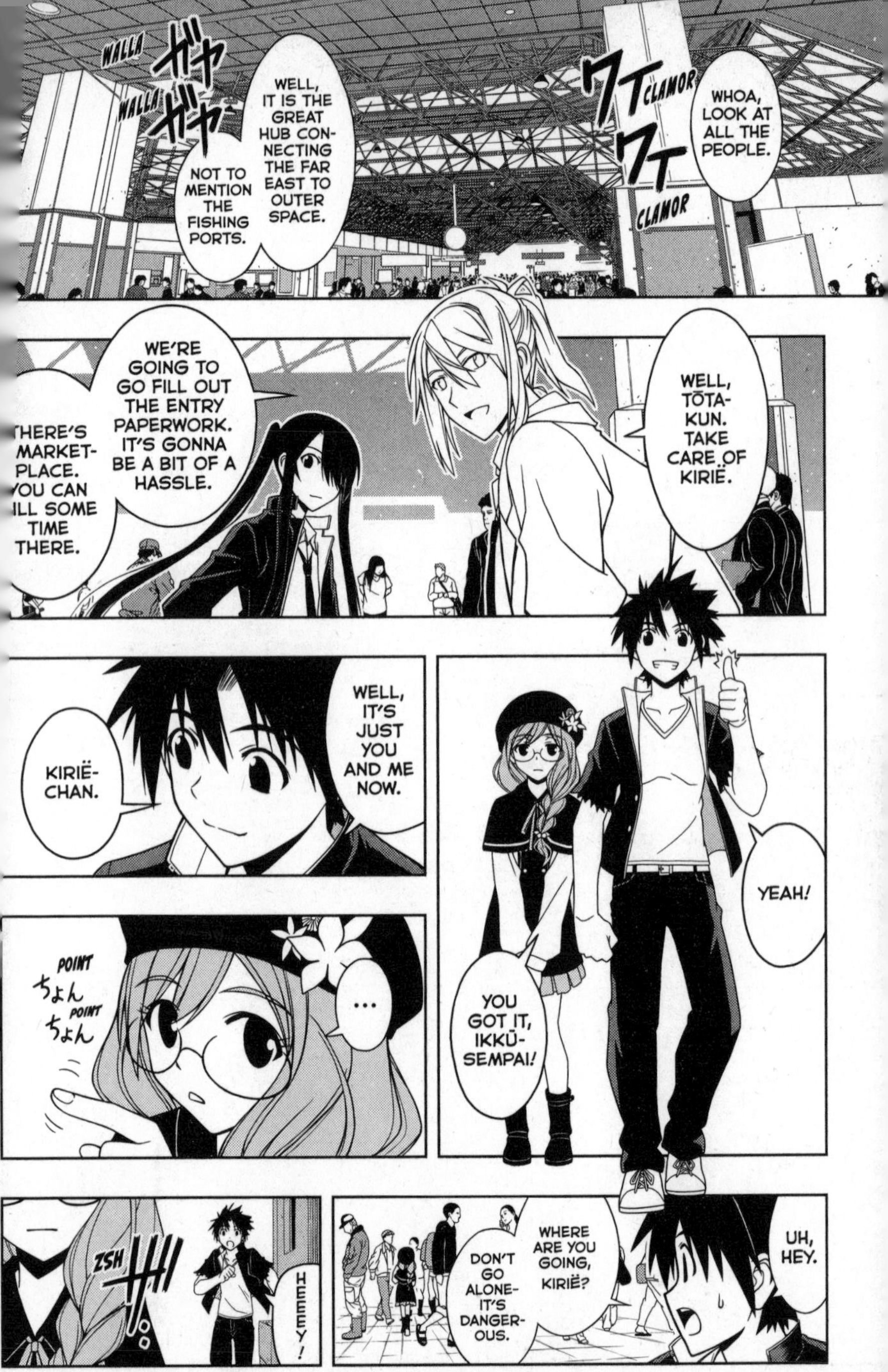

WHOA, LOOK AT ALL THE PEOPLE.
CLAMOR
CLAMOR
WELL, IT IS THE GREAT HUB CONNECTING THE FAR EAST TO OUTER SPACE.
NOT TO MENTION THE FISHING PORTS.
WALLA
WALLA
WELL, TŌTA-KUN. TAKE CARE OF KIRIË.
WE'RE GOING TO GO FILL OUT THE ENTRY PAPERWORK. IT'S GONNA BE A BIT OF A HASSLE.
THERE'S MARKETPLACE. YOU CAN ILL SOME TIME THERE.
YEAH!
YOU GOT IT, IKKŪ-SEMPAI!
WELL, IT'S JUST YOU AND ME NOW.
KIRIË-CHAN.
...
POINT ちょん
POINT ちょん
UH, HEY.
WHERE ARE YOU GOING, KIRIË?
DON'T GO ALONE-IT'S DANGEROUS.
HEEEEY!
ZSH
—

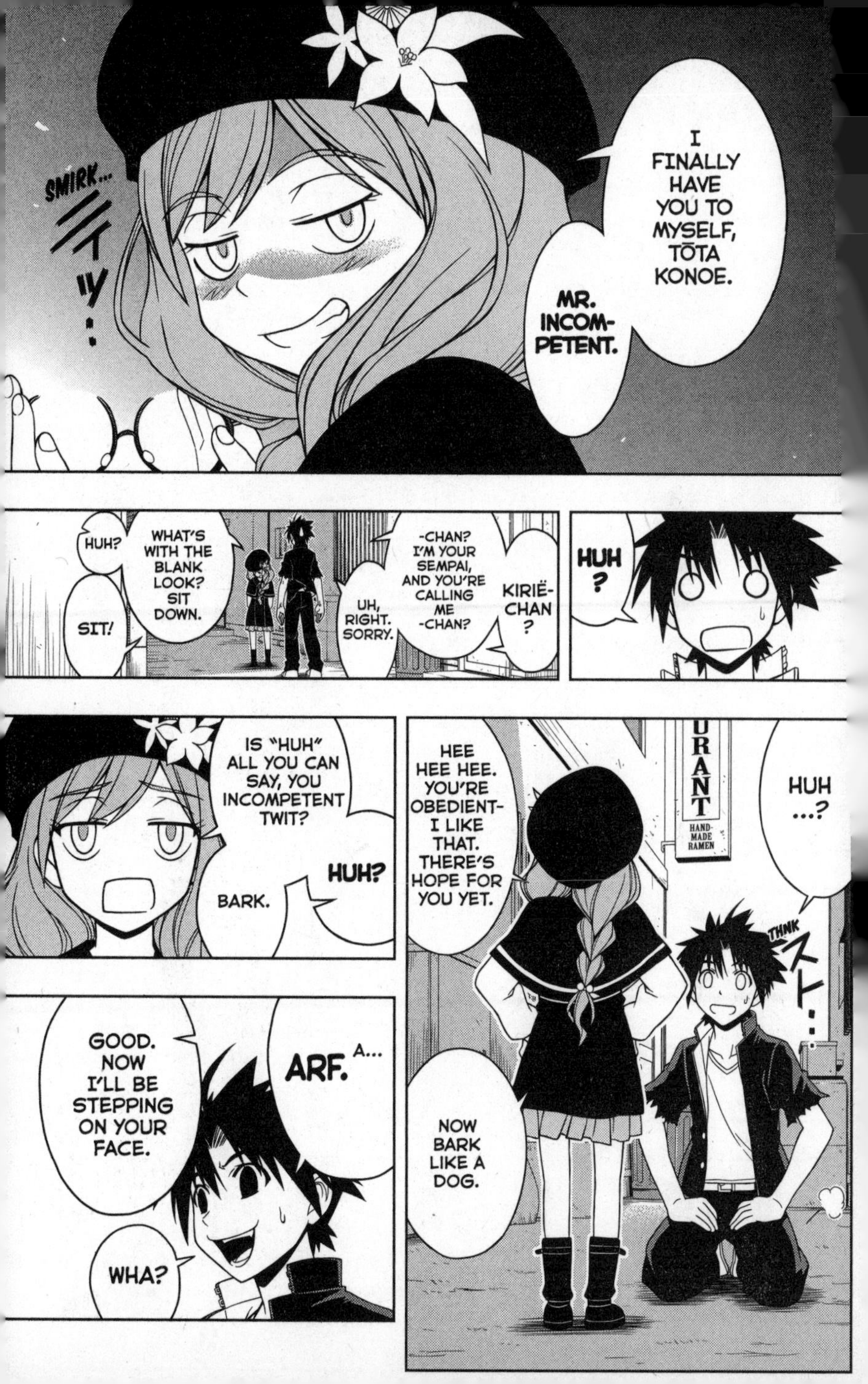
I FINALLY HAVE YOU TO MYSELF, TŌTA KONOE.
MR. INCOMPETENT.
SMIRK...
ニイッ..
HUH?
KIRIË-CHAN?
-CHAN? I'M YOUR SEMPAI, AND YOU'RE CALLING ME -CHAN?
UH, RIGHT. SORRY.
WHAT'S WITH THE BLANK LOOK? SIT DOWN.
HUH?
SIT!
URANT
HAND-MADE RAMEN
HUH...?
HEE HEE HEE. YOU'RE OBEDIENT- I LIKE THAT. THERE'S HOPE FOR YOU YET.
THNK
ストッ..
NOW BARK LIKE A DOG.
IS "HUH" ALL YOU CAN SAY, YOU INCOMPETENT TWIT?
HUH?
BARK.
ARF.
A...
GOOD. NOW I'LL BE STEPPING ON YOUR FACE.
WHA?

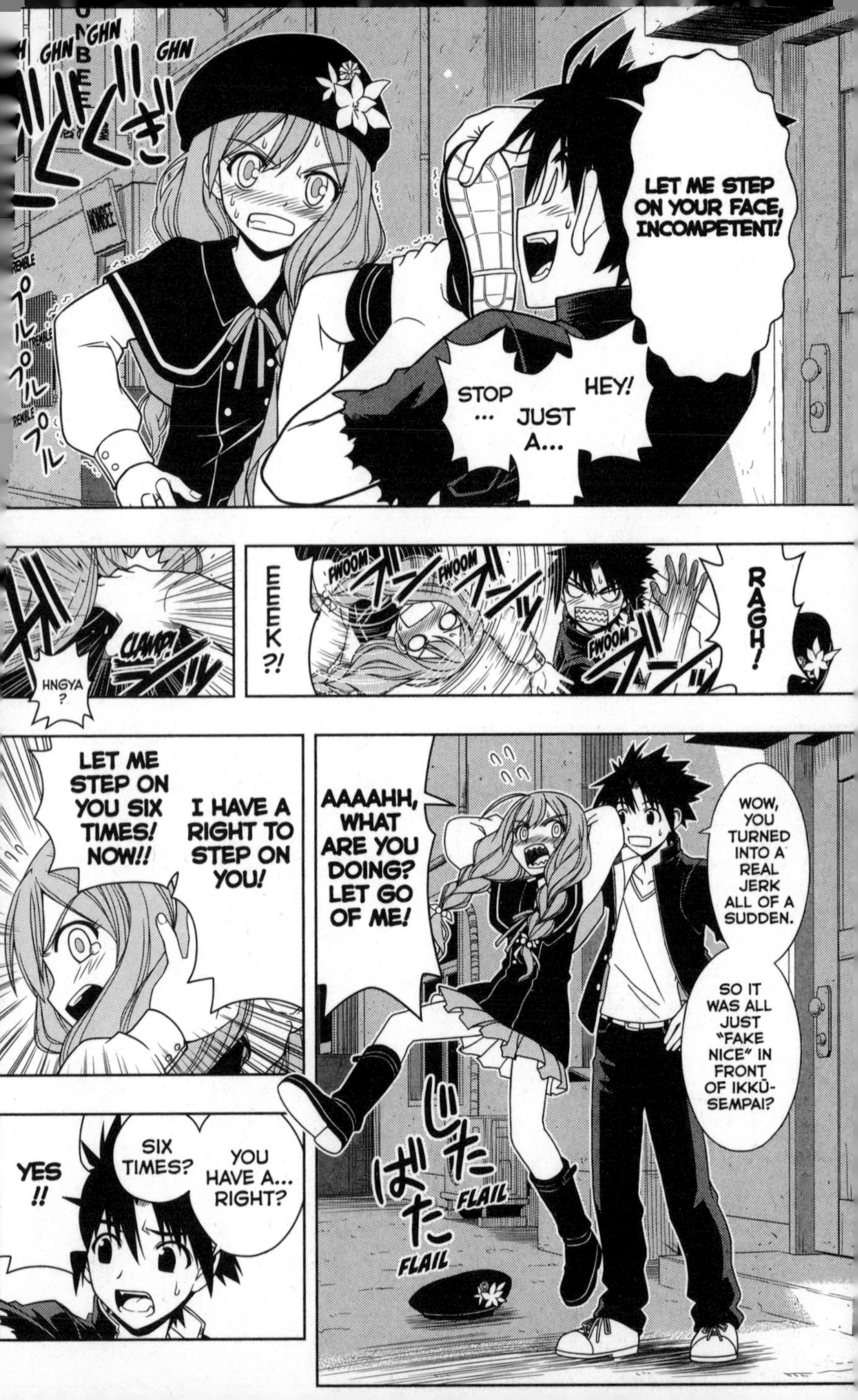
LET ME STEP ON YOUR FACE, INCOMPETENT!
HEY!
JUST A...
STOP...
GHN
GHN
GHN
TREMBLE
TREMBLE
TREMBLE
RAGH!
FWOOM
FWOOM
FWOOM
EEEEK?!
CLAMP!
HNGYA?
WOW, YOU TURNED INTO A REAL JERK ALL OF A SUDDEN.
SO IT WAS ALL JUST "FAKE NICE" IN FRONT OF IKKŪ-SEMPAI?
AAAAHH, WHAT ARE YOU DOING? LET GO OF ME!
FLAIL
FLAIL
I HAVE A RIGHT TO STEP ON YOU!
LET ME STEP ON YOU SIX TIMES! NOW!!
YOU HAVE A... RIGHT?
SIX TIMES?
YES!!

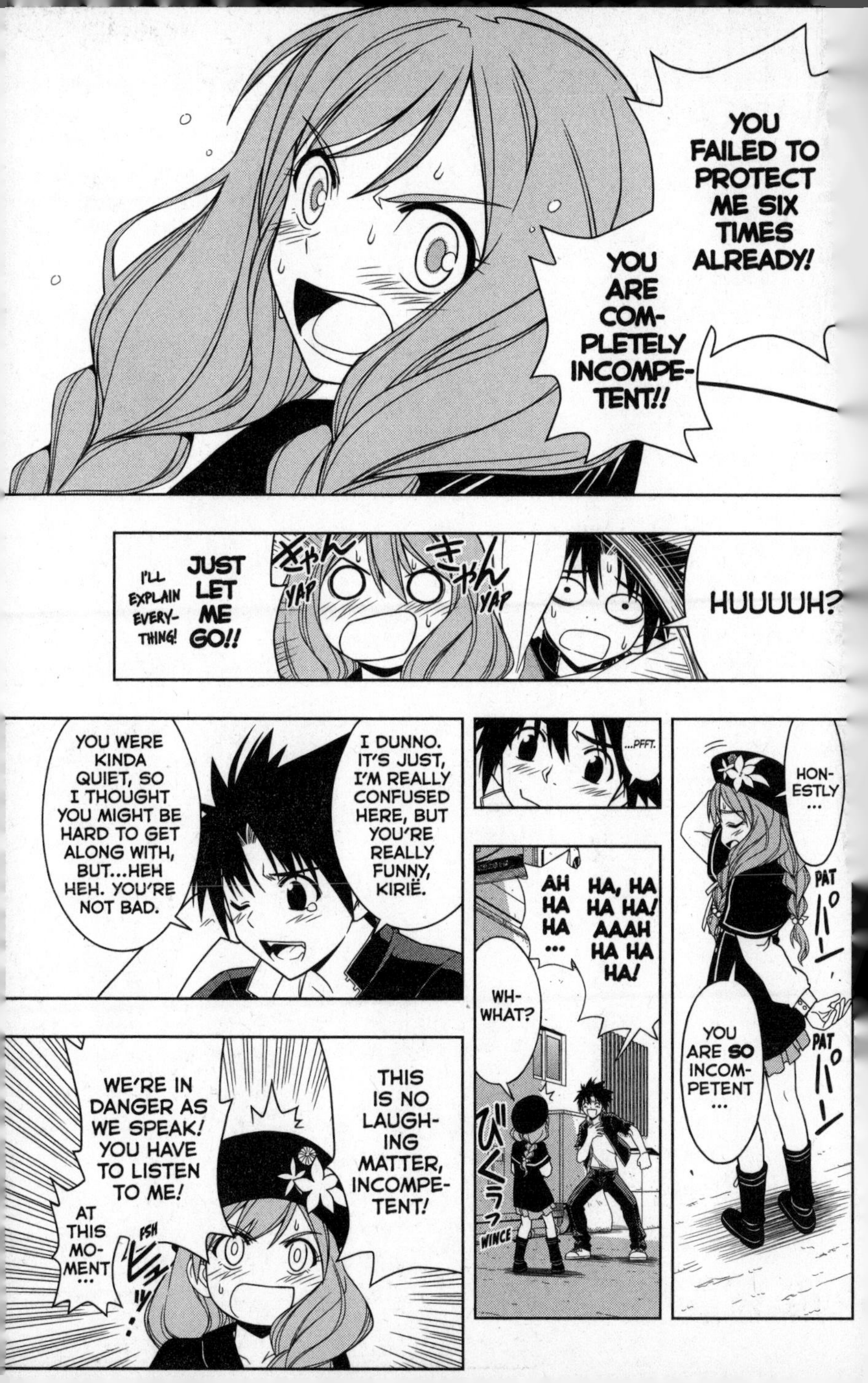
YOU FAILED TO PROTECT ME SIX TIMES ALREADY!
YOU ARE COMPLETELY INCOMPETENT!!
HUUUUH?
きゃん YAP
きゃん YAP
JUST LET ME GO!!
I'LL EXPLAIN EVERYTHING!
HONESTLY...
PAT パー
PAT パー
YOU ARE SO INCOMPETENT...
...PFFT.
HA, HA HA HA! AAAH HA HA HA!
AH HA HA...
WH-WHAT?
びくっ WINCE
I DUNNO. IT'S JUST, I'M REALLY CONFUSED HERE, BUT YOU'RE REALLY FUNNY, KIRIË.
YOU WERE KINDA QUIET, SO I THOUGHT YOU MIGHT BE HARD TO GET ALONG WITH, BUT...HEH HEH. YOU'RE NOT BAD.
THIS IS NO LAUGHING MATTER, INCOMPETENT!
WE'RE IN DANGER AS WE SPEAK! YOU HAVE TO LISTEN TO ME!
AT THIS MOMENT...
FSH ビッ

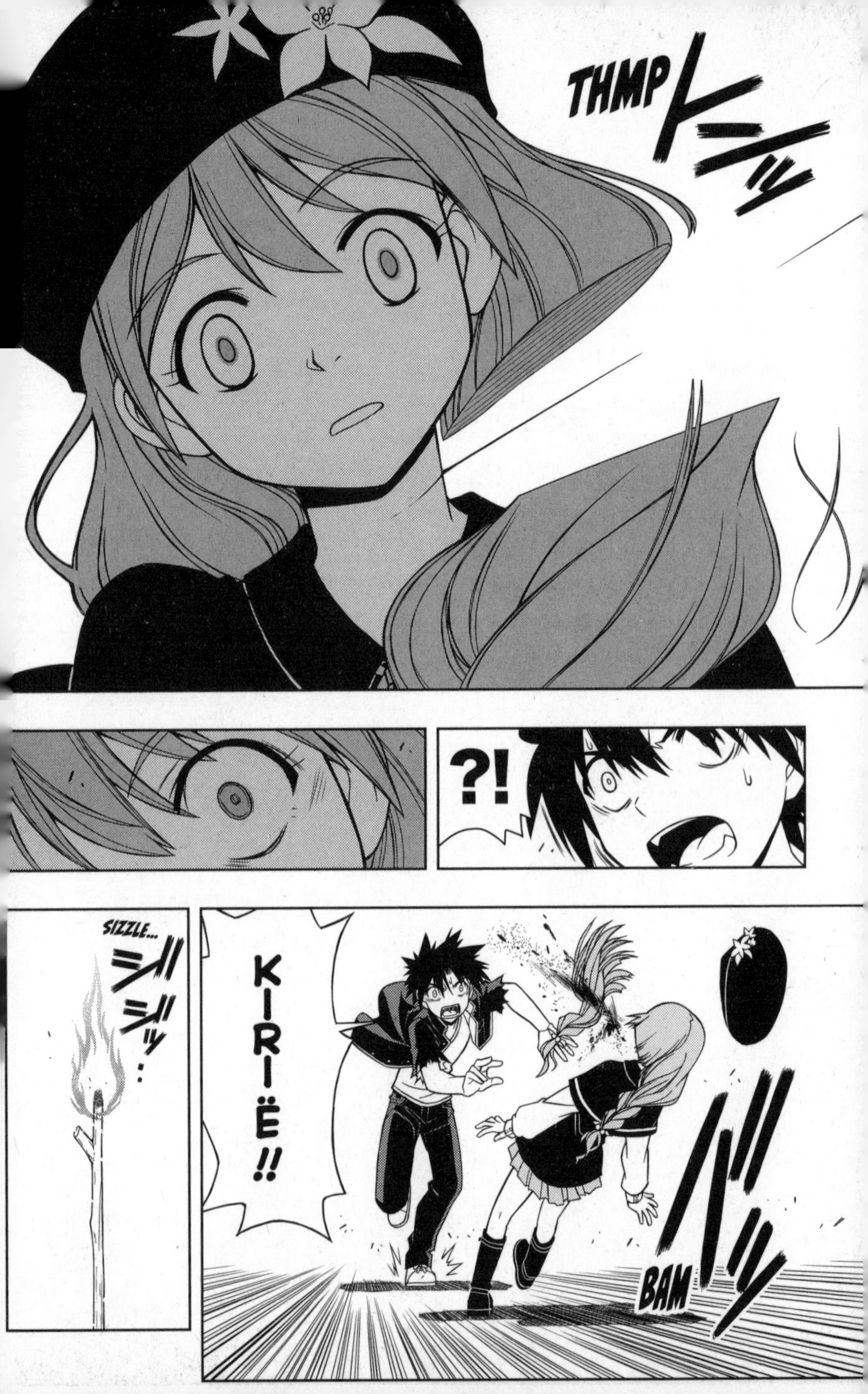
THMP
?!
KIRIË!!
BAM
SIZZLE...

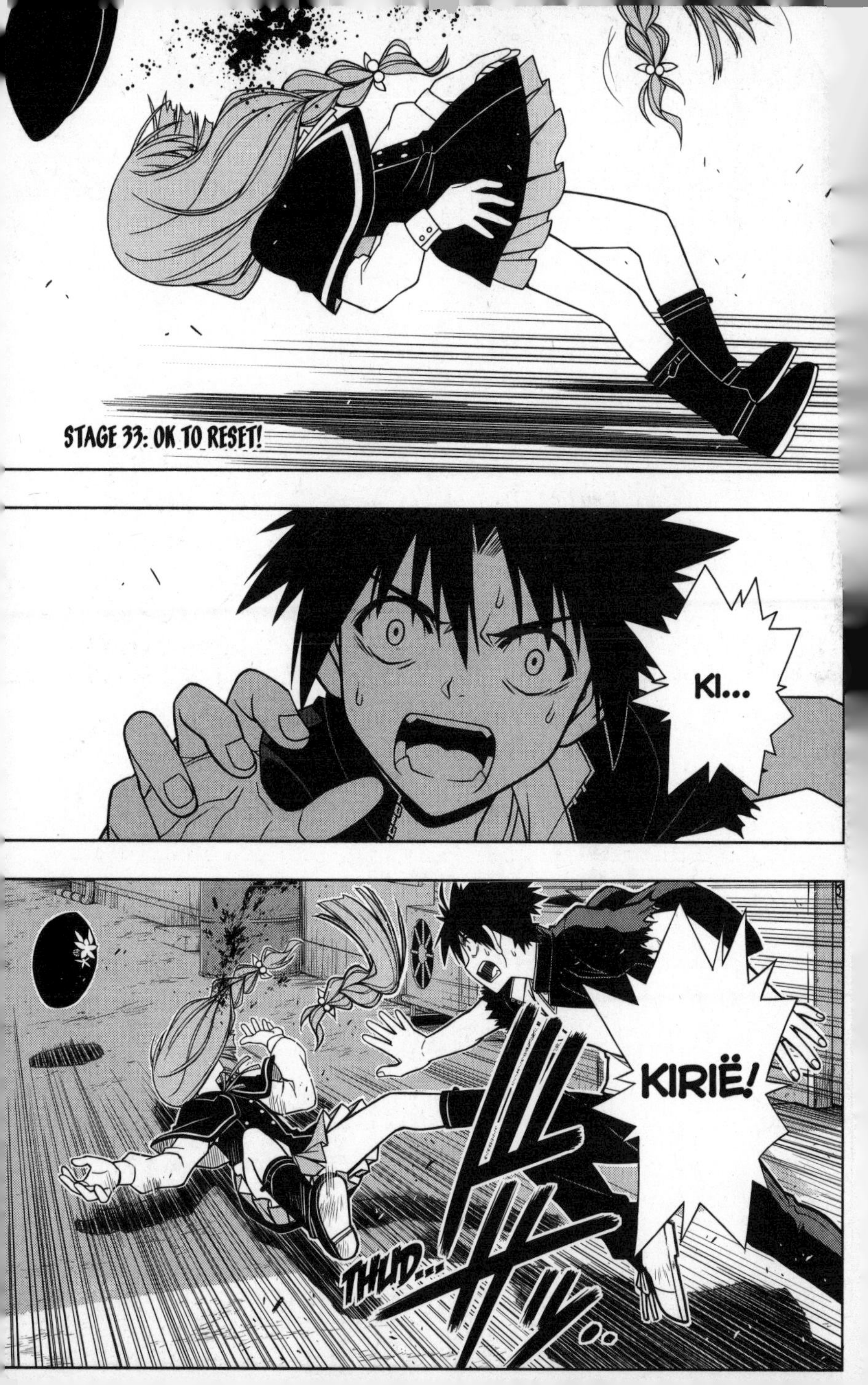
STAGE 33: OK TO RESET!
KI...
KIRIË!
THUD...

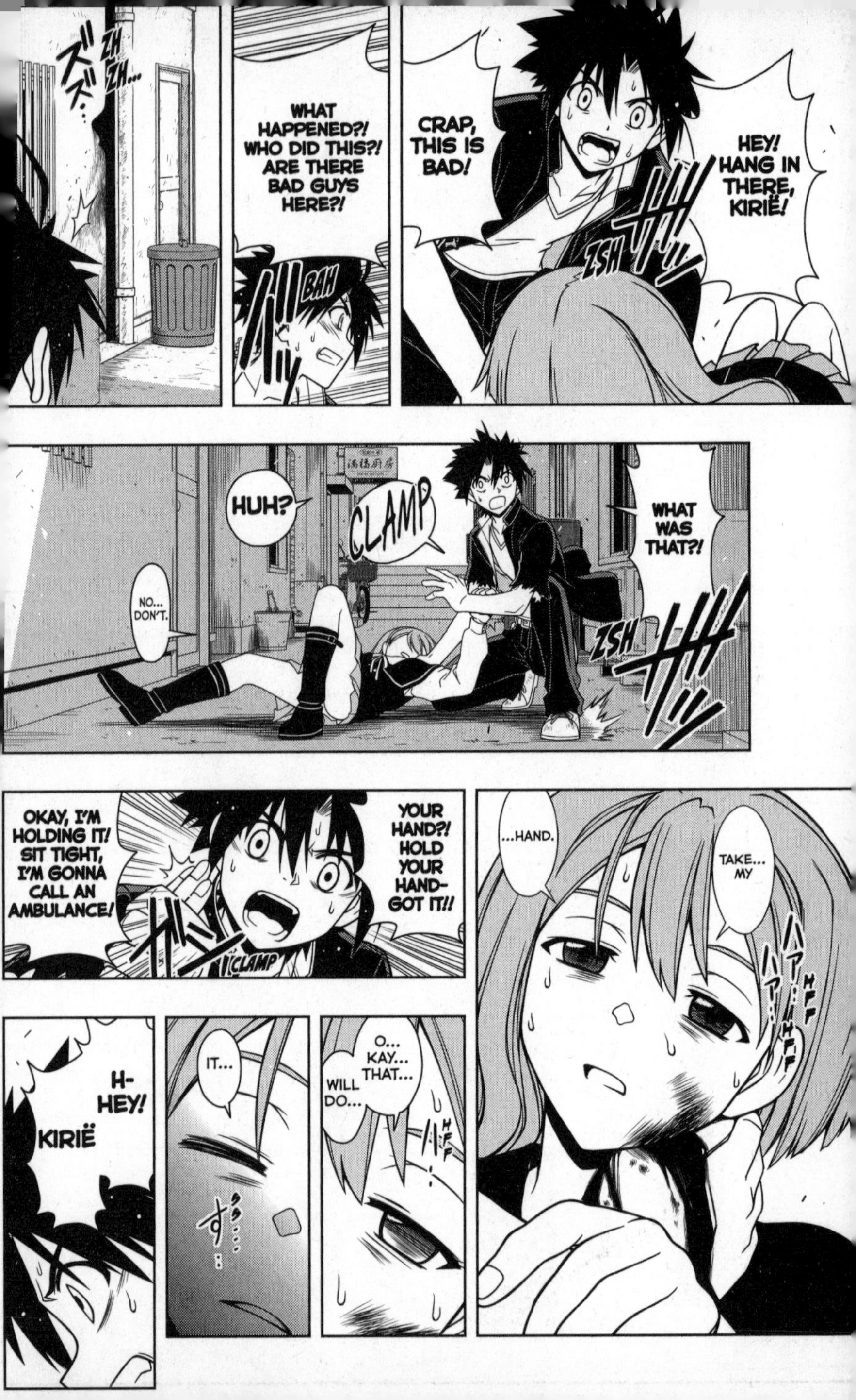
HEY! HANG IN THERE, KIRIË!
CRAP, THIS IS BAD!
ZSH
WHAT HAPPENED?! WHO DID THIS?! ARE THERE BAD GUYS HERE?!
BAH
ズズ…
ZH ZH...
WHAT WAS THAT?!
ZSH
CLAMP
HUH?
NO... DON'T.
TAKE... MY
...HAND.
ハァ ハァ
HFF HFF
YOUR HAND?! HOLD YOUR HAND-GOT IT!!
OKAY, I'M HOLDING IT! SIT TIGHT, I'M GONNA CALL AN AMBULANCE!
CLAMP
O... KAY... THAT... WILL DO...
ハ
HFF
IT...
H-HEY! KIRIË

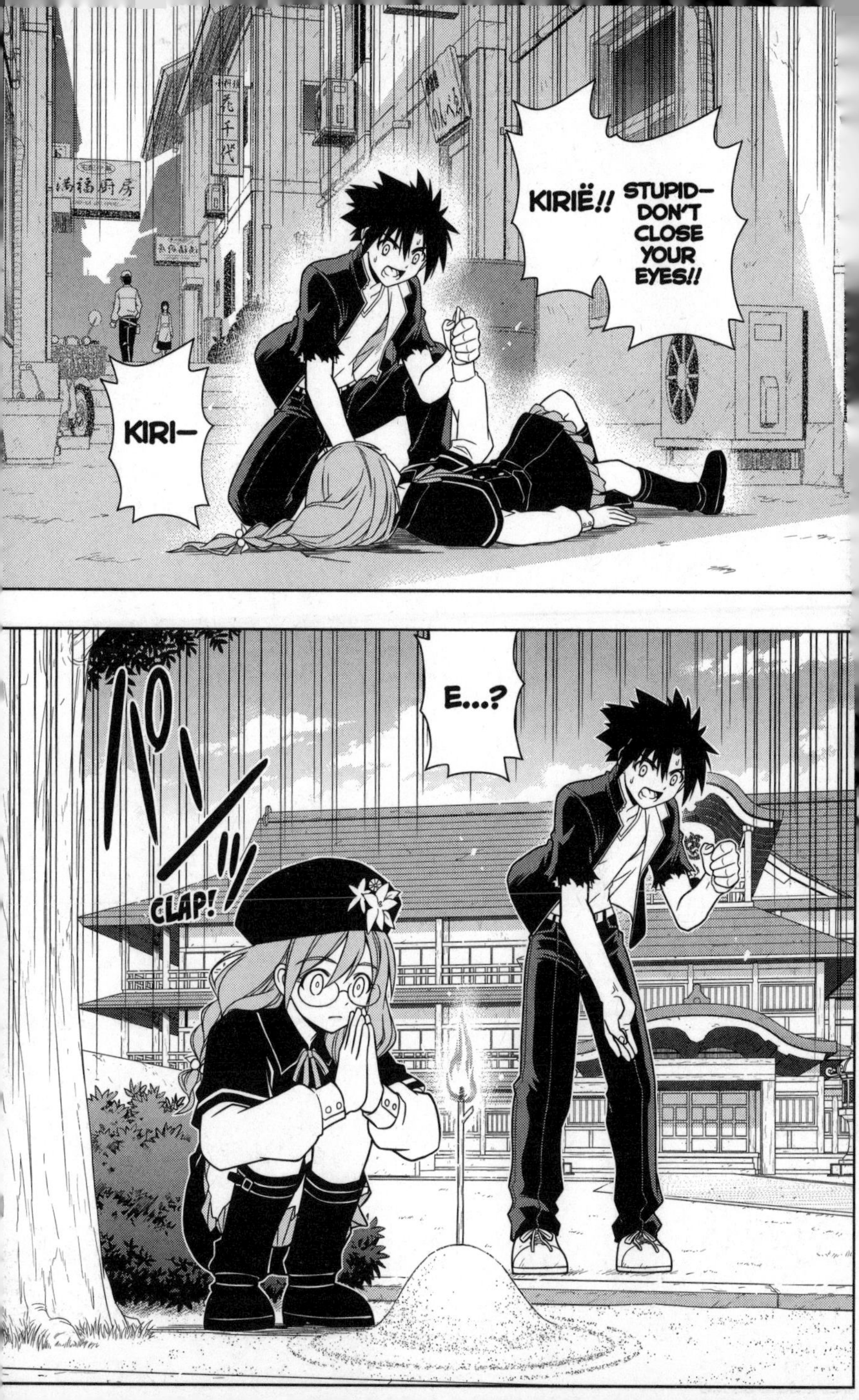
KIRIË!!
STUPID—DON'T CLOSE YOUR EYES!!
KIRI—
E...?
パン
CLAP!

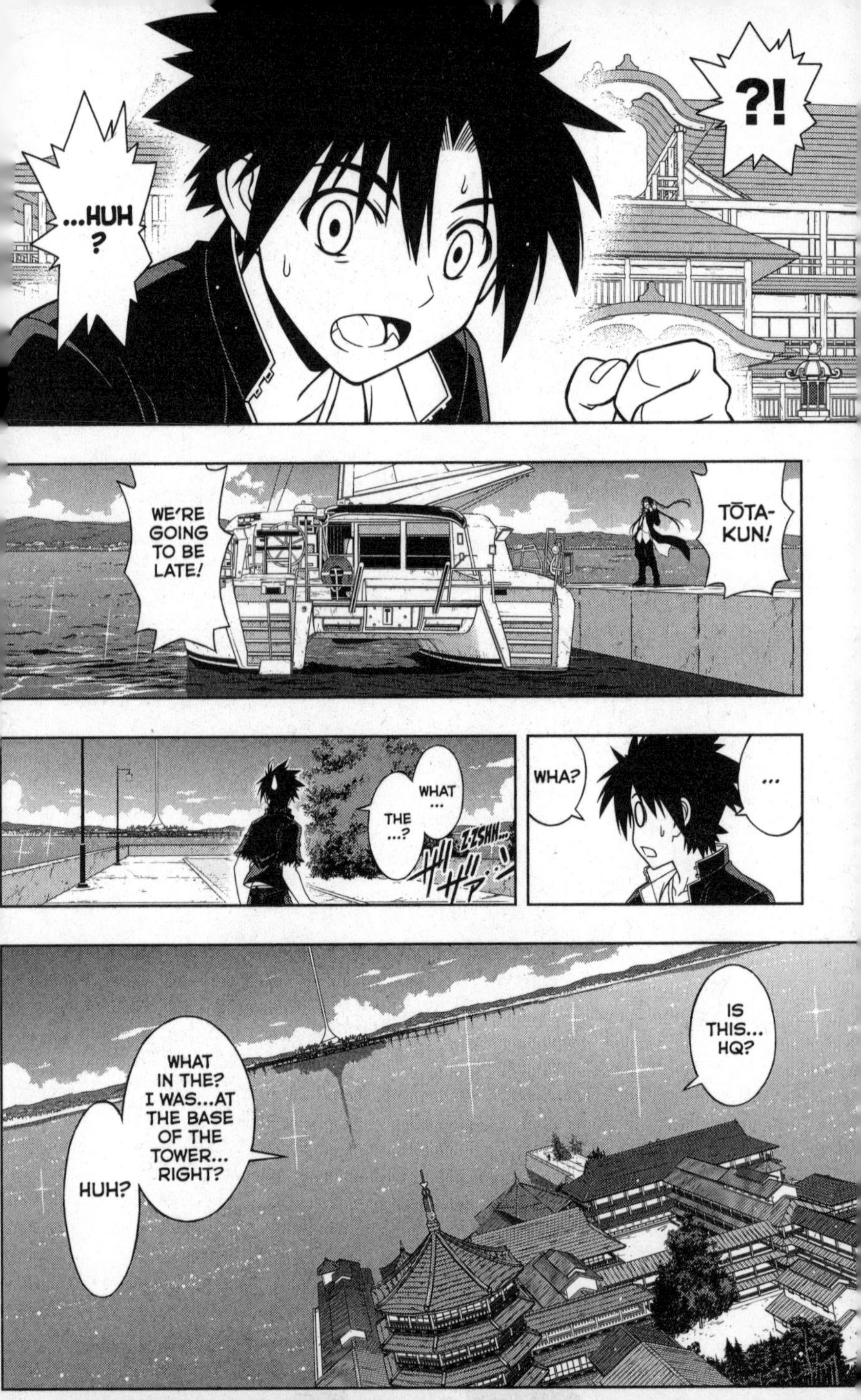
?!
...HUH ?
TŌTA-KUN!
WE'RE GOING TO BE LATE!
...
WHA?
WHAT ... THE ...?
Z-ZSHH...
IS THIS... HQ?
WHAT IN THE? I WAS...AT THE BASE OF THE TOWER... RIGHT?
HUH?

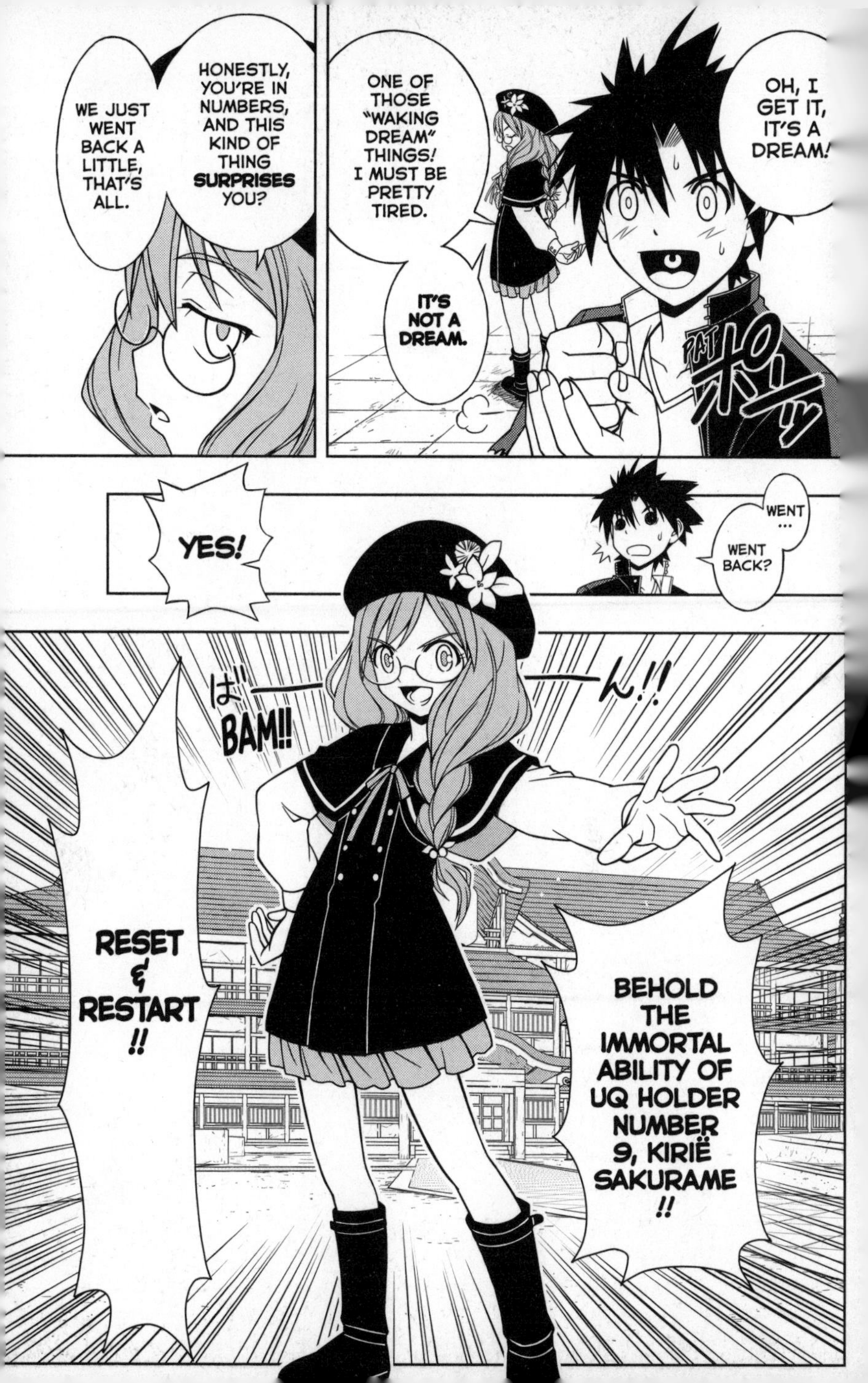

OH, I GET IT, IT'S A DREAM!
ONE OF THOSE "WAKING DREAM" THINGS! I MUST BE PRETTY TIRED.
PAT ポンッ
IT'S NOT A DREAM.
HONESTLY, YOU'RE IN NUMBERS, AND THIS KIND OF THING **SURPRISES** YOU?
WE JUST WENT BACK A LITTLE, THAT'S ALL.
WENT... WENT BACK?
YES!
ば――――ん!!
BAM!!
BEHOLD THE IMMORTAL ABILITY OF UQ HOLDER NUMBER 9, KIRIË SAKURAME!!
RESET & RESTART!!

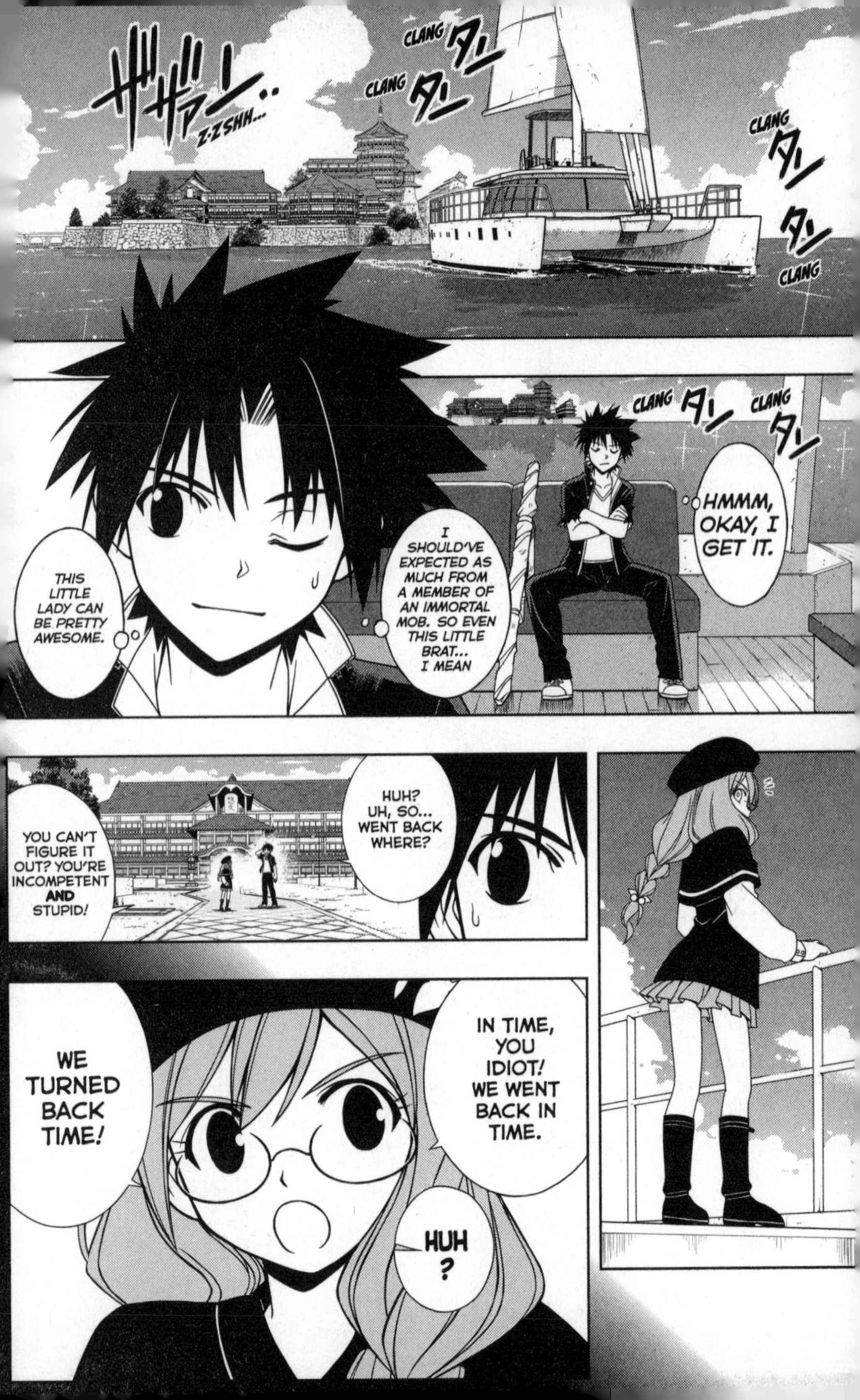
ザザァー…
Z-ZSHH...
CLANG タン
CLANG タン
CLANG タン
タン CLANG
CLANG タン
CLANG タン
HMMM, OKAY, I GET IT.
I SHOULD'VE EXPECTED AS MUCH FROM A MEMBER OF AN IMMORTAL MOB. SO EVEN THIS LITTLE BRAT... I MEAN
THIS LITTLE LADY CAN BE PRETTY AWESOME.
HUH? UH, SO... WENT BACK WHERE?
YOU CAN'T FIGURE IT OUT? YOU'RE INCOMPETENT **AND** STUPID!
IN TIME, YOU IDIOT! WE WENT BACK IN TIME.
WE TURNED BACK TIME!
HUH?

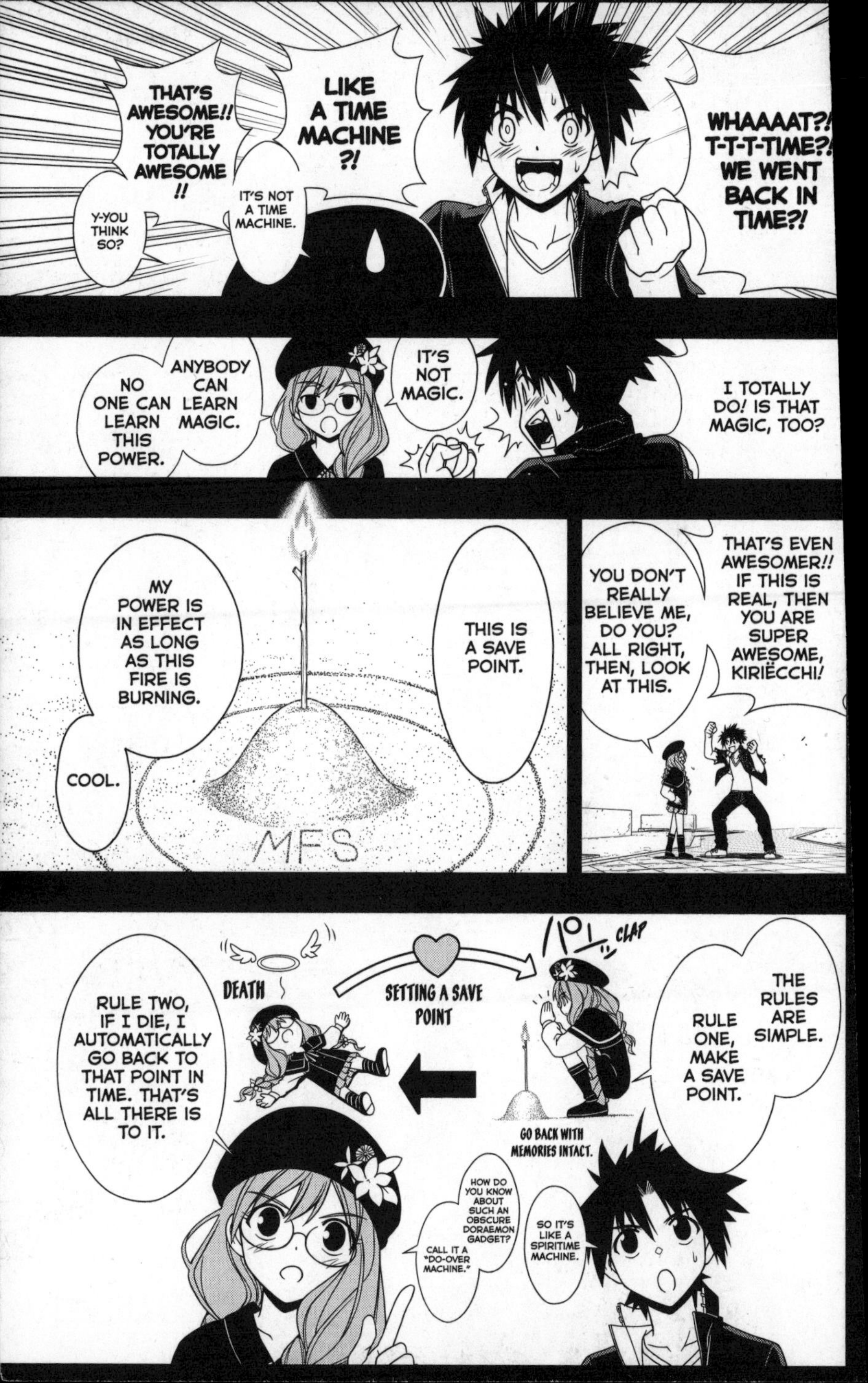
WHAAAAT?! T-T-T-TIME?! WE WENT BACK IN TIME?!
LIKE A TIME MACHINE ?!
IT'S NOT A TIME MACHINE.
THAT'S AWESOME!! YOU'RE TOTALLY AWESOME !!
Y-YOU THINK SO?
I TOTALLY DO! IS THAT MAGIC, TOO?
IT'S NOT MAGIC.
ANYBODY CAN LEARN MAGIC.
NO ONE CAN LEARN THIS POWER.
THAT'S EVEN AWESOMER!! IF THIS IS REAL, THEN YOU ARE SUPER AWESOME, KIRIËCCHI!
YOU DON'T REALLY BELIEVE ME, DO YOU? ALL RIGHT, THEN, LOOK AT THIS.
THIS IS A SAVE POINT.
MY POWER IS IN EFFECT AS LONG AS THIS FIRE IS BURNING.
COOL.
MFS
THE RULES ARE SIMPLE.
RULE ONE, MAKE A SAVE POINT.
CLAP
SETTING A SAVE POINT
DEATH
GO BACK WITH MEMORIES INTACT.
RULE TWO, IF I DIE, I AUTOMATICALLY GO BACK TO THAT POINT IN TIME. THAT'S ALL THERE IS TO IT.
SO IT'S LIKE A SPIRITIME MACHINE.
HOW DO YOU KNOW ABOUT SUCH AN OBSCURE DORAEMON GADGET?
CALL IT A "DO-OVER MACHINE."

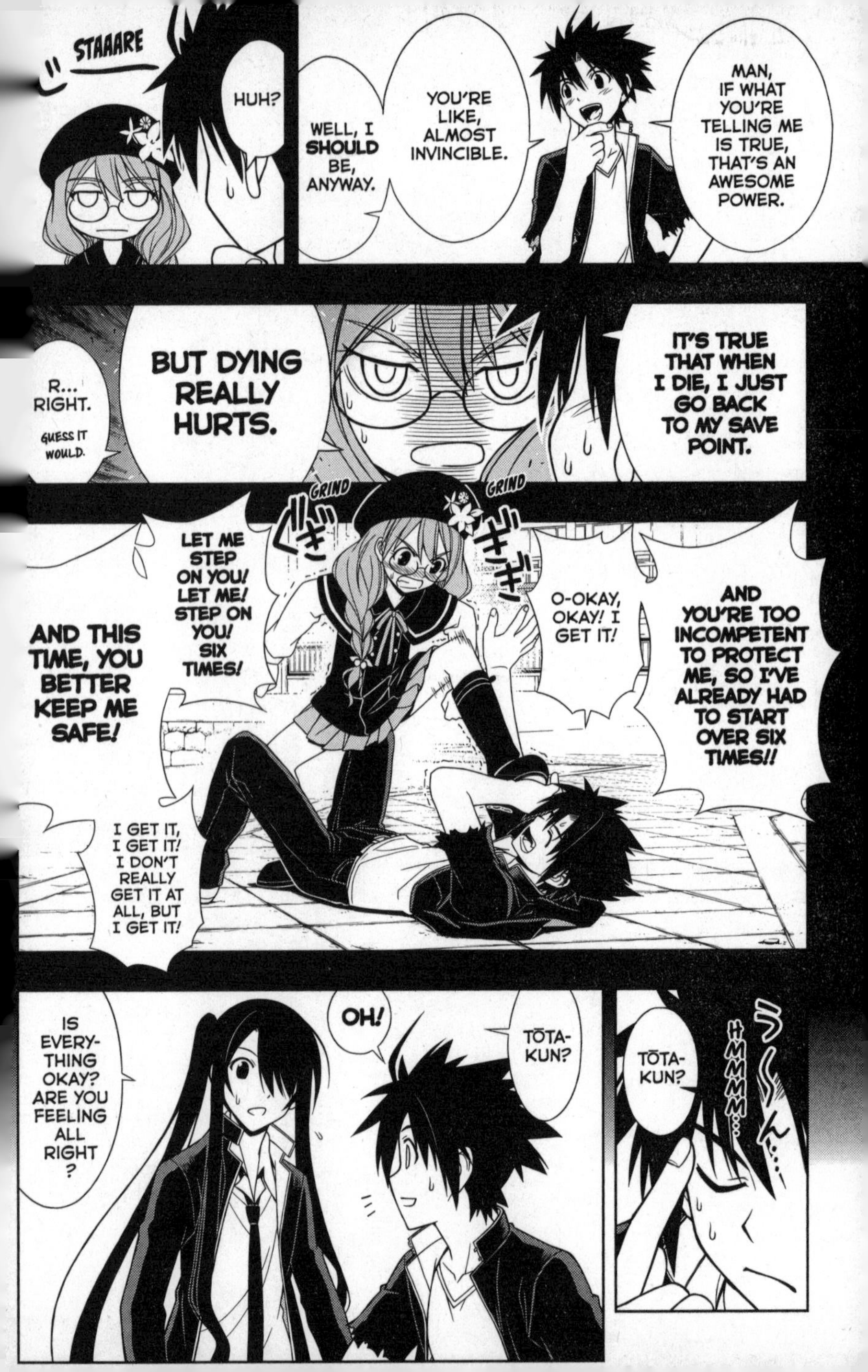
MAN, IF WHAT YOU'RE TELLING ME IS TRUE, THAT'S AN AWESOME POWER.
YOU'RE LIKE, ALMOST INVINCIBLE.
WELL, I SHOULD BE, ANYWAY.
HUH?
STAAARE
IT'S TRUE THAT WHEN I DIE, I JUST GO BACK TO MY SAVE POINT.
BUT DYING REALLY HURTS.
R... RIGHT.
GUESS IT WOULD.
GRIND
GRIND
AND YOU'RE TOO INCOMPETENT TO PROTECT ME, SO I'VE ALREADY HAD TO START OVER SIX TIMES!!
O-OKAY, OKAY! I GET IT!
LET ME STEP ON YOU! LET ME! STEP ON YOU! SIX TIMES!
AND THIS TIME, YOU BETTER KEEP ME SAFE!
I GET IT, I GET IT! I DON'T REALLY GET IT AT ALL, BUT I GET IT!
HMMMM...
TŌTA-KUN?
TŌTA-KUN?
OH!
IS EVERY-THING OKAY? ARE YOU FEELING ALL RIGHT?

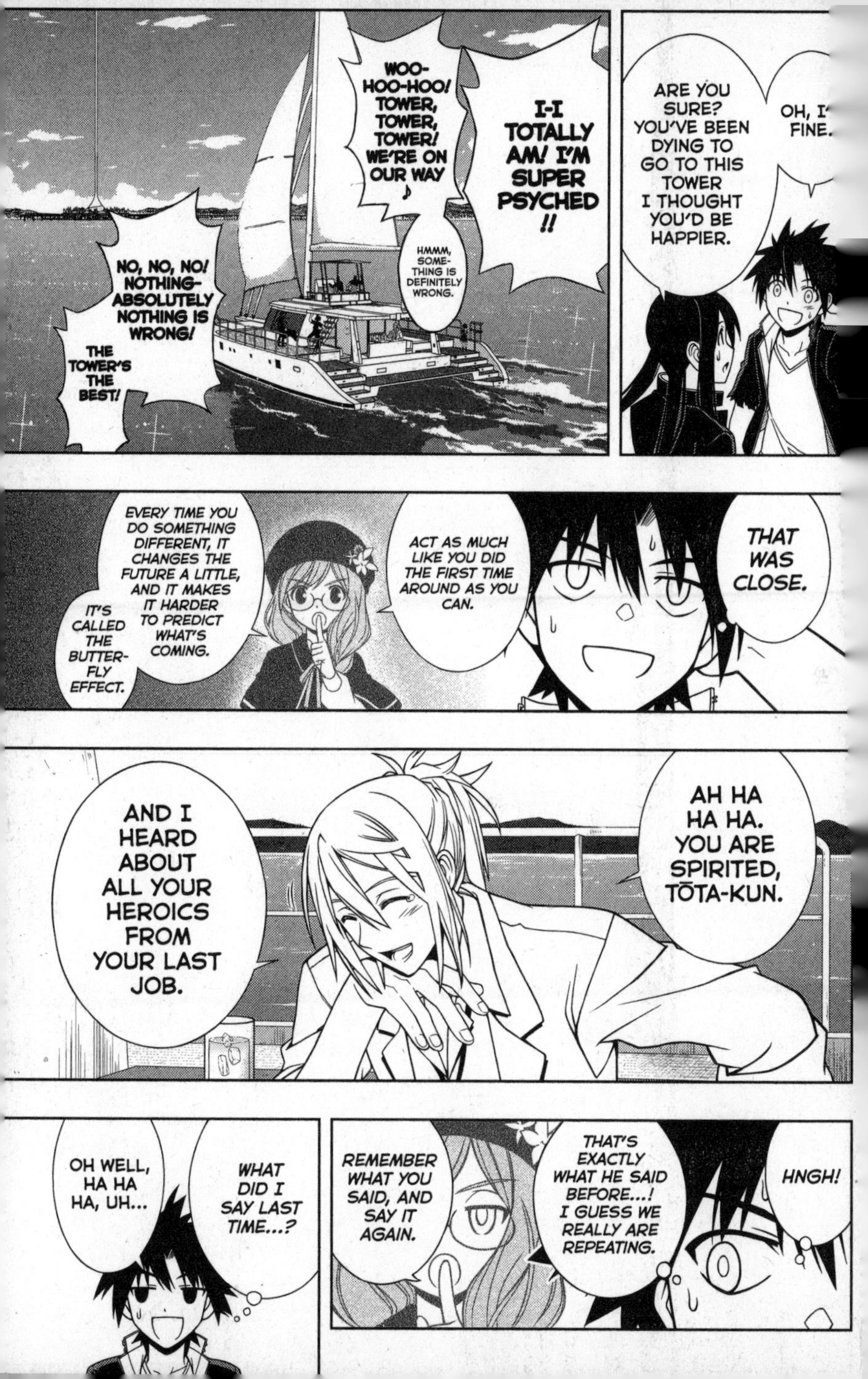
OH, I’ FINE.
ARE YOU SURE? YOU’VE BEEN DYING TO GO TO THIS TOWER I THOUGHT YOU’D BE HAPPIER.
I-I TOTALLY AM! I’M SUPER PSYCHED!!
WOO-HOO-HOO! TOWER, TOWER, TOWER! WE’RE ON OUR WAY ♪
HMMM, SOMETHING IS DEFINITELY WRONG.
NO, NO, NO! NOTHING-ABSOLUTELY NOTHING IS WRONG!
THE TOWER’S THE BEST!
THAT WAS CLOSE.
ACT AS MUCH LIKE YOU DID THE FIRST TIME AROUND AS YOU CAN.
EVERY TIME YOU DO SOMETHING DIFFERENT, IT CHANGES THE FUTURE A LITTLE, AND IT MAKES IT HARDER TO PREDICT WHAT’S COMING.
IT’S CALLED THE BUTTERFLY EFFECT.
AH HA HA HA. YOU ARE SPIRITED, TŌTA-KUN.
AND I HEARD ABOUT ALL YOUR HEROICS FROM YOUR LAST JOB.
HNGH!
THAT’S EXACTLY WHAT HE SAID BEFORE...! I GUESS WE REALLY ARE REPEATING.
REMEMBER WHAT YOU SAID, AND SAY IT AGAIN.
WHAT DID I SAY LAST TIME...?
OH WELL, HA HA HA, UH...

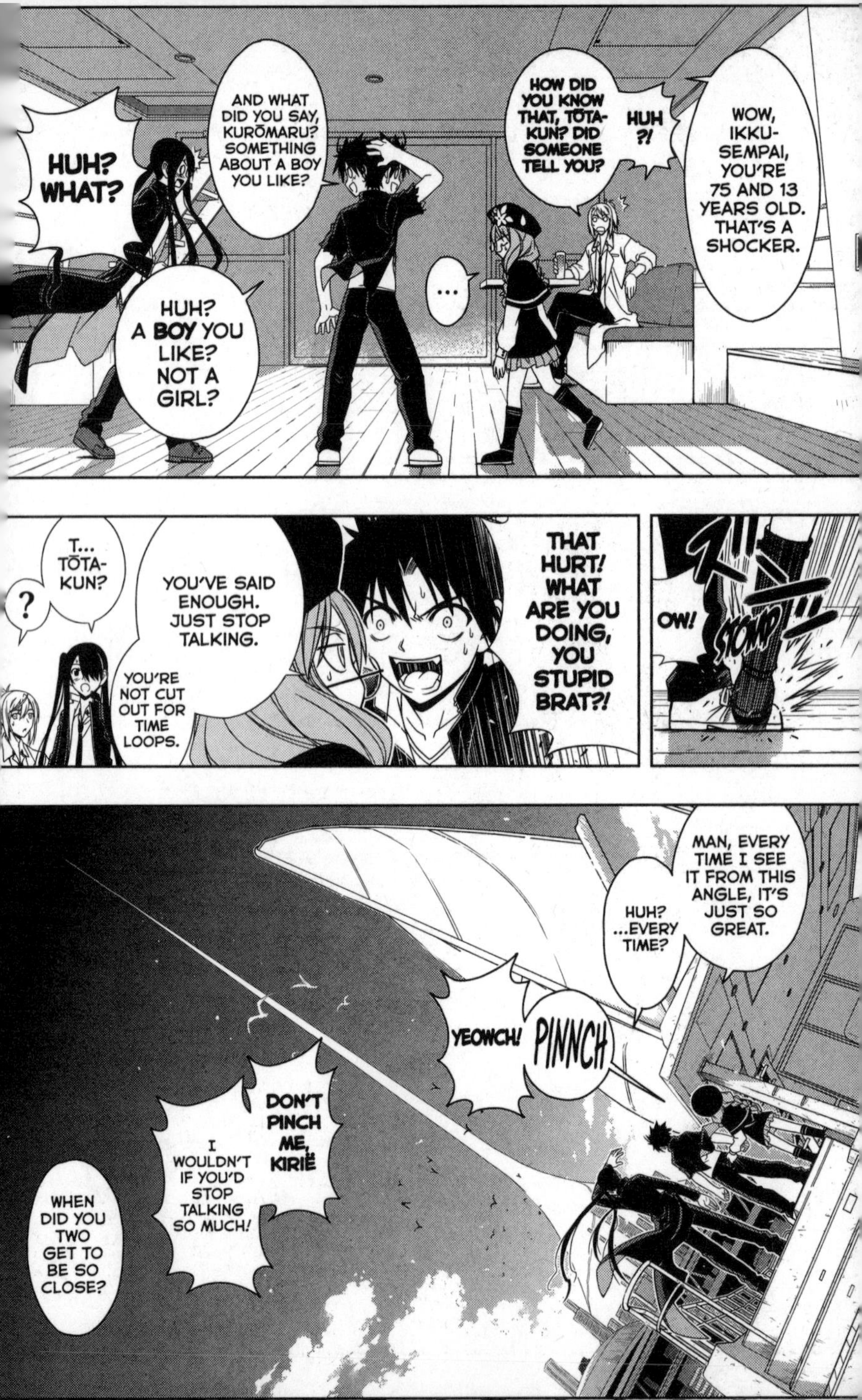
WOW, IKKU-SEMPAI, YOU'RE 75 AND 13 YEARS OLD. THAT'S A SHOCKER.
HUH ?!
HOW DID YOU KNOW THAT, TŌTA-KUN? DID SOMEONE TELL YOU?
...
AND WHAT DID YOU SAY, KURŌMARU? SOMETHING ABOUT A BOY YOU LIKE?
HUH? WHAT?
HUH? A BOY YOU LIKE? NOT A GIRL?
OW!
STOMP
THAT HURT! WHAT ARE YOU DOING, YOU STUPID BRAT?!
YOU'VE SAID ENOUGH. JUST STOP TALKING.
YOU'RE NOT CUT OUT FOR TIME LOOPS.
T... TŌTA-KUN?
?
MAN, EVERY TIME I SEE IT FROM THIS ANGLE, IT'S JUST SO GREAT.
HUH? ...EVERY TIME?
PINNCH
YEOWCH!
DON'T PINCH ME, KIRIË
I WOULDN'T IF YOU'D STOP TALKING SO MUCH!
WHEN DID YOU TWO GET TO BE SO CLOSE?

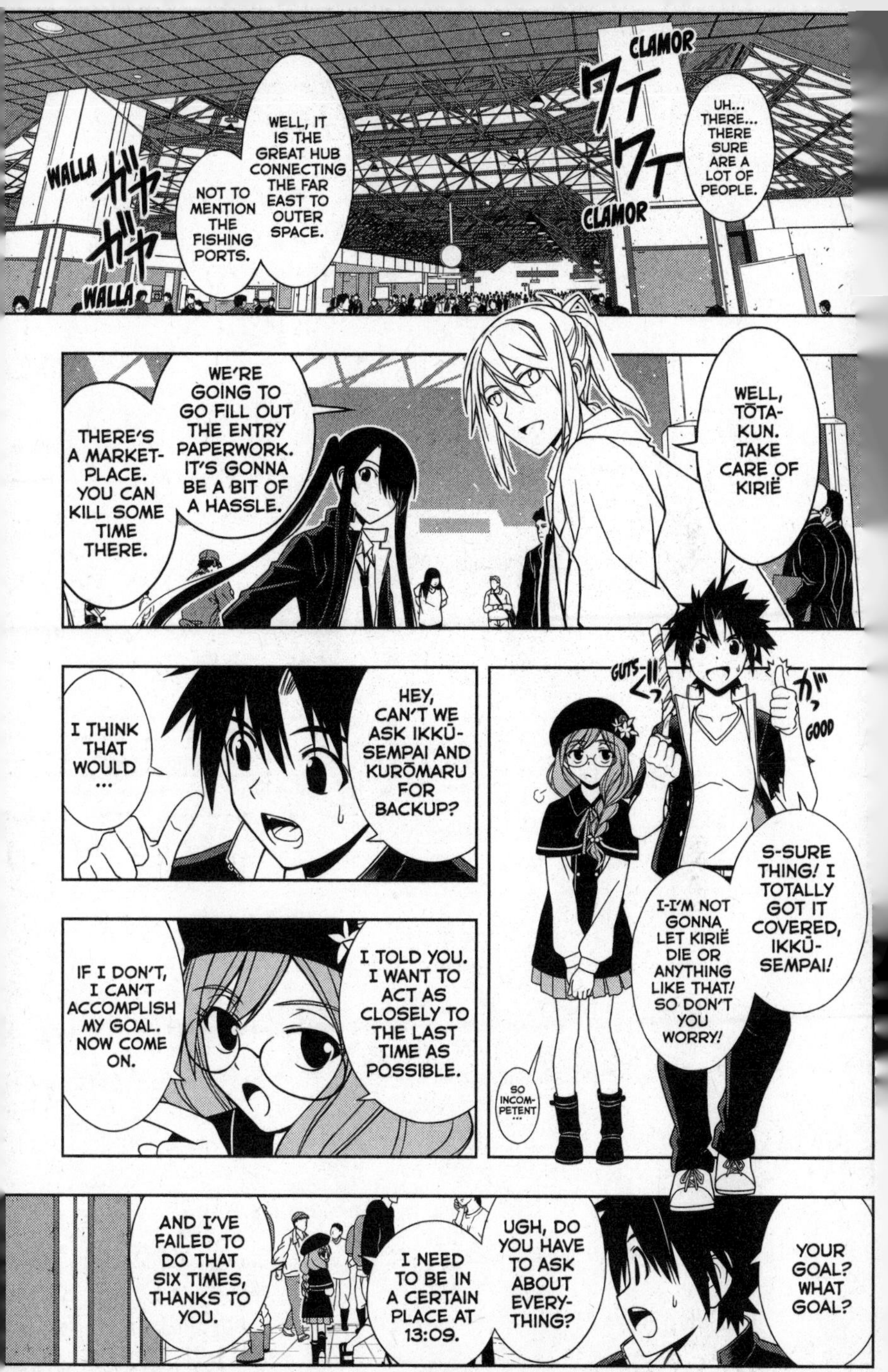
CLAMOR
CLAMOR
UH... THERE... THERE SURE ARE A LOT OF PEOPLE.
WELL, IT IS THE GREAT HUB CONNECTING THE FAR EAST TO OUTER SPACE.
NOT TO MENTION THE FISHING PORTS.
WALLA
WALLA
WELL, TŌTA-KUN. TAKE CARE OF KIRIË
WE'RE GOING TO GO FILL OUT THE ENTRY PAPERWORK. IT'S GONNA BE A BIT OF A HASSLE.
THERE'S A MARKET-PLACE. YOU CAN KILL SOME TIME THERE.
GUTS
GOOD
S-SURE THING! I TOTALLY GOT IT COVERED, IKKŪ-SEMPAI!
I-I'M NOT GONNA LET KIRIË DIE OR ANYTHING LIKE THAT! SO DON'T YOU WORRY!
SO INCOM-PETENT ...
HEY, CAN'T WE ASK IKKŪ-SEMPAI AND KURŌMARU FOR BACKUP?
I THINK THAT WOULD ...
I TOLD YOU. I WANT TO ACT AS CLOSELY TO THE LAST TIME AS POSSIBLE.
IF I DON'T, I CAN'T ACCOMPLISH MY GOAL. NOW COME ON.
YOUR GOAL? WHAT GOAL?
UGH, DO YOU HAVE TO ASK ABOUT EVERY-THING?
I NEED TO BE IN A CERTAIN PLACE AT 13:09.
AND I'VE FAILED TO DO THAT SIX TIMES, THANKS TO YOU.

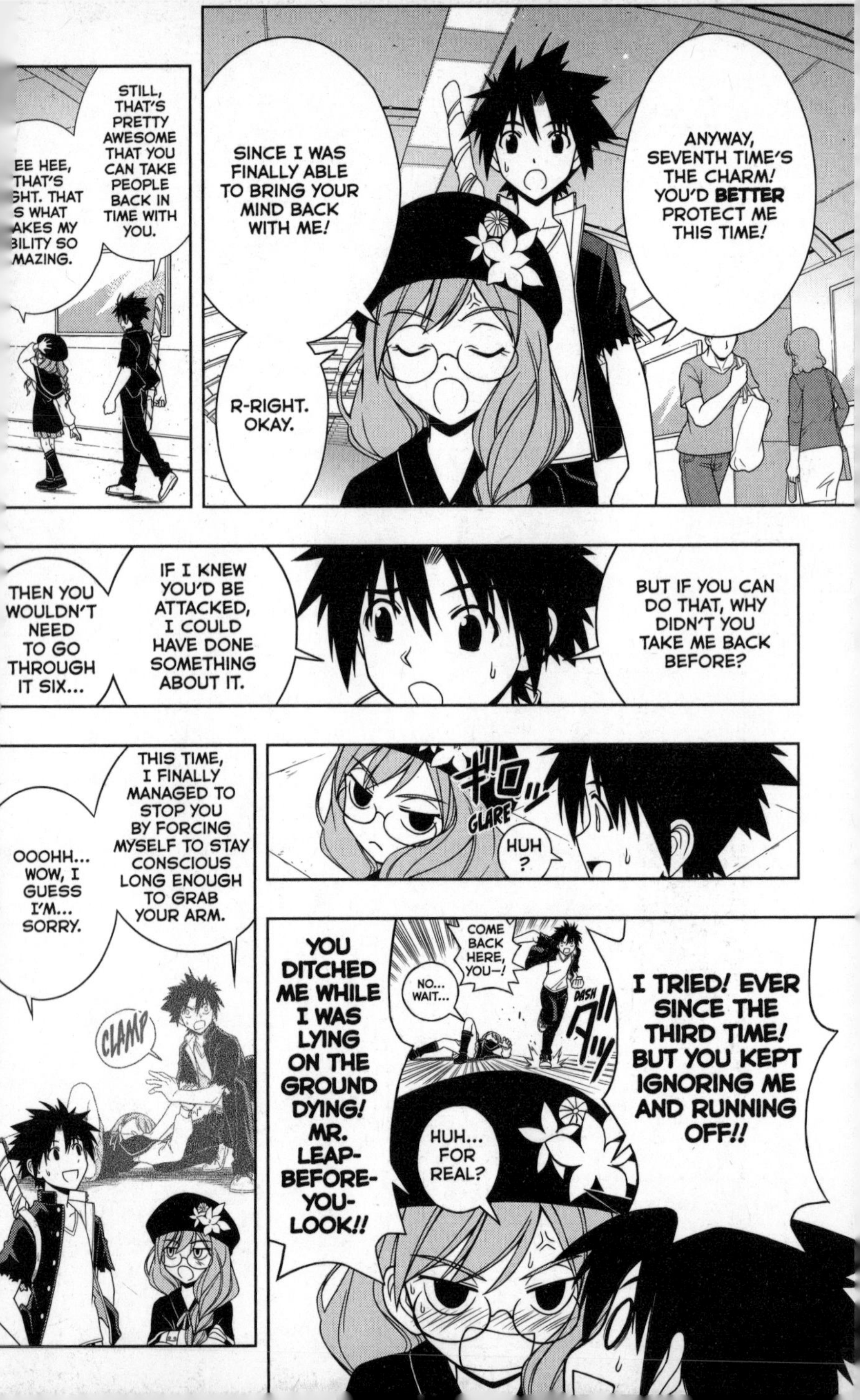
ANYWAY, SEVENTH TIME'S THE CHARM! YOU'D **BETTER** PROTECT ME THIS TIME!
SINCE I WAS FINALLY ABLE TO BRING YOUR MIND BACK WITH ME!
R-RIGHT. OKAY.
STILL, THAT'S PRETTY AWESOME THAT YOU CAN TAKE PEOPLE BACK IN TIME WITH YOU.
EE HEE, THAT'S GHT. THAT S WHAT AKES MY BILITY SO MAZING.
BUT IF YOU CAN DO THAT, WHY DIDN'T YOU TAKE ME BACK BEFORE?
IF I KNEW YOU'D BE ATTACKED, I COULD HAVE DONE SOMETHING ABOUT IT.
THEN YOU WOULDN'T NEED TO GO THROUGH IT SIX...
GLARE
HUH?
I TRIED! EVER SINCE THE THIRD TIME! BUT YOU KEPT IGNORING ME AND RUNNING OFF!!
COME BACK HERE, YOU—!
DASH
NO... WAIT...
YOU DITCHED ME WHILE I WAS LYING ON THE GROUND DYING! MR. LEAP-BEFORE-YOU-LOOK!!
HUH... FOR REAL?
THIS TIME, I FINALLY MANAGED TO STOP YOU BY FORCING MYSELF TO STAY CONSCIOUS LONG ENOUGH TO GRAB YOUR ARM.
OOOHH... WOW, I GUESS I'M... SORRY.
CLAMP

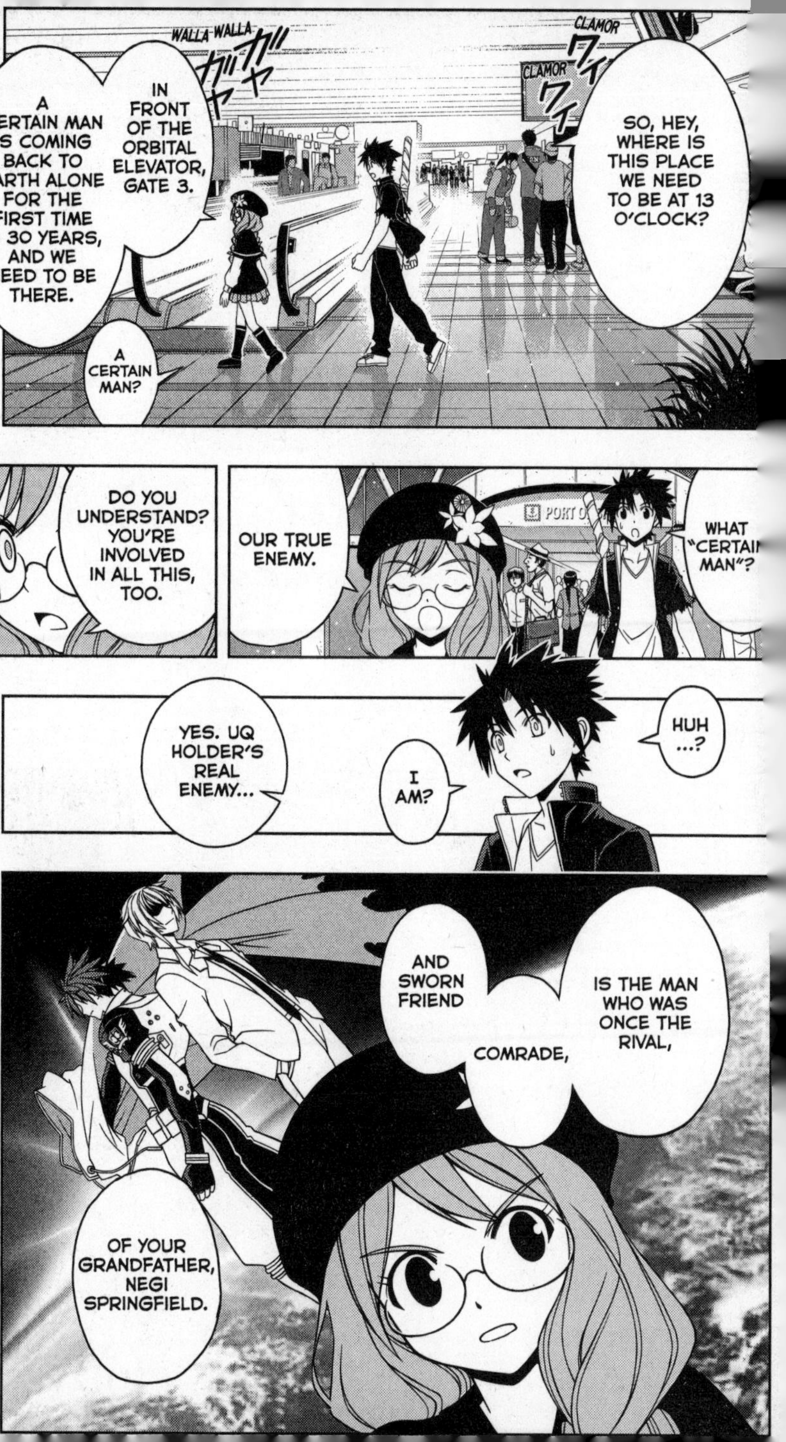
CLAMOR ワイ
CLAMOR ワイ
WALLA WALLA ガヤ ガヤ
SO, HEY, WHERE IS THIS PLACE WE NEED TO BE AT 13 O'CLOCK?
IN FRONT OF THE ORBITAL ELEVATOR, GATE 3.
A CERTAIN MAN IS COMING BACK TO EARTH ALONE FOR THE FIRST TIME IN 30 YEARS, AND WE NEED TO BE THERE.
A CERTAIN MAN?
WHAT "CERTAI MAN"?
PORT O
OUR TRUE ENEMY.
DO YOU UNDERSTAND? YOU'RE INVOLVED IN ALL THIS, TOO.
HUH ...?
I AM?
YES. UQ HOLDER'S REAL ENEMY...
IS THE MAN WHO WAS ONCE THE RIVAL,
COMRADE,
AND SWORN FRIEND
OF YOUR GRANDFATHER, NEGI SPRINGFIELD.

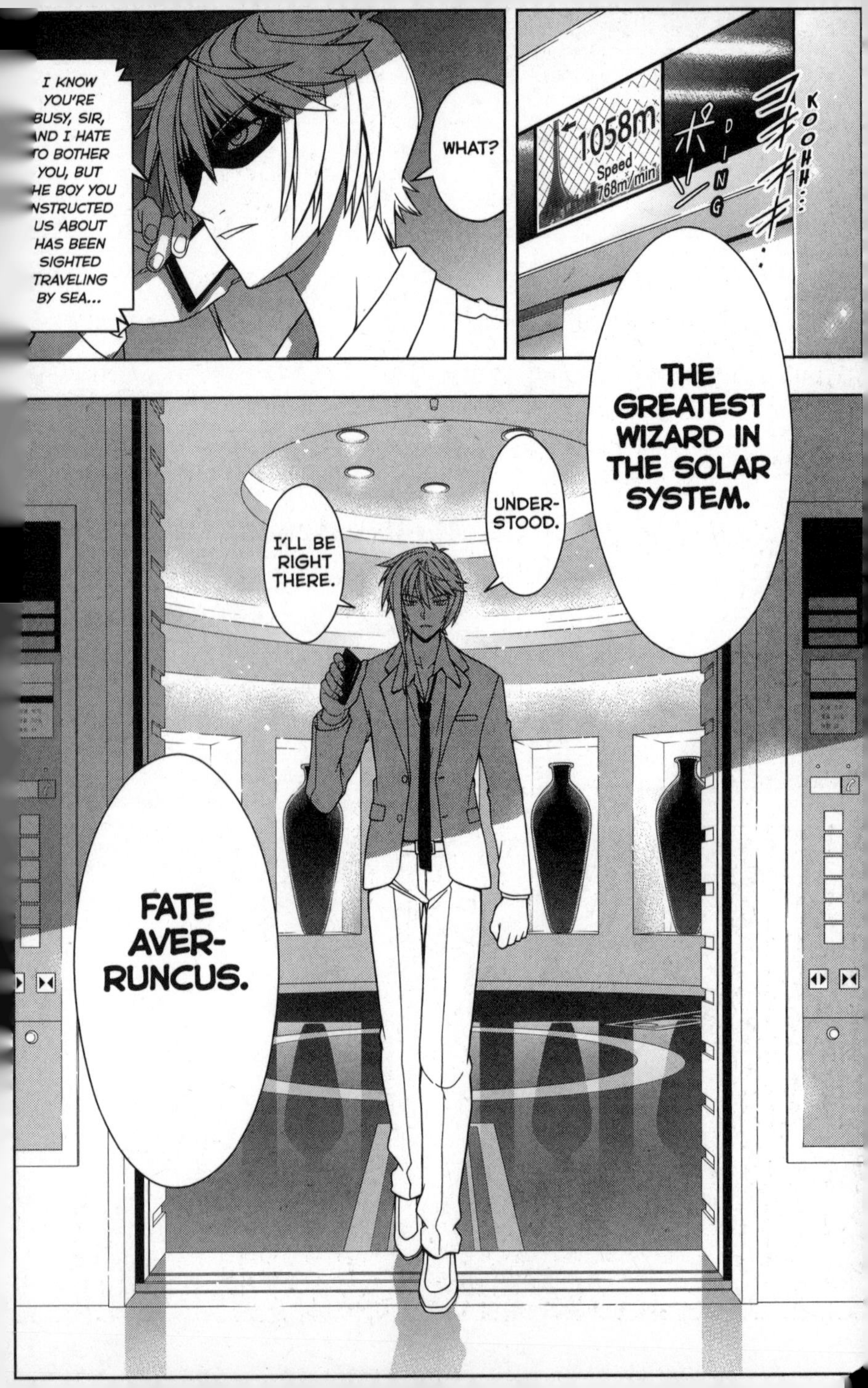

1058m
Speed
768m/min
KOOHH...
DING
I KNOW YOU'RE BUSY, SIR, AND I HATE TO BOTHER YOU, BUT THE BOY YOU INSTRUCTED US ABOUT HAS BEEN SIGHTED TRAVELING BY SEA...
WHAT?
THE GREATEST WIZARD IN THE SOLAR SYSTEM.
UNDER-STOOD.
I'LL BE RIGHT THERE.
FATE AVER-RUNCUS.

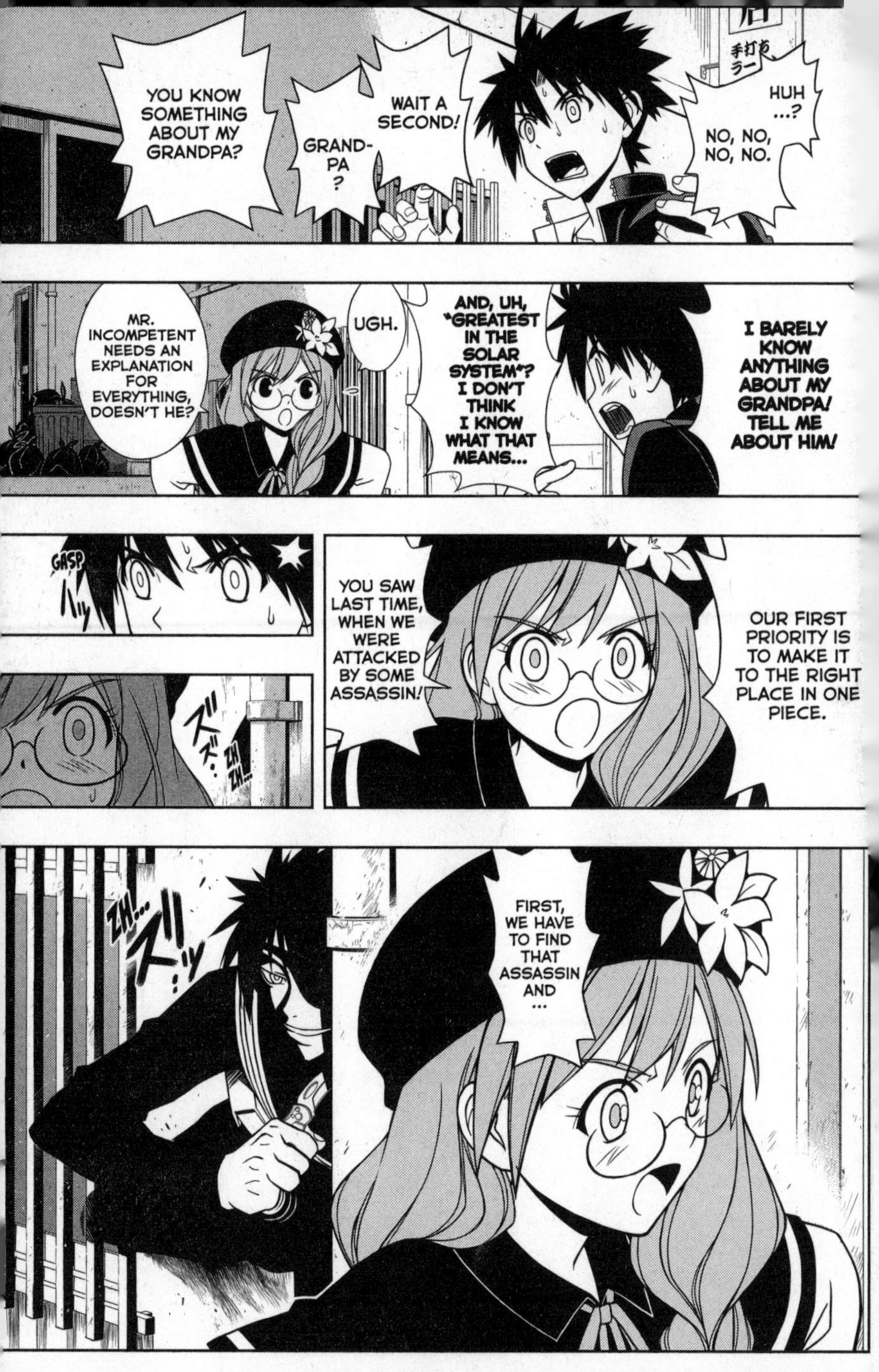
手打ち
ラー
HUH ...?
NO, NO, NO, NO.
WAIT A SECOND!
GRANDPA?
YOU KNOW SOMETHING ABOUT MY GRANDPA?
I BARELY KNOW ANYTHING ABOUT MY GRANDPA! TELL ME ABOUT HIM!
AND, UH, "GREATEST IN THE SOLAR SYSTEM"? I DON'T THINK I KNOW WHAT THAT MEANS...
UGH.
MR. INCOMPETENT NEEDS AN EXPLANATION FOR EVERYTHING, DOESN'T HE?
OUR FIRST PRIORITY IS TO MAKE IT TO THE RIGHT PLACE IN ONE PIECE.
YOU SAW LAST TIME, WHEN WE WERE ATTACKED BY SOME ASSASSIN!
GASP
ハッ
ズズ…
ZH ZH...
FIRST, WE HAVE TO FIND THAT ASSASSIN AND ...
ZH!...
ズリッ

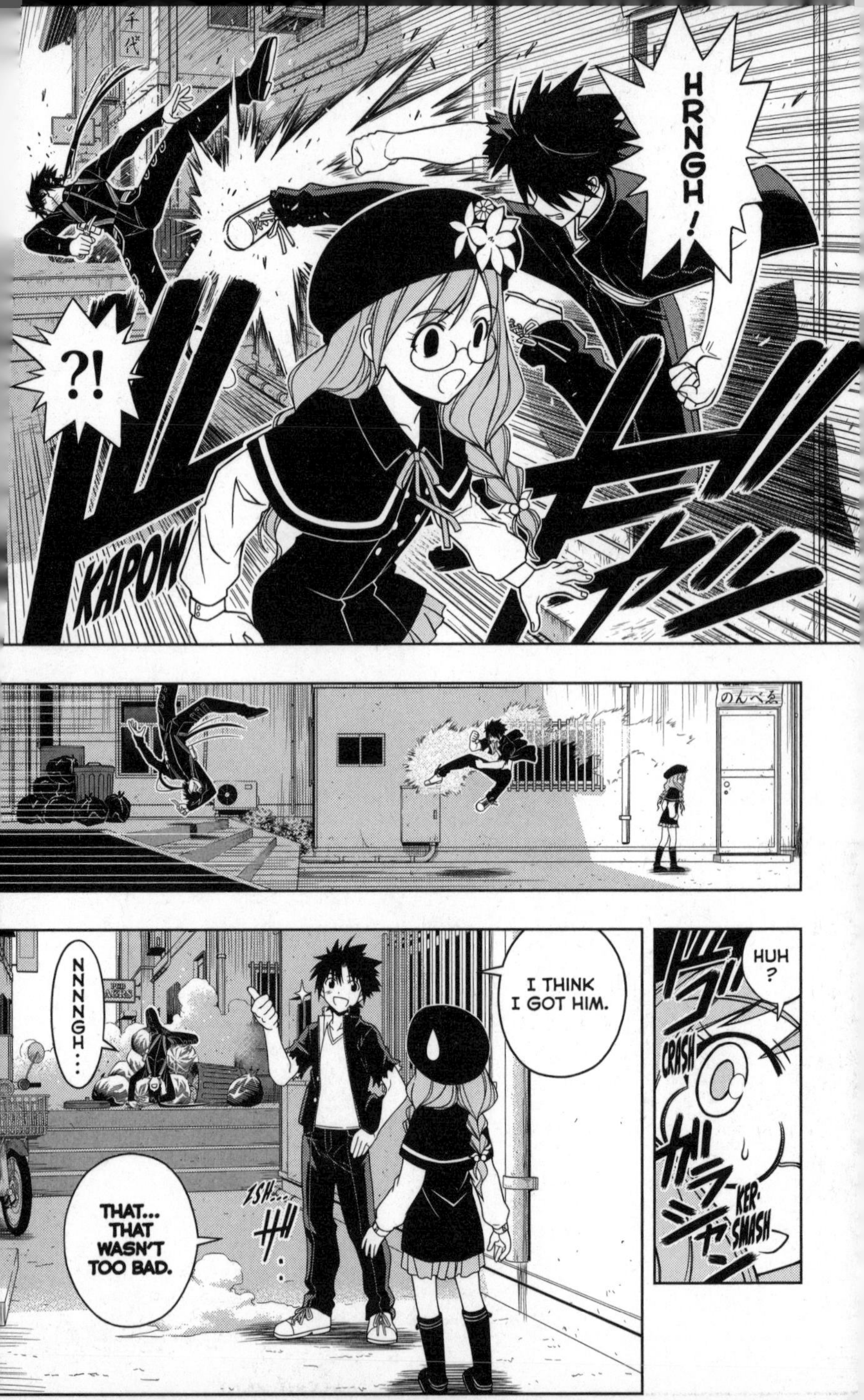
HRNGH!
?!
KAPOW
のんべゑ
HUH?
CRASH
KER-SMASH
I THINK I GOT HIM.
NNNNGH...
TSH...
THAT... THAT WASN'T TOO BAD.

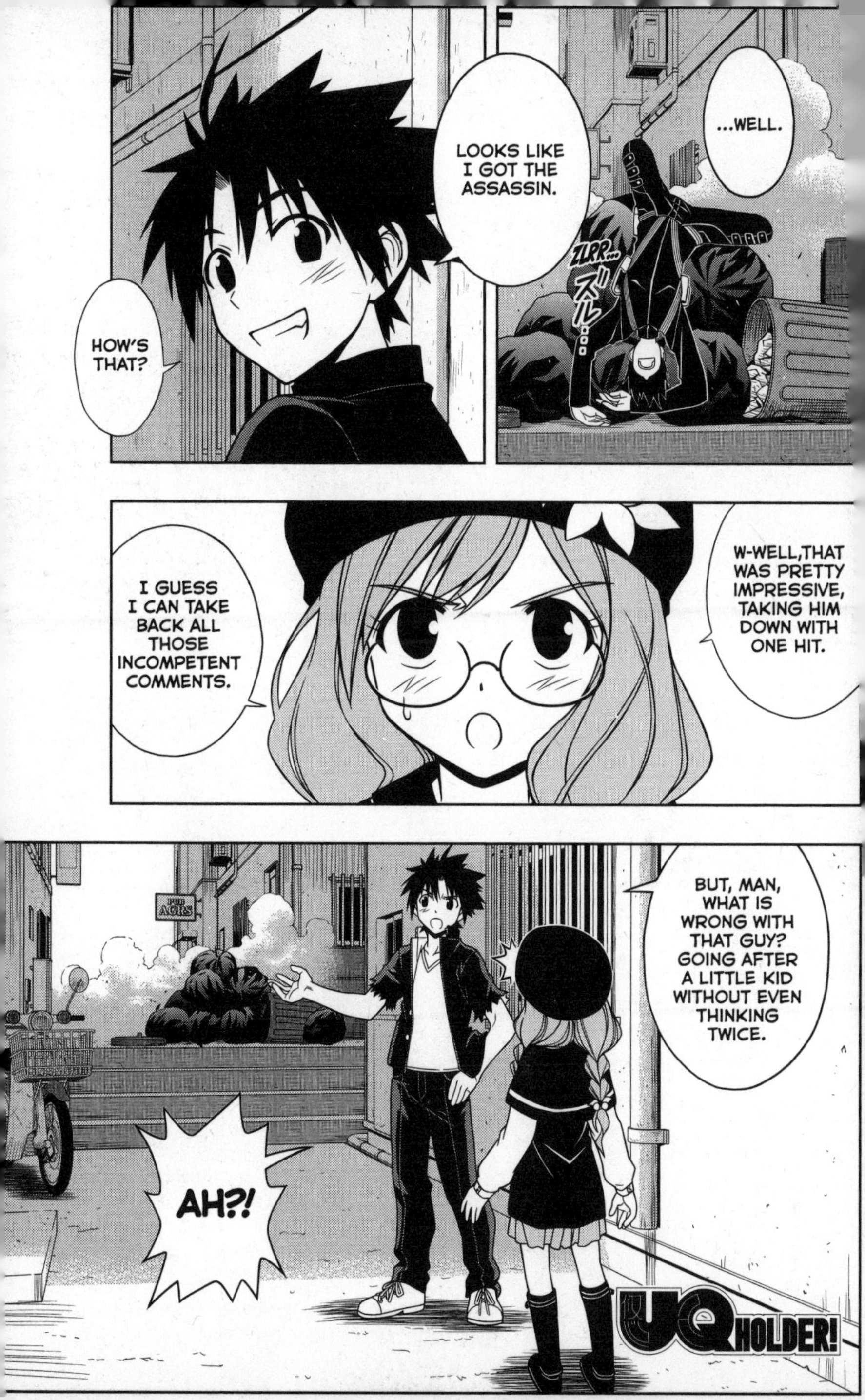
...WELL.
ZLRR...
ズル…
LOOKS LIKE I GOT THE ASSASSIN.
HOW'S THAT?
W-WELL,THAT WAS PRETTY IMPRESSIVE, TAKING HIM DOWN WITH ONE HIT.
I GUESS I CAN TAKE BACK ALL THOSE INCOMPETENT COMMENTS.
BUT, MAN, WHAT IS WRONG WITH THAT GUY? GOING AFTER A LITTLE KID WITHOUT EVEN THINKING TWICE.
AH?!

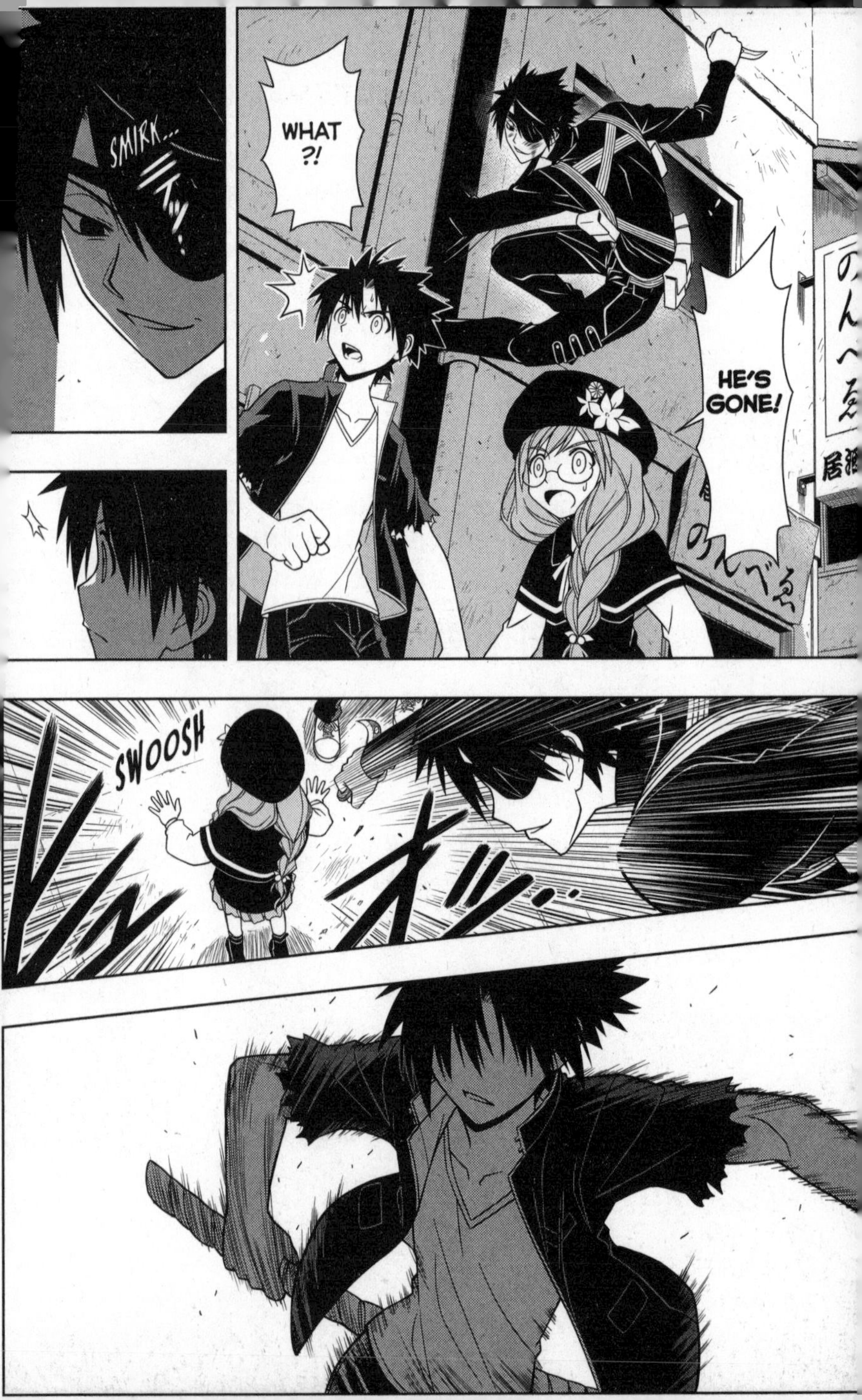
WHAT ?!
HE'S GONE!
SMIRK...
SWOOSH

STAGE 34: RETURN OF THE CREEPY ASSASSIN!

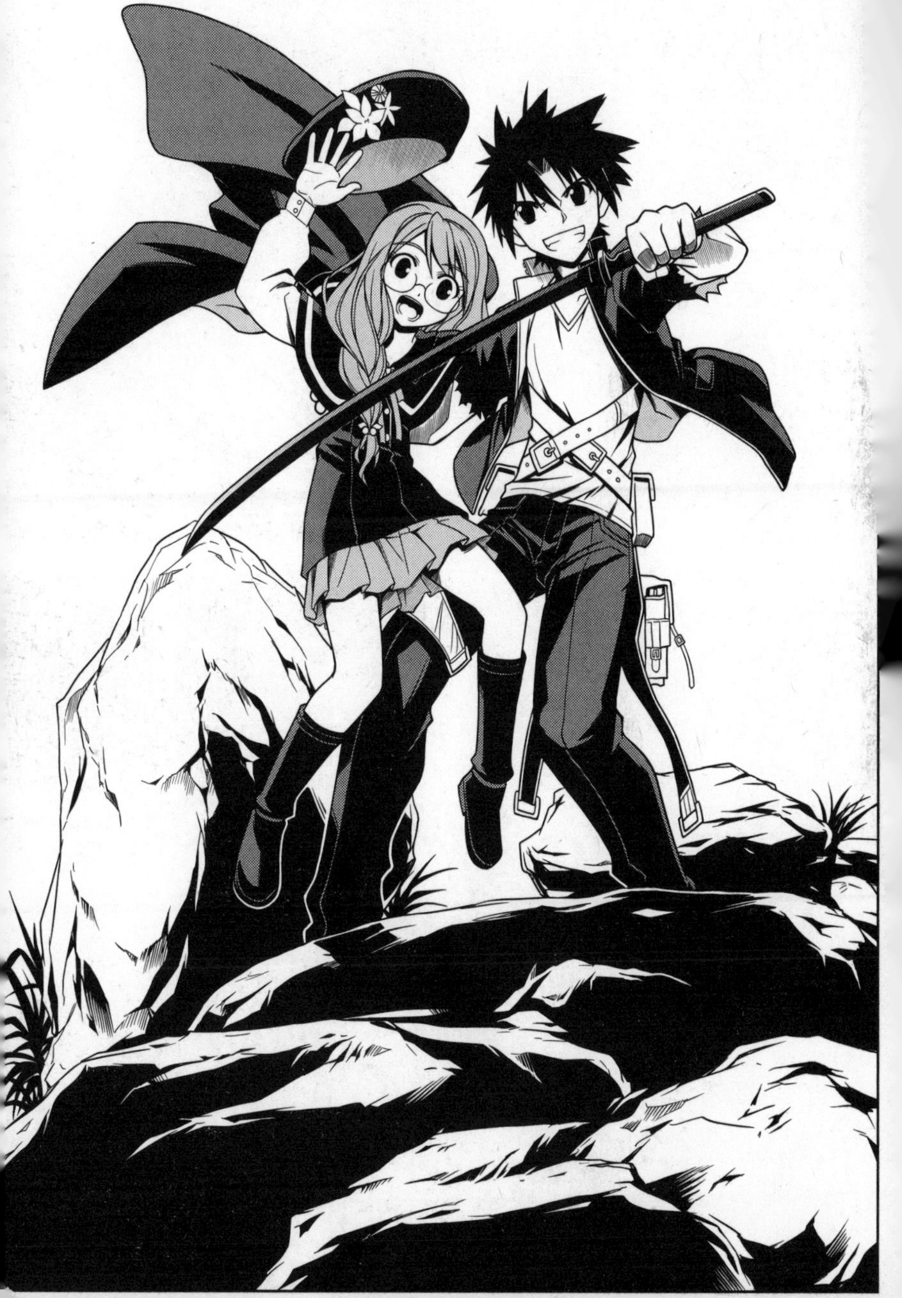

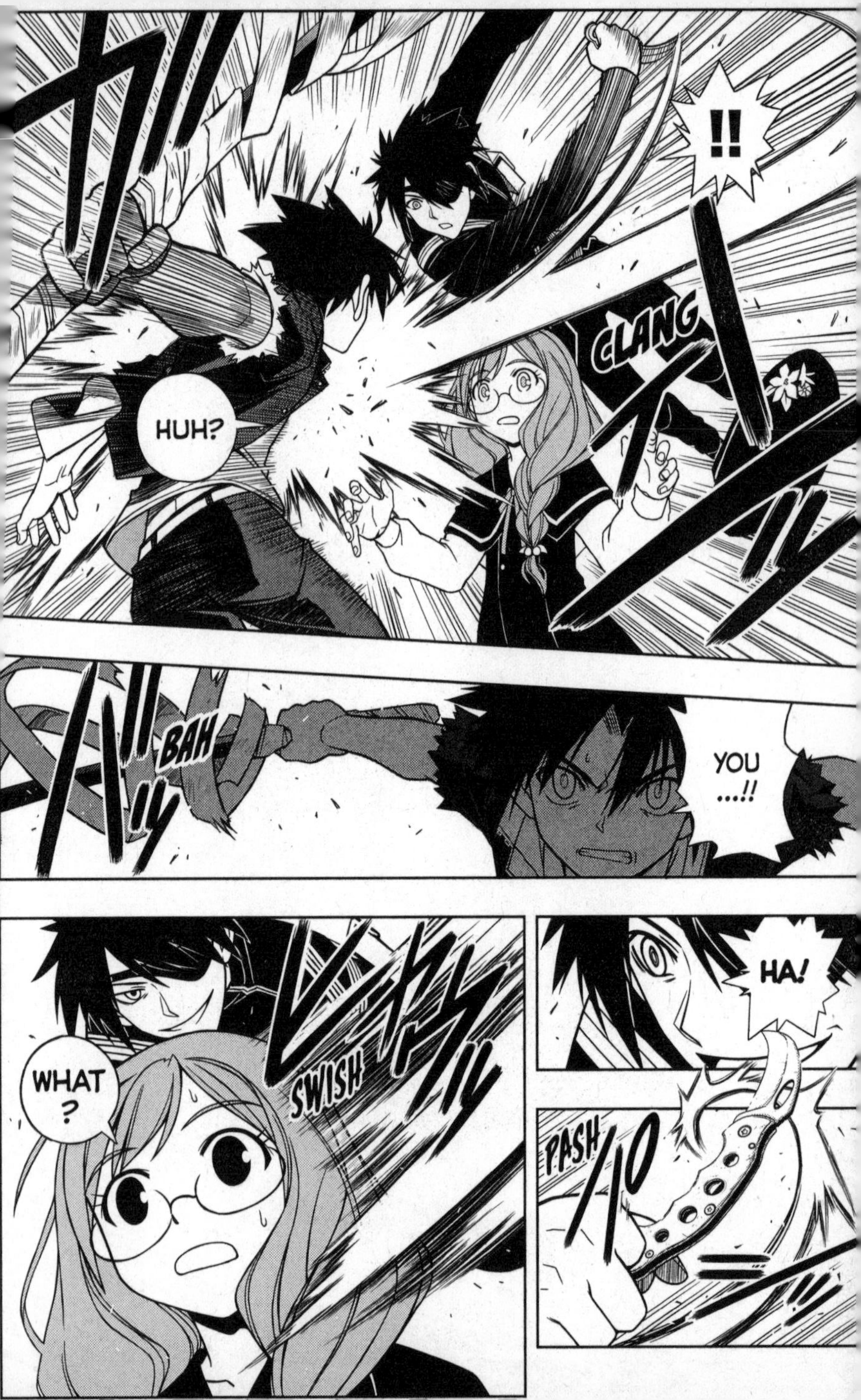
!!
CLANG
HUH?
YOU ...!!
BAH
HA!
PASH
SWISH
WHAT ?

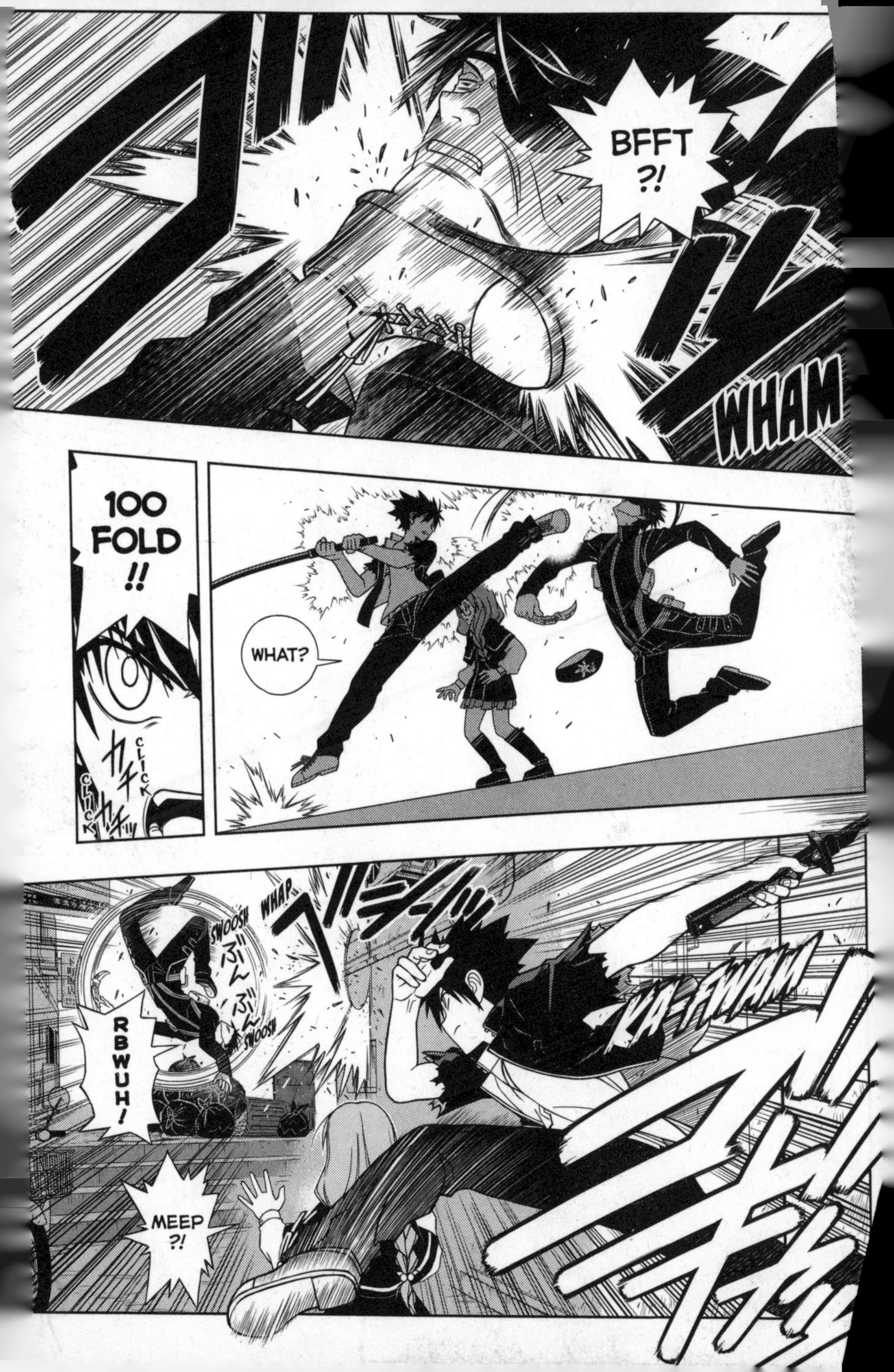

BFFT ?!
WHAM
WHAT?
100 FOLD !!
CLICK CLICK
KA-FWAM
WHAP
SWOOSH SWOOSH
RBWUH!
MEEP ?!

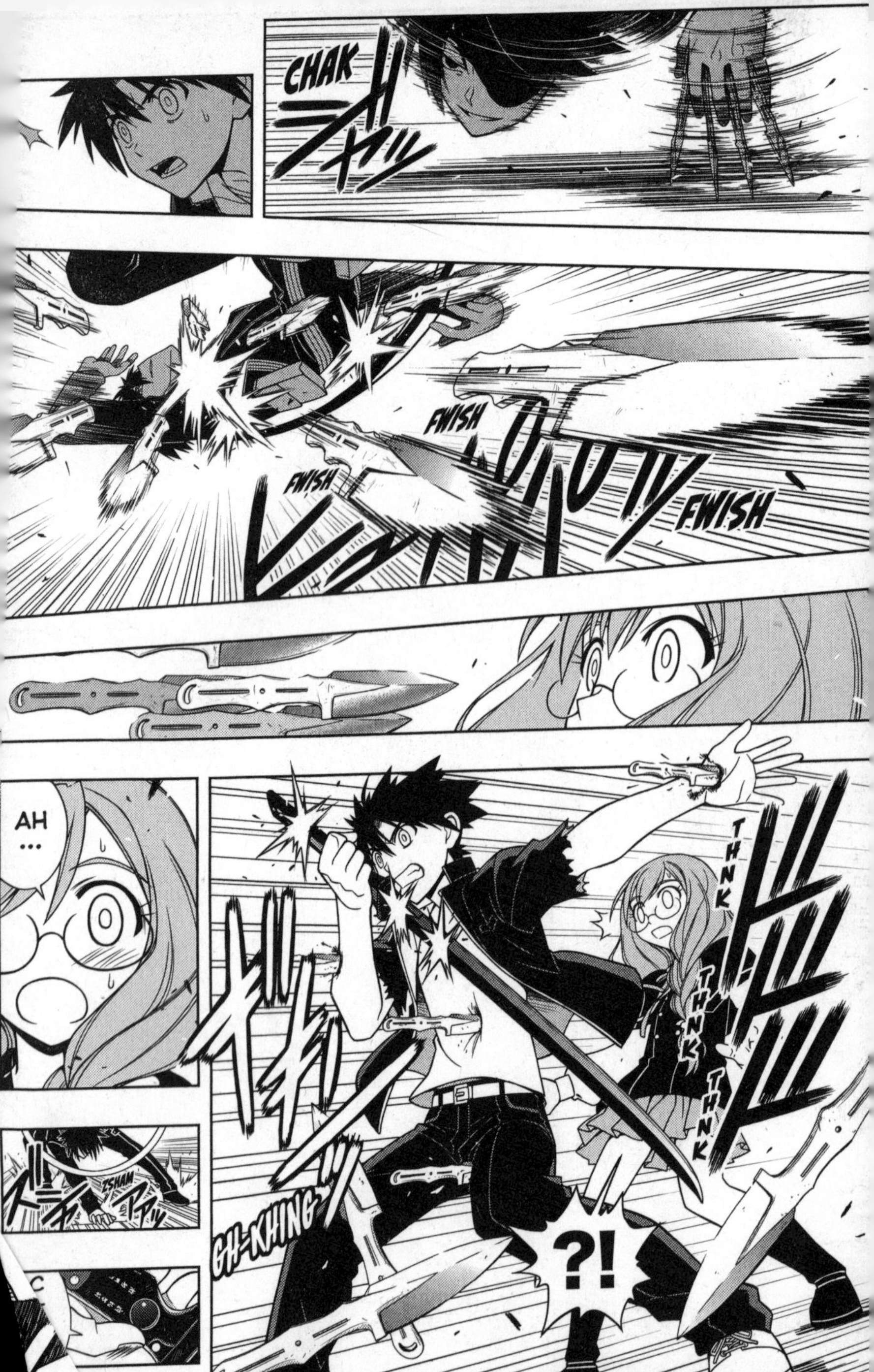
CHAK
FWISH
FWISH
FWISH
THNK
THNK
THNK
GH-KHING
?!
AH ...
ZSHAM

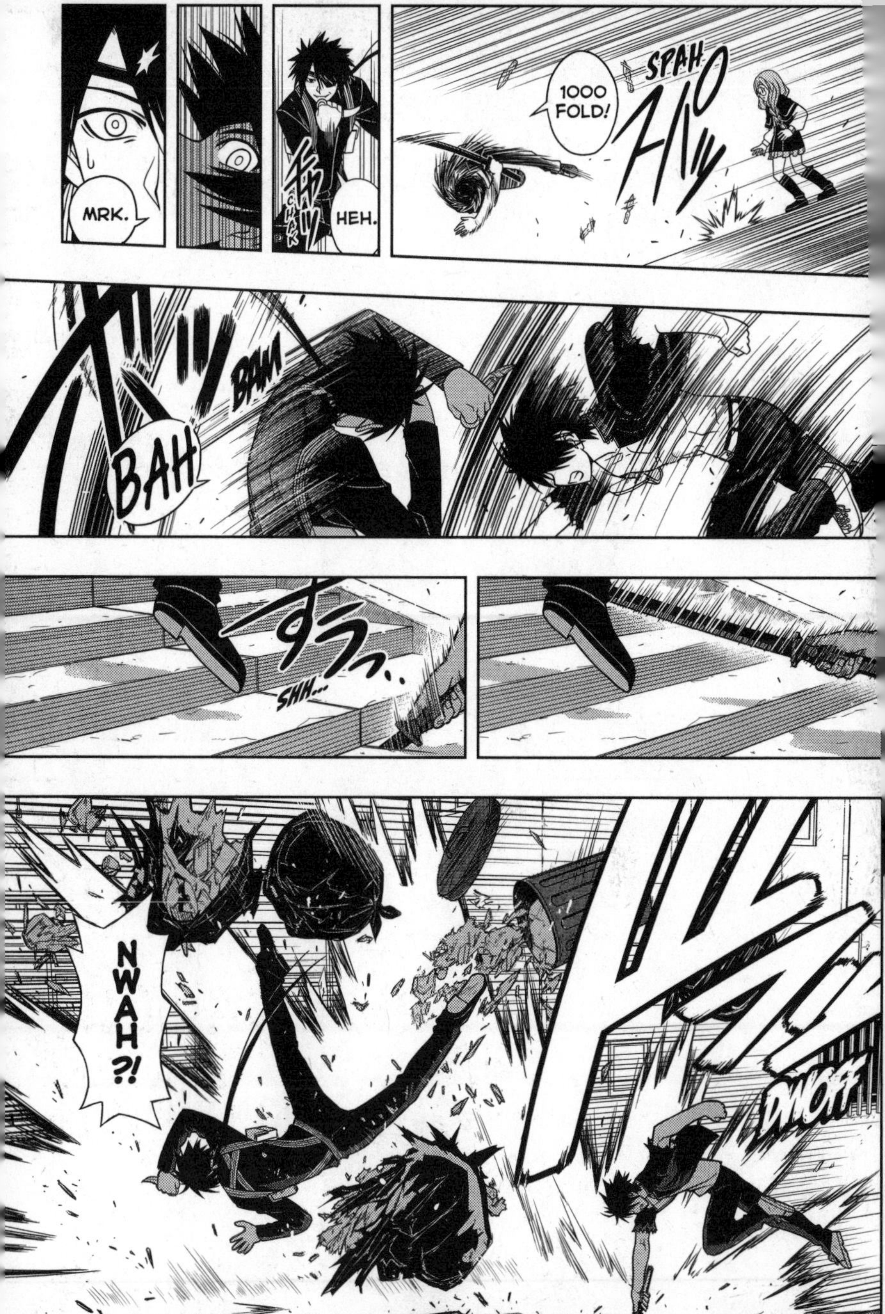
SPAH
1000 FOLD!
CHAK
HEH.
MRK.
BAM
BAH
SHH...
DWOFF
NWAH?!

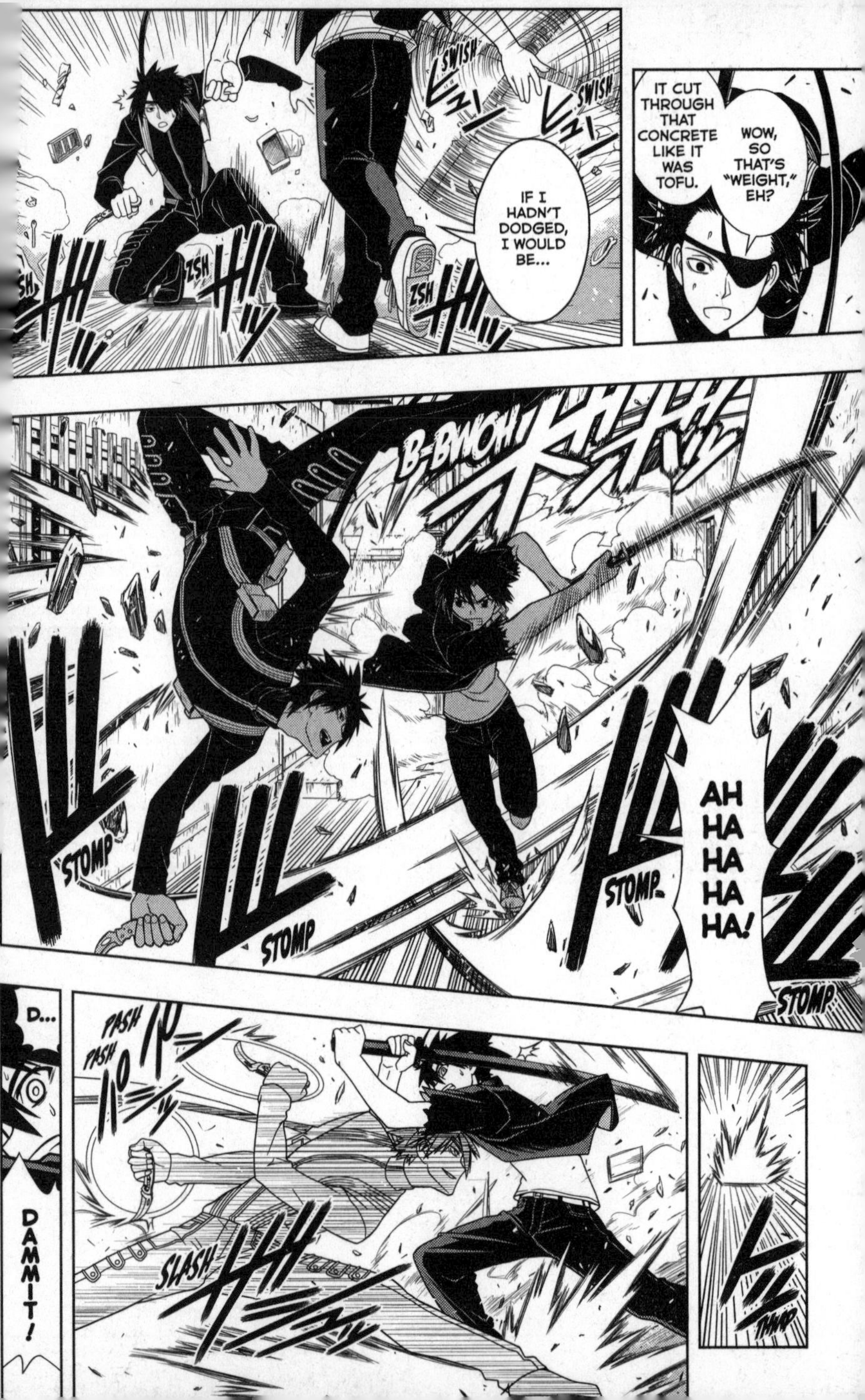
IT CUT THROUGH THAT CONCRETE LIKE IT WAS TOFU.
WOW, SO THAT'S "WEIGHT," EH?
SWISH
SWISH
IF I HADN'T DODGED, I WOULD BE...
ZSH
ZSH
SH
B-BWOH
AH HA HA HA HA HA!
STOMP
STOMP
STOMP
STOMP
THWAP
PASH
PASH
SLASH
D...
DAMMIT!

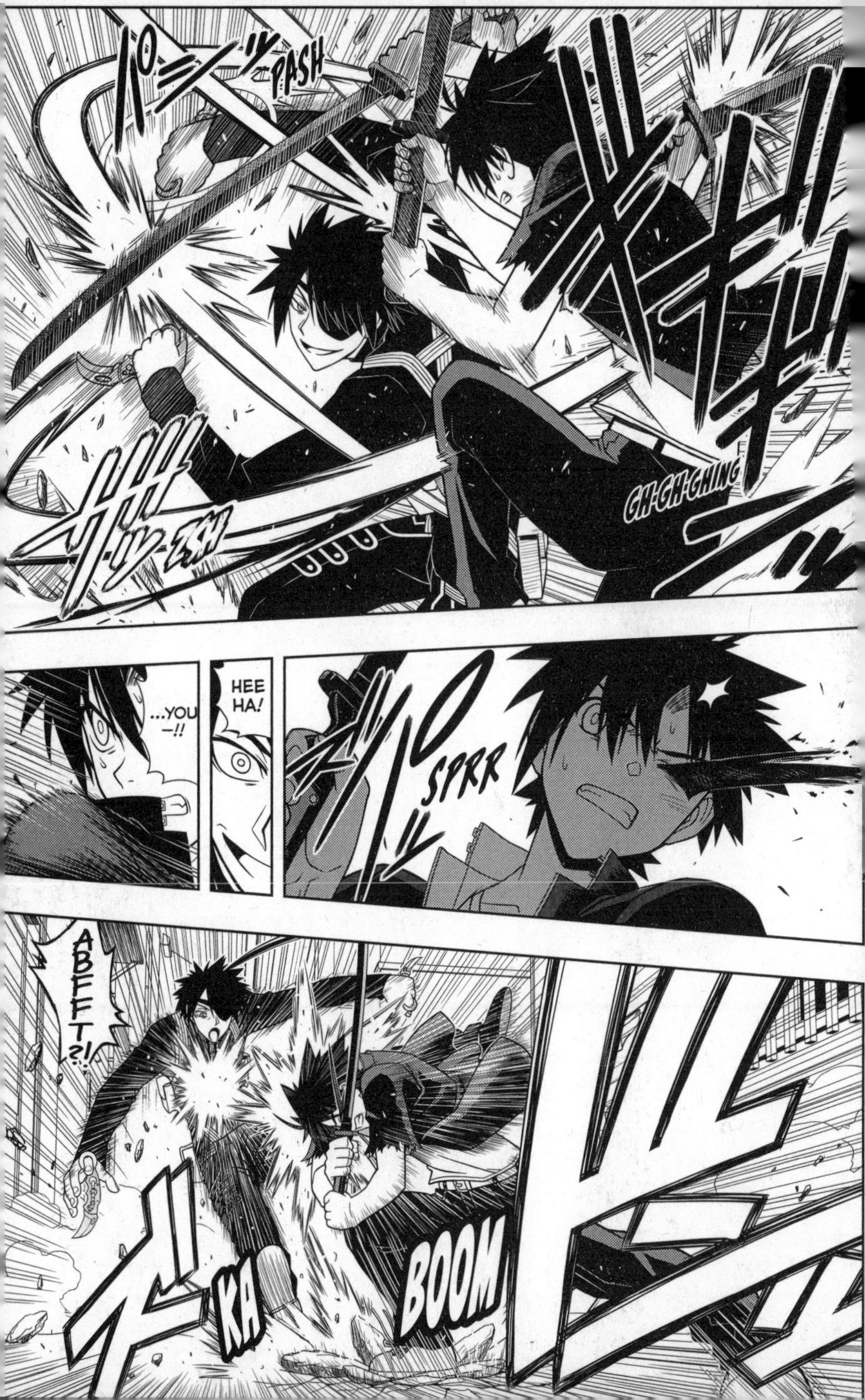
PASH
GH-GH-GHING
ZSH
SPRR
HEE HA!
...YOU—!!
ABFFFT?!
KA
BOOM

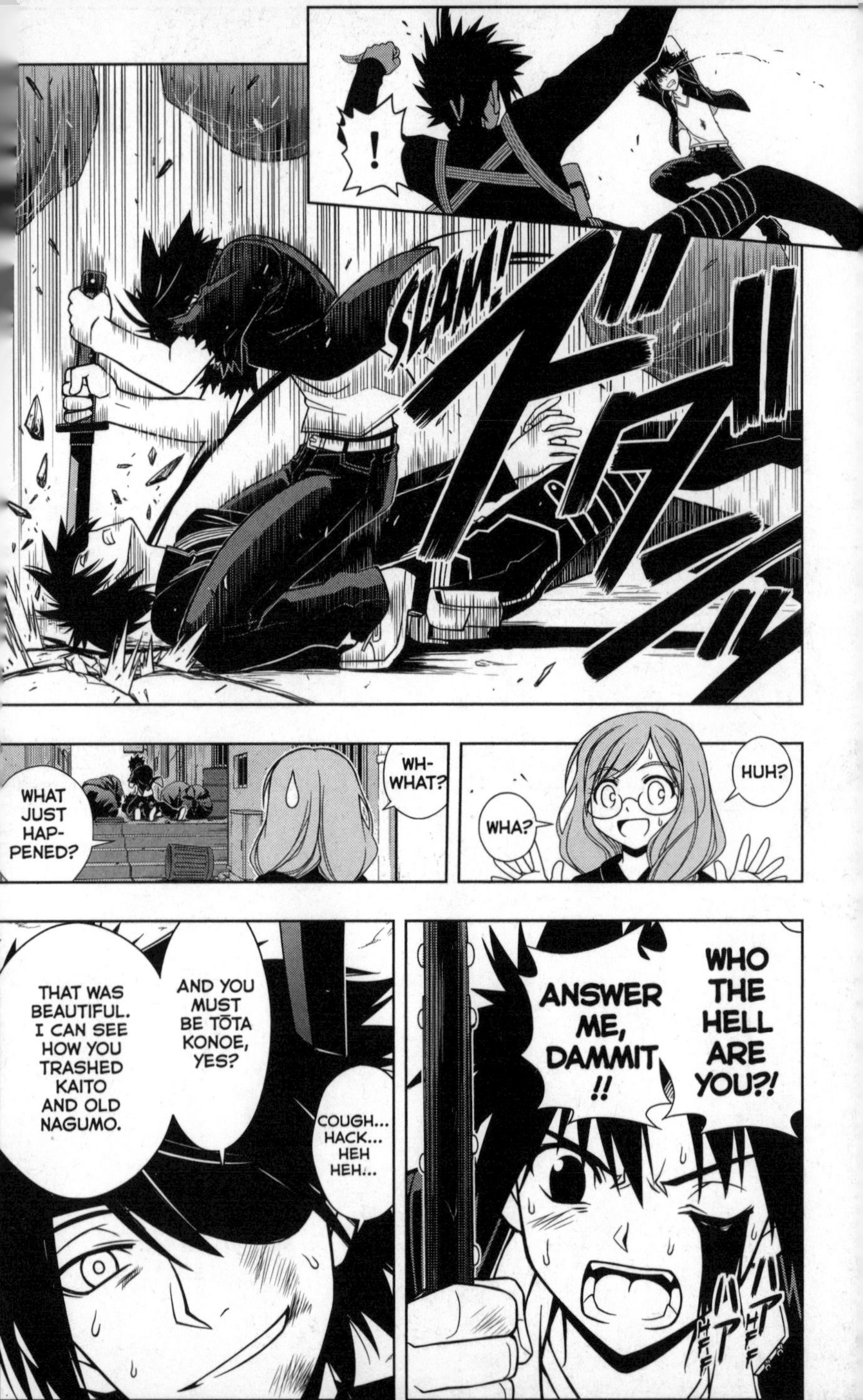
!
SLAM!
HUH?
WHA?
WH- WHAT?
WHAT JUST HAPPENED?
WHO THE HELL ARE YOU?!
ANSWER ME, DAMMIT!!
HFF HFF
HFF HFF
COUGH... HACK... HEH HEH...
AND YOU MUST BE TŌTA KONOE, YES?
THAT WAS BEAUTIFUL. I CAN SEE HOW YOU TRASHED KAITO AND OLD NAGUMO.

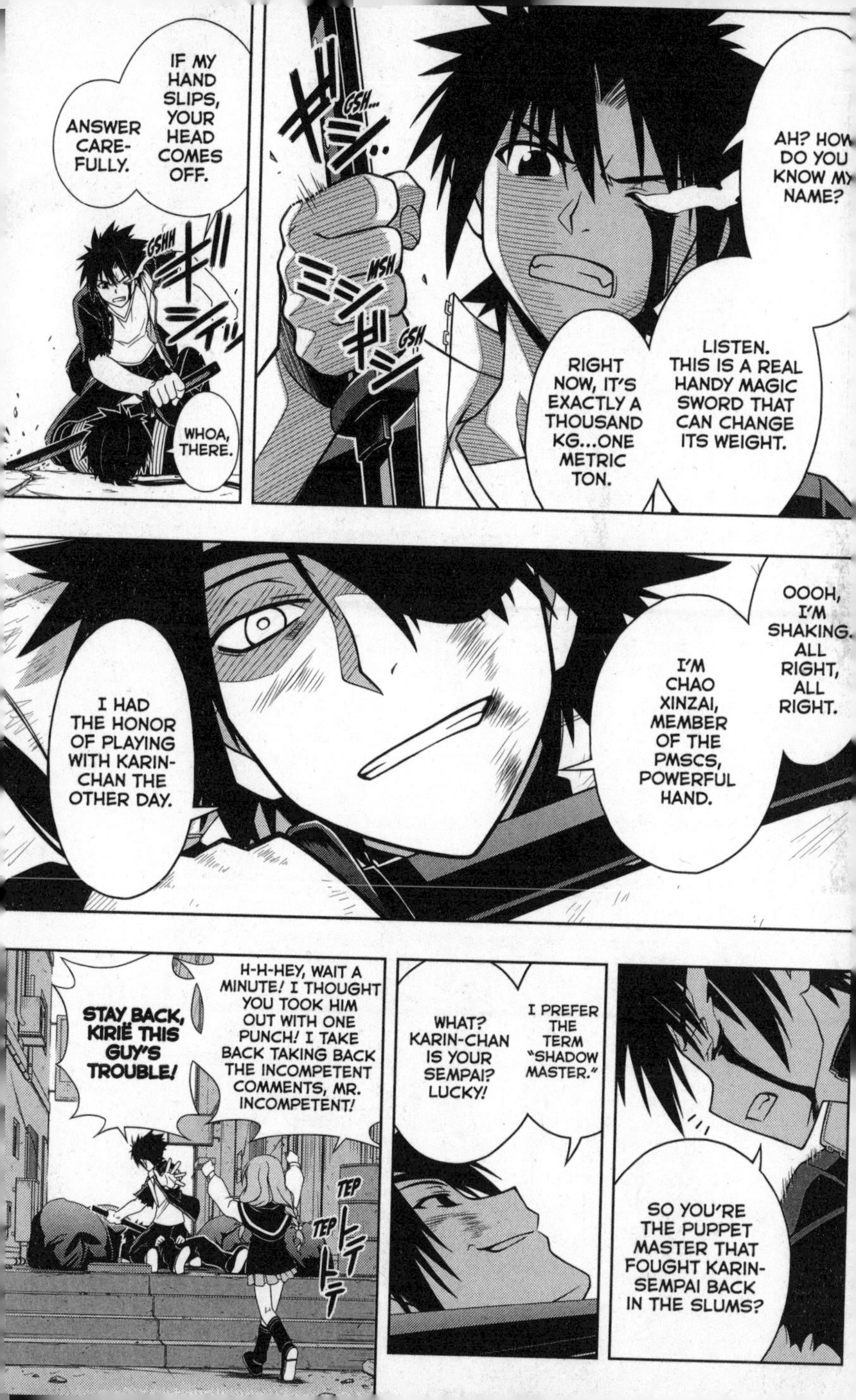
AH? HOW DO YOU KNOW MY NAME?
GSH...
MSH
GSH
LISTEN. THIS IS A REAL HANDY MAGIC SWORD THAT CAN CHANGE ITS WEIGHT.
RIGHT NOW, IT'S EXACTLY A THOUSAND KG...ONE METRIC TON.
IF MY HAND SLIPS, YOUR HEAD COMES OFF.
ANSWER CAREFULLY.
GSHH
WHOA, THERE.
OOOH, I'M SHAKING. ALL RIGHT, ALL RIGHT.
I'M CHAO XINZAI, MEMBER OF THE PMSCS, POWERFUL HAND.
I HAD THE HONOR OF PLAYING WITH KARIN-CHAN THE OTHER DAY.
SO YOU'RE THE PUPPET MASTER THAT FOUGHT KARIN-SEMPAI BACK IN THE SLUMS?
I PREFER THE TERM "SHADOW MASTER."
WHAT? KARIN-CHAN IS YOUR SEMPAI? LUCKY!
H-H-HEY, WAIT A MINUTE! I THOUGHT YOU TOOK HIM OUT WITH ONE PUNCH! I TAKE BACK TAKING BACK THE INCOMPETENT COMMENTS, MR. INCOMPETENT!
STAY BACK, KIRIE! THIS GUY'S TROUBLE!
TEP
TEP

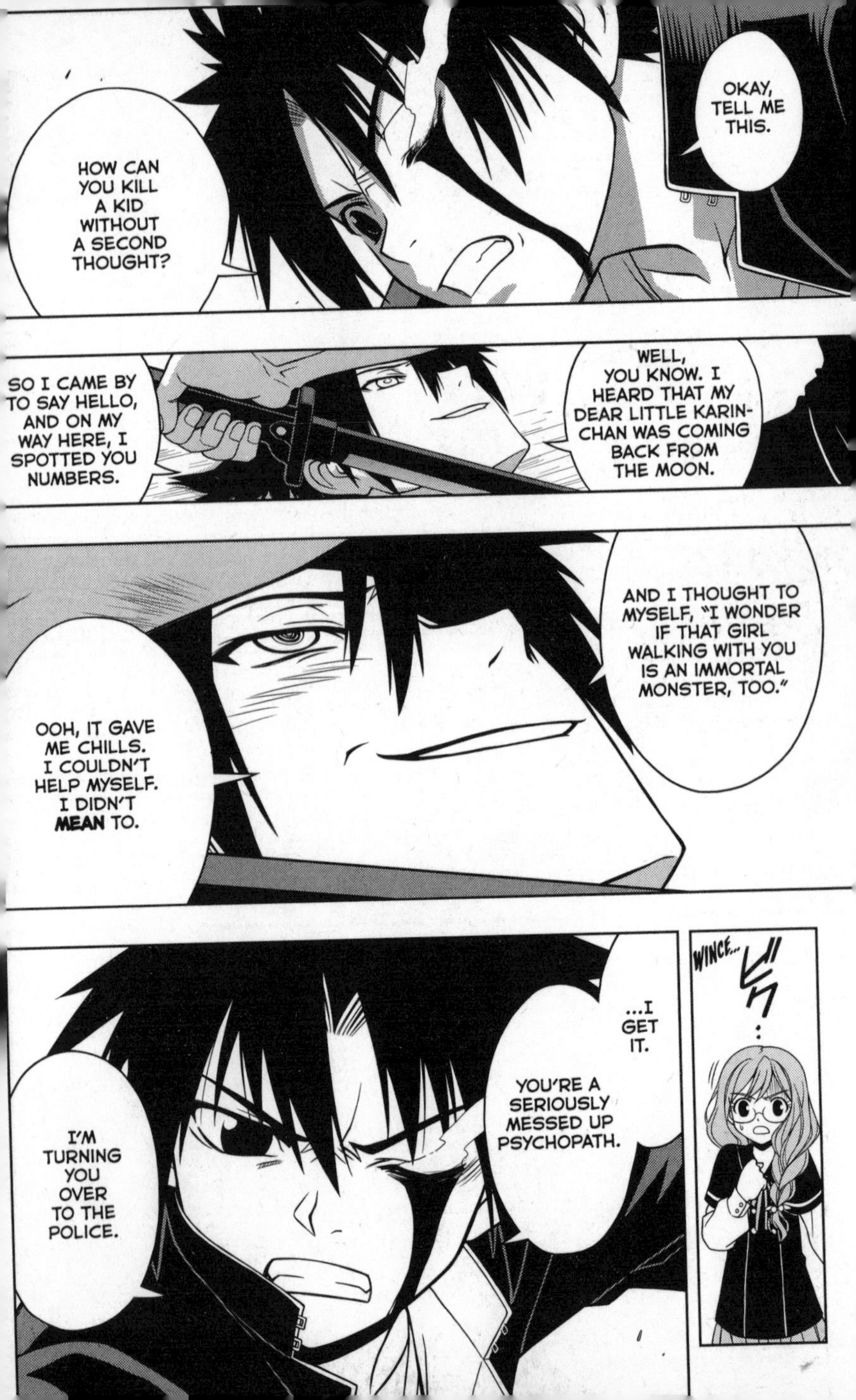
OKAY, TELL ME THIS.
HOW CAN YOU KILL A KID WITHOUT A SECOND THOUGHT?
WELL, YOU KNOW. I HEARD THAT MY DEAR LITTLE KARIN-CHAN WAS COMING BACK FROM THE MOON.
SO I CAME BY TO SAY HELLO, AND ON MY WAY HERE, I SPOTTED YOU NUMBERS.
AND I THOUGHT TO MYSELF, "I WONDER IF THAT GIRL WALKING WITH YOU IS AN IMMORTAL MONSTER, TOO."
OOH, IT GAVE ME CHILLS. I COULDN'T HELP MYSELF. I DIDN'T **MEAN** TO.
WINCE...
ビク
...I GET IT.
YOU'RE A SERIOUSLY MESSED UP PSYCHOPATH.
I'M TURNING YOU OVER TO THE POLICE.

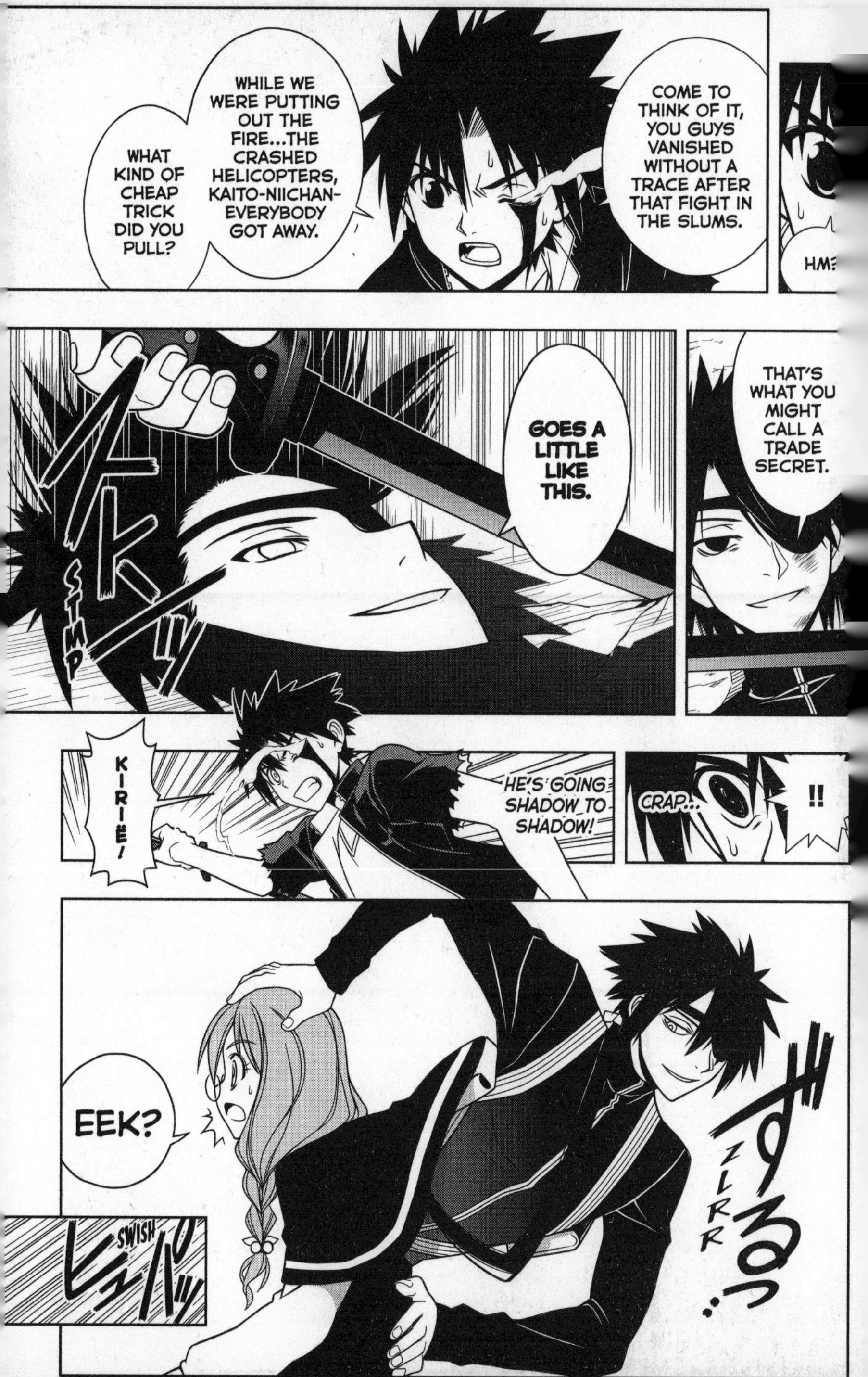
HM?
COME TO THINK OF IT, YOU GUYS VANISHED WITHOUT A TRACE AFTER THAT FIGHT IN THE SLUMS.
WHILE WE WERE PUTTING OUT THE FIRE...THE CRASHED HELICOPTERS, KAITO-NIICHAN-EVERYBODY GOT AWAY.
WHAT KIND OF CHEAP TRICK DID YOU PULL?
THAT'S WHAT YOU MIGHT CALL A TRADE SECRET.
GOES A LITTLE LIKE THIS.
STMP
!!
CRAP...
HE'S GOING SHADOW TO SHADOW!
KIRIË!
ZLRR
EEK?
SWISH

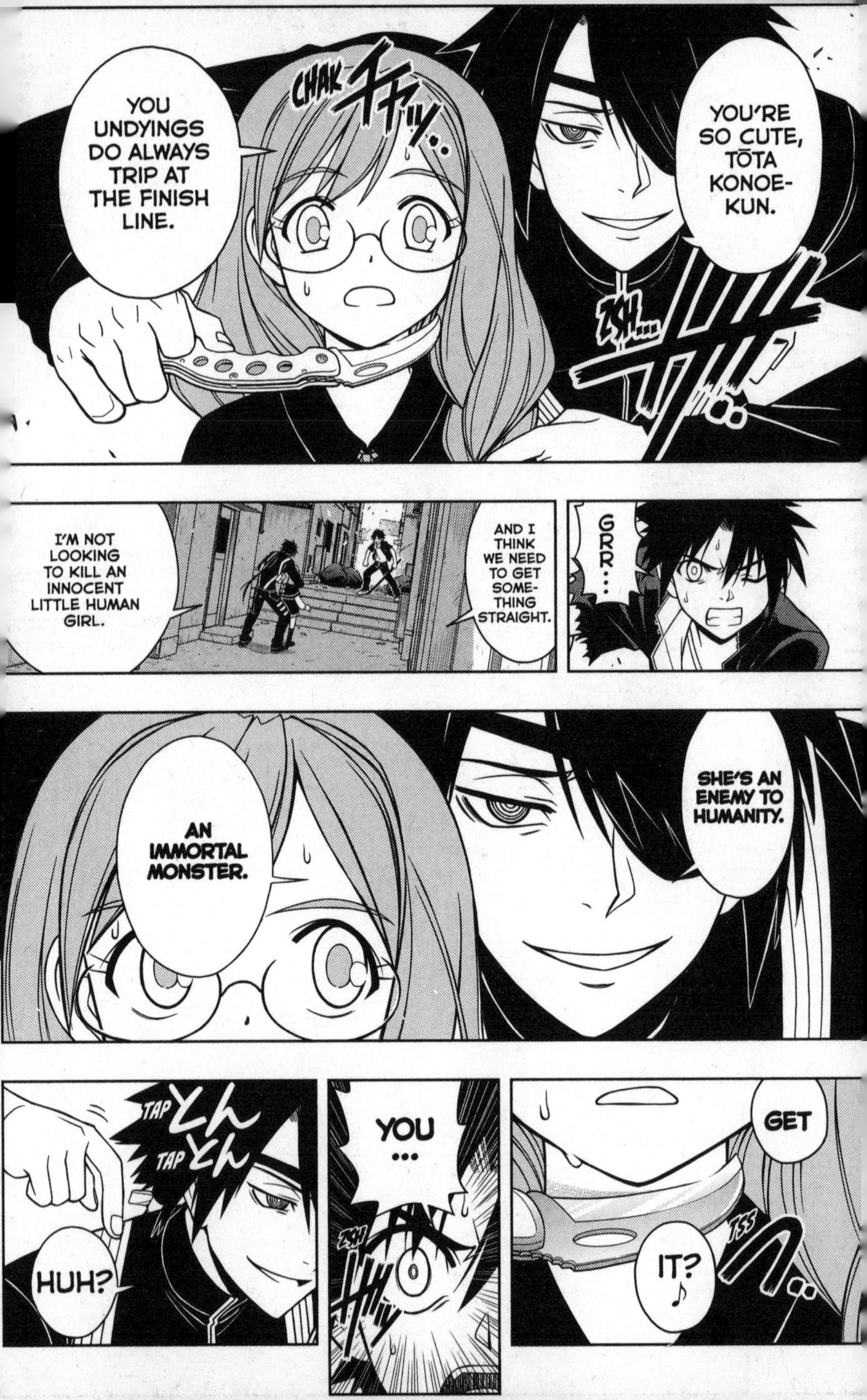
YOU'RE SO CUTE, TŌTA KONOE-KUN.
CHAK
YOU UNDYINGS DO ALWAYS TRIP AT THE FINISH LINE.
ZSH...
GRR...
AND I THINK WE NEED TO GET SOME-THING STRAIGHT.
I'M NOT LOOKING TO KILL AN INNOCENT LITTLE HUMAN GIRL.
SHE'S AN ENEMY TO HUMANITY.
AN IMMORTAL MONSTER.
GET
IT?♪
TSS
YOU...
ZSH
TAP
TAP
HUH?

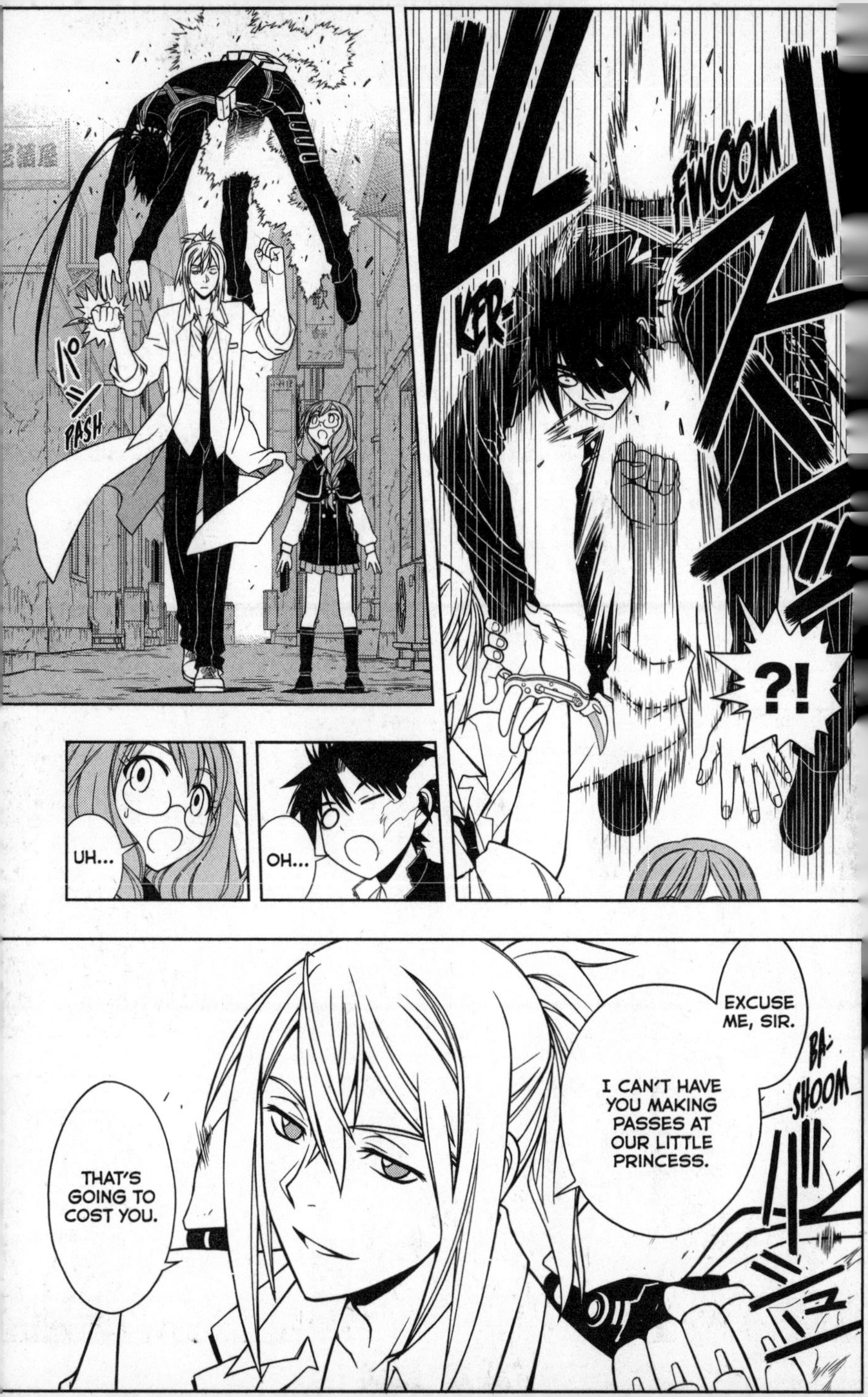
KER-
FWOOM
?!
PASH
OH...
UH...
EXCUSE ME, SIR.
I CAN'T HAVE YOU MAKING PASSES AT OUR LITTLE PRINCESS.
BA-SHOOM
THAT'S GOING TO COST YOU.

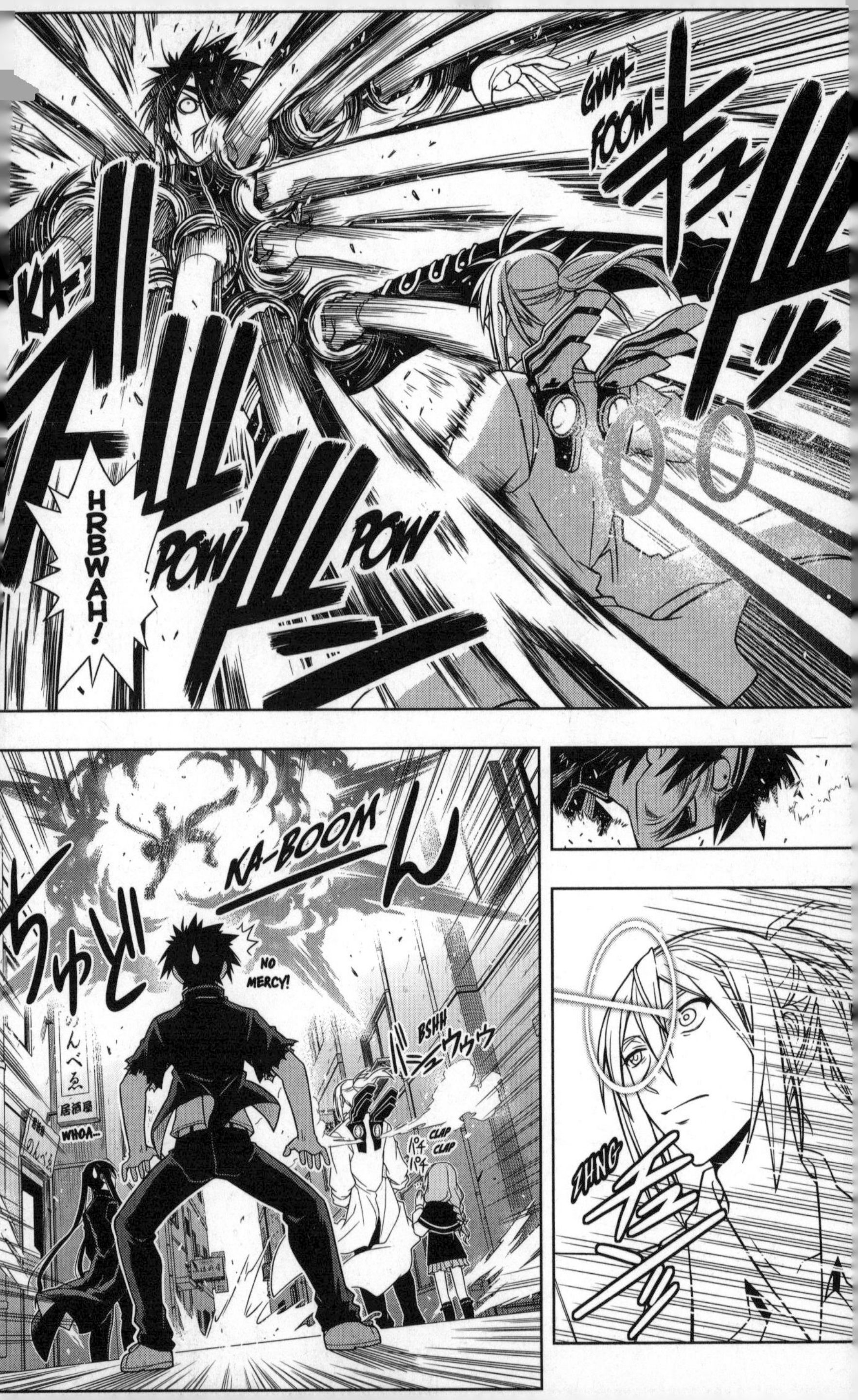
GWA-FOOM
KA-
POW
POW
HRBWAH!
ZHING
KA-BOOM
NO MERCY!
BSHH
CLAP CLAP
WHOA...

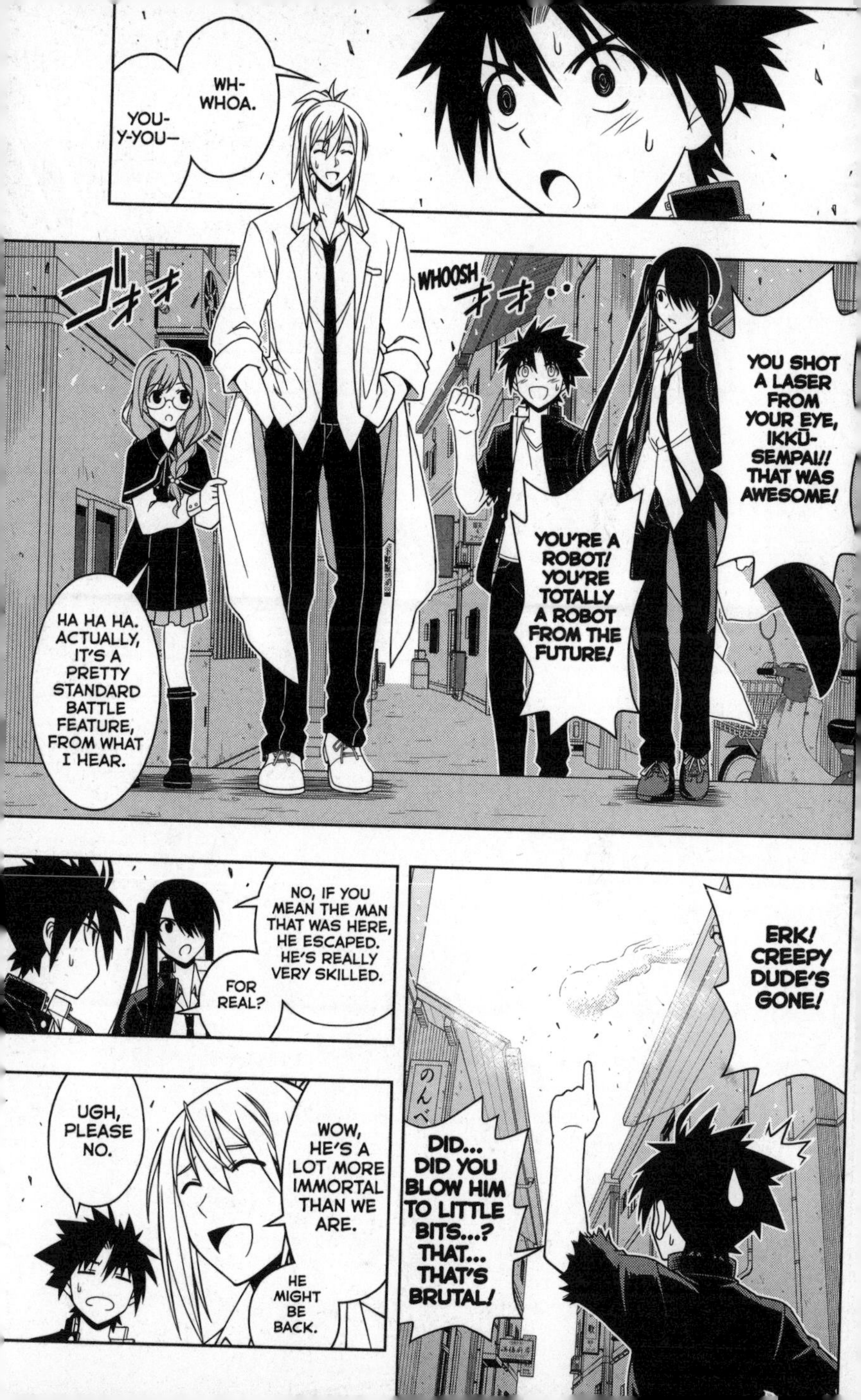

WH- WHOA.
YOU- Y-YOU—
WHOOSH
YOU SHOT A LASER FROM YOUR EYE, IKKŪ-SEMPAI!! THAT WAS AWESOME!
YOU'RE A ROBOT! YOU'RE TOTALLY A ROBOT FROM THE FUTURE!
HA HA HA. ACTUALLY, IT'S A PRETTY STANDARD BATTLE FEATURE, FROM WHAT I HEAR.
ERK! CREEPY DUDE'S GONE!
のんべ
DID... DID YOU BLOW HIM TO LITTLE BITS...? THAT... THAT'S BRUTAL!
NO, IF YOU MEAN THE MAN THAT WAS HERE, HE ESCAPED. HE'S REALLY VERY SKILLED.
FOR REAL?
WOW, HE'S A LOT MORE IMMORTAL THAN WE ARE.
HE MIGHT BE BACK.
UGH, PLEASE NO.

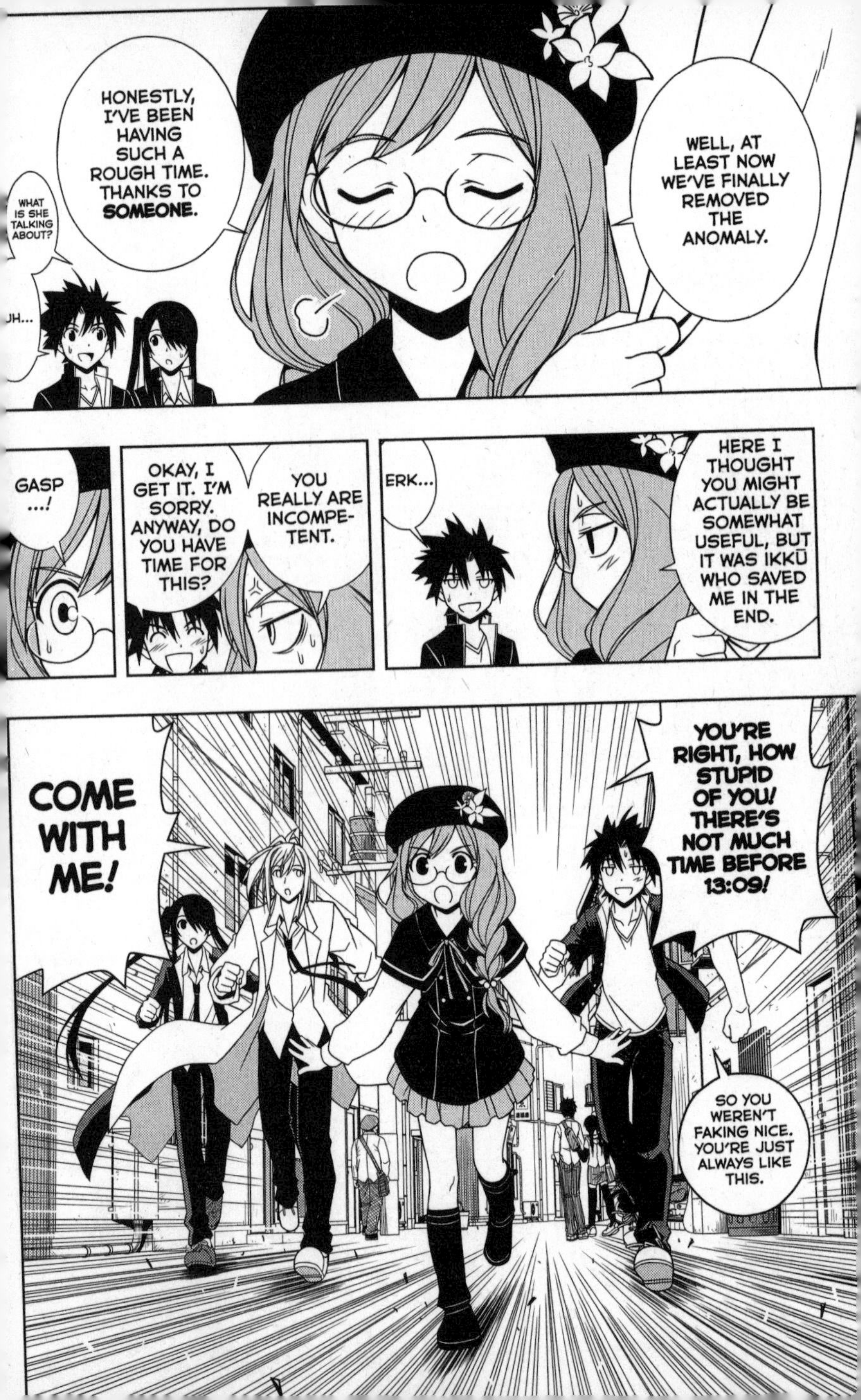

WELL, AT LEAST NOW WE'VE FINALLY REMOVED THE ANOMALY.
HONESTLY, I'VE BEEN HAVING SUCH A ROUGH TIME. THANKS TO **SOMEONE.**
WHAT IS SHE TALKING ABOUT?
HERE I THOUGHT YOU MIGHT ACTUALLY BE SOMEWHAT USEFUL, BUT IT WAS IKKŪ WHO SAVED ME IN THE END.
ERK...
YOU REALLY ARE INCOMPETENT.
OKAY, I GET IT. I'M SORRY. ANYWAY, DO YOU HAVE TIME FOR THIS?
GASP ...!
YOU'RE RIGHT, HOW STUPID OF YOU! THERE'S NOT MUCH TIME BEFORE 13:09!
COME WITH ME!
SO YOU WEREN'T FAKING NICE. YOU'RE JUST ALWAYS LIKE THIS.

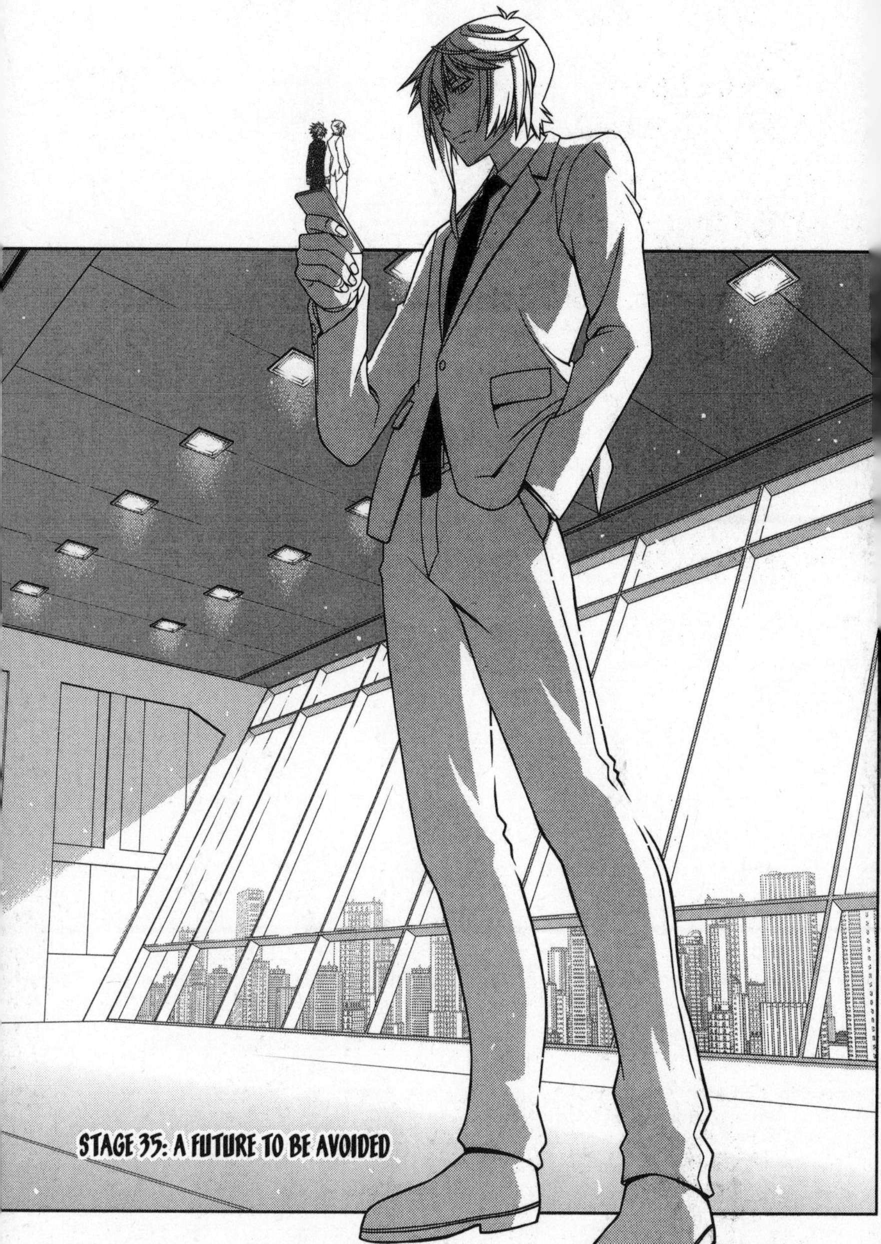
STAGE 35: A FUTURE TO BE AVOIDED

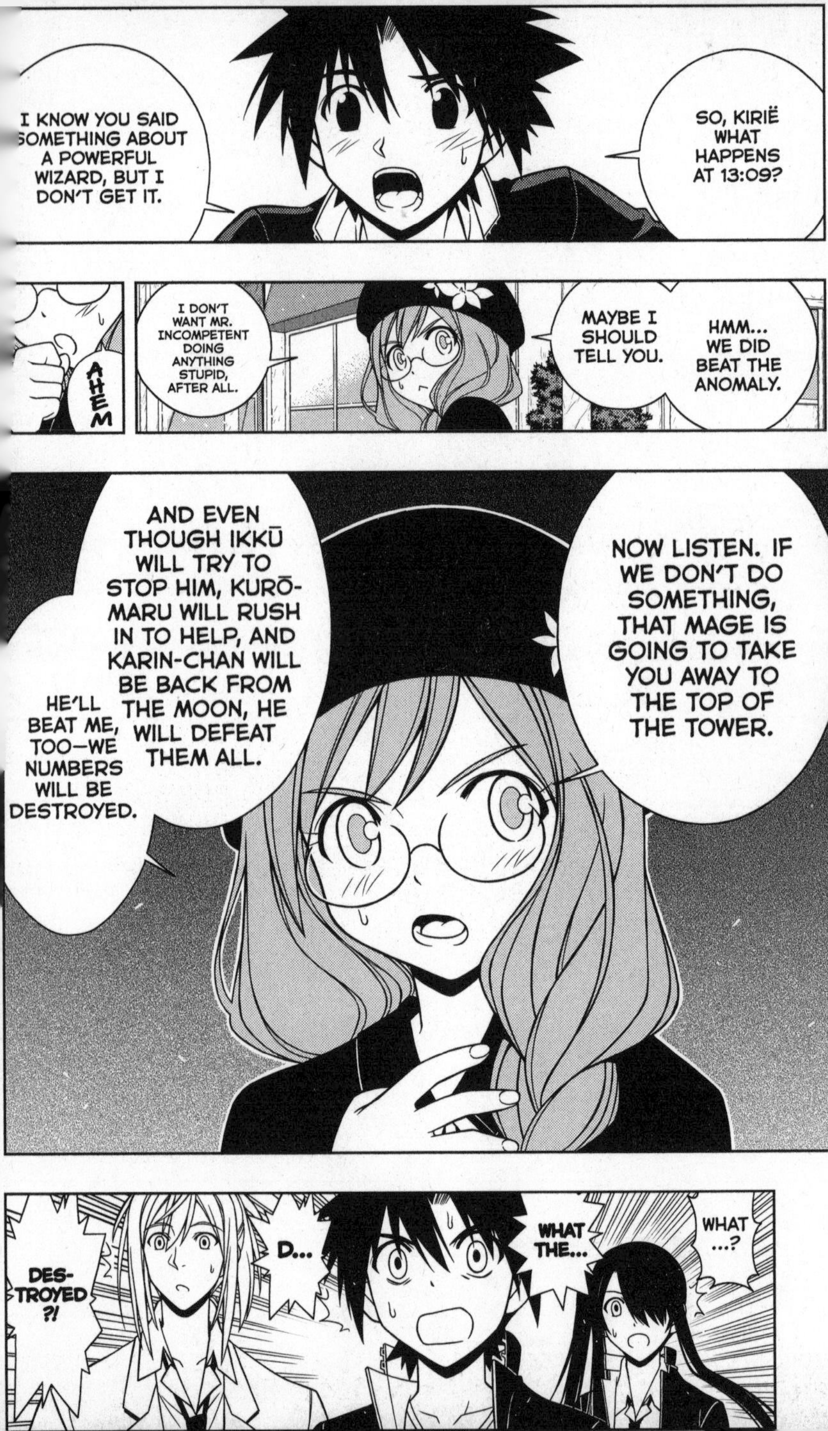
SO, KIRIË WHAT HAPPENS AT 13:09?
I KNOW YOU SAID SOMETHING ABOUT A POWERFUL WIZARD, BUT I DON'T GET IT.
HMM... WE DID BEAT THE ANOMALY.
MAYBE I SHOULD TELL YOU.
I DON'T WANT MR. INCOMPETENT DOING ANYTHING STUPID, AFTER ALL.
AHEM
NOW LISTEN. IF WE DON'T DO SOMETHING, THAT MAGE IS GOING TO TAKE YOU AWAY TO THE TOP OF THE TOWER.
AND EVEN THOUGH IKKŪ WILL TRY TO STOP HIM, KURŌMARU WILL RUSH IN TO HELP, AND KARIN-CHAN WILL BE BACK FROM THE MOON, HE WILL DEFEAT THEM ALL.
HE'LL BEAT ME, TOO—WE NUMBERS WILL BE DESTROYED.
WHAT ...?
WHAT THE...
D...
DES-TROYED?!

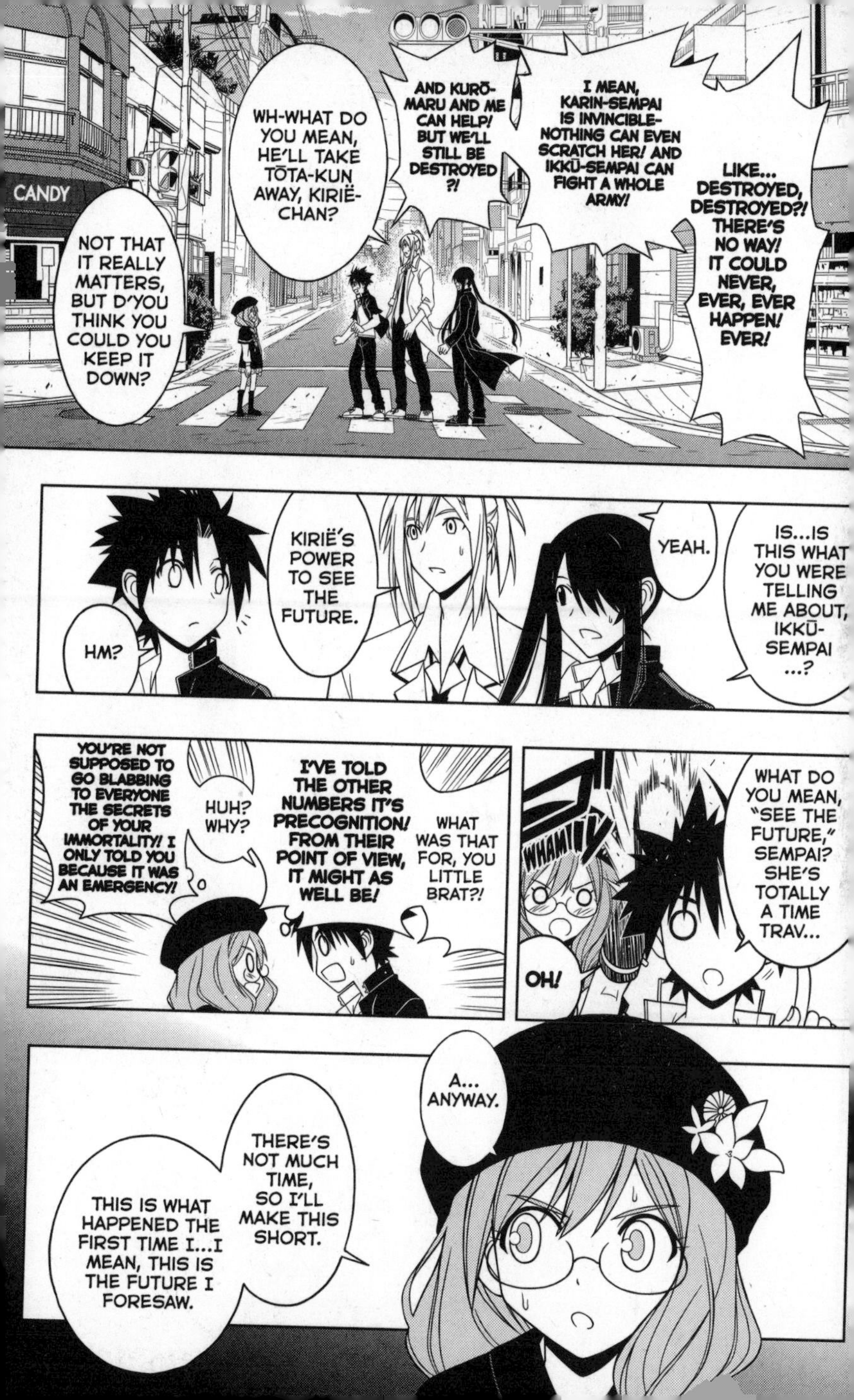
LIKE... DESTROYED, DESTROYED?! THERE'S NO WAY! IT COULD NEVER, EVER, EVER HAPPEN! EVER!
I MEAN, KARIN-SEMPAI IS INVINCIBLE- NOTHING CAN EVEN SCRATCH HER! AND IKKŪ-SEMPAI CAN FIGHT A WHOLE ARMY!
AND KURŌ-MARU AND ME CAN HELP! BUT WE'LL STILL BE DESTROYED?!
WH-WHAT DO YOU MEAN, HE'LL TAKE TŌTA-KUN AWAY, KIRIË-CHAN?
CANDY
NOT THAT IT REALLY MATTERS, BUT D'YOU THINK YOU COULD YOU KEEP IT DOWN?
IS...IS THIS WHAT YOU WERE TELLING ME ABOUT, IKKŪ-SEMPAI...?
YEAH.
KIRIË'S POWER TO SEE THE FUTURE.
HM?
WHAT DO YOU MEAN, "SEE THE FUTURE," SEMPAI? SHE'S TOTALLY A TIME TRAV...
WHAM!!
OH!
WHAT WAS THAT FOR, YOU LITTLE BRAT?!
YOU'RE NOT SUPPOSED TO GO BLABBING TO EVERYONE THE SECRETS OF YOUR IMMORTALITY! I ONLY TOLD YOU BECAUSE IT WAS AN EMERGENCY!
HUH? WHY?
I'VE TOLD THE OTHER NUMBERS IT'S PRECOGNITION! FROM THEIR POINT OF VIEW, IT MIGHT AS WELL BE!
A... ANYWAY.
THERE'S NOT MUCH TIME, SO I'LL MAKE THIS SHORT.
THIS IS WHAT HAPPENED THE FIRST TIME I...I MEAN, THIS IS THE FUTURE I FORESAW.

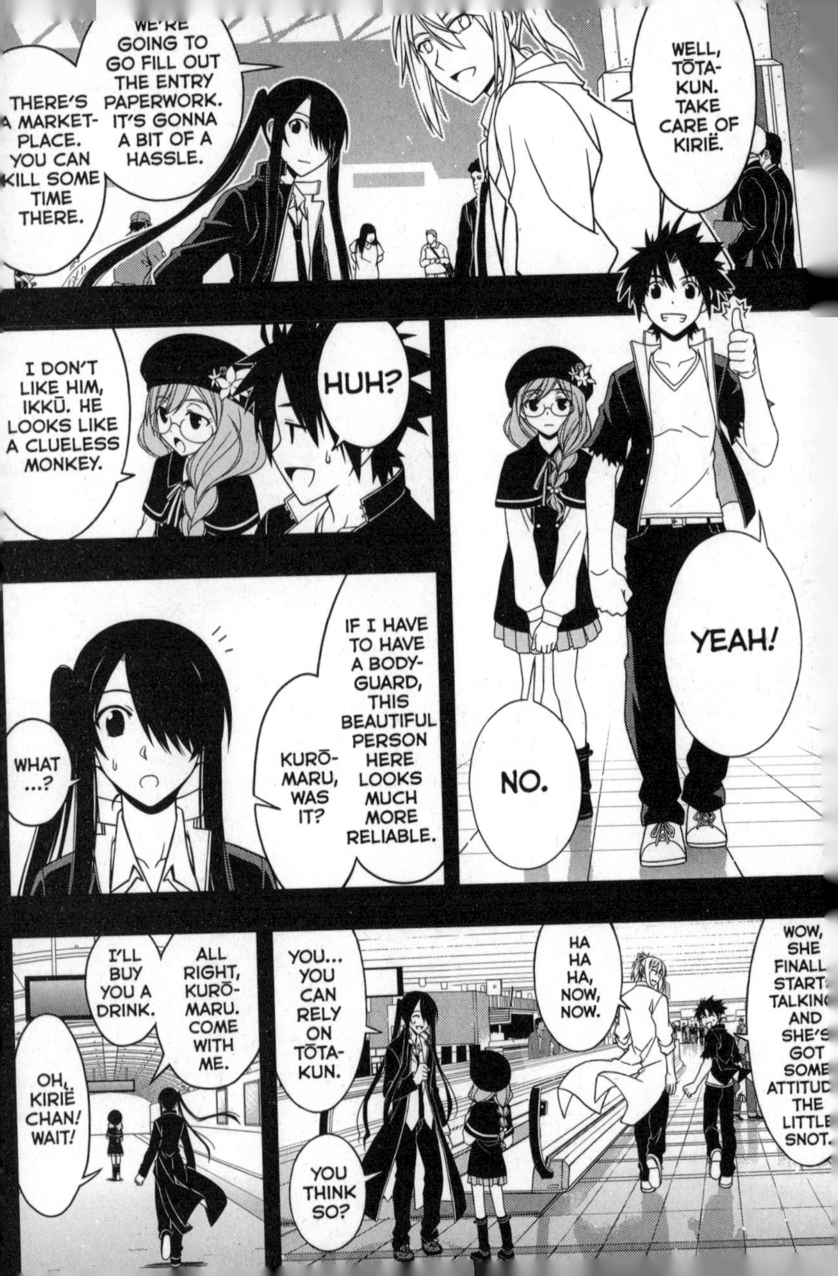
WELL, TŌTA-KUN. TAKE CARE OF KIRIË.
WE'RE GOING TO GO FILL OUT THE ENTRY PAPERWORK. IT'S GONNA A BIT OF A HASSLE.
THERE'S A MARKET-PLACE. YOU CAN KILL SOME TIME THERE.
YEAH!
NO.
HUH?
I DON'T LIKE HIM, IKKŪ. HE LOOKS LIKE A CLUELESS MONKEY.
IF I HAVE TO HAVE A BODY-GUARD, THIS BEAUTIFUL PERSON HERE LOOKS MUCH MORE RELIABLE.
KURŌ-MARU, WAS IT?
WHAT ...?
WOW, SHE FINALL STARTS TALKING AND SHE'S GOT SOME ATTITUD THE LITTLE SNOT.
HA HA HA, NOW, NOW.
YOU... YOU CAN RELY ON TŌTA-KUN.
YOU THINK SO?
ALL RIGHT, KURŌ-MARU. COME WITH ME.
I'LL BUY YOU A DRINK.
OH, KIRIË-CHAN! WAIT!

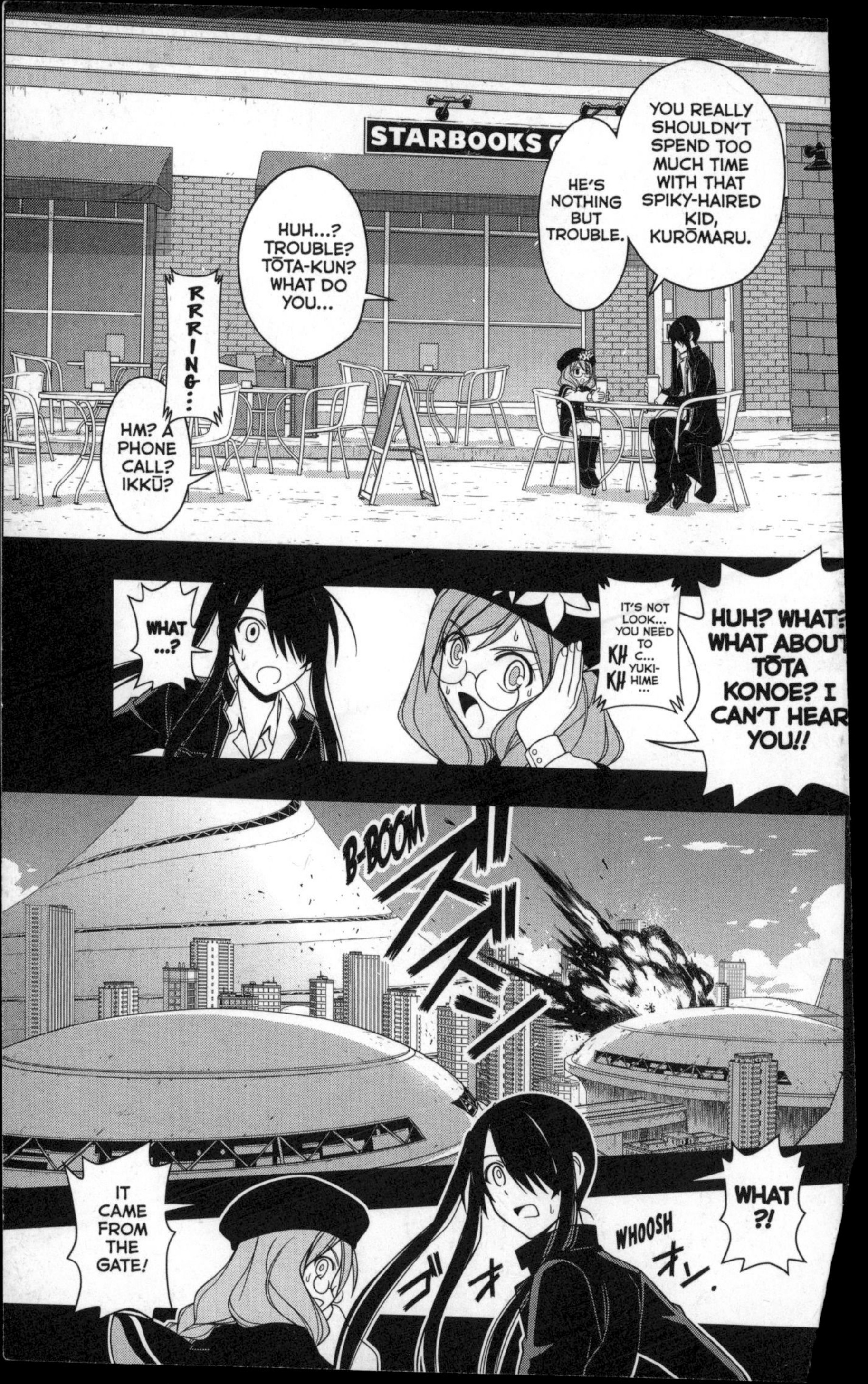
YOU REALLY SHOULDN'T SPEND TOO MUCH TIME WITH THAT SPIKY-HAIRED KID, KURŌMARU.
HE'S NOTHING BUT TROUBLE.
STARBOOKS
HUH...? TROUBLE? TŌTA-KUN? WHAT DO YOU...
RRRING...
HM? A PHONE CALL? IKKŪ?
HUH? WHAT? WHAT ABOUT TŌTA KONOE? I CAN'T HEAR YOU!!
IT'S NOT LOOK... YOU NEED TO C... YUKI-HIME...
KH KH
WHAT ...?
B-BOOM
WHAT ?!
WHOOSH
ゴオン
IT CAME FROM THE GATE!

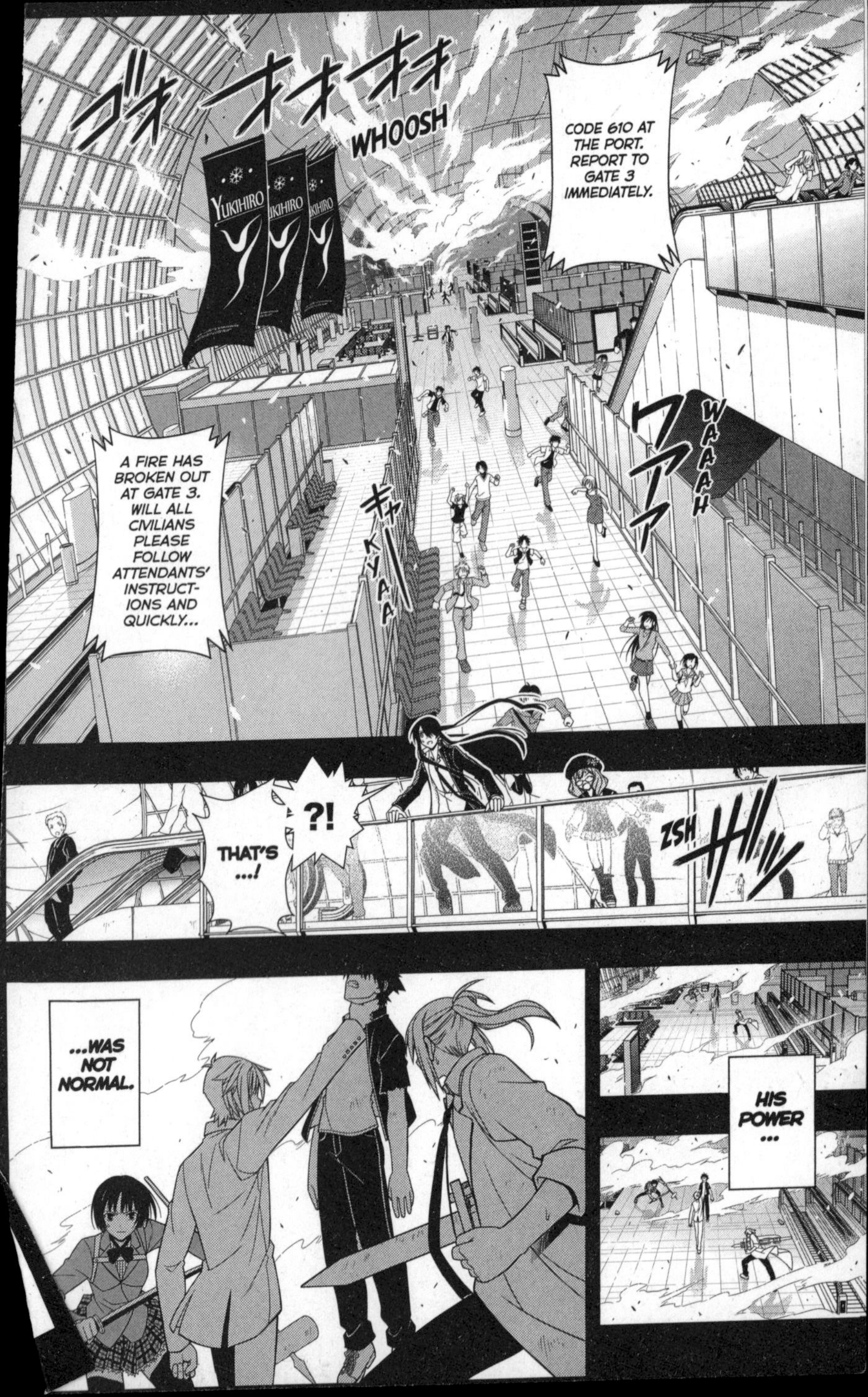
WHOOSH
CODE 610 AT THE PORT. REPORT TO GATE 3 IMMEDIATELY.
WAAAH
A FIRE HAS BROKEN OUT AT GATE 3. WILL ALL CIVILIANS PLEASE FOLLOW ATTENDANTS' INSTRUCTIONS AND QUICKLY...
KYAAA
ZSH
?!
THAT'S ...!
HIS POWER ...
...WAS NOT NORMAL.

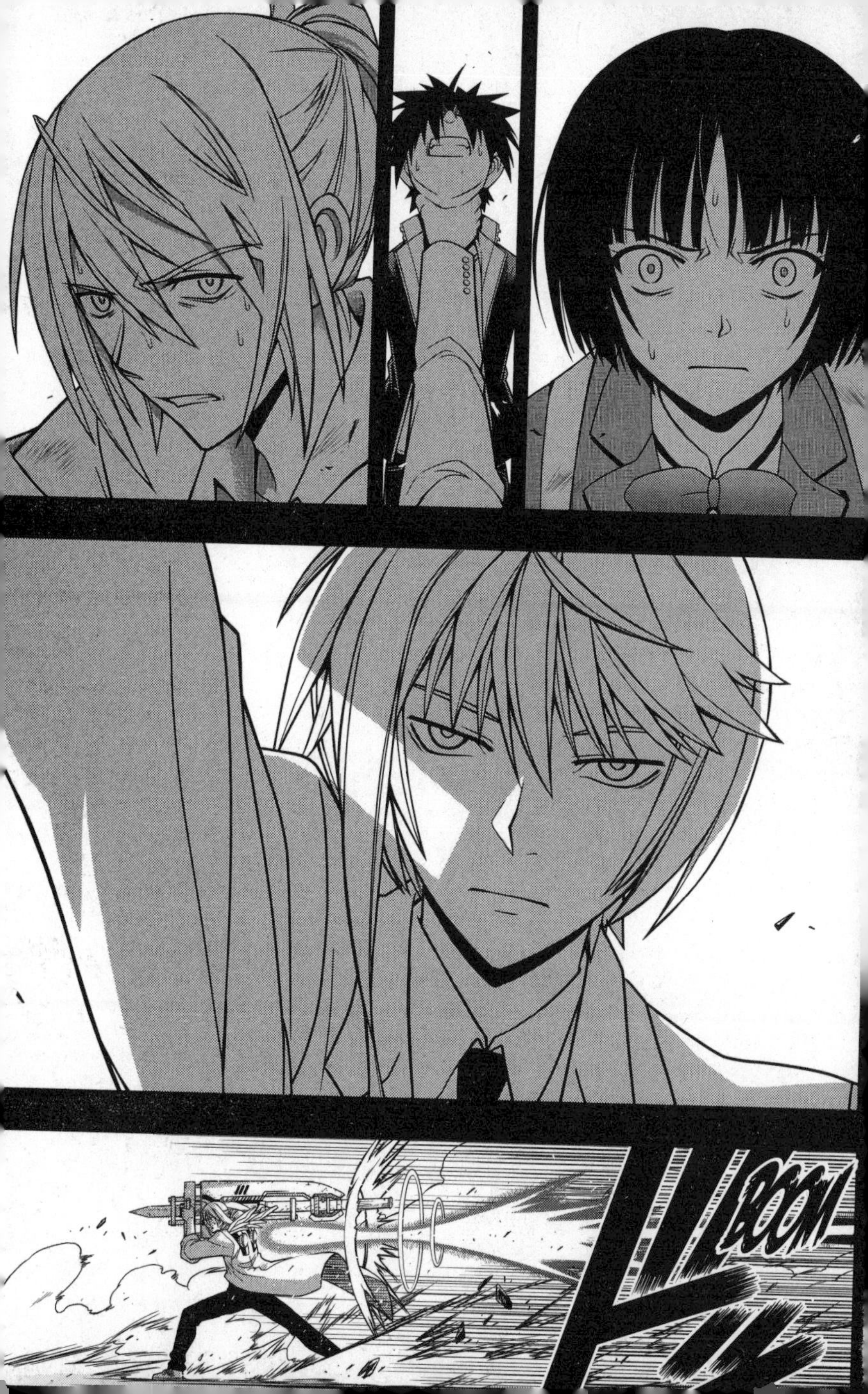
BOOM

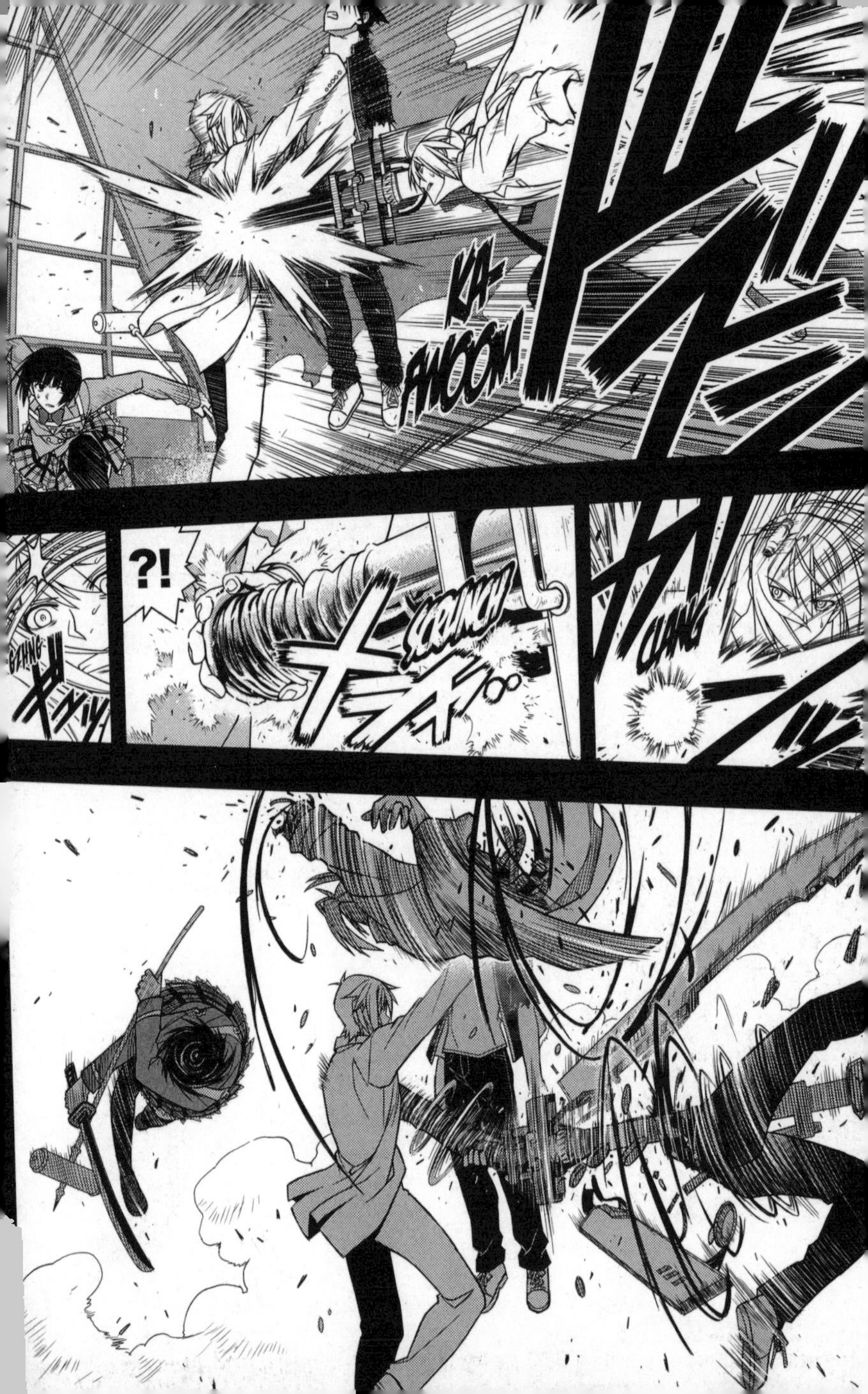
KA-FWOOM
CLANG
SCRUNCH
?!
GZHNG

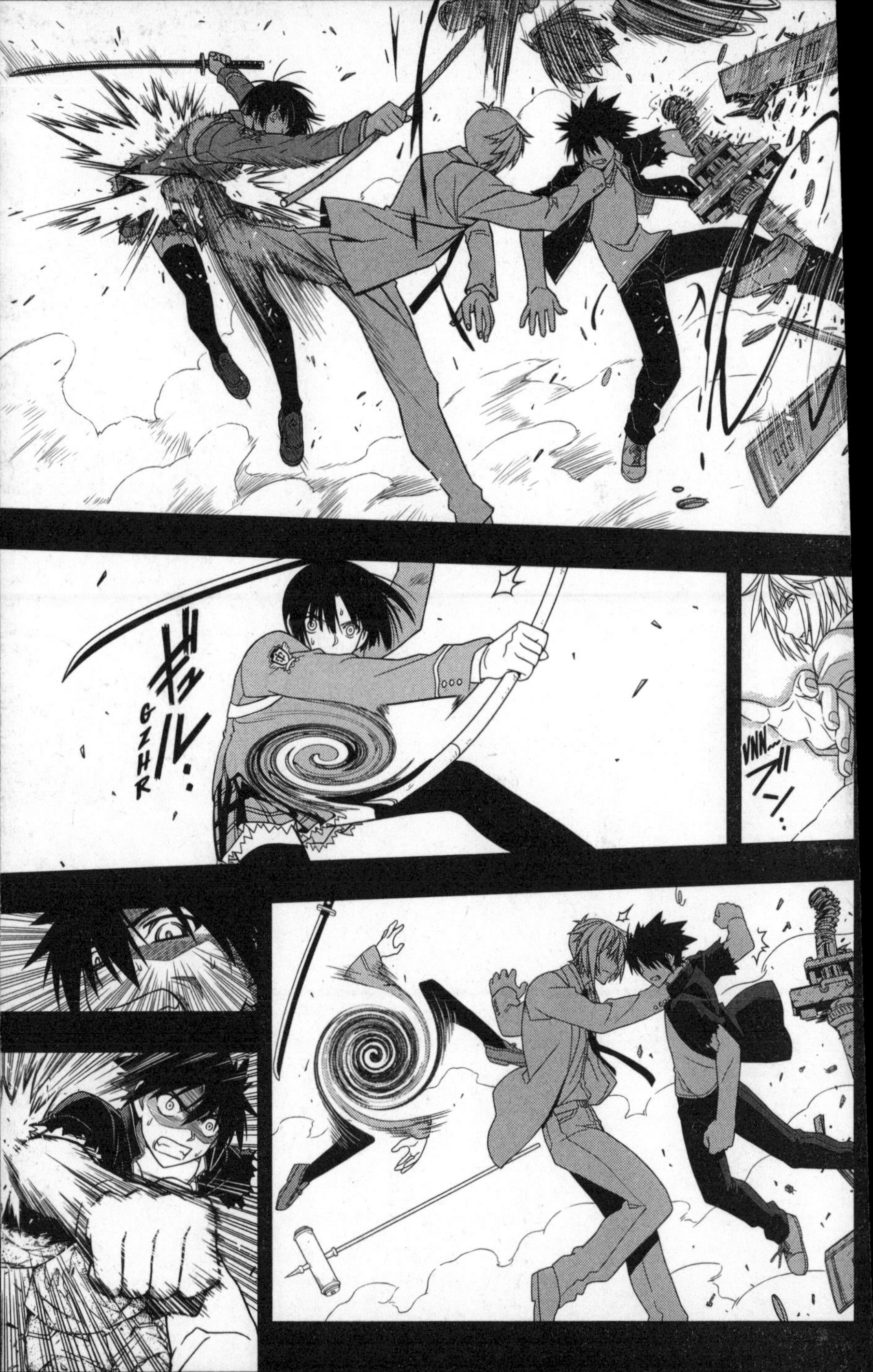
VNN...
GZHR

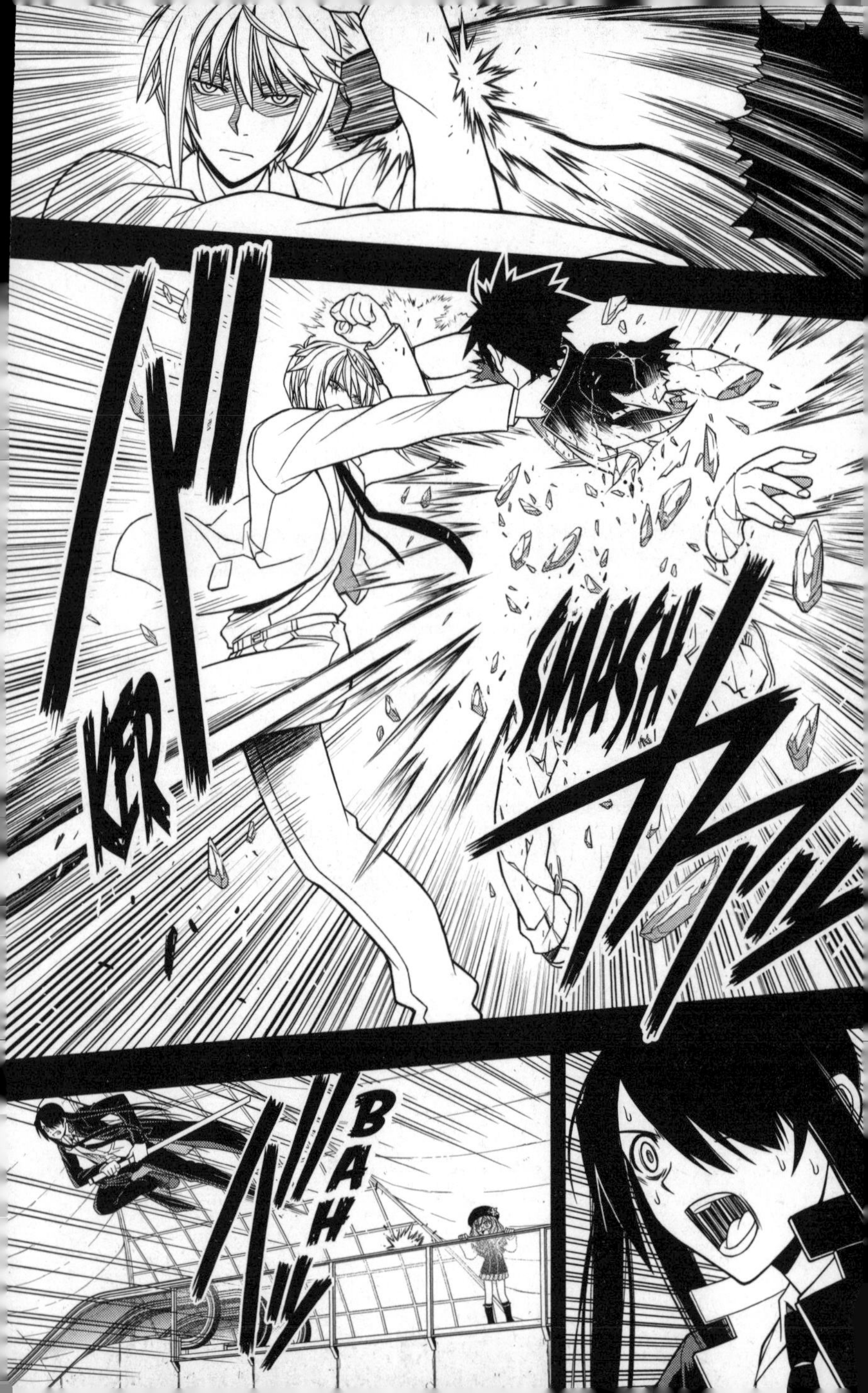

KER
SMASH
BAH

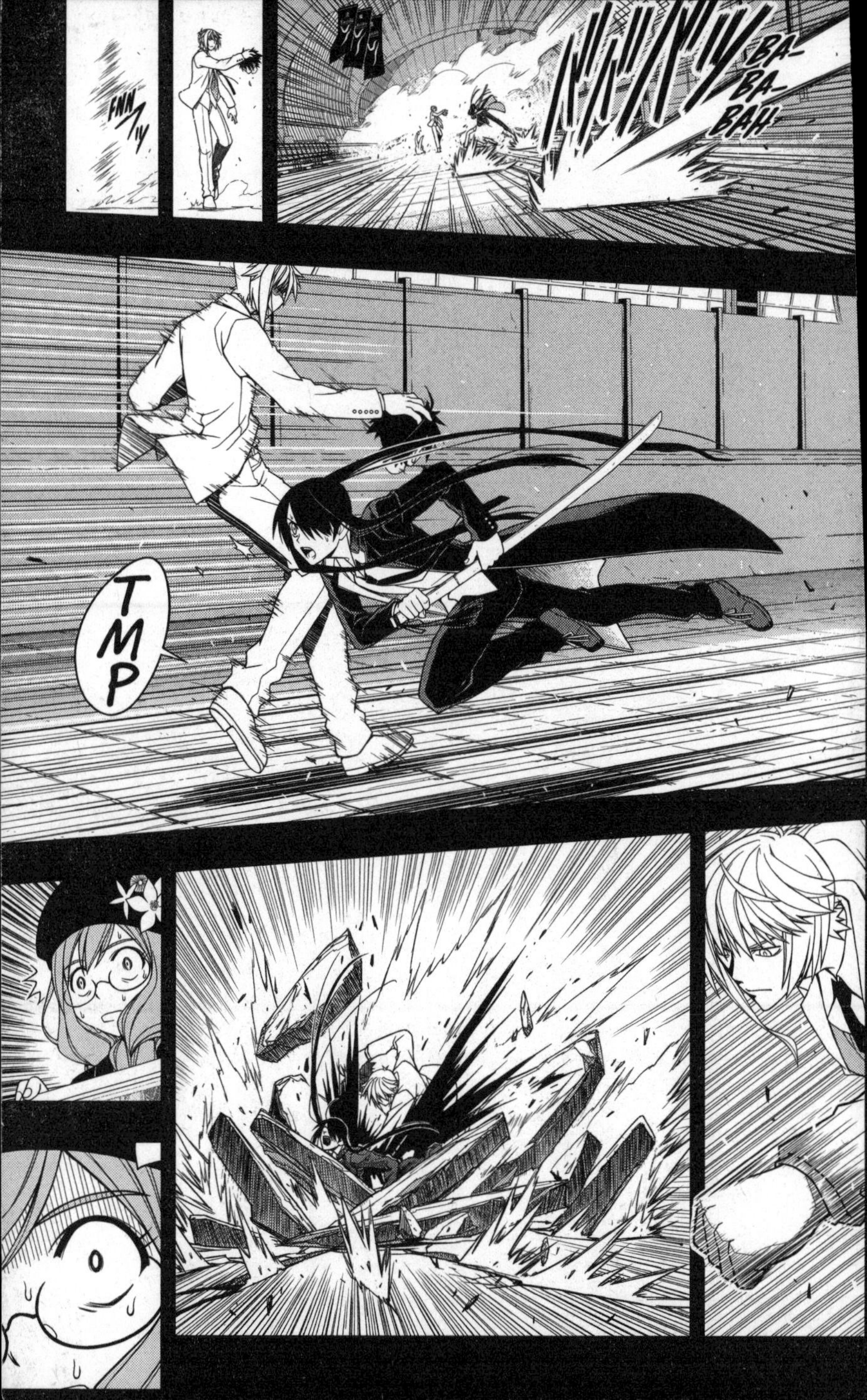
BA-BA-BAH
FNN
TMP

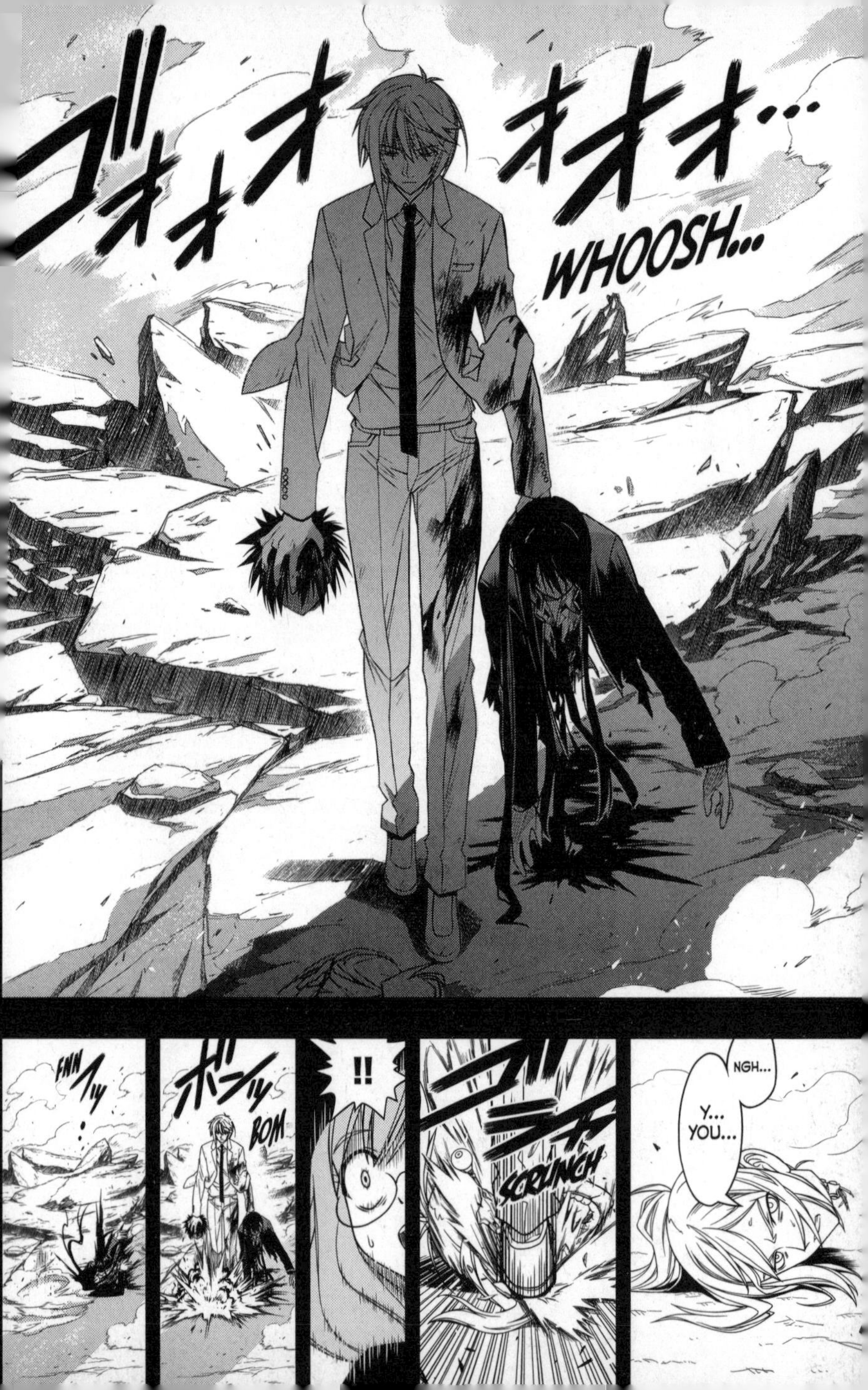
WHOOSH...
NGH...
Y... YOU...
SCRUNCH
!!
BOM
FNN

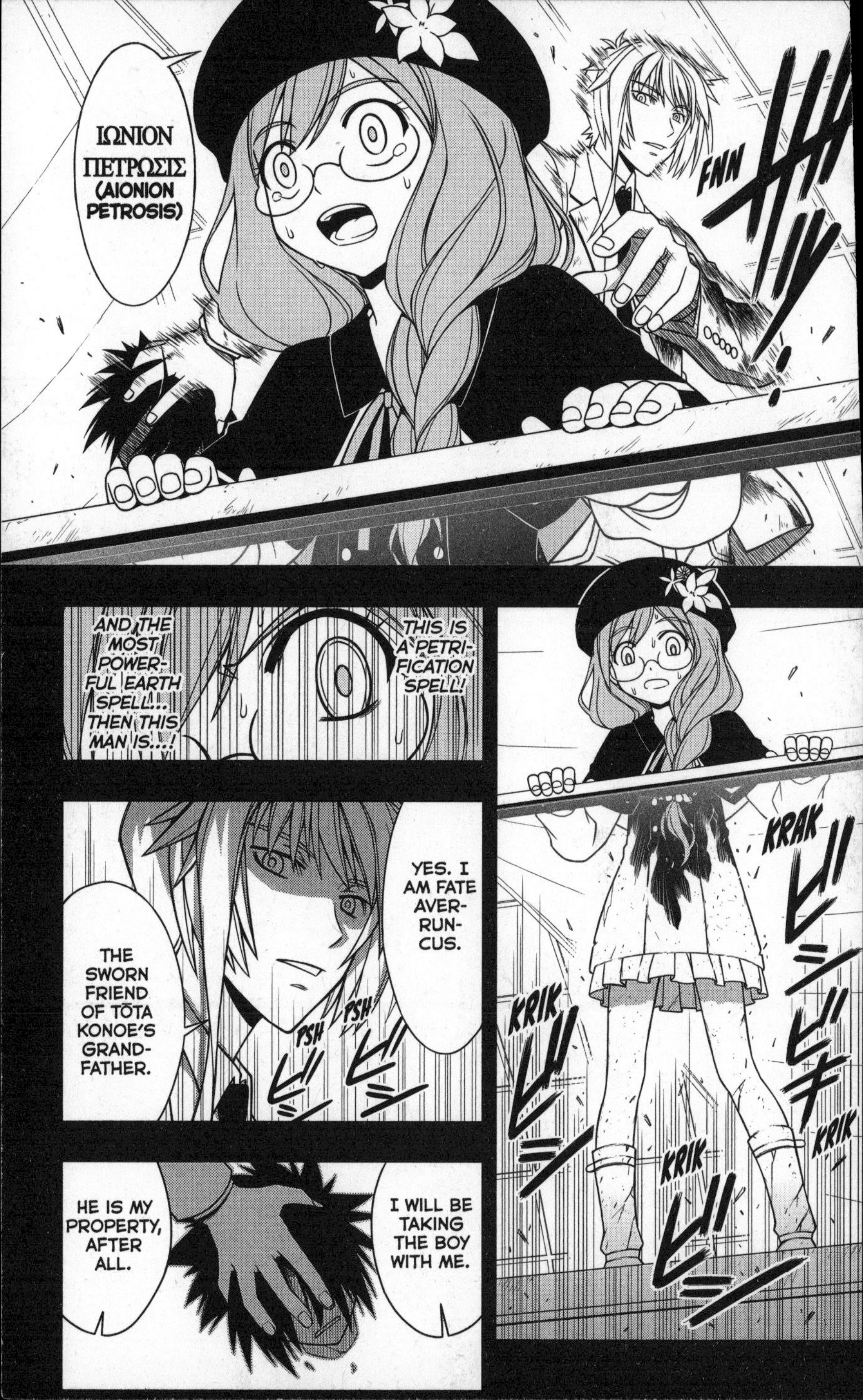
ΙΩΝΙΟΝ ΠΕΤΡΩΣΙΣ (AIONION PETROSIS)
FNN
KRAK
KRIK
KRIK
KRIK
THIS IS A PETRIFICATION SPELL!
AND THE MOST POWERFUL EARTH SPELL... THEN THIS MAN IS...!
YES. I AM FATE AVERRUNCUS.
THE SWORN FRIEND OF TŌTA KONOE'S GRANDFATHER.
PSH
PSH
I WILL BE TAKING THE BOY WITH ME.
HE IS MY PROPERTY, AFTER ALL.

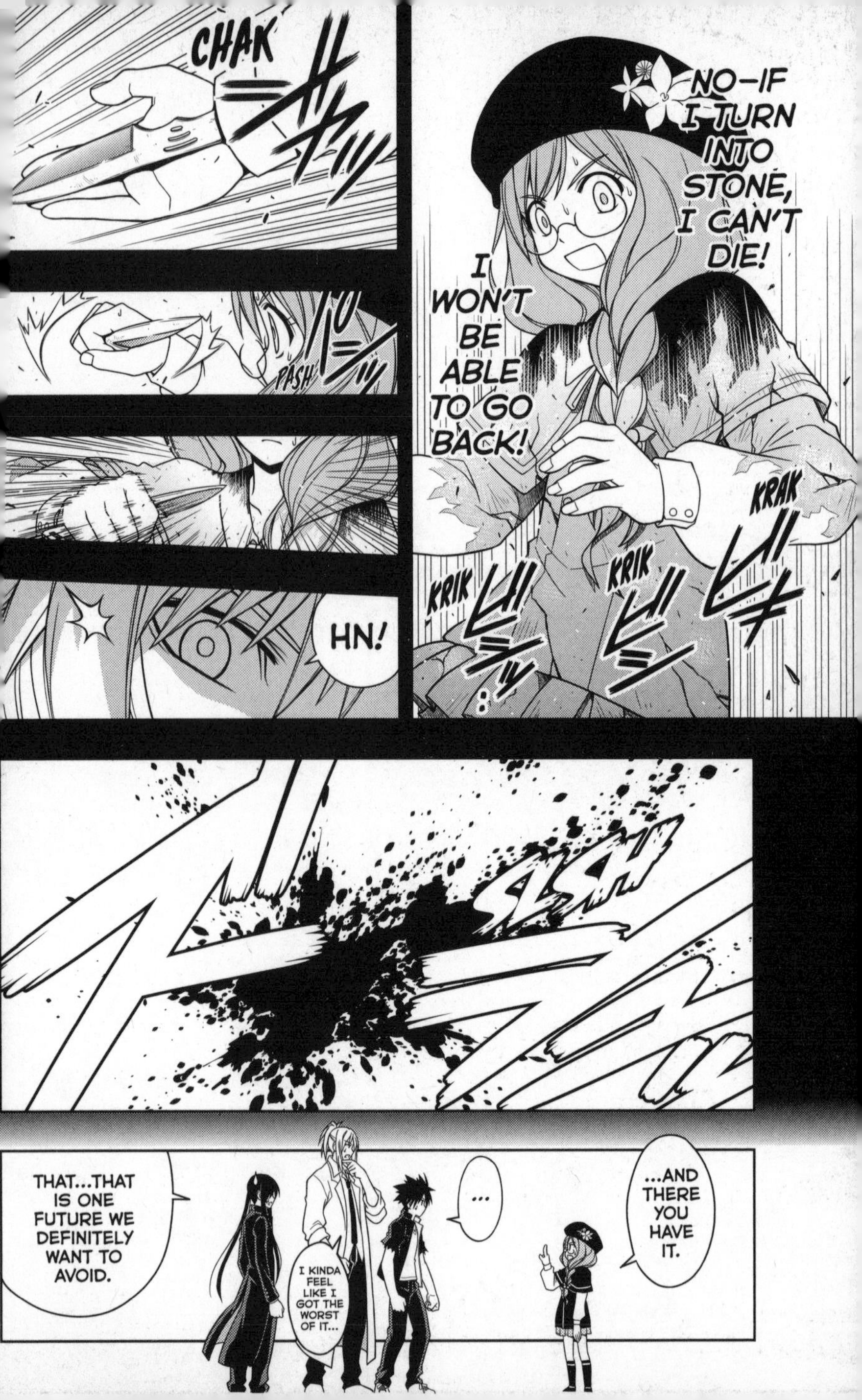
NO—IF I TURN INTO STONE, I CAN'T DIE!
I WON'T BE ABLE TO GO BACK!
KRAK
KRIK
KRIK
CHAK
PASH
HN!
...AND THERE YOU HAVE IT.
...
I KINDA FEEL LIKE I GOT THE WORST OF IT...
THAT...THAT IS ONE FUTURE WE DEFINITELY WANT TO AVOID.

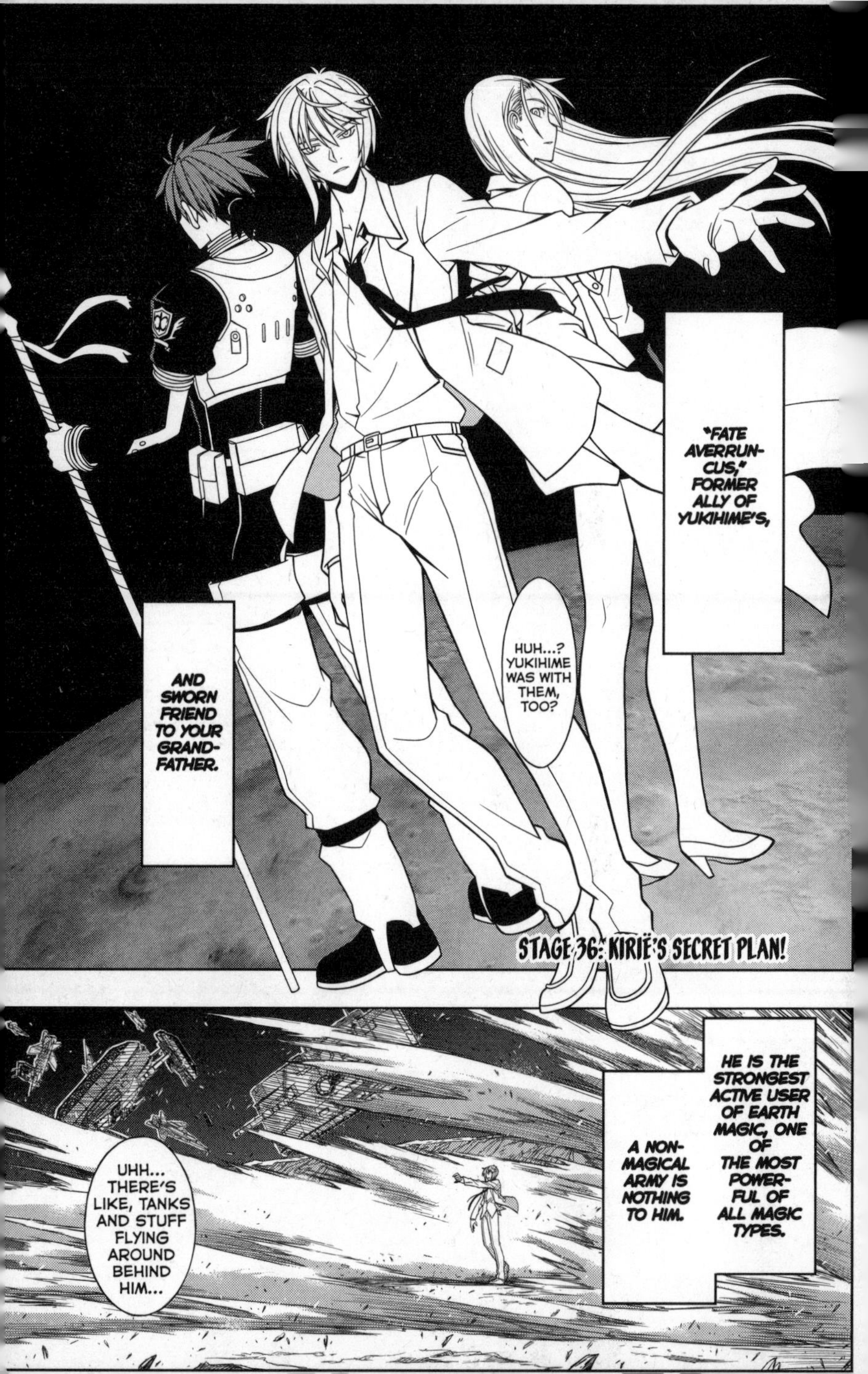
"FATE AVERRUNCUS," FORMER ALLY OF YUKIHIME'S,
HUH...? YUKIHIME WAS WITH THEM, TOO?
AND SWORN FRIEND TO YOUR GRANDFATHER.
STAGE 36: KIRIË'S SECRET PLAN!
HE IS THE STRONGEST ACTIVE USER OF EARTH MAGIC, ONE OF THE MOST POWERFUL OF ALL MAGIC TYPES.
A NON-MAGICAL ARMY IS NOTHING TO HIM.
UHH... THERE'S LIKE, TANKS AND STUFF FLYING AROUND BEHIND HIM...

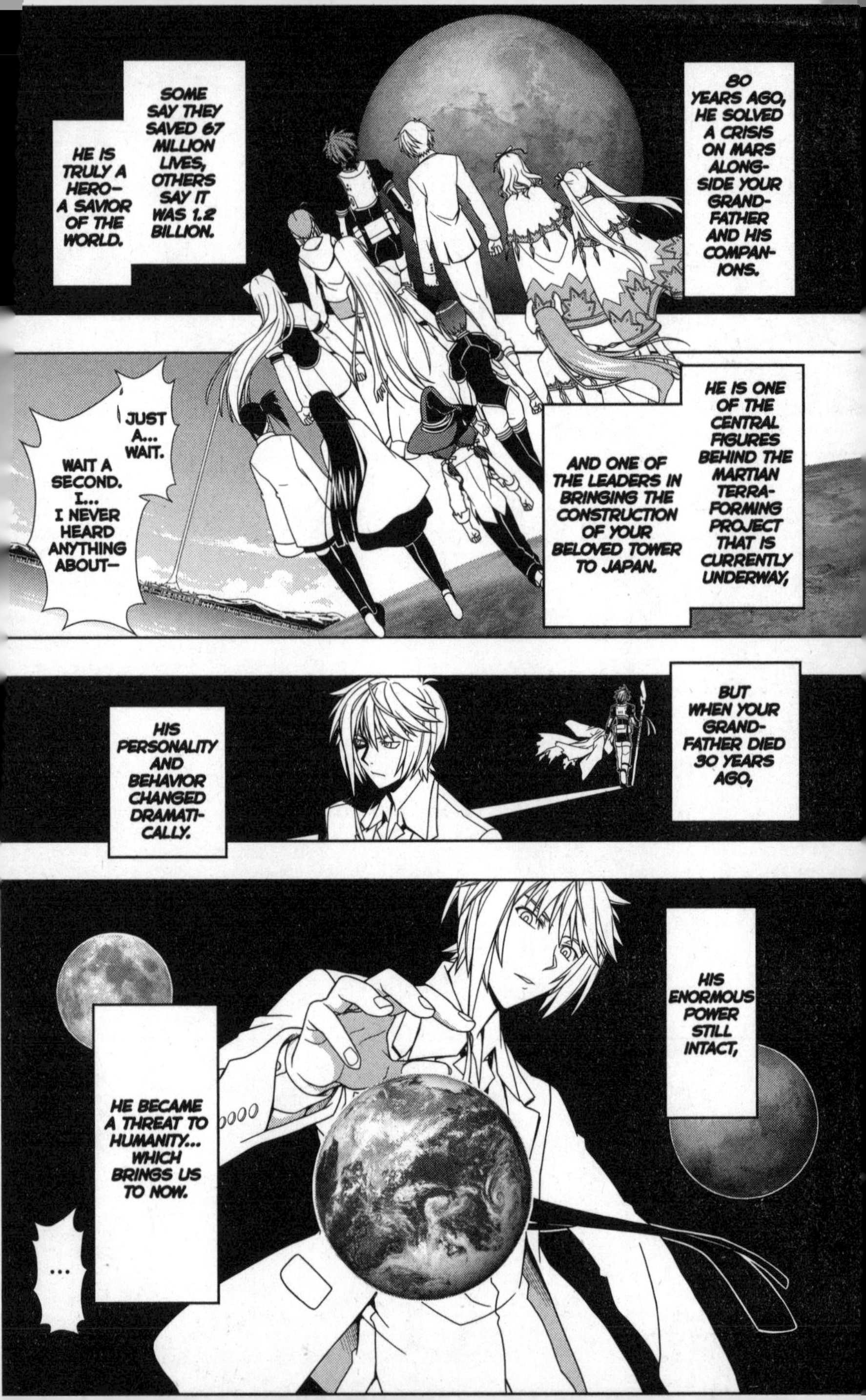
80 YEARS AGO, HE SOLVED A CRISIS ON MARS ALONGSIDE YOUR GRANDFATHER AND HIS COMPANIONS.
SOME SAY THEY SAVED 67 MILLION LIVES, OTHERS SAY IT WAS 1.2 BILLION.
HE IS TRULY A HERO—A SAVIOR OF THE WORLD.
HE IS ONE OF THE CENTRAL FIGURES BEHIND THE MARTIAN TERRAFORMING PROJECT THAT IS CURRENTLY UNDERWAY,
AND ONE OF THE LEADERS IN BRINGING THE CONSTRUCTION OF YOUR BELOVED TOWER TO JAPAN.
JUST A... WAIT.
WAIT A SECOND. I... I NEVER HEARD ANYTHING ABOUT—
BUT WHEN YOUR GRANDFATHER DIED 30 YEARS AGO,
HIS PERSONALITY AND BEHAVIOR CHANGED DRAMATICALLY.
HIS ENORMOUS POWER STILL INTACT,
HE BECAME A THREAT TO HUMANITY... WHICH BRINGS US TO NOW.
...

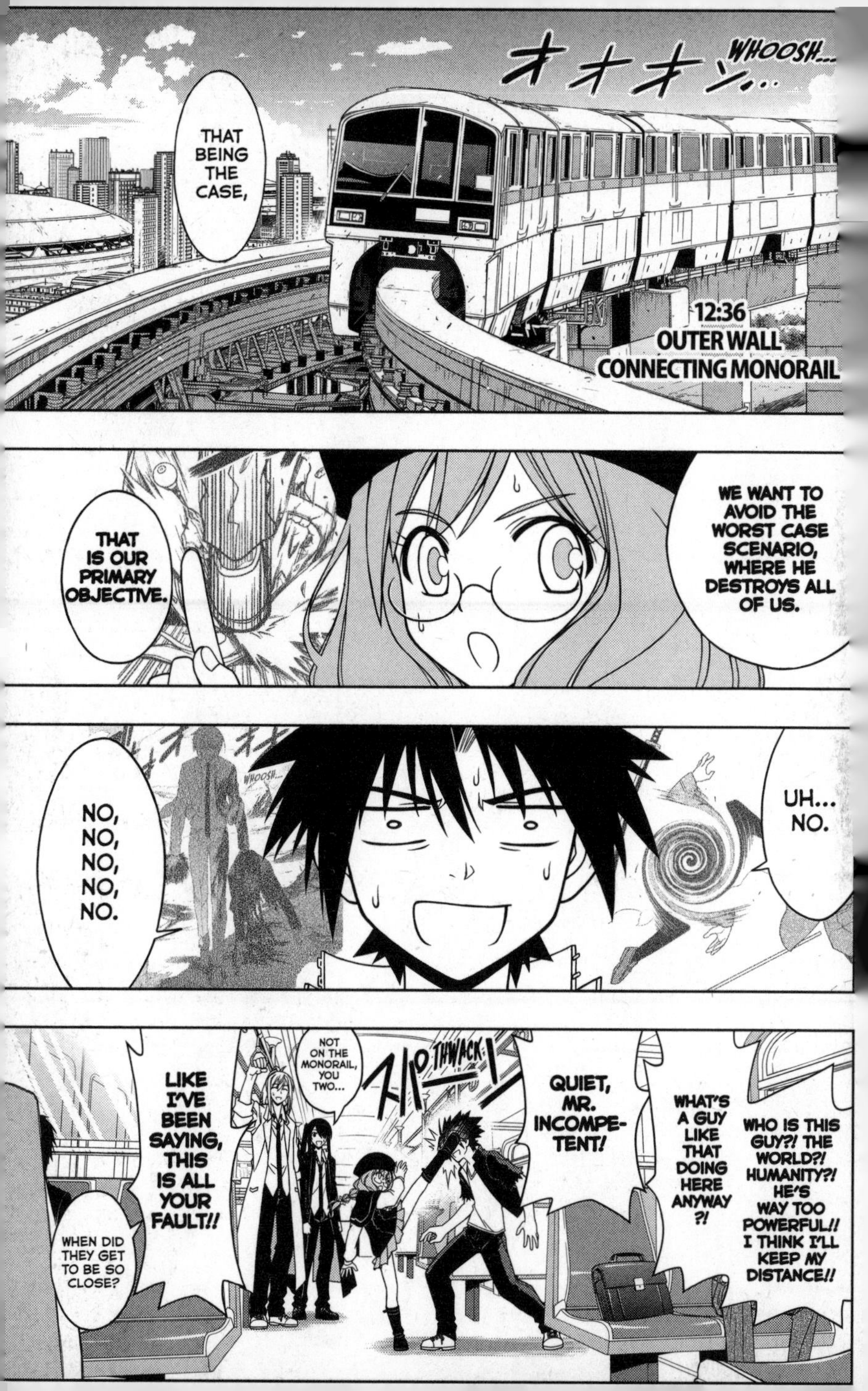

オオオン…
WHOOSH...
12:36
OUTER WALL
CONNECTING MONORAIL
THAT BEING THE CASE,
WE WANT TO AVOID THE WORST CASE SCENARIO, WHERE HE DESTROYS ALL OF US.
THAT IS OUR PRIMARY OBJECTIVE.
UH... NO.
WHOOSH...
NO, NO, NO, NO, NO.
WHO IS THIS GUY?! THE WORLD?! HUMANITY?! HE'S WAY TOO POWERFUL!! I THINK I'LL KEEP MY DISTANCE!!
WHAT'S A GUY LIKE THAT DOING HERE ANYWAY?!
QUIET, MR. INCOMPETENT!
THWACK
NOT ON THE MONORAIL, YOU TWO...
LIKE I'VE BEEN SAYING, THIS IS ALL YOUR FAULT!!
WHEN DID THEY GET TO BE SO CLOSE?

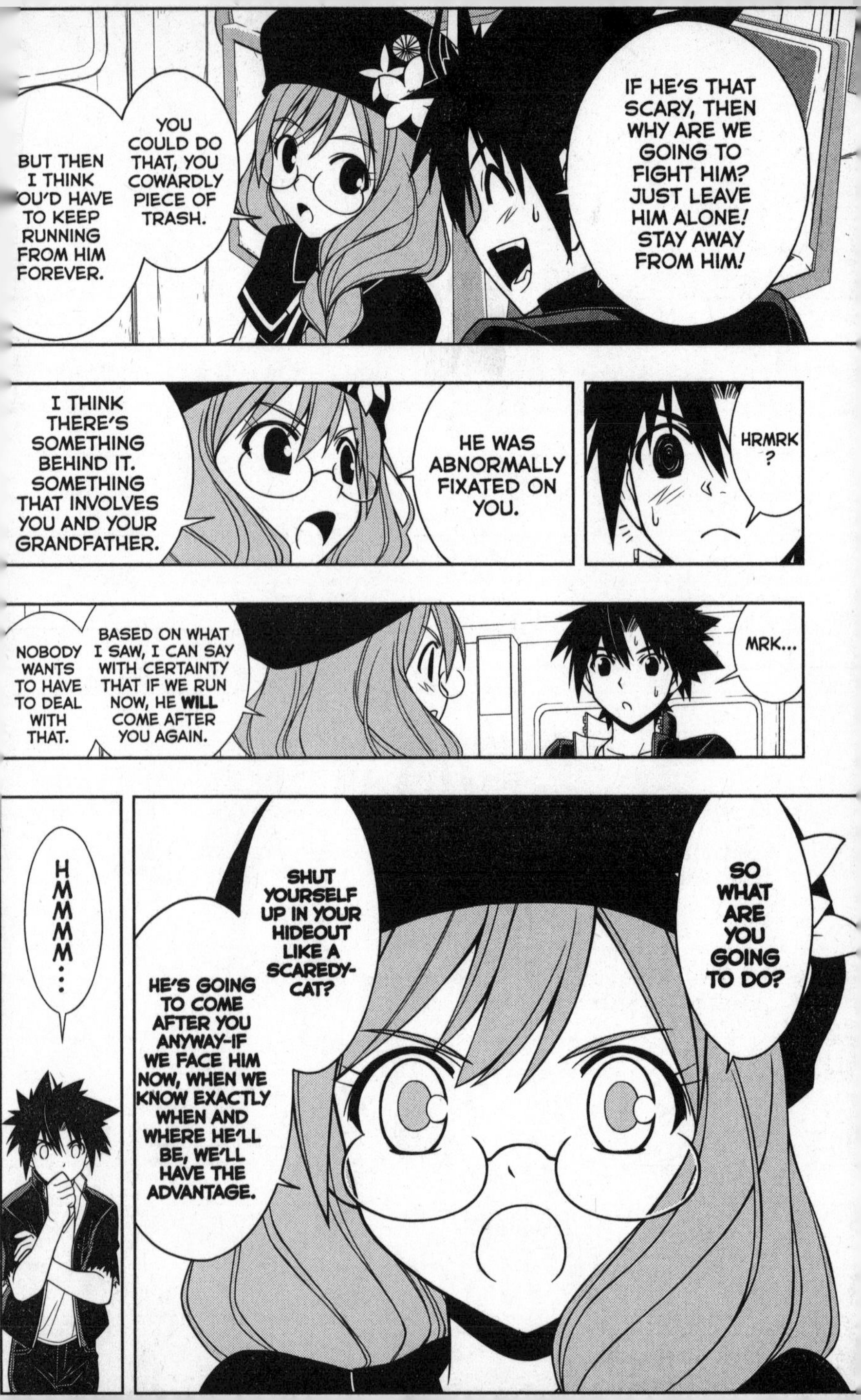
IF HE'S THAT SCARY, THEN WHY ARE WE GOING TO FIGHT HIM? JUST LEAVE HIM ALONE! STAY AWAY FROM HIM!
YOU COULD DO THAT, YOU COWARDLY PIECE OF TRASH.
BUT THEN I THINK OU'D HAVE TO KEEP RUNNING FROM HIM FOREVER.
HRMRK?
HE WAS ABNORMALLY FIXATED ON YOU.
I THINK THERE'S SOMETHING BEHIND IT. SOMETHING THAT INVOLVES YOU AND YOUR GRANDFATHER.
MRK...
BASED ON WHAT I SAW, I CAN SAY WITH CERTAINTY THAT IF WE RUN NOW, HE **WILL** COME AFTER YOU AGAIN.
NOBODY WANTS TO HAVE TO DEAL WITH THAT.
SO WHAT ARE YOU GOING TO DO?
SHUT YOURSELF UP IN YOUR HIDEOUT LIKE A SCAREDY-CAT?
HE'S GOING TO COME AFTER YOU ANYWAY-IF WE FACE HIM NOW, WHEN WE KNOW EXACTLY WHEN AND WHERE HE'LL BE, WE'LL HAVE THE ADVANTAGE.
HMMMM...

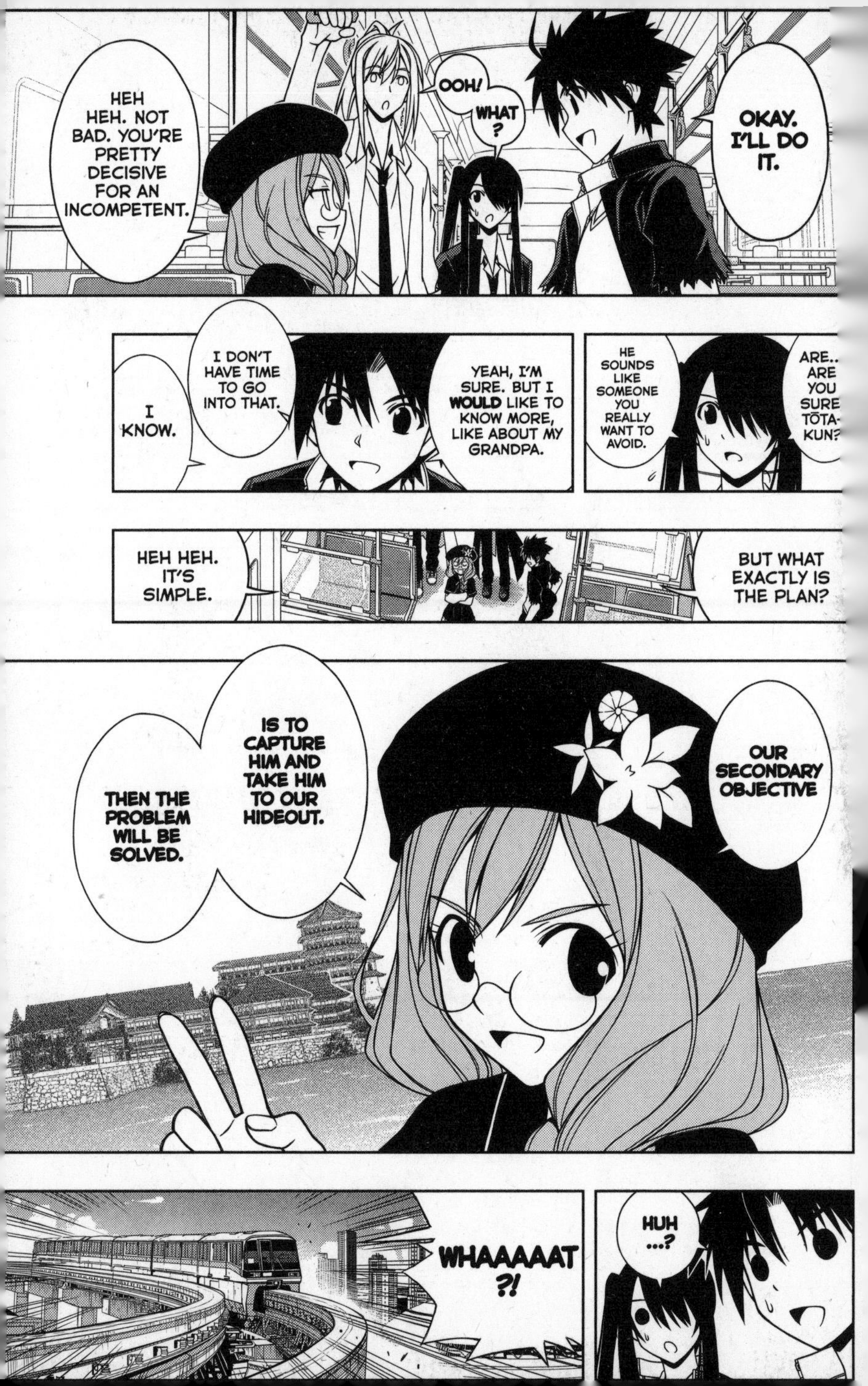
OKAY. I'LL DO IT.
OOH!
WHAT?
HEH HEH. NOT BAD. YOU'RE PRETTY DECISIVE FOR AN INCOMPETENT.
ARE... ARE YOU SURE TŌTA-KUN?
HE SOUNDS LIKE SOMEONE YOU REALLY WANT TO AVOID.
YEAH, I'M SURE. BUT I **WOULD** LIKE TO KNOW MORE, LIKE ABOUT MY GRANDPA.
I DON'T HAVE TIME TO GO INTO THAT.
I KNOW.
BUT WHAT EXACTLY IS THE PLAN?
HEH HEH. IT'S SIMPLE.
OUR SECONDARY OBJECTIVE
IS TO CAPTURE HIM AND TAKE HIM TO OUR HIDEOUT.
THEN THE PROBLEM WILL BE SOLVED.
HUH ...?
WHAAAAAT ?!

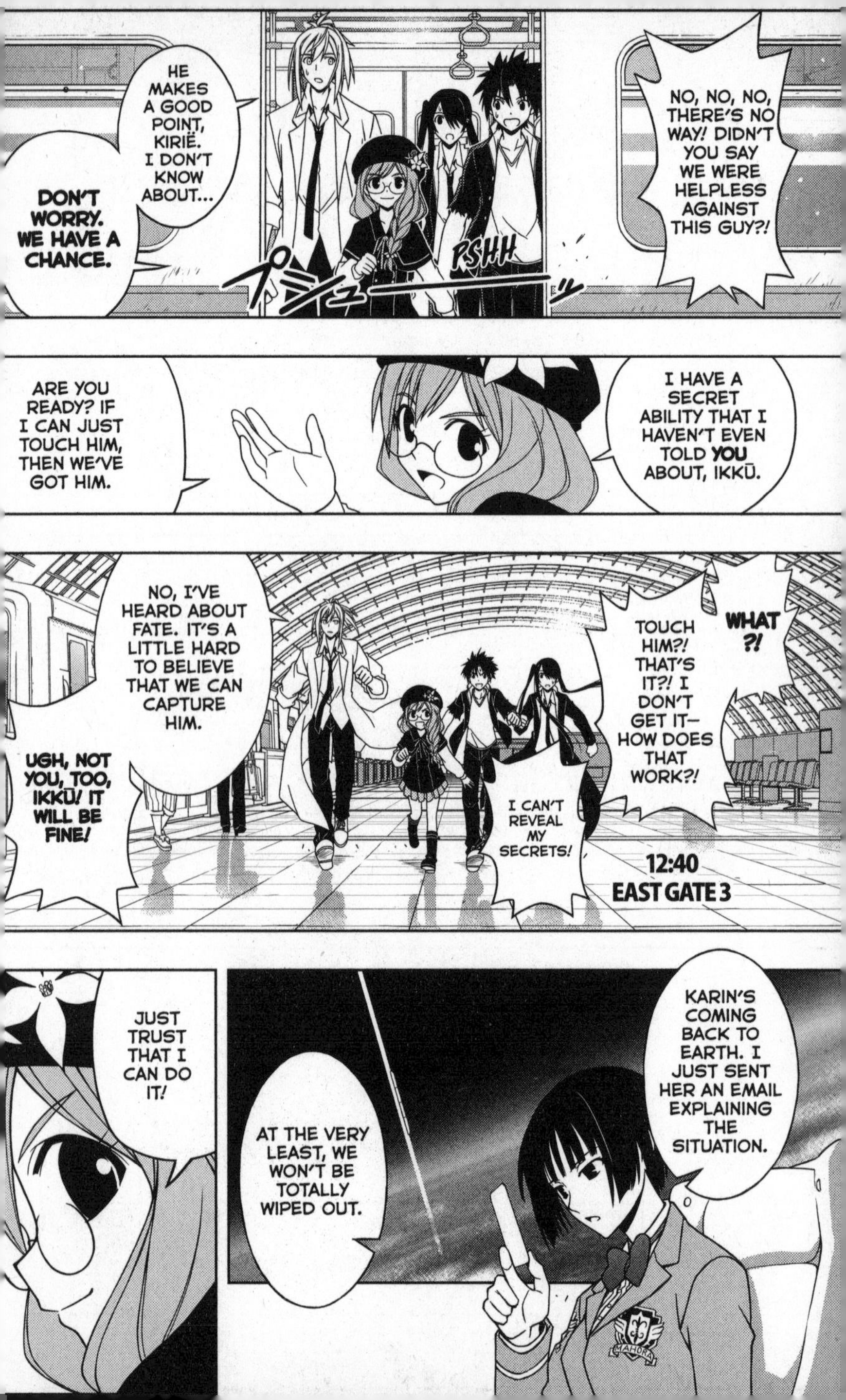
NO, NO, NO, THERE'S NO WAY! DIDN'T YOU SAY WE WERE HELPLESS AGAINST THIS GUY?!
PSHH
HE MAKES A GOOD POINT, KIRIË. I DON'T KNOW ABOUT...
DON'T WORRY. WE HAVE A CHANCE.
I HAVE A SECRET ABILITY THAT I HAVEN'T EVEN TOLD **YOU** ABOUT, IKKŪ.
ARE YOU READY? IF I CAN JUST TOUCH HIM, THEN WE'VE GOT HIM.
WHAT?!
TOUCH HIM?! THAT'S IT?! I DON'T GET IT—HOW DOES THAT WORK?!
12:40 EAST GATE 3
I CAN'T REVEAL MY SECRETS!
NO, I'VE HEARD ABOUT FATE. IT'S A LITTLE HARD TO BELIEVE THAT WE CAN CAPTURE HIM.
UGH, NOT YOU, TOO, IKKŪ! IT WILL BE FINE!
KARIN'S COMING BACK TO EARTH. I JUST SENT HER AN EMAIL EXPLAINING THE SITUATION.
AT THE VERY LEAST, WE WON'T BE TOTALLY WIPED OUT.
MAHORA
JUST TRUST THAT I CAN DO IT!

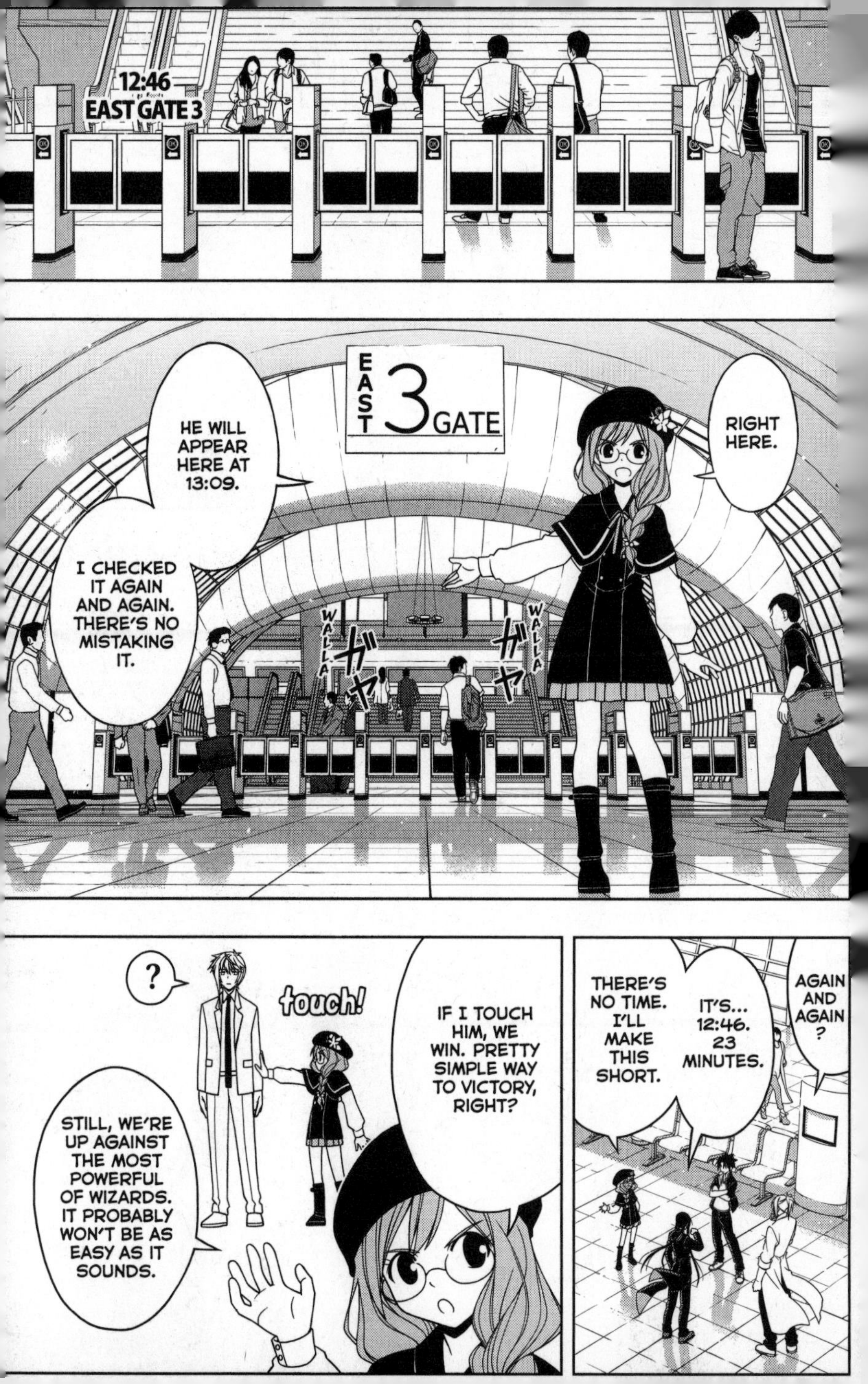
12:46
EAST GATE 3
EAST 3 GATE
RIGHT HERE.
HE WILL APPEAR HERE AT 13:09.
I CHECKED IT AGAIN AND AGAIN. THERE'S NO MISTAKING IT.
WALLA
WALLA
AGAIN AND AGAIN?
IT'S... 12:46. 23 MINUTES.
THERE'S NO TIME. I'LL MAKE THIS SHORT.
IF I TOUCH HIM, WE WIN. PRETTY SIMPLE WAY TO VICTORY, RIGHT?
touch!
?
STILL, WE'RE UP AGAINST THE MOST POWERFUL OF WIZARDS. IT PROBABLY WON'T BE AS EASY AS IT SOUNDS.

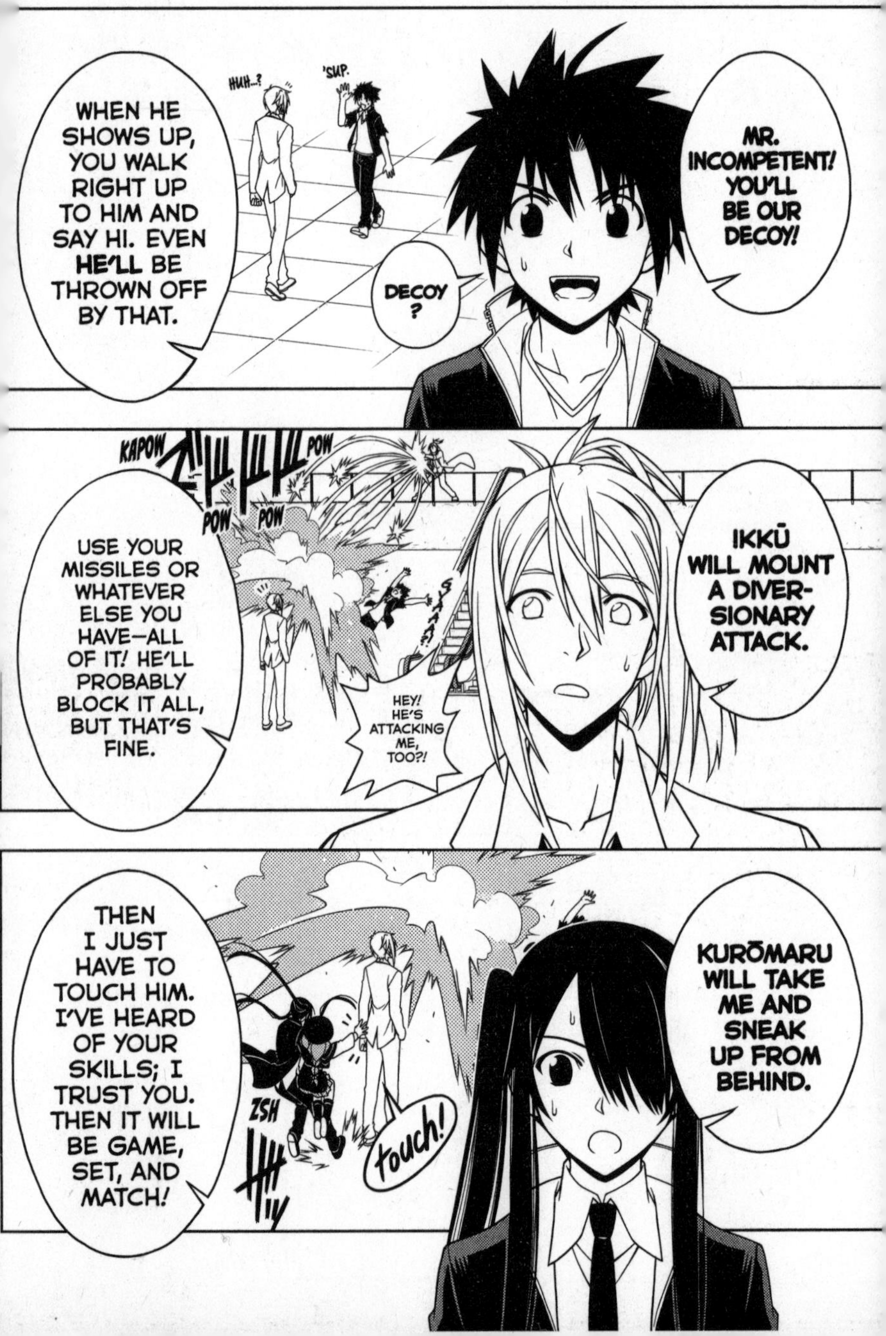
MR. INCOMPETENT! YOU'LL BE OUR DECOY!
DECOY?
'SUP.
HUH...?
WHEN HE SHOWS UP, YOU WALK RIGHT UP TO HIM AND SAY HI. EVEN **HE'LL** BE THROWN OFF BY THAT.
IKKŪ WILL MOUNT A DIVER-SIONARY ATTACK.
POW
KAPOW
POW
POW
HEY! HE'S ATTACKING ME, TOO?!
USE YOUR MISSILES OR WHATEVER ELSE YOU HAVE—ALL OF IT! HE'LL PROBABLY BLOCK IT ALL, BUT THAT'S FINE.
KURŌMARU WILL TAKE ME AND SNEAK UP FROM BEHIND.
touch!
ZSH
THEN I JUST HAVE TO TOUCH HIM. I'VE HEARD OF YOUR SKILLS; I TRUST YOU. THEN IT WILL BE GAME, SET, AND MATCH!

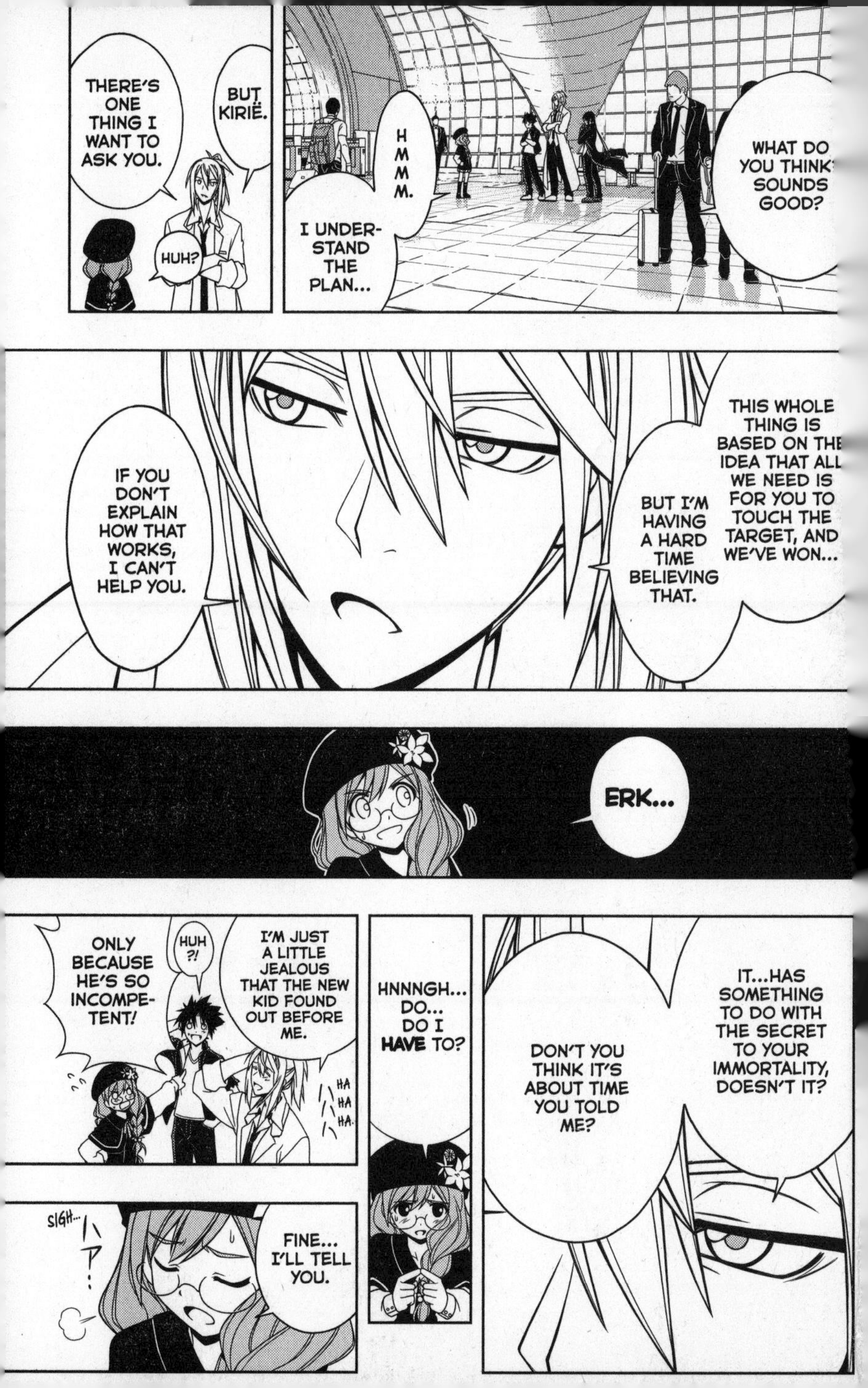

WHAT DO YOU THINK SOUNDS GOOD?
HMMM.
I UNDERSTAND THE PLAN...
BUT KIRIË.
THERE'S ONE THING I WANT TO ASK YOU.
HUH?
THIS WHOLE THING IS BASED ON THE IDEA THAT ALL WE NEED IS FOR YOU TO TOUCH THE TARGET, AND WE'VE WON...
BUT I'M HAVING A HARD TIME BELIEVING THAT.
IF YOU DON'T EXPLAIN HOW THAT WORKS, I CAN'T HELP YOU.
ERK...
IT...HAS SOMETHING TO DO WITH THE SECRET TO YOUR IMMORTALITY, DOESN'T IT?
DON'T YOU THINK IT'S ABOUT TIME YOU TOLD ME?
HNNNGH... DO... DO I **HAVE** TO?
I'M JUST A LITTLE JEALOUS THAT THE NEW KID FOUND OUT BEFORE ME.
HUH ?!
ONLY BECAUSE HE'S SO INCOMPETENT!
HA HA HA.
FINE... I'LL TELL YOU.
SIGH...

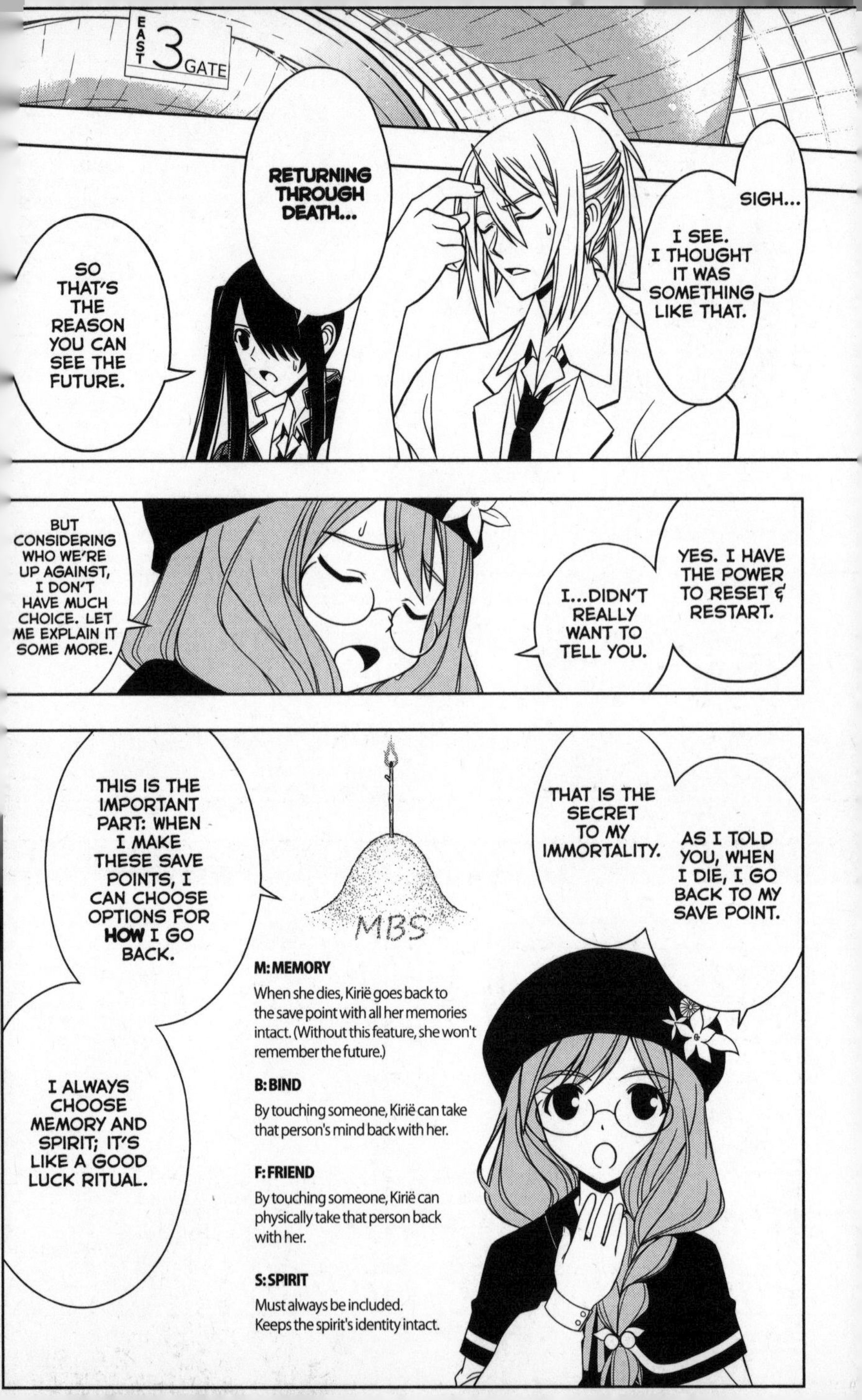
EAST 3 GATE
SIGH...
I SEE. I THOUGHT IT WAS SOMETHING LIKE THAT.
RETURNING THROUGH DEATH...
SO THAT'S THE REASON YOU CAN SEE THE FUTURE.
YES. I HAVE THE POWER TO RESET & RESTART.
I...DIDN'T REALLY WANT TO TELL YOU.
BUT CONSIDERING WHO WE'RE UP AGAINST, I DON'T HAVE MUCH CHOICE. LET ME EXPLAIN IT SOME MORE.
AS I TOLD YOU, WHEN I DIE, I GO BACK TO MY SAVE POINT.
THAT IS THE SECRET TO MY IMMORTALITY.
THIS IS THE IMPORTANT PART: WHEN I MAKE THESE SAVE POINTS, I CAN CHOOSE OPTIONS FOR **HOW** I GO BACK.
MBS
M: MEMORY
When she dies, Kiriё goes back to the save point with all her memories intact. (Without this feature, she won't remember the future.)
B: BIND
By touching someone, Kiriё can take that person's mind back with her.
F: FRIEND
By touching someone, Kiriё can physically take that person back with her.
S: SPIRIT
Must always be included. Keeps the spirit's identity intact.
I ALWAYS CHOOSE MEMORY AND SPIRIT; IT'S LIKE A GOOD LUCK RITUAL.

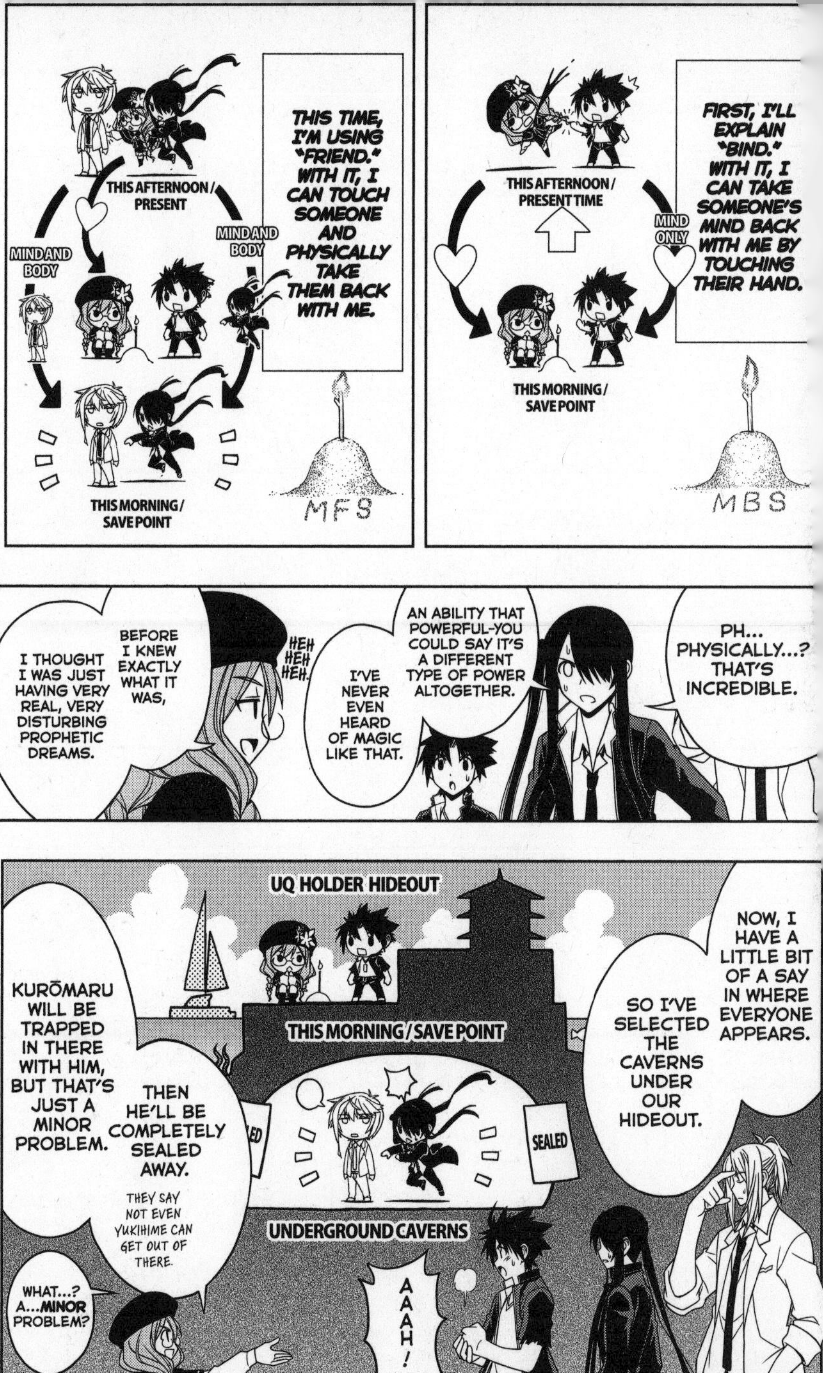
FIRST, I'LL EXPLAIN "BIND." WITH IT, I CAN TAKE SOMEONE'S MIND BACK WITH ME BY TOUCHING THEIR HAND.
THIS AFTERNOON / PRESENT TIME
MIND ONLY
THIS MORNING / SAVE POINT
MBS
THIS TIME, I'M USING "FRIEND." WITH IT, I CAN TOUCH SOMEONE AND PHYSICALLY TAKE THEM BACK WITH ME.
THIS AFTERNOON / PRESENT
MIND AND BODY
MIND AND BODY
THIS MORNING / SAVE POINT
MFS
PH... PHYSICALLY...? THAT'S INCREDIBLE.
AN ABILITY THAT POWERFUL-YOU COULD SAY IT'S A DIFFERENT TYPE OF POWER ALTOGETHER.
I'VE NEVER EVEN HEARD OF MAGIC LIKE THAT.
HEH HEH HEH.
BEFORE I KNEW EXACTLY WHAT IT WAS,
I THOUGHT I WAS JUST HAVING VERY REAL, VERY DISTURBING PROPHETIC DREAMS.
NOW, I HAVE A LITTLE BIT OF A SAY IN WHERE EVERYONE APPEARS.
SO I'VE SELECTED THE CAVERNS UNDER OUR HIDEOUT.
UQ HOLDER HIDEOUT
THIS MORNING / SAVE POINT
SEALED
UNDERGROUND CAVERNS
THEN HE'LL BE COMPLETELY SEALED AWAY.
THEY SAY NOT EVEN YUKIHIME CAN GET OUT OF THERE.
KURŌMARU WILL BE TRAPPED IN THERE WITH HIM, BUT THAT'S JUST A MINOR PROBLEM.
AAAH!
WHAT...? A...MINOR PROBLEM?

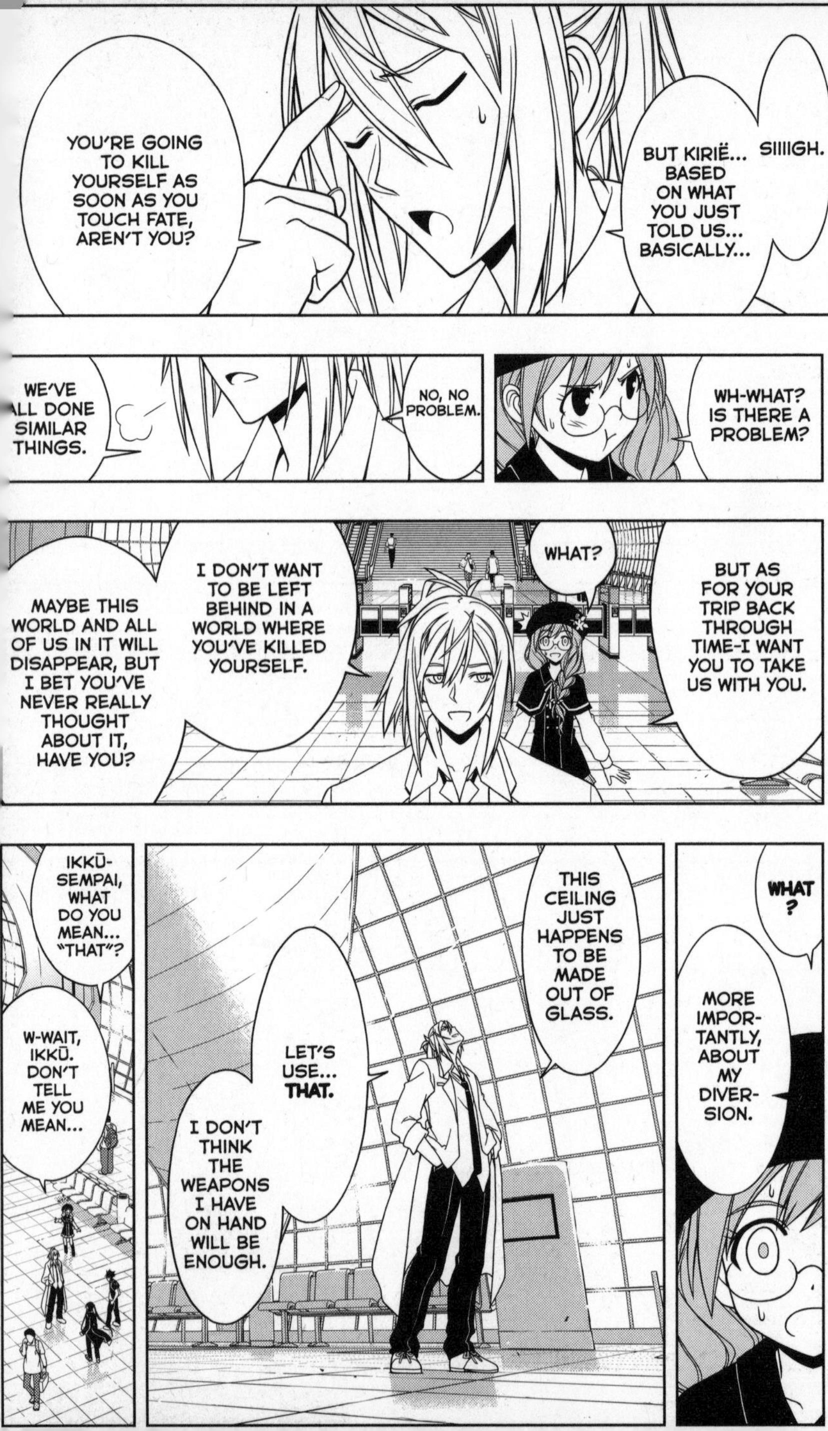
SIIIGH.
BUT KIRIË... BASED ON WHAT YOU JUST TOLD US... BASICALLY...
YOU'RE GOING TO KILL YOURSELF AS SOON AS YOU TOUCH FATE, AREN'T YOU?
WH-WHAT? IS THERE A PROBLEM?
NO, NO PROBLEM.
WE'VE ALL DONE SIMILAR THINGS.
BUT AS FOR YOUR TRIP BACK THROUGH TIME—I WANT YOU TO TAKE US WITH YOU.
WHAT?
I DON'T WANT TO BE LEFT BEHIND IN A WORLD WHERE YOU'VE KILLED YOURSELF.
MAYBE THIS WORLD AND ALL OF US IN IT WILL DISAPPEAR, BUT I BET YOU'VE NEVER REALLY THOUGHT ABOUT IT, HAVE YOU?
WHAT?
MORE IMPORTANTLY, ABOUT MY DIVERSION.
THIS CEILING JUST HAPPENS TO BE MADE OUT OF GLASS.
I DON'T THINK THE WEAPONS I HAVE ON HAND WILL BE ENOUGH.
LET'S USE... THAT.
IKKŪ-SEMPAI, WHAT DO YOU MEAN... "THAT"?
W-WAIT, IKKŪ. DON'T TELL ME YOU MEAN...

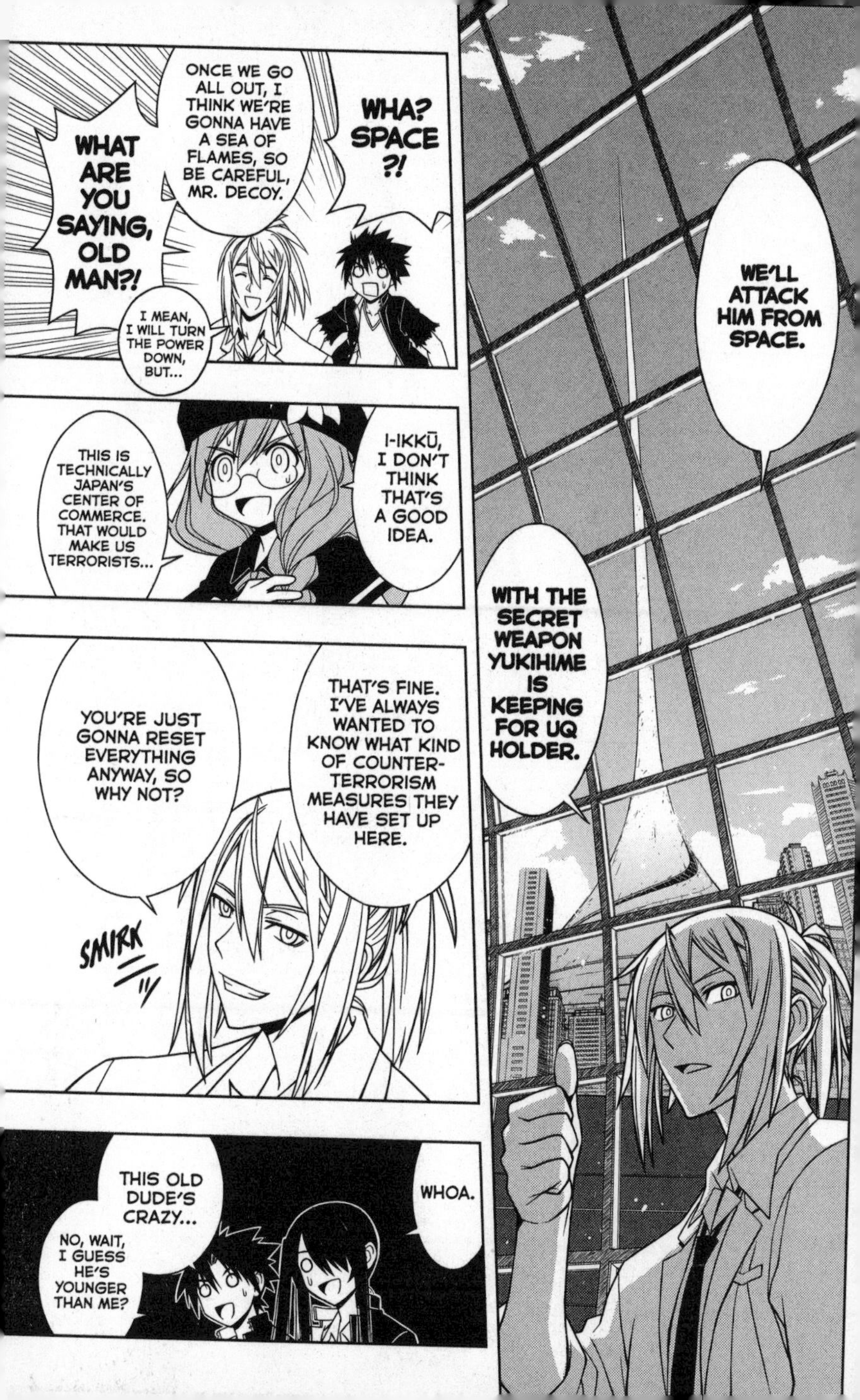
WE'LL ATTACK HIM FROM SPACE.
WITH THE SECRET WEAPON YUKIHIME IS KEEPING FOR UQ HOLDER.
WHA? SPACE?!
ONCE WE GO ALL OUT, I THINK WE'RE GONNA HAVE A SEA OF FLAMES, SO BE CAREFUL, MR. DECOY.
WHAT ARE YOU SAYING, OLD MAN?!
I MEAN, I WILL TURN THE POWER DOWN, BUT...
I-IKKŪ, I DON'T THINK THAT'S A GOOD IDEA.
THIS IS TECHNICALLY JAPAN'S CENTER OF COMMERCE. THAT WOULD MAKE US TERRORISTS...
THAT'S FINE. I'VE ALWAYS WANTED TO KNOW WHAT KIND OF COUNTER-TERRORISM MEASURES THEY HAVE SET UP HERE.
YOU'RE JUST GONNA RESET EVERYTHING ANYWAY, SO WHY NOT?
SMIRK
WHOA.
THIS OLD DUDE'S CRAZY...
NO, WAIT, I GUESS HE'S YOUNGER THAN ME?

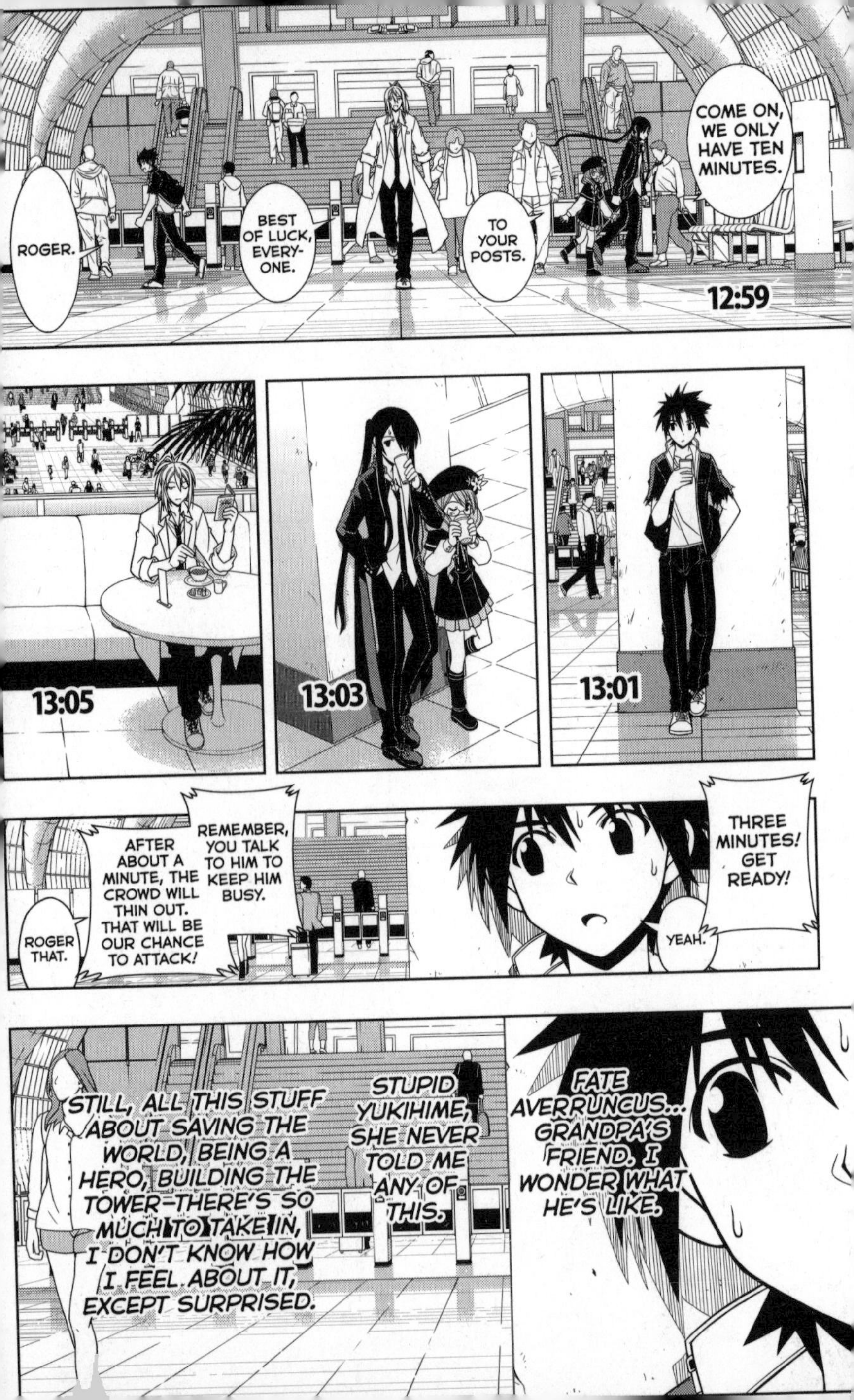

COME ON, WE ONLY HAVE TEN MINUTES.
12:59
TO YOUR POSTS.
BEST OF LUCK, EVERY-ONE.
ROGER.
13:01
13:03
13:05
THREE MINUTES! GET READY!
YEAH.
REMEMBER, YOU TALK TO HIM TO KEEP HIM BUSY.
AFTER ABOUT A MINUTE, THE CROWD WILL THIN OUT. THAT WILL BE OUR CHANCE TO ATTACK!
ROGER THAT.
FATE AVERRUNCUS... GRANDPA'S FRIEND. I WONDER WHAT HE'S LIKE.
STUPID YUKIHIME, SHE NEVER TOLD ME ANY OF THIS.
STILL, ALL THIS STUFF ABOUT SAVING THE WORLD, BEING A HERO, BUILDING THE TOWER—THERE'S SO MUCH TO TAKE IN, I DON'T KNOW HOW I FEEL ABOUT IT, EXCEPT SURPRISED.

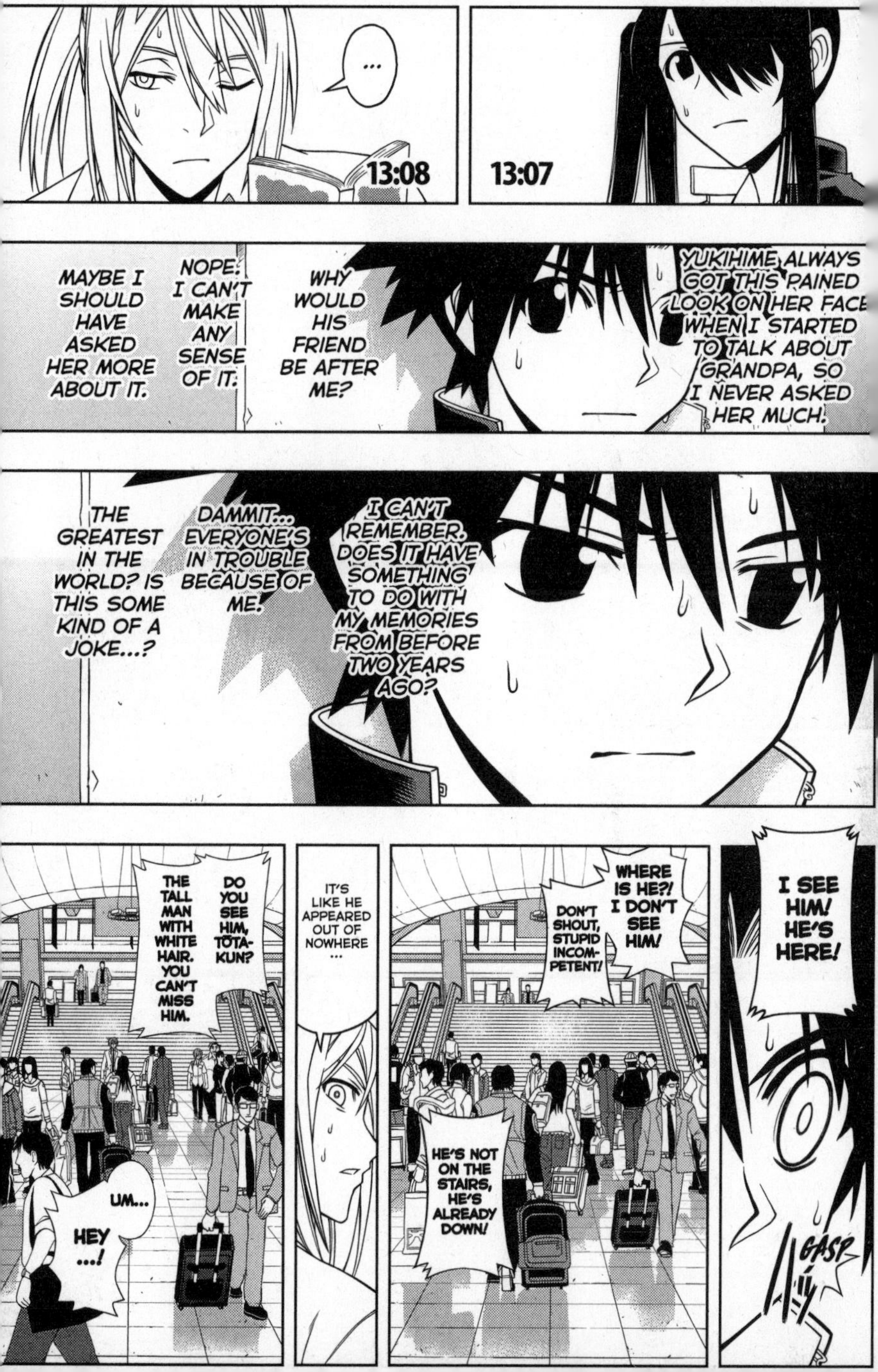
13:07
...
13:08
YUKIHIME ALWAYS GOT THIS PAINED LOOK ON HER FACE WHEN I STARTED TO TALK ABOUT GRANDPA, SO I NEVER ASKED HER MUCH.
WHY WOULD HIS FRIEND BE AFTER ME?
NOPE. I CAN'T MAKE ANY SENSE OF IT.
MAYBE I SHOULD HAVE ASKED HER MORE ABOUT IT.
I CAN'T REMEMBER. DOES IT HAVE SOMETHING TO DO WITH MY MEMORIES FROM BEFORE TWO YEARS AGO?
DAMMIT... EVERYONE'S IN TROUBLE BECAUSE OF ME.
THE GREATEST IN THE WORLD? IS THIS SOME KIND OF A JOKE...?
I SEE HIM! HE'S HERE!
GASP
WHERE IS HE?! I DON'T SEE HIM!
DON'T SHOUT, STUPID INCOMPETENT!
HE'S NOT ON THE STAIRS, HE'S ALREADY DOWN!
IT'S LIKE HE APPEARED OUT OF NOWHERE...
DO YOU SEE HIM, TOTA-KUN?
THE TALL MAN WITH WHITE HAIR. YOU CAN'T MISS HIM.
UM...
HEY ...!

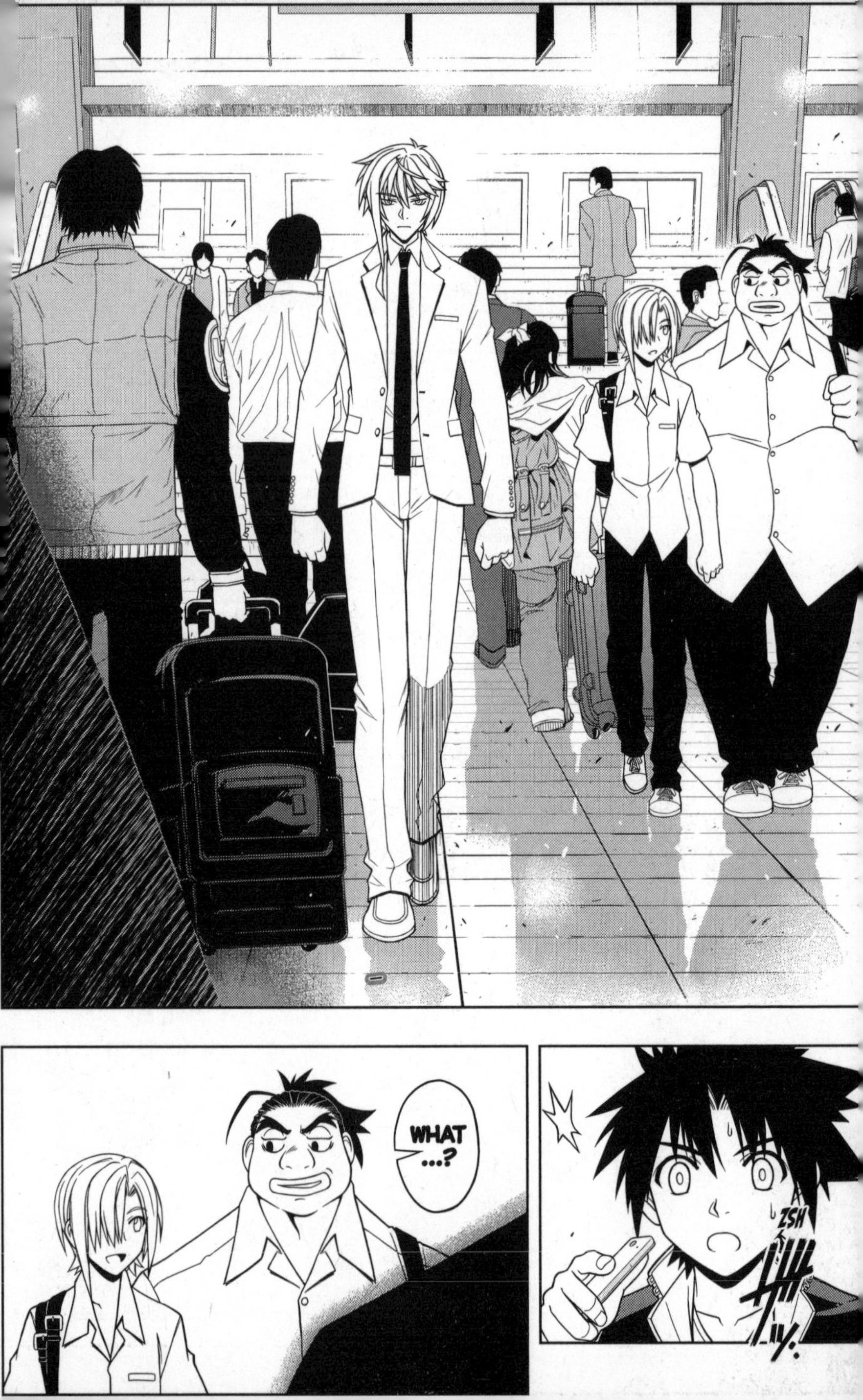
ZSH
WHAT ...?

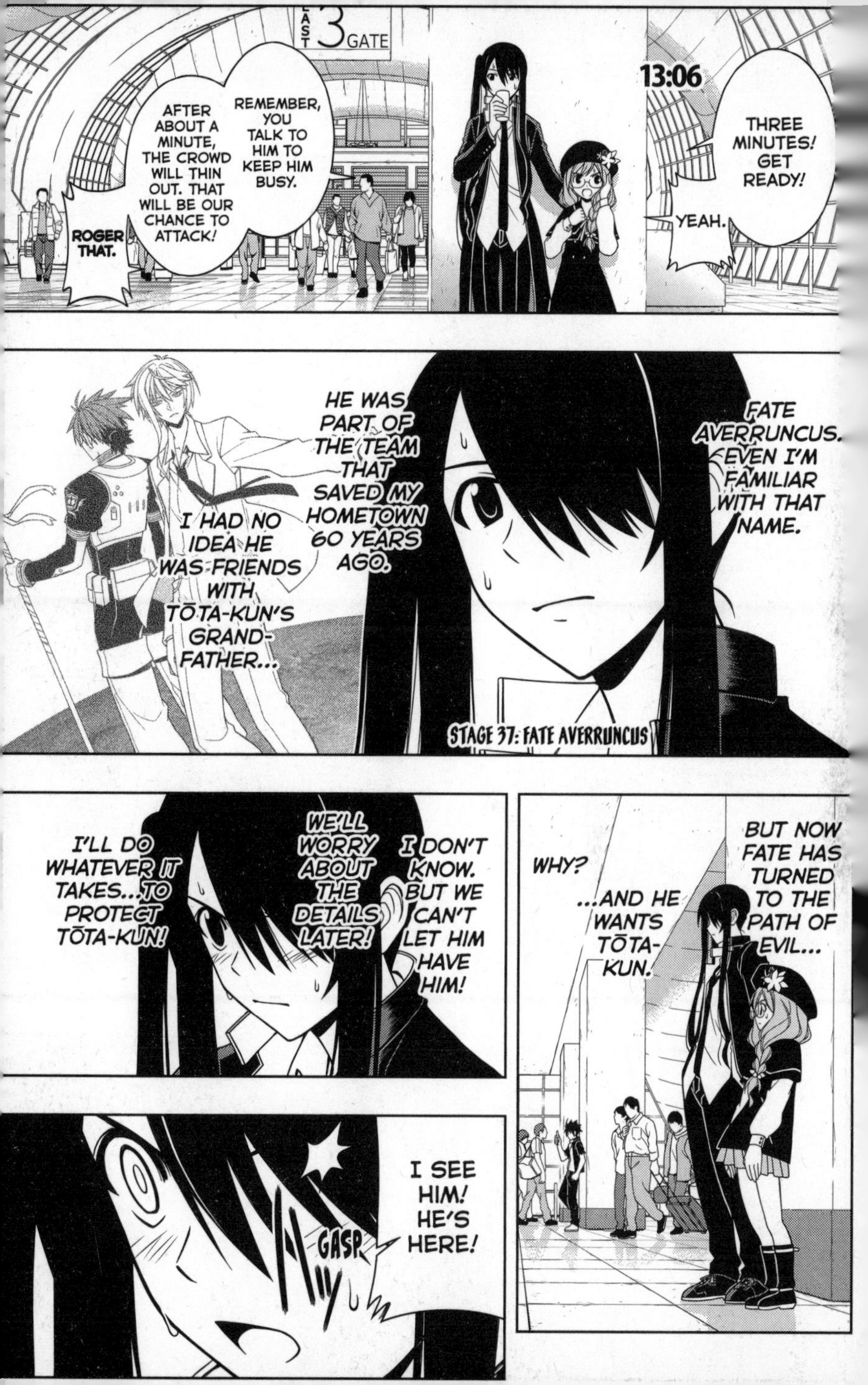
13:06
THREE MINUTES! GET READY!
YEAH.
LAST 3 GATE
REMEMBER, YOU TALK TO HIM TO KEEP HIM BUSY.
AFTER ABOUT A MINUTE, THE CROWD WILL THIN OUT. THAT WILL BE OUR CHANCE TO ATTACK!
ROGER THAT.
FATE AVERRUNCUS. EVEN I'M FAMILIAR WITH THAT NAME.
HE WAS PART OF THE TEAM THAT SAVED MY HOMETOWN 60 YEARS AGO.
I HAD NO IDEA HE WAS FRIENDS WITH TŌTA-KUN'S GRAND-FATHER...
STAGE 37: FATE AVERRUNCUS
BUT NOW FATE HAS TURNED TO THE PATH OF EVIL...
...AND HE WANTS TŌTA-KUN.
WHY?
I DON'T KNOW. BUT WE CAN'T LET HIM HAVE HIM!
WE'LL WORRY ABOUT THE DETAILS LATER!
I'LL DO WHATEVER IT TAKES...TO PROTECT TŌTA-KUN!
I SEE HIM! HE'S HERE!
GASP

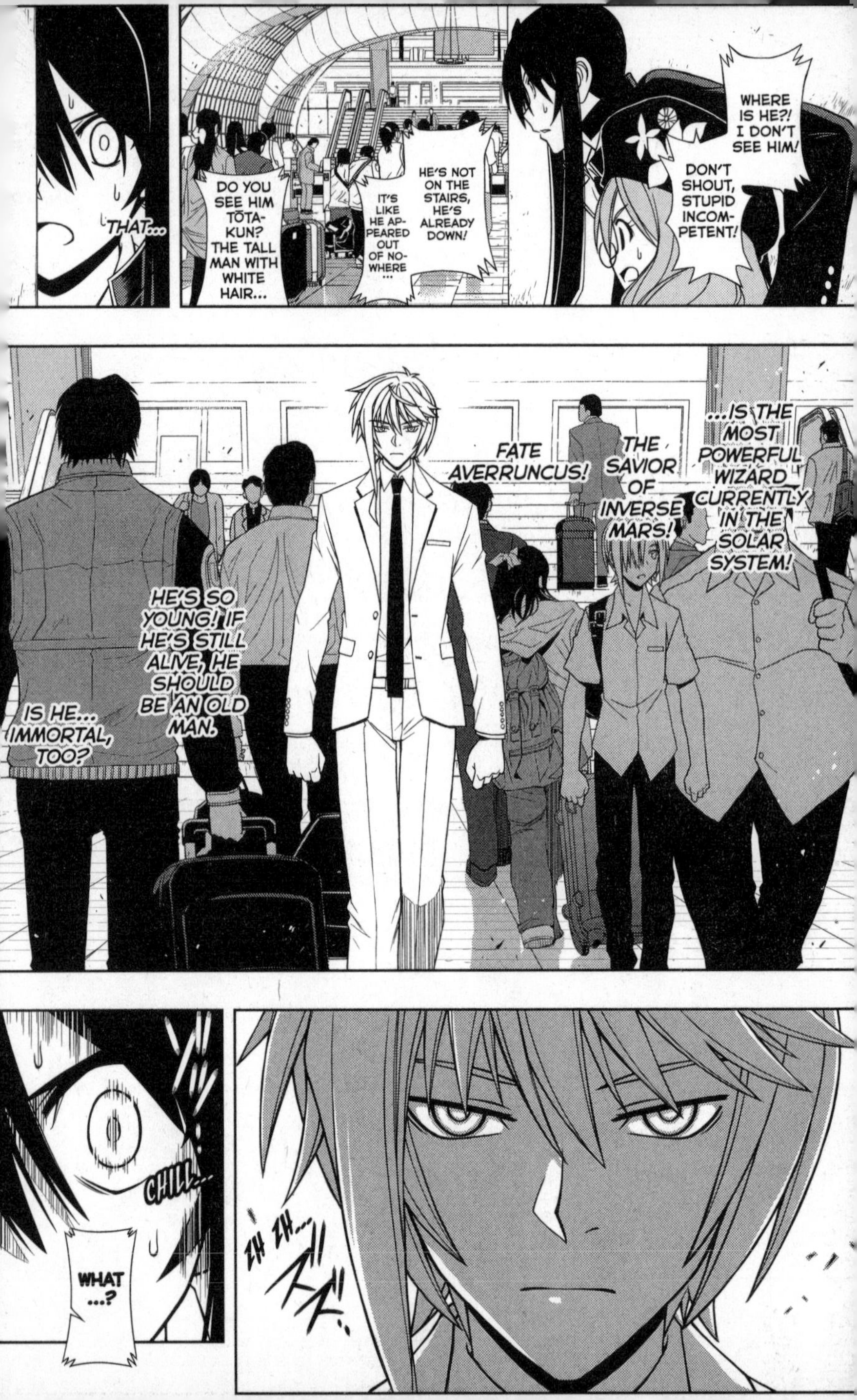
WHERE IS HE?! I DON'T SEE HIM!
DON'T SHOUT, STUPID INCOMPETENT!
HE'S NOT ON THE STAIRS, HE'S ALREADY DOWN!
IT'S LIKE HE APPEARED OUT OF NOWHERE...
DO YOU SEE HIM TŌTA-KUN? THE TALL MAN WITH WHITE HAIR...
THAT...
...IS THE MOST POWERFUL WIZARD CURRENTLY IN THE SOLAR SYSTEM!
THE SAVIOR OF INVERSE MARS!
FATE AVERRUNCUS!
HE'S SO YOUNG! IF HE'S STILL ALIVE, HE SHOULD BE AN OLD MAN.
IS HE... IMMORTAL, TOO?
ZH ZH...
CHILL...
WHAT...?

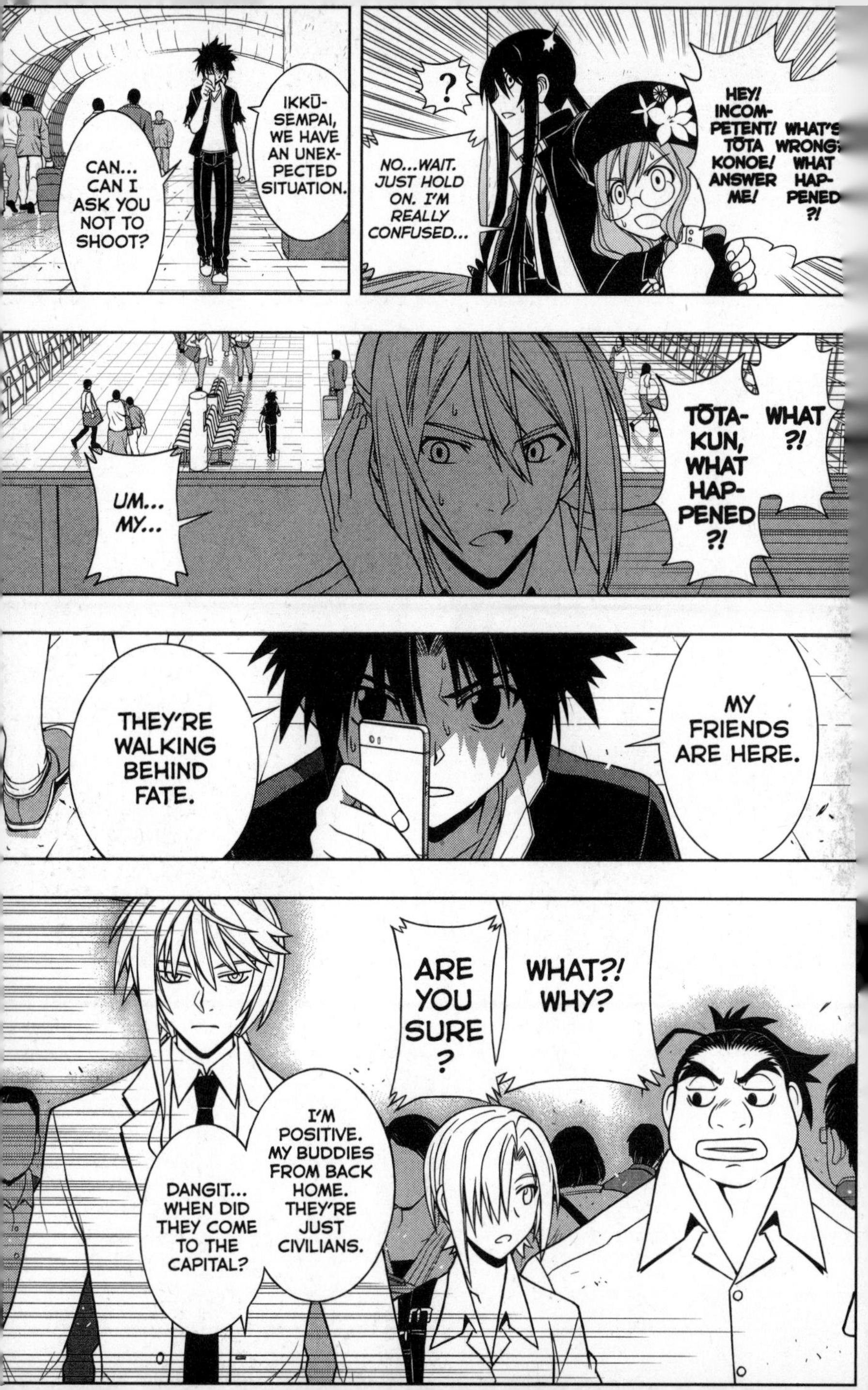

HEY! INCOMPETENT! TŌTA KONOE! ANSWER ME!
WHAT'S WRONG? WHAT HAPPENED?!
?
NO...WAIT. JUST HOLD ON. I'M REALLY CONFUSED...
IKKŪ-SEMPAI, WE HAVE AN UNEXPECTED SITUATION.
CAN... CAN I ASK YOU NOT TO SHOOT?
WHAT?!
TŌTA-KUN, WHAT HAPPENED?!
UM... MY...
MY FRIENDS ARE HERE.
THEY'RE WALKING BEHIND FATE.
WHAT?! WHY?
ARE YOU SURE?
I'M POSITIVE. MY BUDDIES FROM BACK HOME. THEY'RE JUST CIVILIANS.
DANGIT... WHEN DID THEY COME TO THE CAPITAL?

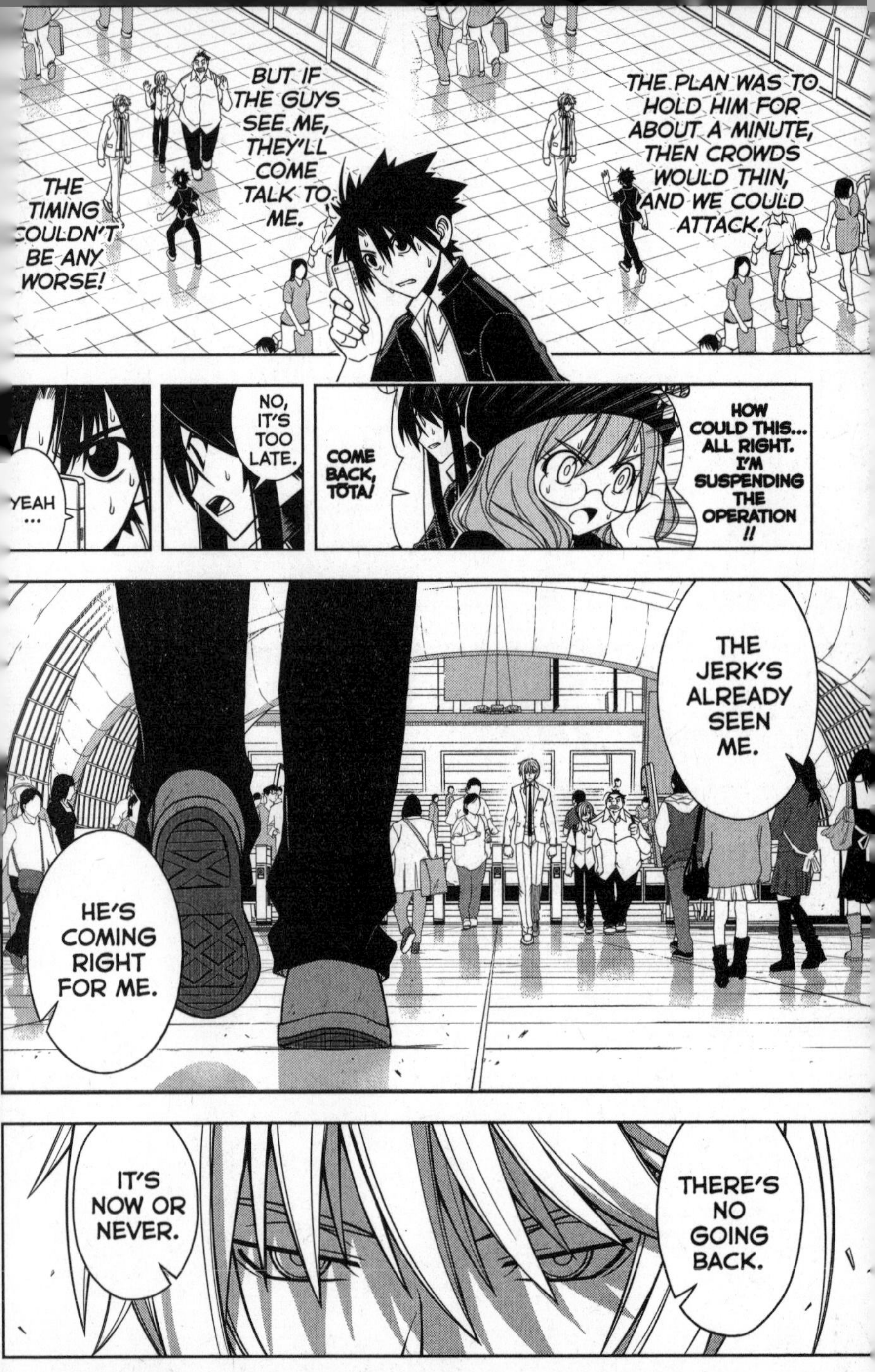
THE PLAN WAS TO HOLD HIM FOR ABOUT A MINUTE, THEN CROWDS WOULD THIN, AND WE COULD ATTACK.
BUT IF THE GUYS SEE ME, THEY'LL COME TALK TO ME.
THE TIMING COULDN'T BE ANY WORSE!
HOW COULD THIS... ALL RIGHT. I'M SUSPENDING THE OPERATION !!
COME BACK, TOTA!
NO, IT'S TOO LATE.
YEAH ...
THE JERK'S ALREADY SEEN ME.
HE'S COMING RIGHT FOR ME.
THERE'S NO GOING BACK.
IT'S NOW OR NEVER.

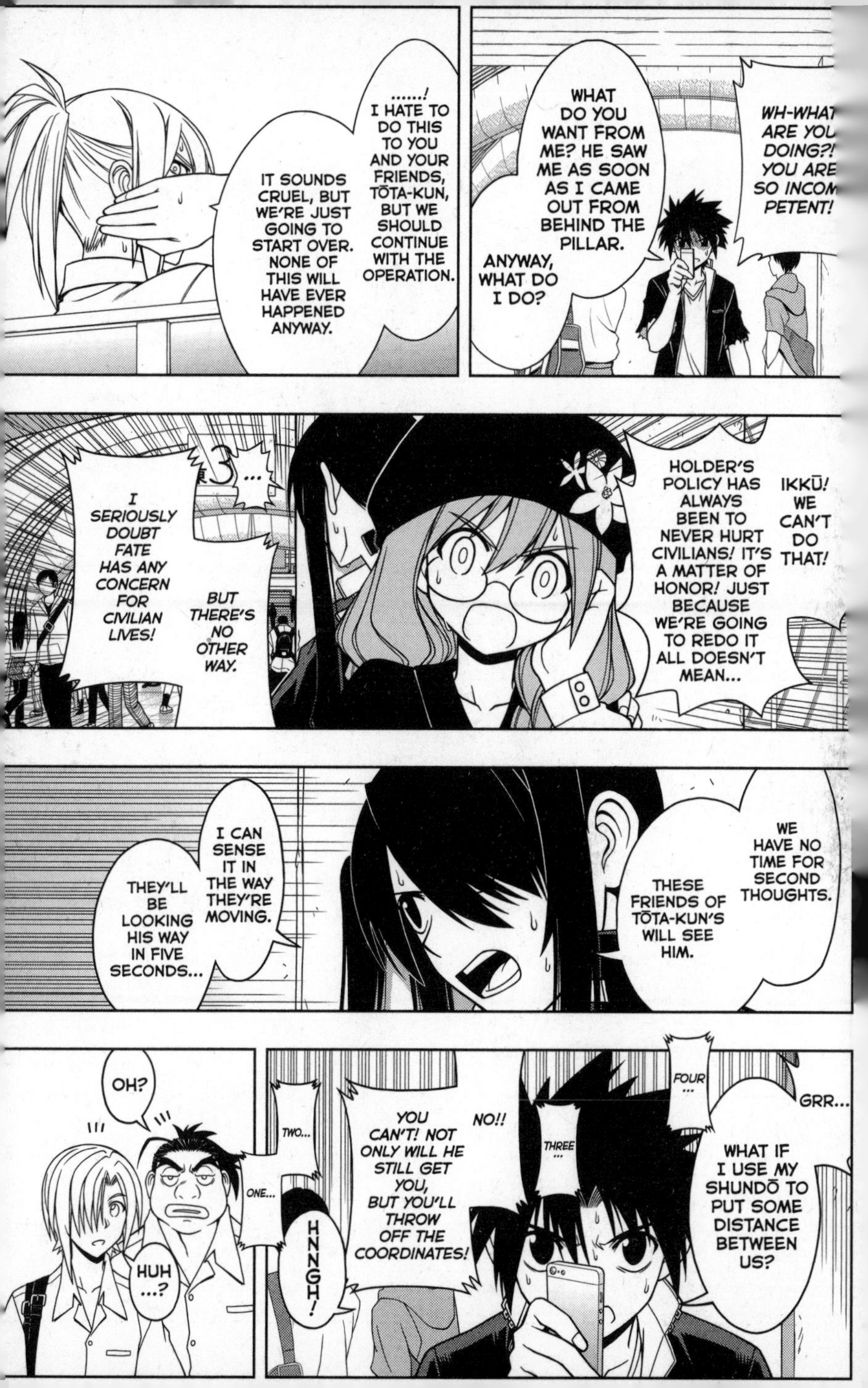
WH-WHAT ARE YOU DOING?! YOU ARE SO INCOMPETENT!
WHAT DO YOU WANT FROM ME? HE SAW ME AS SOON AS I CAME OUT FROM BEHIND THE PILLAR.
ANYWAY, WHAT DO I DO?
......! I HATE TO DO THIS TO YOU AND YOUR FRIENDS, TŌTA-KUN, BUT WE SHOULD CONTINUE WITH THE OPERATION.
IT SOUNDS CRUEL, BUT WE'RE JUST GOING TO START OVER. NONE OF THIS WILL HAVE EVER HAPPENED ANYWAY.
IKKŪ! WE CAN'T DO THAT!
HOLDER'S POLICY HAS ALWAYS BEEN TO NEVER HURT CIVILIANS! IT'S A MATTER OF HONOR! JUST BECAUSE WE'RE GOING TO REDO IT ALL DOESN'T MEAN...
3...
I SERIOUSLY DOUBT FATE HAS ANY CONCERN FOR CIVILIAN LIVES!
BUT THERE'S NO OTHER WAY.
WE HAVE NO TIME FOR SECOND THOUGHTS.
THESE FRIENDS OF TŌTA-KUN'S WILL SEE HIM.
I CAN SENSE IT IN THE WAY THEY'RE MOVING.
THEY'LL BE LOOKING HIS WAY IN FIVE SECONDS...
GRR...
FOUR...
WHAT IF I USE MY SHUNDŌ TO PUT SOME DISTANCE BETWEEN US?
THREE...
NO!!
YOU CAN'T! NOT ONLY WILL HE STILL GET YOU, BUT YOU'LL THROW OFF THE COORDINATES!
TWO...
HNNGH!
ONE...
OH?
HUH...?

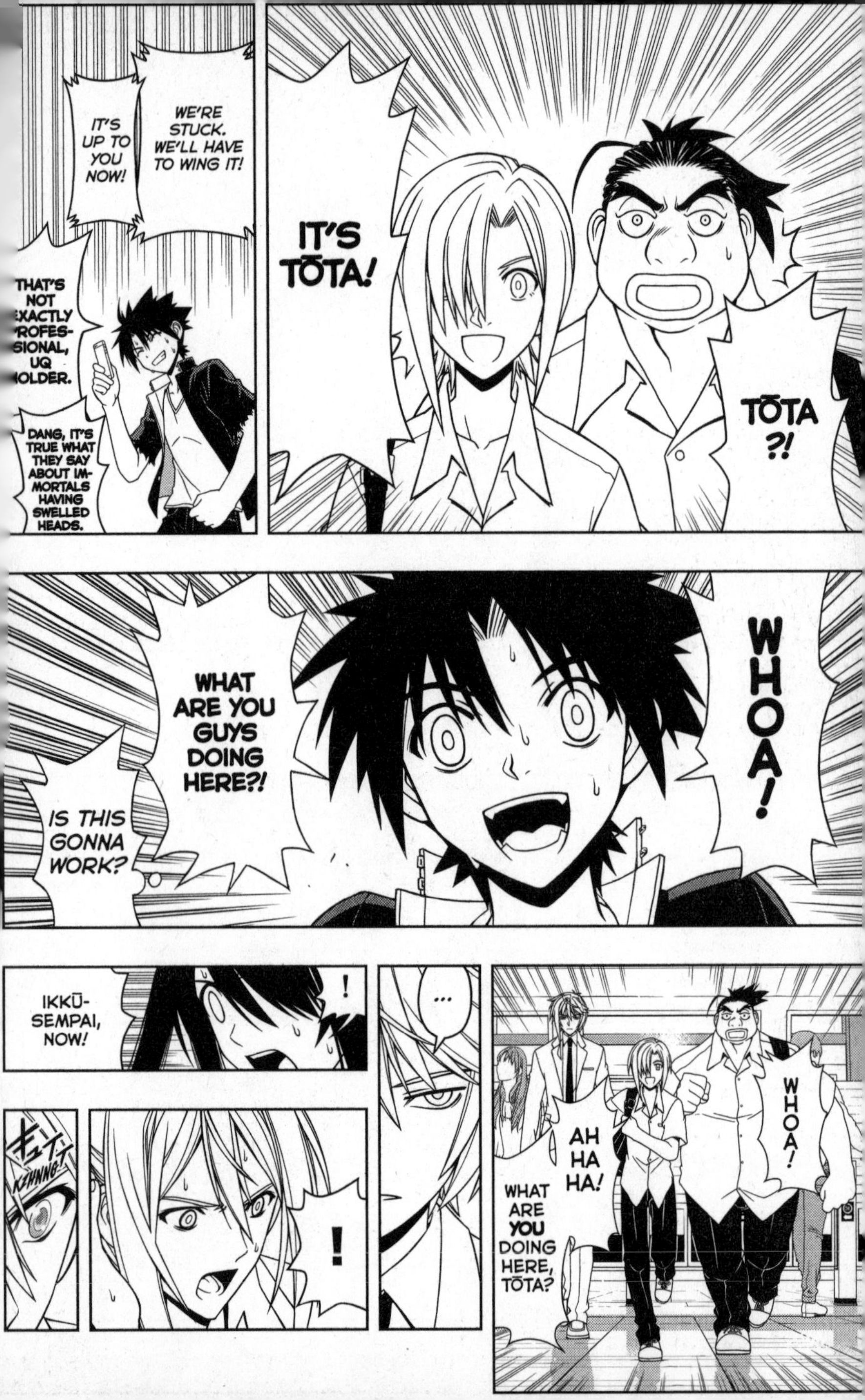
TŌTA ?!
IT'S TŌTA!
WE'RE STUCK. WE'LL HAVE TO WING IT!
IT'S UP TO YOU NOW!
THAT'S NOT EXACTLY PROFES-SIONAL, UQ HOLDER.
DANG, IT'S TRUE WHAT THEY SAY ABOUT IM-MORTALS HAVING SWELLED HEADS.
WHOA!
WHAT ARE YOU GUYS DOING HERE?!
IS THIS GONNA WORK?
WHOA!
AH HA HA!
WHAT ARE YOU DOING HERE, TŌTA?
...
!
IKKŪ-SEMPAI, NOW!
!
キュイイ
KCHNNG!

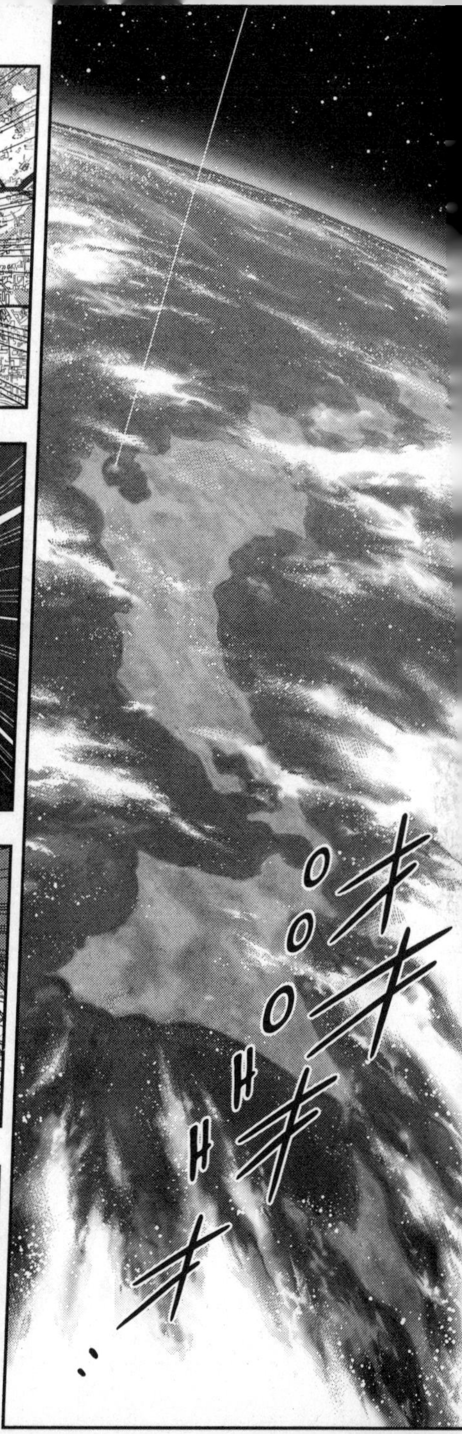

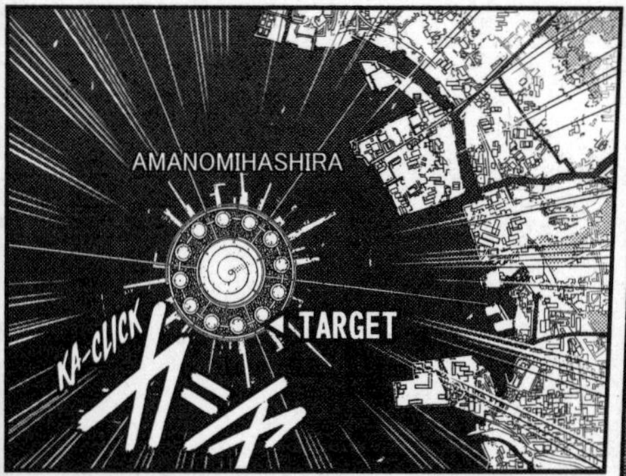
AMANOMIHASHIRA
TARGET
KA-CLICK

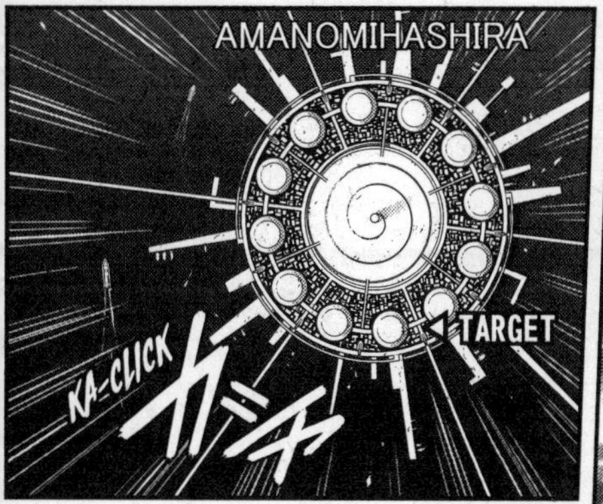
AMANOMIHASHIRA
TARGET
KA-CLICK

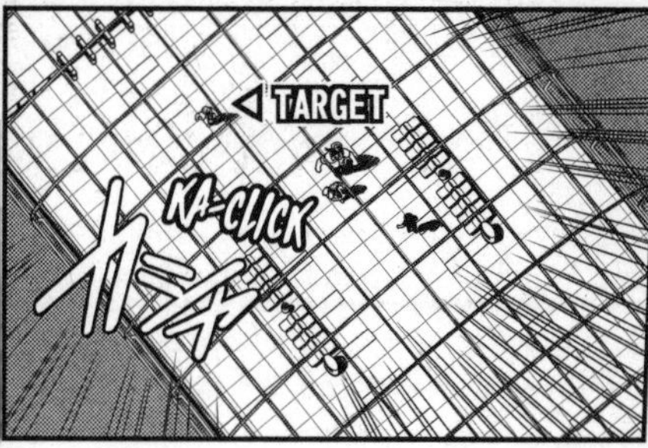
TARGET
KA-CLICK

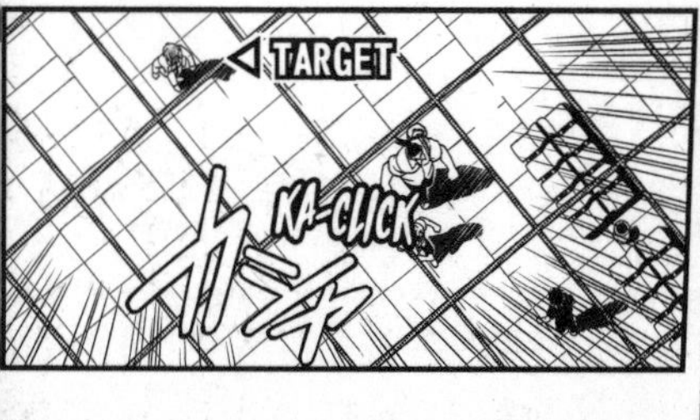
TARGET
KA-CLICK

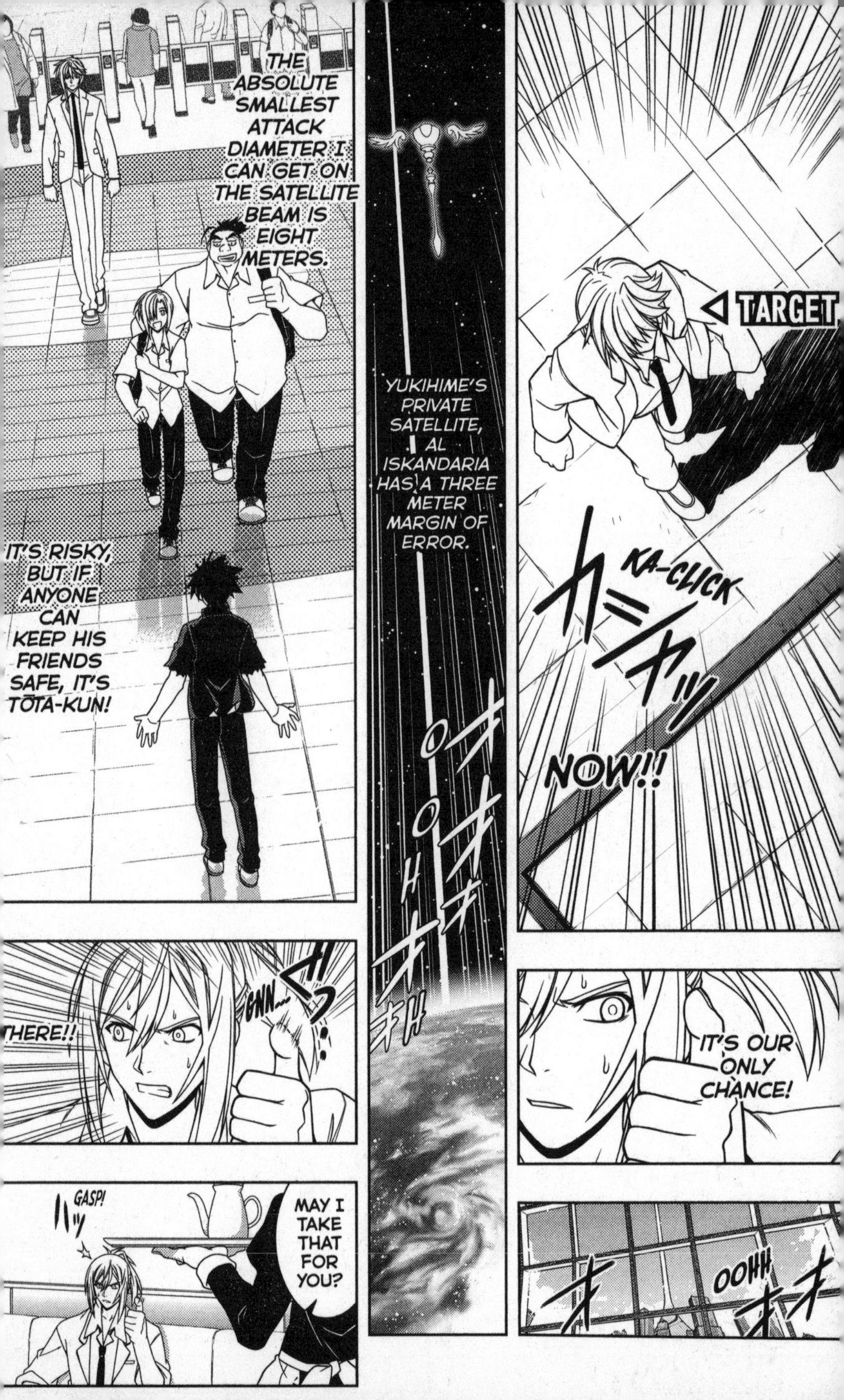
TARGET
KA-CLICK
NOW!!
YUKIHIME'S PRIVATE SATELLITE, AL ISKANDARIA HAS A THREE METER MARGIN OF ERROR.
THE ABSOLUTE SMALLEST ATTACK DIAMETER I CAN GET ON THE SATELLITE BEAM IS EIGHT METERS.
IT'S RISKY, BUT IF ANYONE CAN KEEP HIS FRIENDS SAFE, IT'S TŌTA-KUN!
IT'S OUR ONLY CHANCE!
GNN...
THERE!!
OOHH
GASP!
MAY I TAKE THAT FOR YOU?

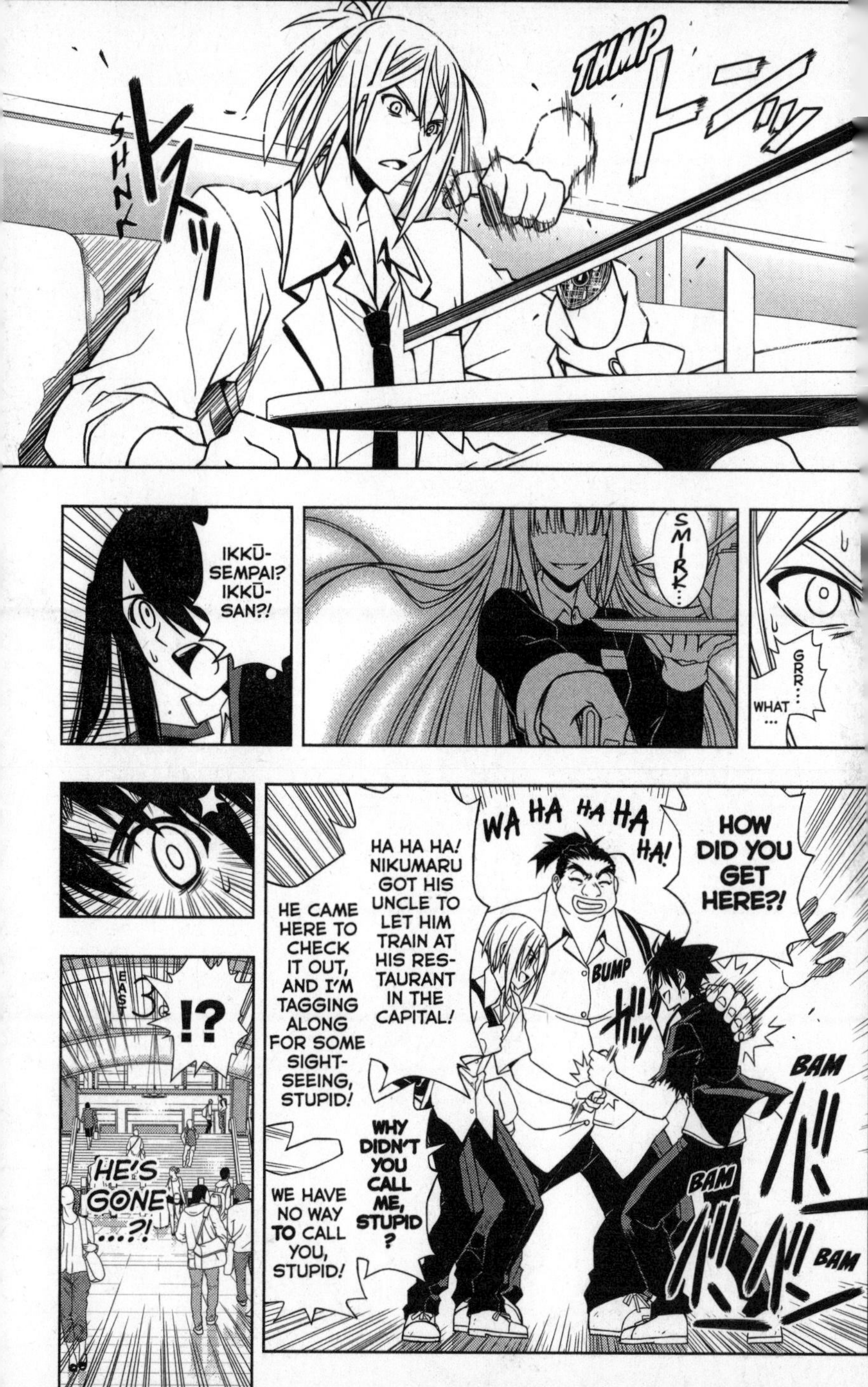
THMP
SHNK
GRR...
WHAT...
SMIRK...
IKKŪ-SEMPAI? IKKŪ-SAN?!
HOW DID YOU GET HERE?!
WA HA HA HA HA HA!
HA HA HA! NIKUMARU GOT HIS UNCLE TO LET HIM TRAIN AT HIS RES-TAURANT IN THE CAPITAL!
HE CAME HERE TO CHECK IT OUT, AND I'M TAGGING ALONG FOR SOME SIGHT-SEEING, STUPID!
BUMP
BAM
BAM
BAM
WHY DIDN'T YOU CALL ME, STUPID?
WE HAVE NO WAY TO CALL YOU, STUPID!
EAST 3
!?
HE'S GONE...?!

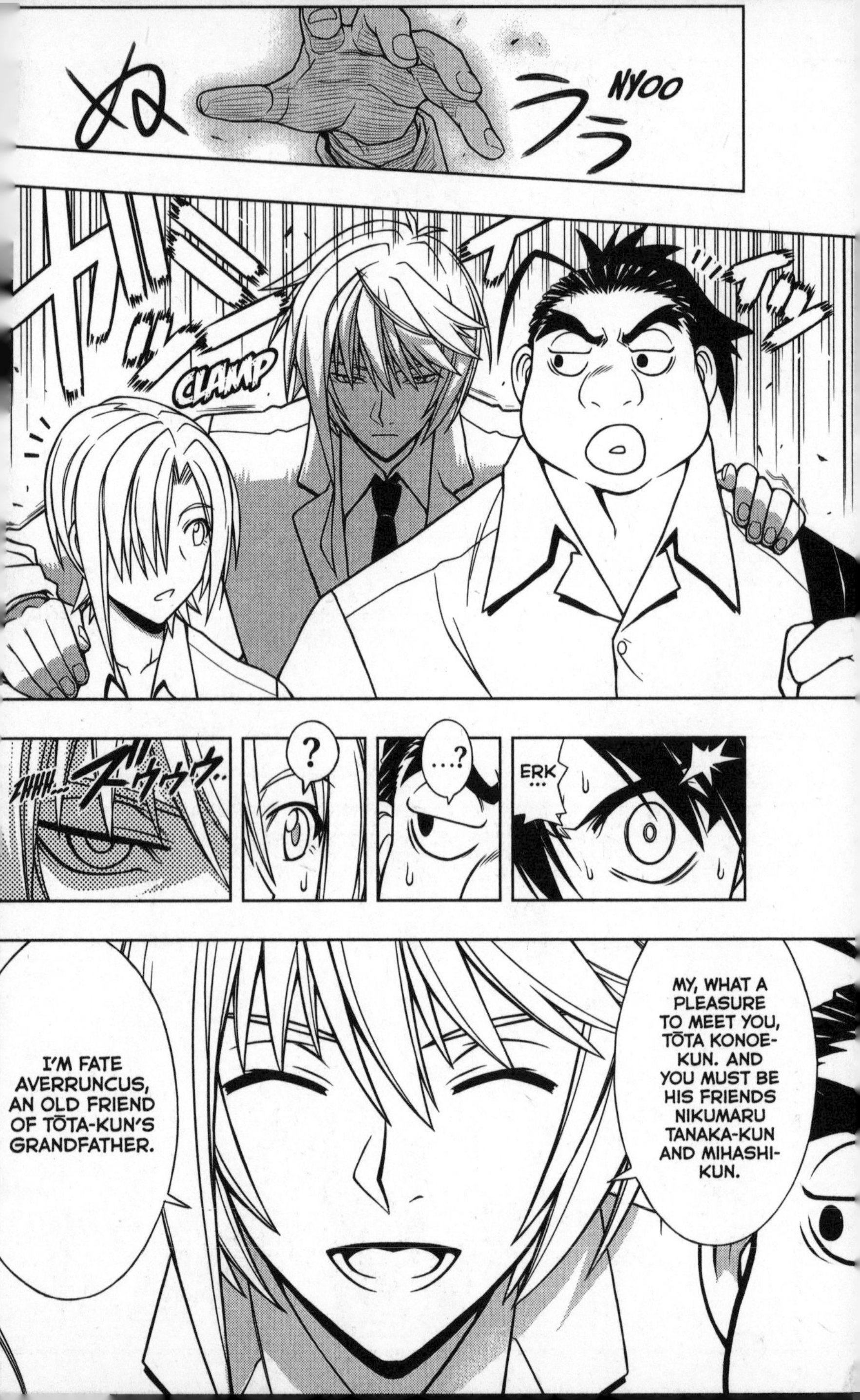
NYOO
CLAMP
ERK...
...?
?
ZHHH...
MY, WHAT A PLEASURE TO MEET YOU, TŌTA KONOE-KUN. AND YOU MUST BE HIS FRIENDS NIKUMARU TANAKA-KUN AND MIHASHI-KUN.
I'M FATE AVERRUNCUS, AN OLD FRIEND OF TŌTA-KUN'S GRANDFATHER.

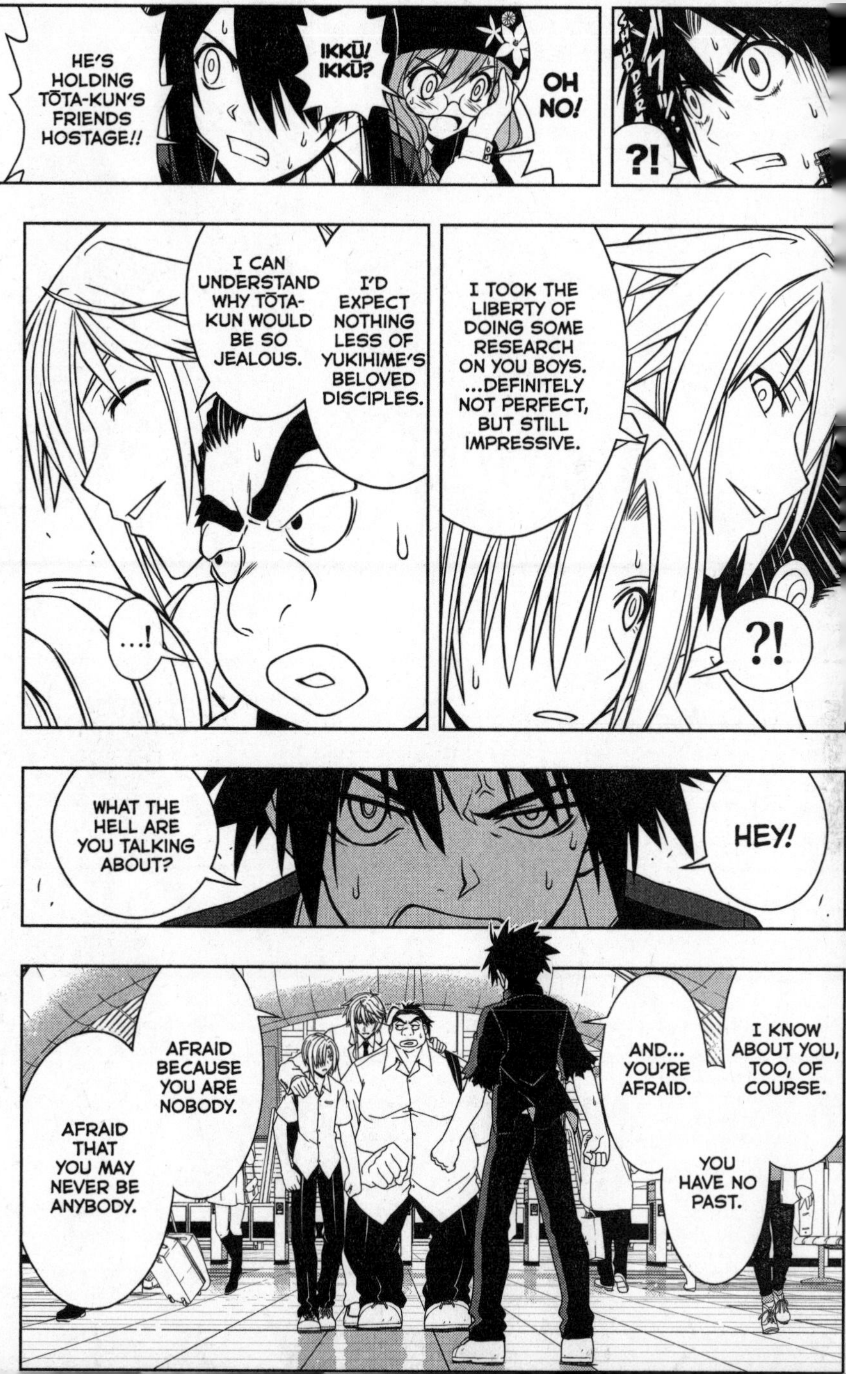
SHUDDER
?!
OH NO!
IKKŪ! IKKŪ?
HE'S HOLDING TŌTA-KUN'S FRIENDS HOSTAGE!!
I TOOK THE LIBERTY OF DOING SOME RESEARCH ON YOU BOYS. ...DEFINITELY NOT PERFECT, BUT STILL IMPRESSIVE.
?!
I'D EXPECT NOTHING LESS OF YUKIHIME'S BELOVED DISCIPLES.
I CAN UNDERSTAND WHY TŌTA-KUN WOULD BE SO JEALOUS.
...!
HEY!
WHAT THE HELL ARE YOU TALKING ABOUT?
I KNOW ABOUT YOU, TOO, OF COURSE.
AND... YOU'RE AFRAID.
YOU HAVE NO PAST.
AFRAID BECAUSE YOU ARE NOBODY.
AFRAID THAT YOU MAY NEVER BE ANYBODY.

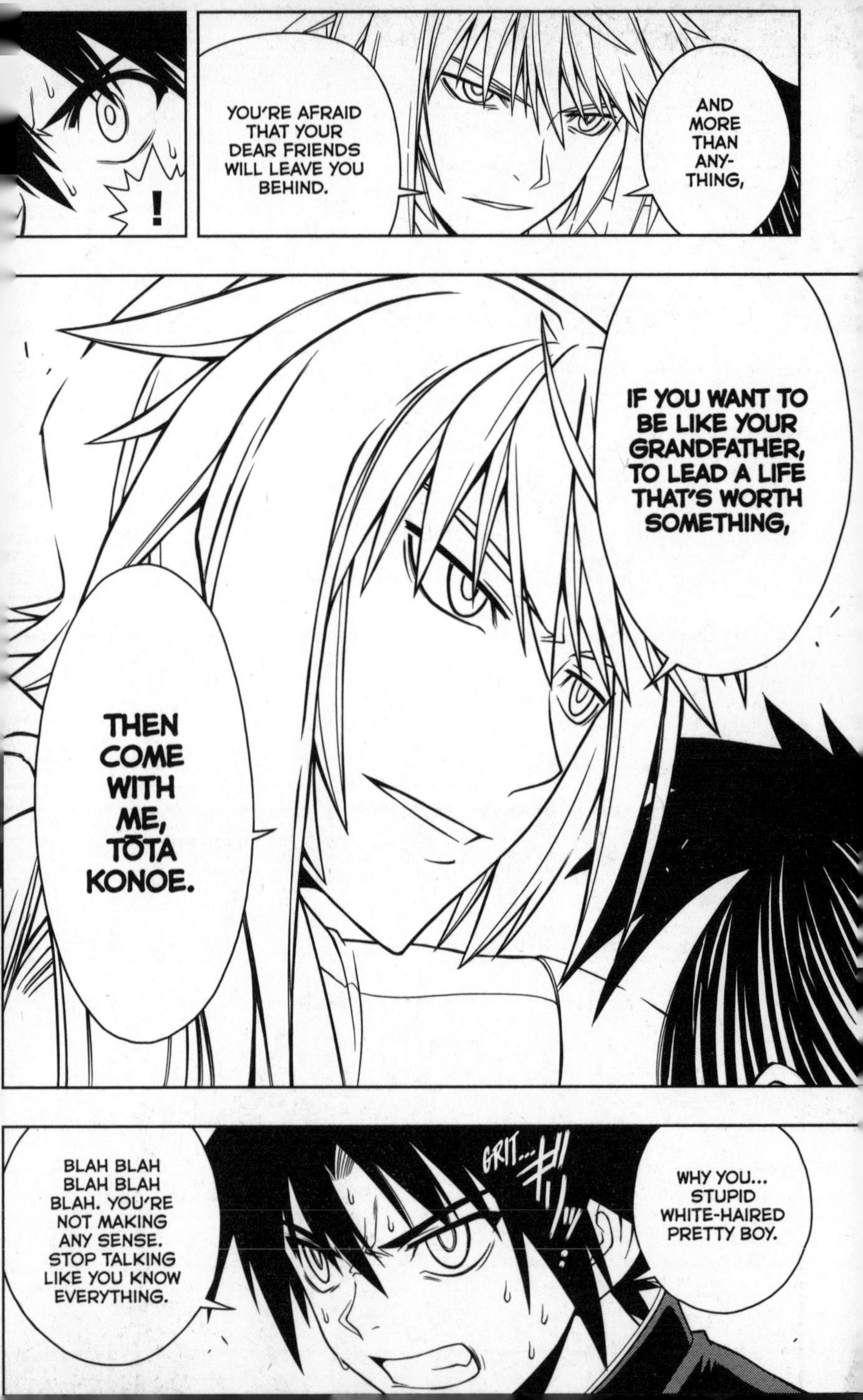
YOU'RE AFRAID THAT YOUR DEAR FRIENDS WILL LEAVE YOU BEHIND.
AND MORE THAN ANY-THING,
!
IF YOU WANT TO BE LIKE YOUR GRANDFATHER, TO LEAD A LIFE THAT'S WORTH SOMETHING,
THEN COME WITH ME, TŌTA KONOE.
WHY YOU... STUPID WHITE-HAIRED PRETTY BOY.
GRIT...
BLAH BLAH BLAH BLAH BLAH. YOU'RE NOT MAKING ANY SENSE. STOP TALKING LIKE YOU KNOW EVERYTHING.

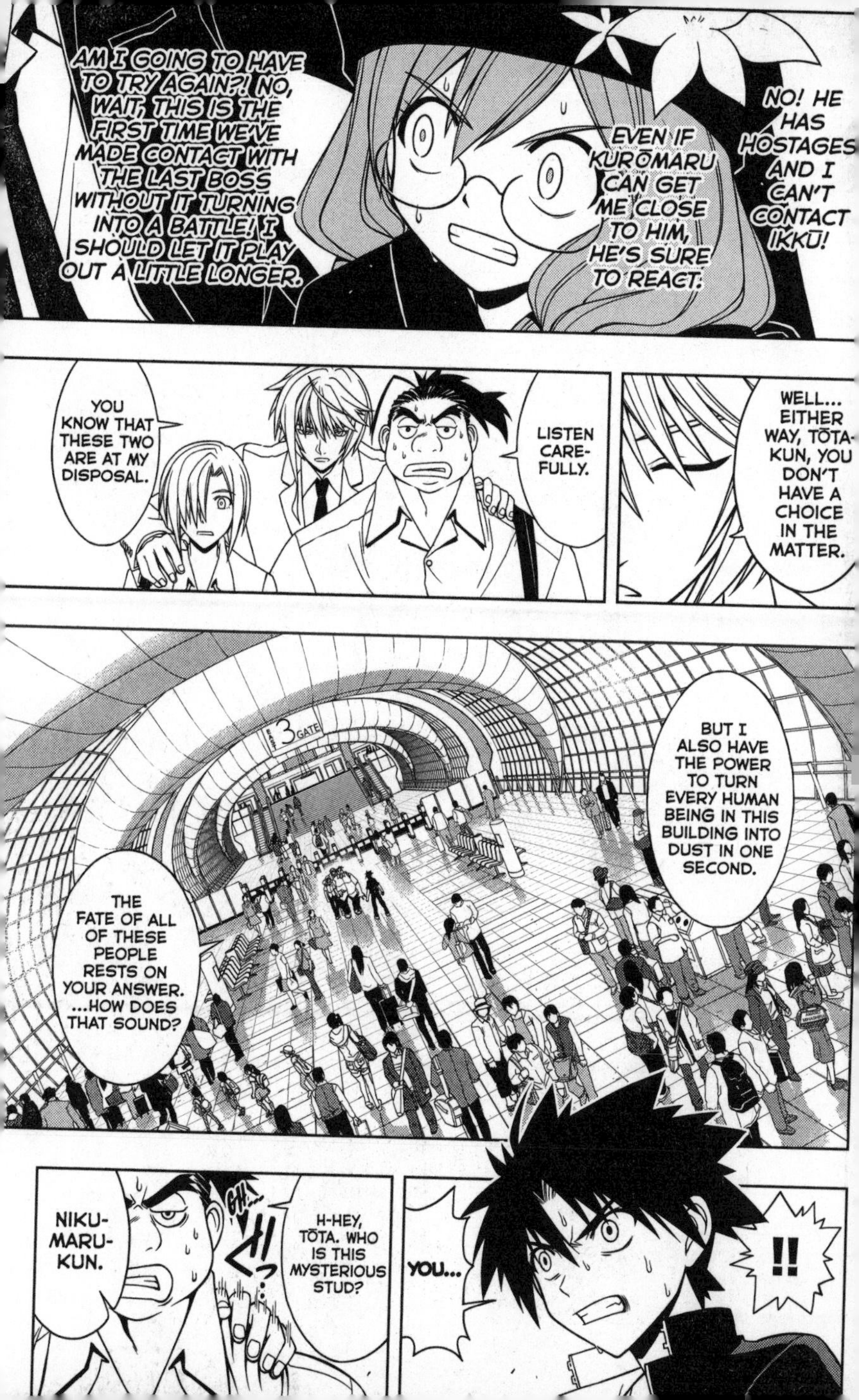
NO! HE HAS HOSTAGES AND I CAN'T CONTACT IKKŪ!
EVEN IF KURŌMARU CAN GET ME CLOSE TO HIM, HE'S SURE TO REACT.
AM I GOING TO HAVE TO TRY AGAIN?! NO, WAIT, THIS IS THE FIRST TIME WE'VE MADE CONTACT WITH THE LAST BOSS WITHOUT IT TURNING INTO A BATTLE! I SHOULD LET IT PLAY OUT A LITTLE LONGER.
WELL... EITHER WAY, TŌTA-KUN, YOU DON'T HAVE A CHOICE IN THE MATTER.
LISTEN CARE-FULLY.
YOU KNOW THAT THESE TWO ARE AT MY DISPOSAL.
3 GATE
BUT I ALSO HAVE THE POWER TO TURN EVERY HUMAN BEING IN THIS BUILDING INTO DUST IN ONE SECOND.
THE FATE OF ALL OF THESE PEOPLE RESTS ON YOUR ANSWER. ...HOW DOES THAT SOUND?
!!
YOU...
H-HEY, TŌTA. WHO IS THIS MYSTERIOUS STUD?
GH!...
NIKU-MARU-KUN.

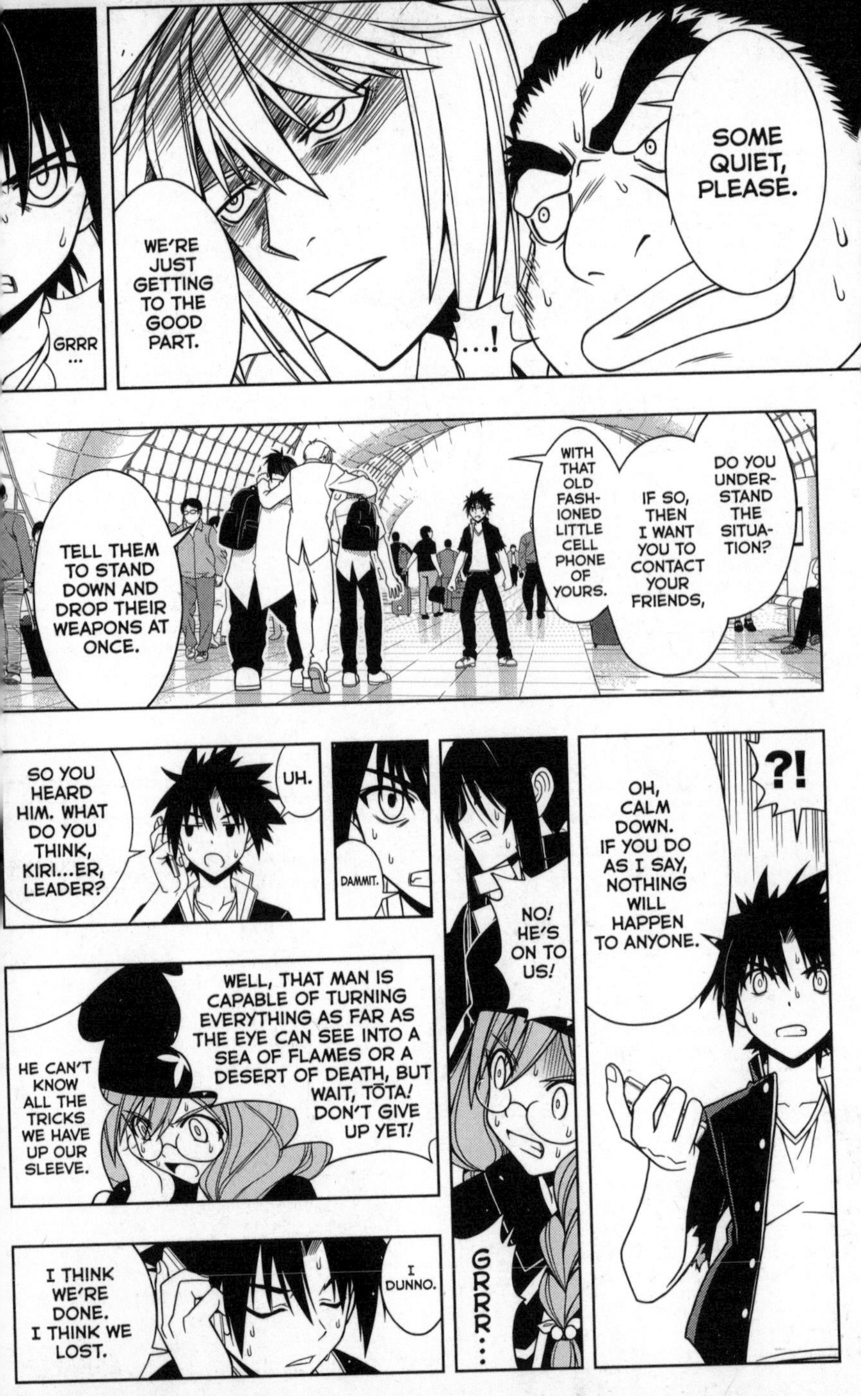
SOME QUIET, PLEASE.
...!
WE'RE JUST GETTING TO THE GOOD PART.
GRRR...
DO YOU UNDERSTAND THE SITUATION?
IF SO, THEN I WANT YOU TO CONTACT YOUR FRIENDS,
WITH THAT OLD FASHIONED LITTLE CELL PHONE OF YOURS.
TELL THEM TO STAND DOWN AND DROP THEIR WEAPONS AT ONCE.
?!
OH, CALM DOWN. IF YOU DO AS I SAY, NOTHING WILL HAPPEN TO ANYONE.
NO! HE'S ON TO US!
GRRR...
DAMMIT.
UH.
SO YOU HEARD HIM. WHAT DO YOU THINK, KIRI...ER, LEADER?
WELL, THAT MAN IS CAPABLE OF TURNING EVERYTHING AS FAR AS THE EYE CAN SEE INTO A SEA OF FLAMES OR A DESERT OF DEATH, BUT WAIT, TŌTA! DON'T GIVE UP YET!
HE CAN'T KNOW ALL THE TRICKS WE HAVE UP OUR SLEEVE.
I DUNNO.
I THINK WE'RE DONE. I THINK WE LOST.

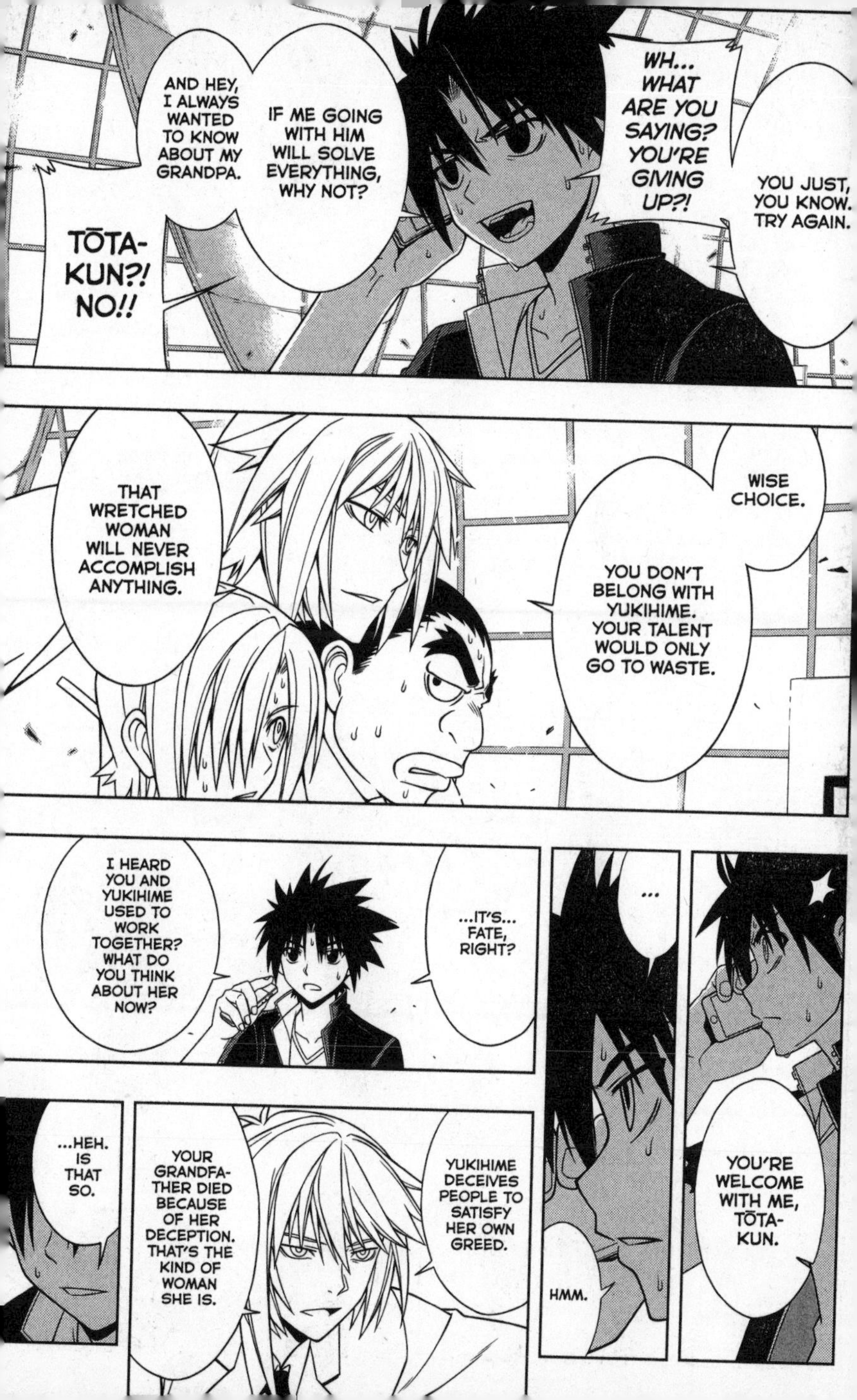
YOU JUST, YOU KNOW. TRY AGAIN.
WH... WHAT ARE YOU SAYING? YOU'RE GIVING UP?!
IF ME GOING WITH HIM WILL SOLVE EVERYTHING, WHY NOT?
AND HEY, I ALWAYS WANTED TO KNOW ABOUT MY GRANDPA.
TŌTA-KUN?! NO!!
WISE CHOICE.
YOU DON'T BELONG WITH YUKIHIME. YOUR TALENT WOULD ONLY GO TO WASTE.
THAT WRETCHED WOMAN WILL NEVER ACCOMPLISH ANYTHING.
YOU'RE WELCOME WITH ME, TŌTA-KUN.
...
HMM.
...IT'S... FATE, RIGHT?
I HEARD YOU AND YUKIHIME USED TO WORK TOGETHER? WHAT DO YOU THINK ABOUT HER NOW?
YUKIHIME DECEIVES PEOPLE TO SATISFY HER OWN GREED.
YOUR GRANDFA-THER DIED BECAUSE OF HER DECEPTION. THAT'S THE KIND OF WOMAN SHE IS.
...HEH. IS THAT SO.

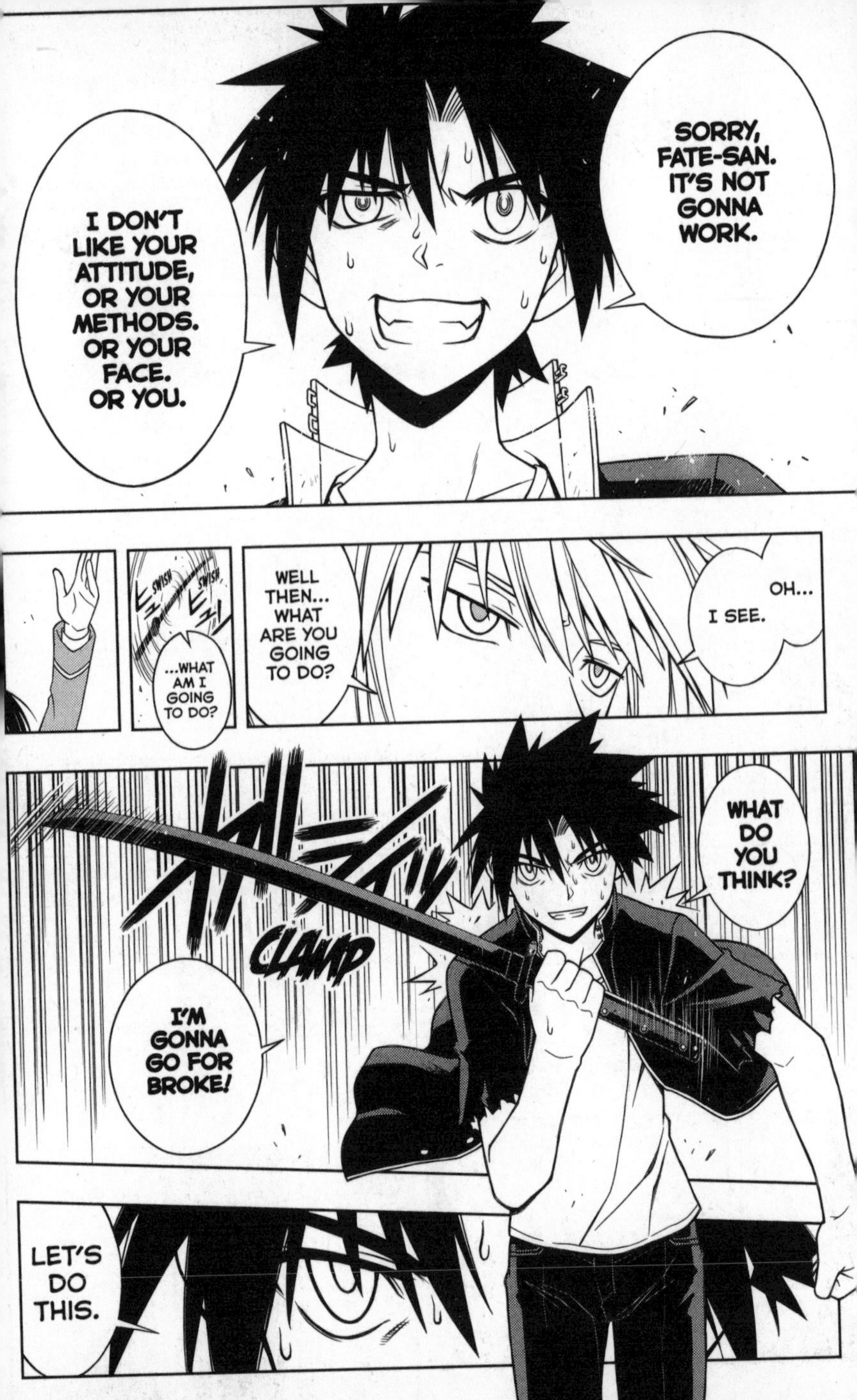
SORRY, FATE-SAN. IT'S NOT GONNA WORK.
I DON'T LIKE YOUR ATTITUDE, OR YOUR METHODS. OR YOUR FACE. OR YOU.
OH... I SEE.
WELL THEN... WHAT ARE YOU GOING TO DO?
SWISH
SWISH
...WHAT AM I GOING TO DO?
WHAT DO YOU THINK?
CLAMP
I'M GONNA GO FOR BROKE!
LET'S DO THIS.

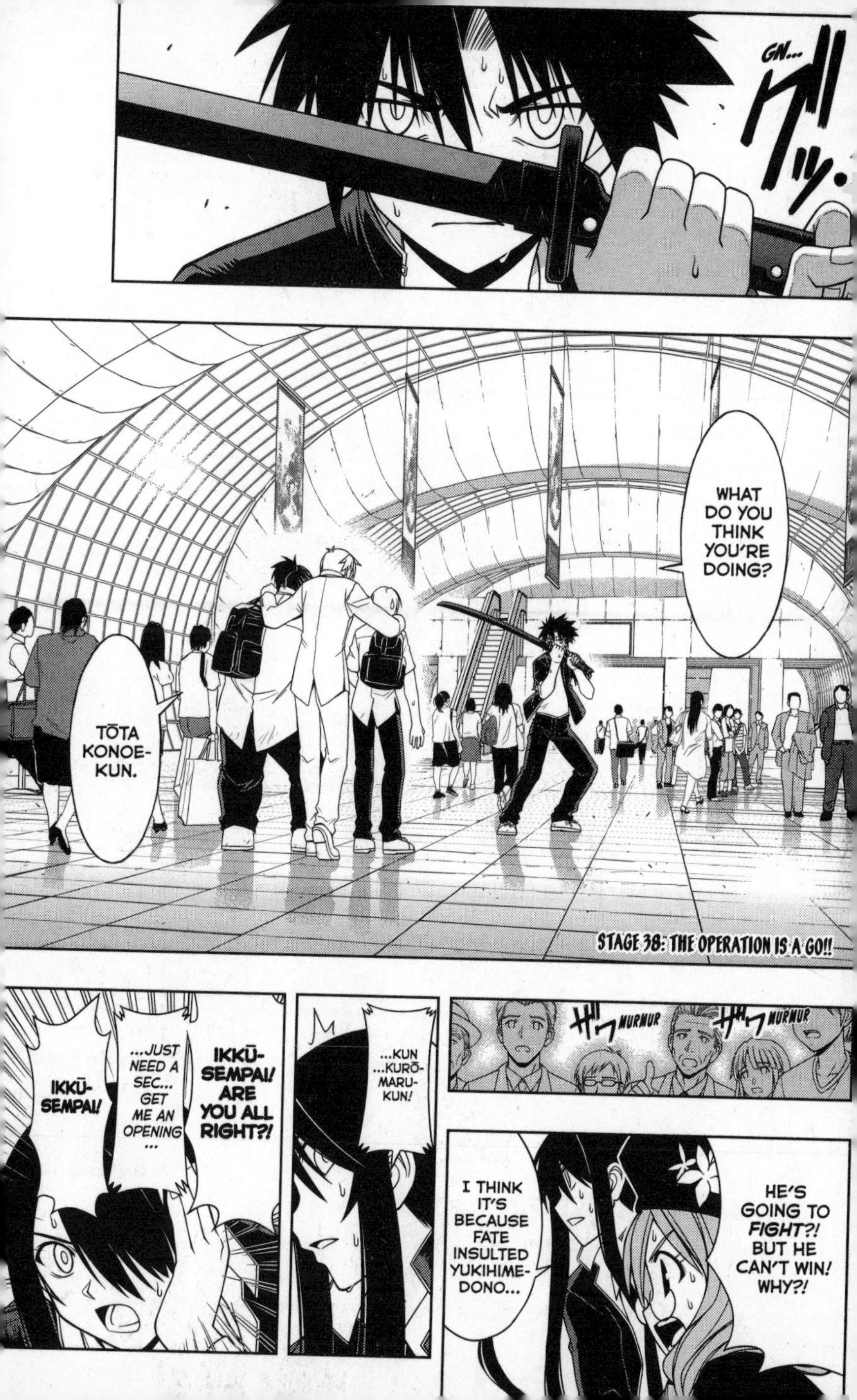
GN...
WHAT DO YOU THINK YOU'RE DOING?
TŌTA KONOE-KUN.
STAGE 38: THE OPERATION IS A GO!!
MURMUR
MURMUR
HE'S GOING TO *FIGHT*?! BUT HE CAN'T WIN! WHY?!
I THINK IT'S BECAUSE FATE INSULTED YUKIHIME-DONO...
...KUN ...KURŌ-MARU-KUN!
IKKŪ-SEMPAI! ARE YOU ALL RIGHT?!
...JUST NEED A SEC... GET ME AN OPENING...
IKKŪ-SEMPAI!

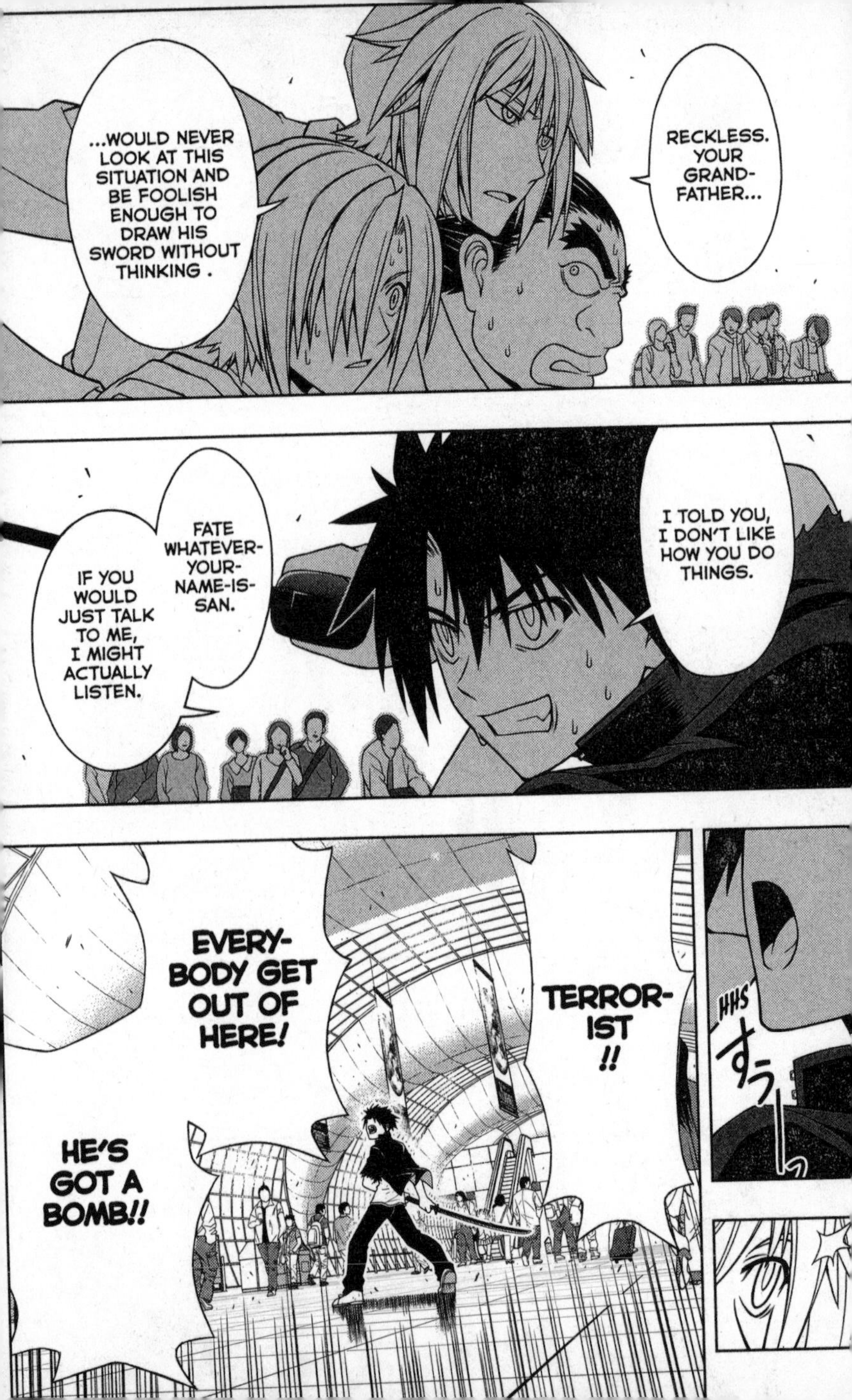
RECKLESS. YOUR GRAND-FATHER...
...WOULD NEVER LOOK AT THIS SITUATION AND BE FOOLISH ENOUGH TO DRAW HIS SWORD WITHOUT THINKING .
I TOLD YOU, I DON'T LIKE HOW YOU DO THINGS.
FATE WHATEVER-YOUR-NAME-IS-SAN.
IF YOU WOULD JUST TALK TO ME, I MIGHT ACTUALLY LISTEN.
HHS
TERROR-IST!!
EVERY-BODY GET OUT OF HERE!
HE'S GOT A BOMB!!

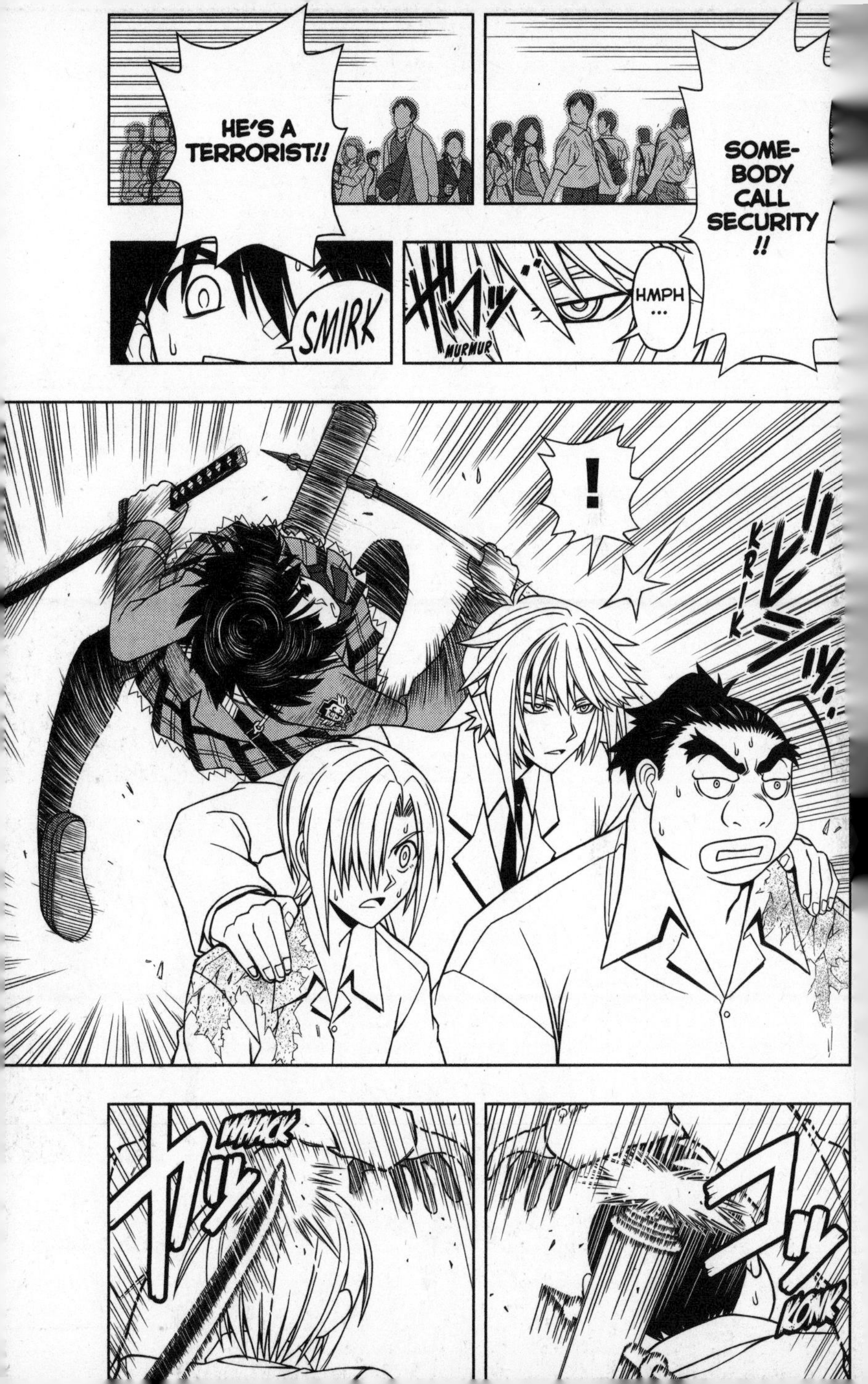
SOME-
BODY
CALL
SECURITY
!!
HE'S A
TERRORIST!!
HMPH
...
MURMUR
SMIRK
!
KRIK
KONK
WHACK

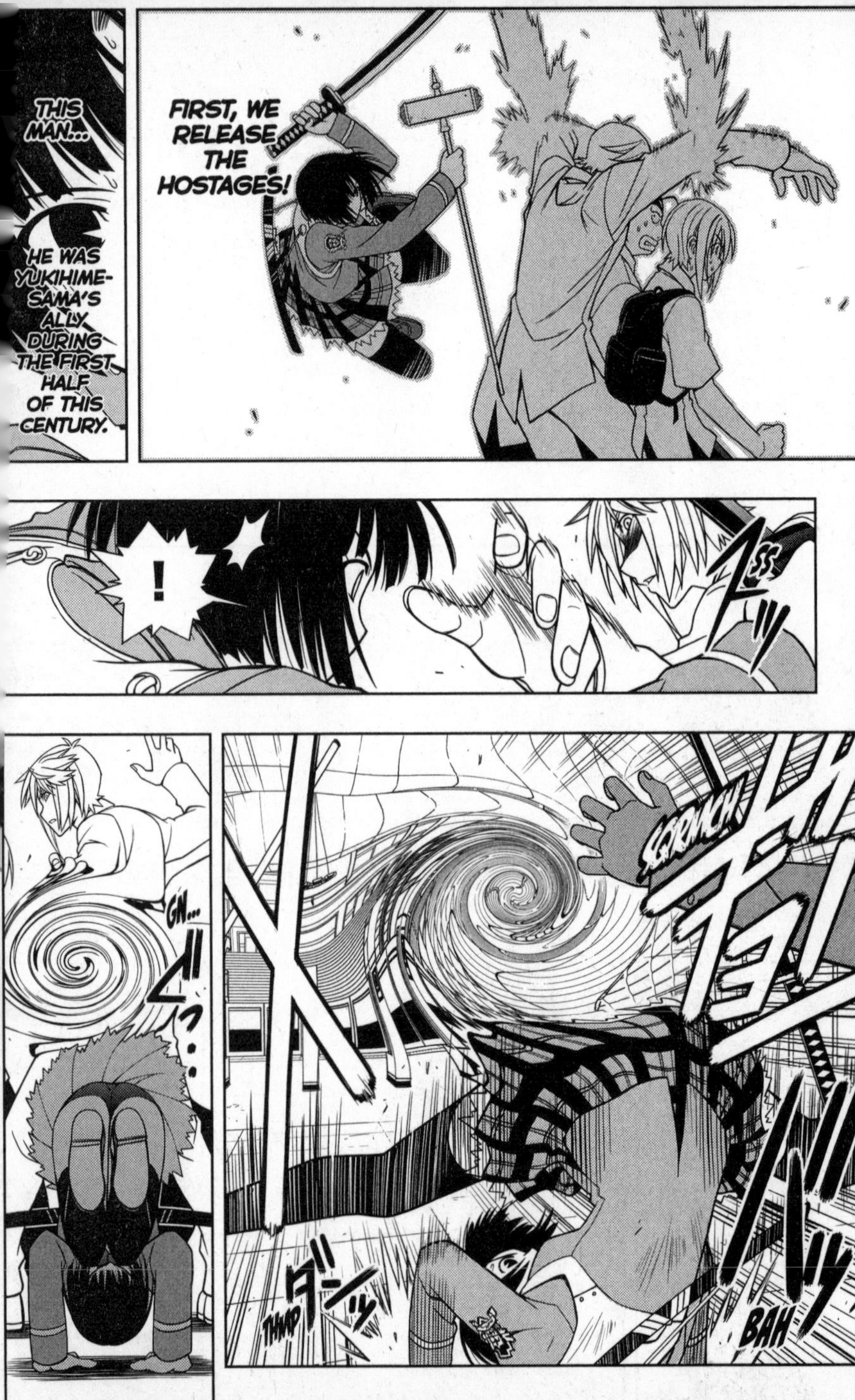
FIRST, WE RELEASE THE HOSTAGES!
THIS MAN...
HE WAS YUKIHIME-SAMA'S ALLY DURING THE FIRST HALF OF THIS CENTURY.
!
SS
SCRUNCH
BAH
THMP
GN...

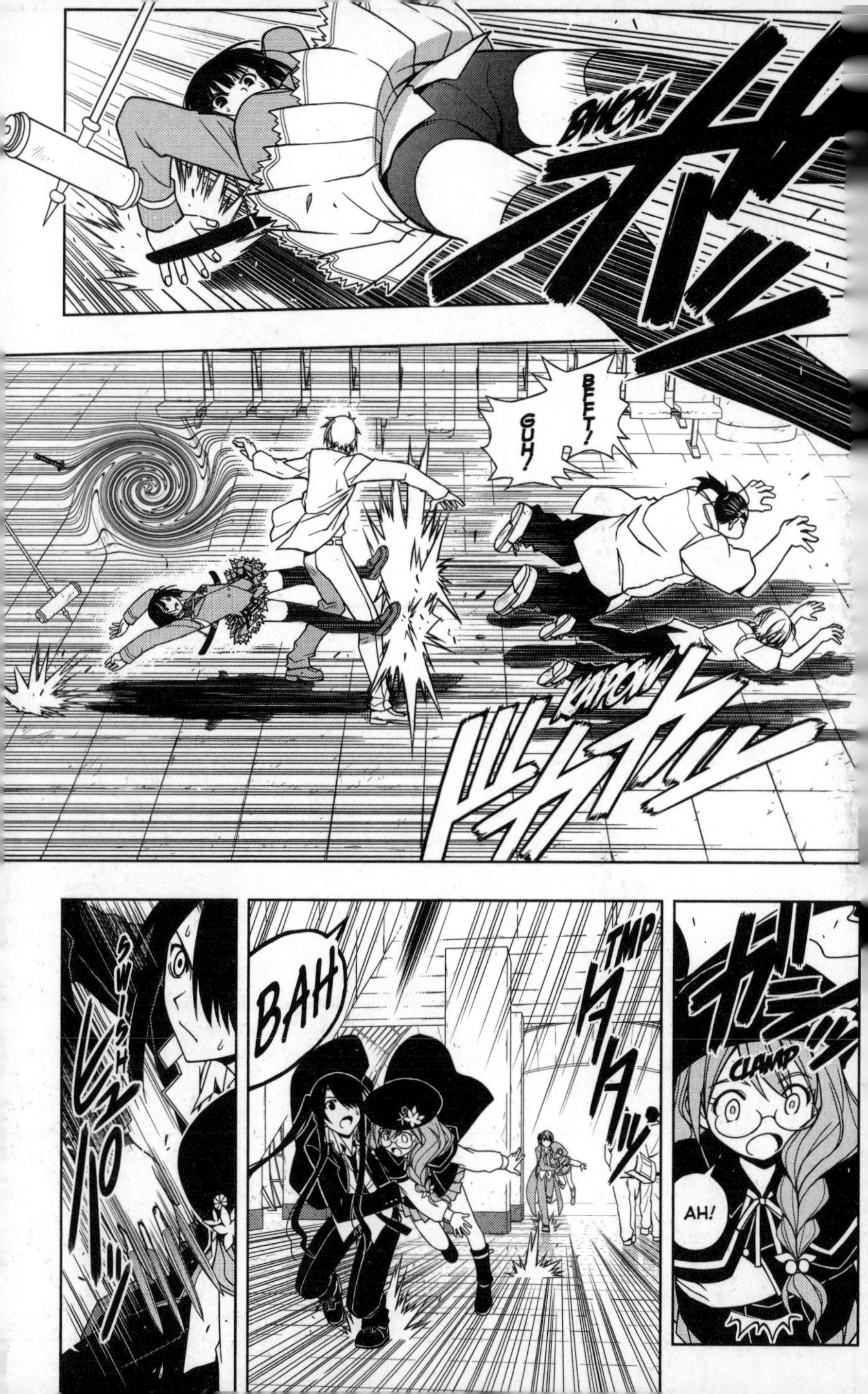
BWOH
BEFT!
GUH!
KAPOW
CLAMP
AH!
TMP
BAH
SWISH

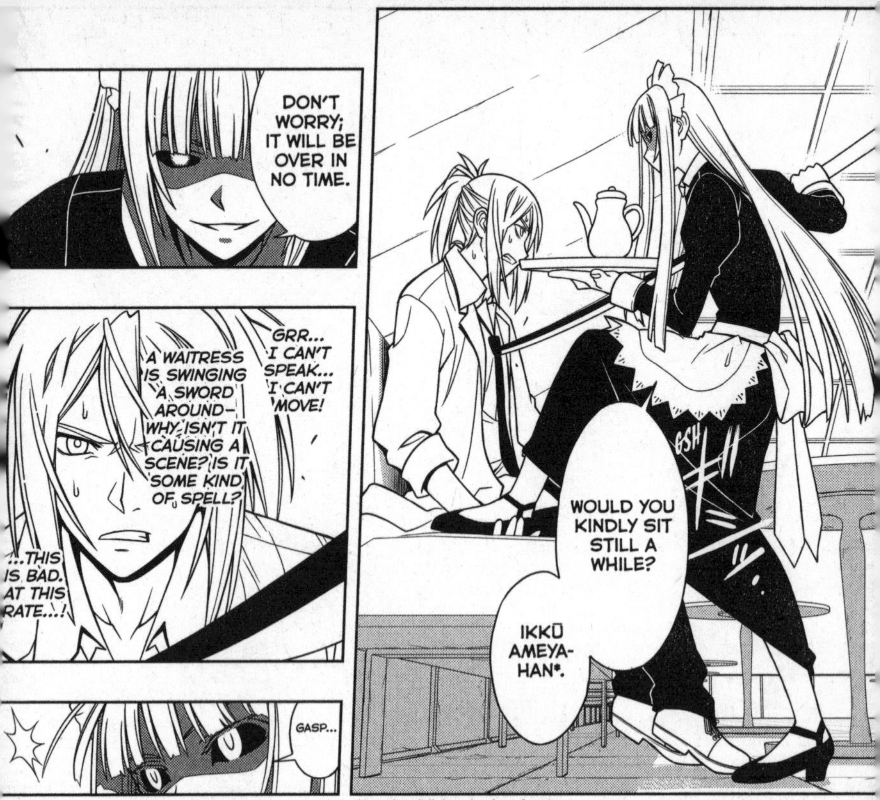
GSH
WOULD YOU KINDLY SIT STILL A WHILE?
IKKŪ AMEYA-HAN*.
DON'T WORRY; IT WILL BE OVER IN NO TIME.
GRR... I CAN'T SPEAK... I CAN'T MOVE!
A WAITRESS IS SWINGING A SWORD AROUND—WHY ISN'T IT CAUSING A SCENE? IS IT SOME KIND OF SPELL?
...THIS IS BAD. AT THIS RATE...!
GASP...

*A regional dialect version of -san.

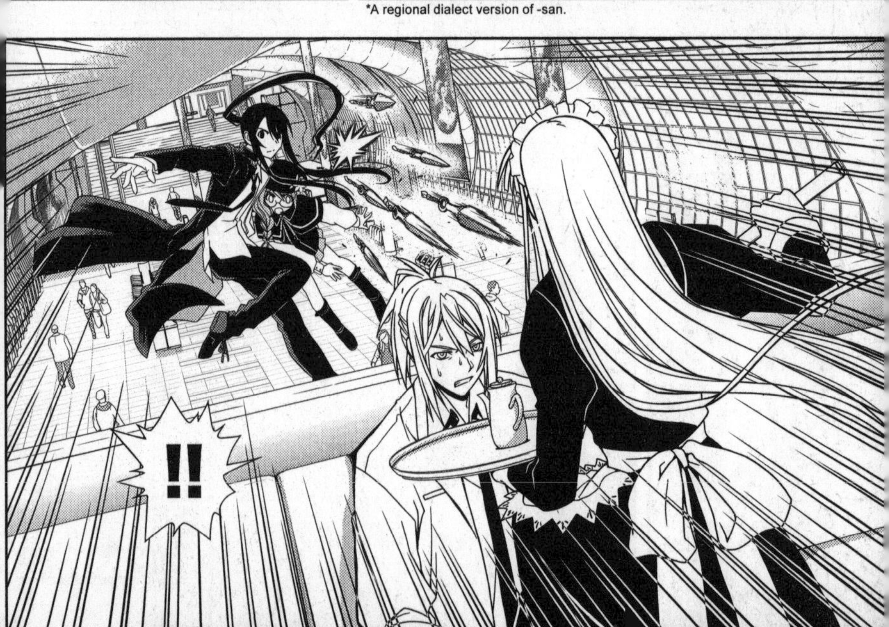
!!

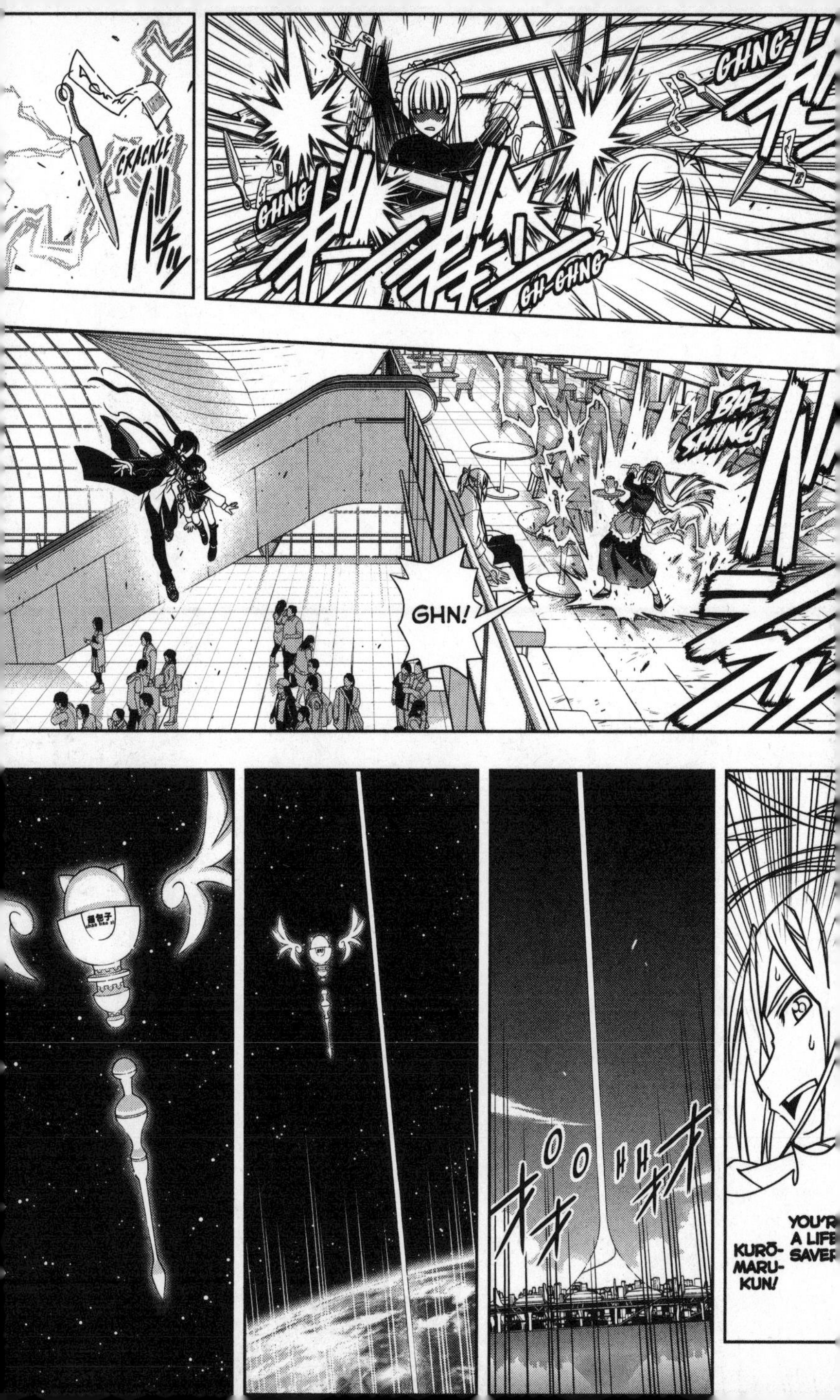
GHNG
GHNG
GH-GHNG
CRACKLE
BA-SHING
GHN!
YOU'R A LIFE SAVER
KURŌ-MARU-KUN!

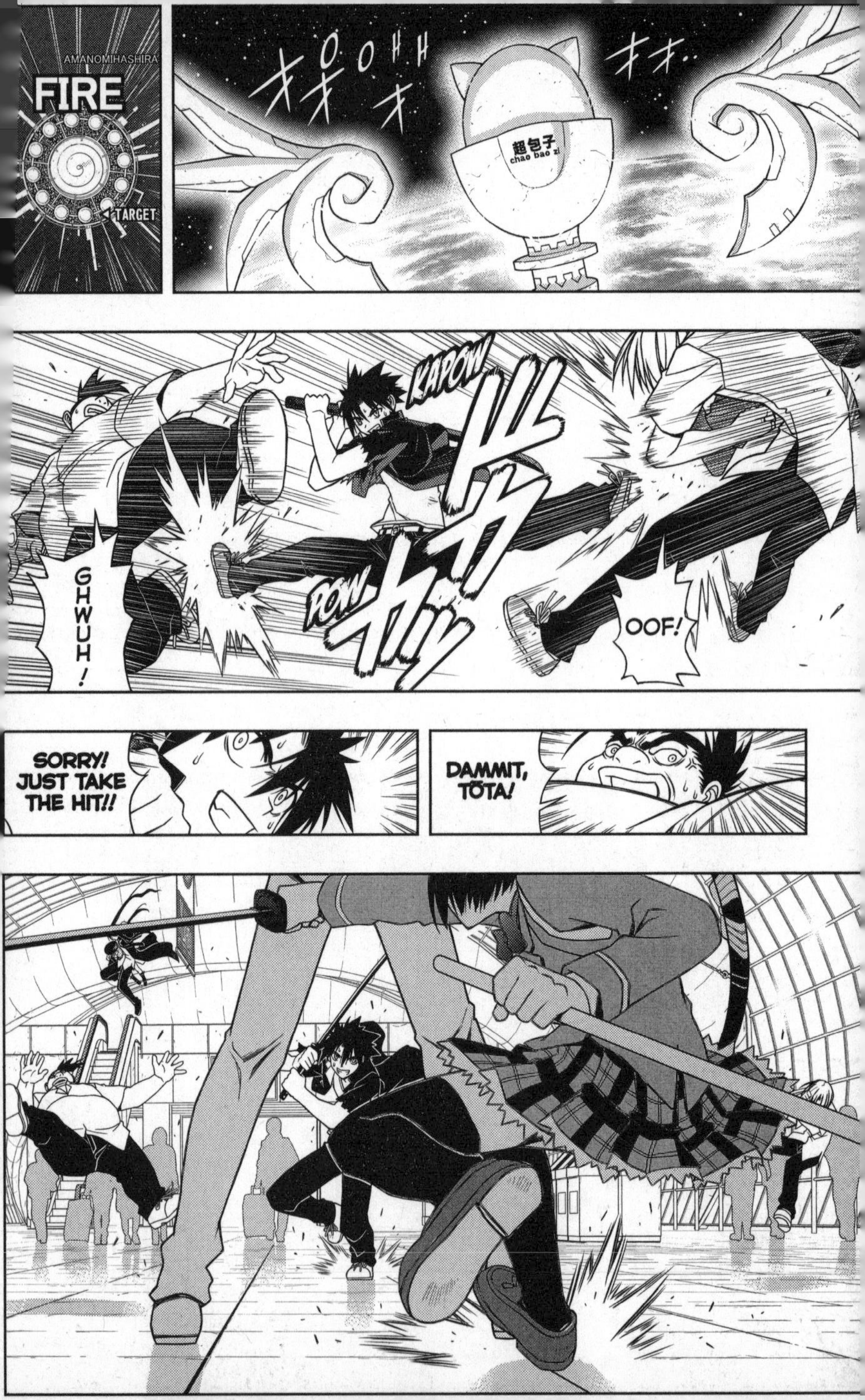

OOHH
超包子
chao bao zi
AMANOMIHASHIRA
FIRE
TARGET
KAPOW
POW
GHWUH!
OOF!
DAMMIT, TŌTA!
SORRY! JUST TAKE THE HIT!!

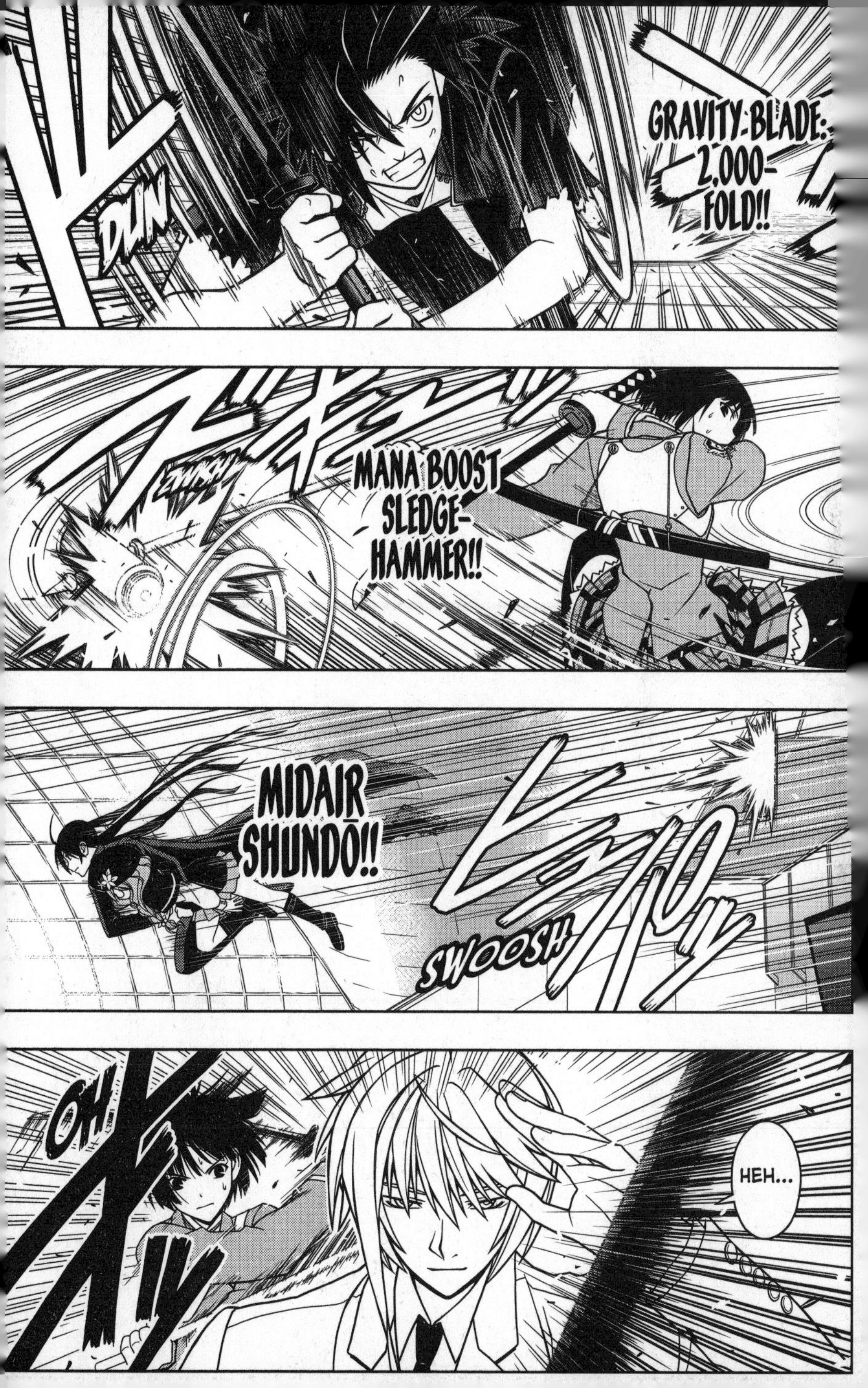
DUN
GRAVITY BLADE: 2,000-FOLD!!
ZWMCH
MANA BOOST SLEDGE-HAMMER!!
MIDAIR SHUNDŌ!!
SWOOSH
OH
HEH...

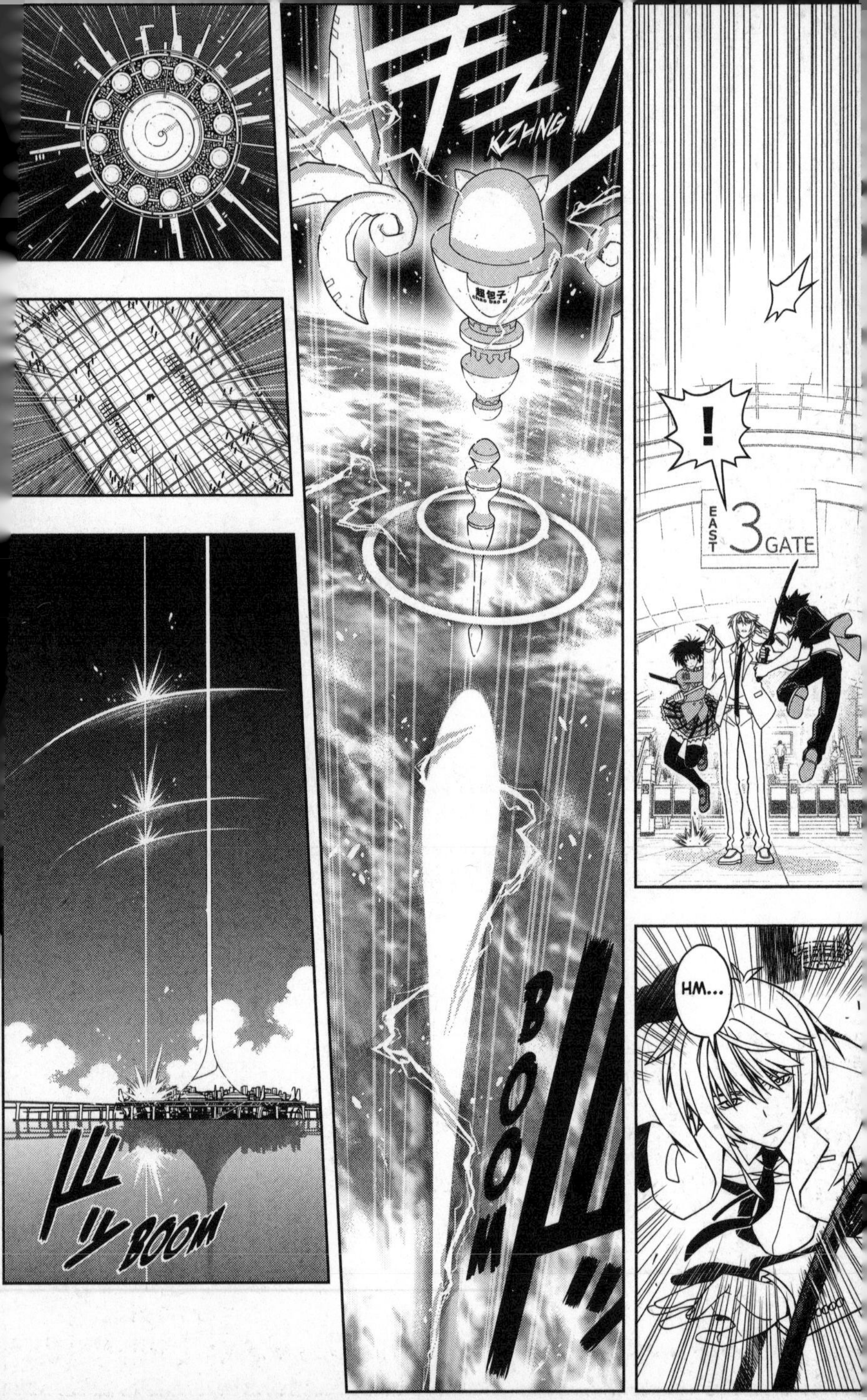
!
EAST 3 GATE
HM...
KZHNG
超包子
CHAO BAO ZI
BOOOOM
BOOM

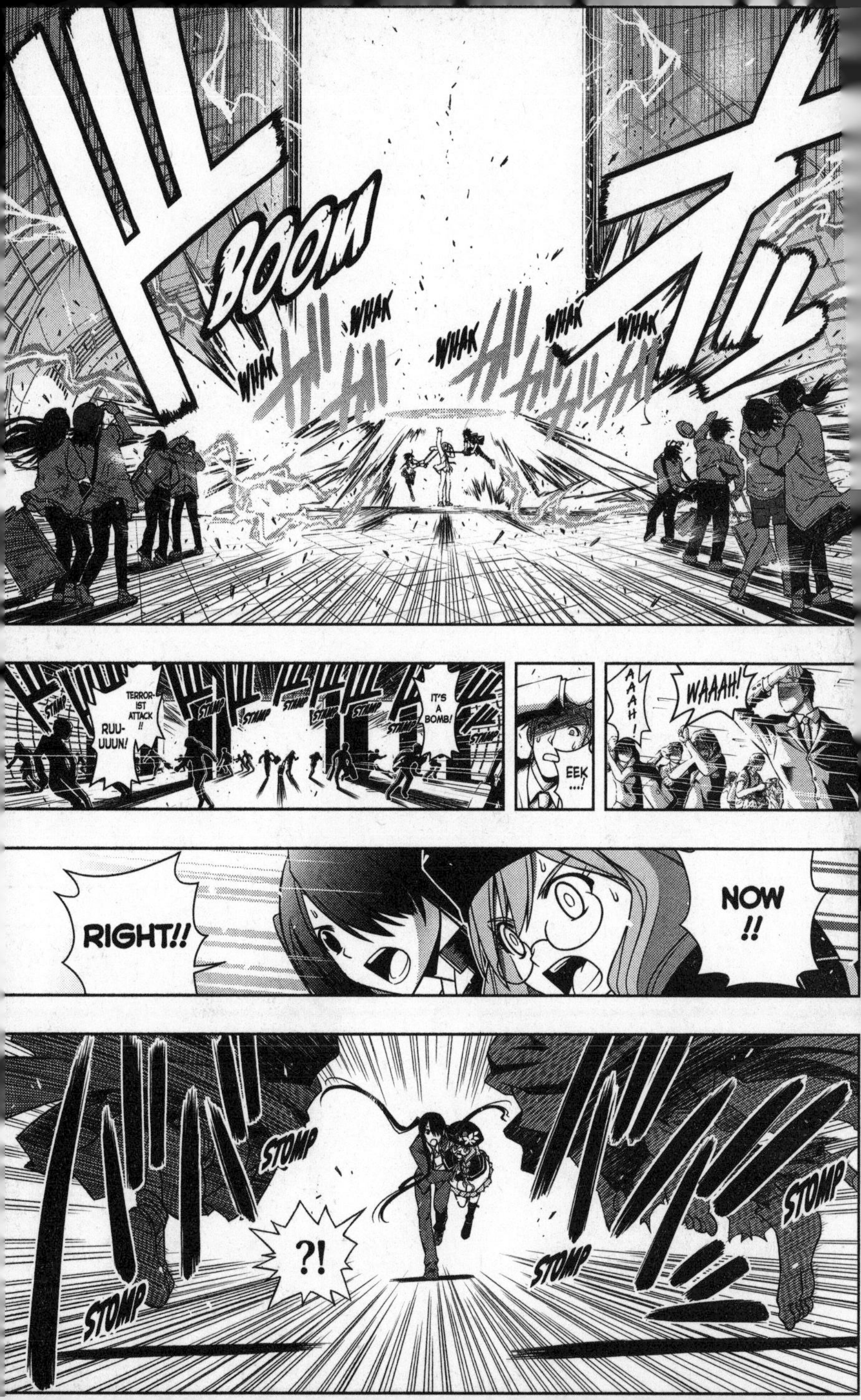

BOOM
WHAK
WHAK
WHAK
WHAK
WHAK
WAAAH!
AAAAH!
EEK...!
IT'S A BOMB!
STAMP
STAMP
STAMP
STAMP
STAMP
STAMP
STAMP
TERROR-IST ATTACK!!
RUU-UUUN!
STAMP
NOW!!
RIGHT!!
STOMP
STOMP
STOMP
?!
STOMP

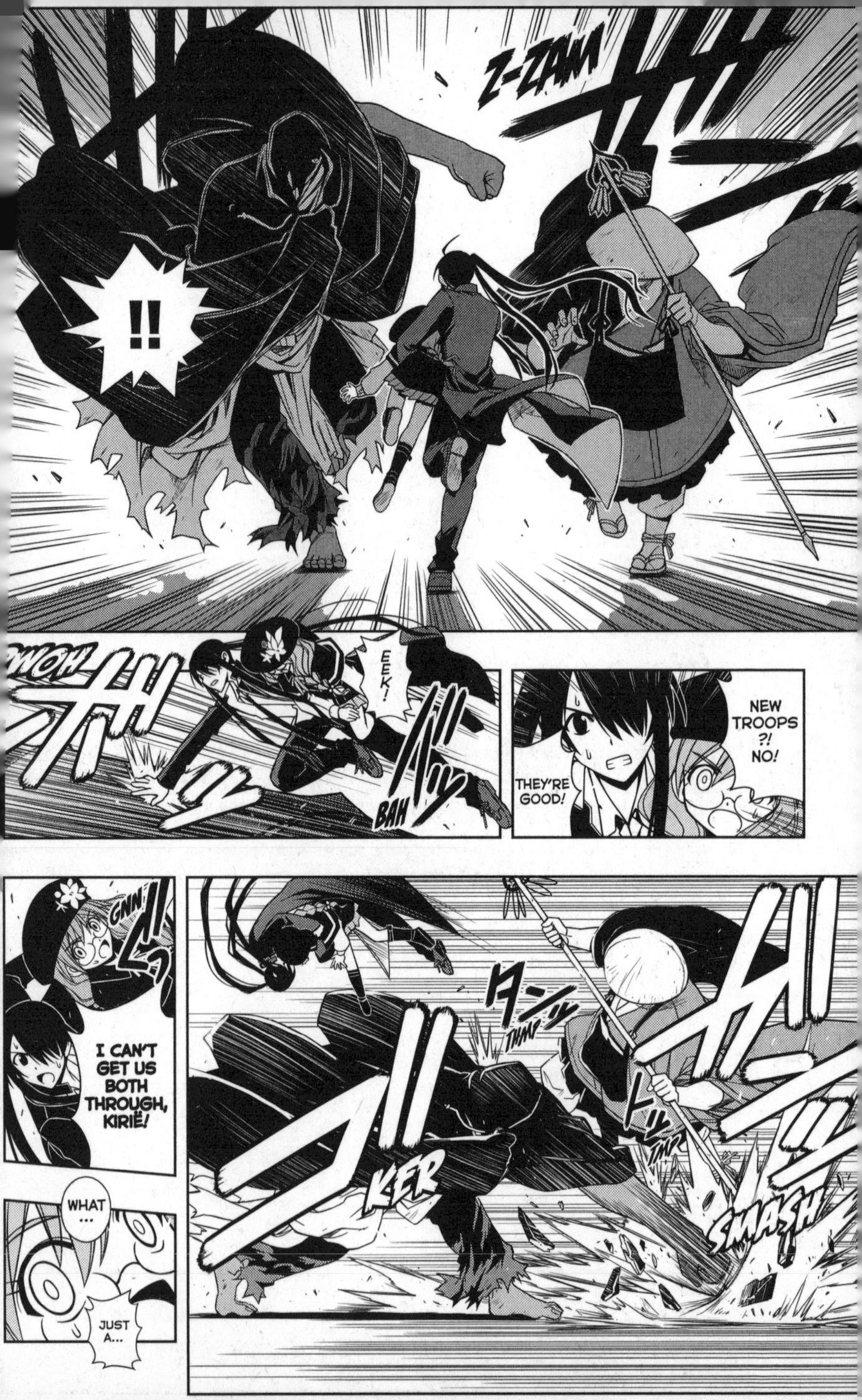
Z-ZAAAAH
!!
NEW TROOPS ?! NO!
THEY'RE GOOD!
EEK!
BAH
WOOOH
タン
THMP
KER
SMASH
I CAN'T GET US BOTH THROUGH, KIRIË!
GNN
WHAT ...
JUST A...

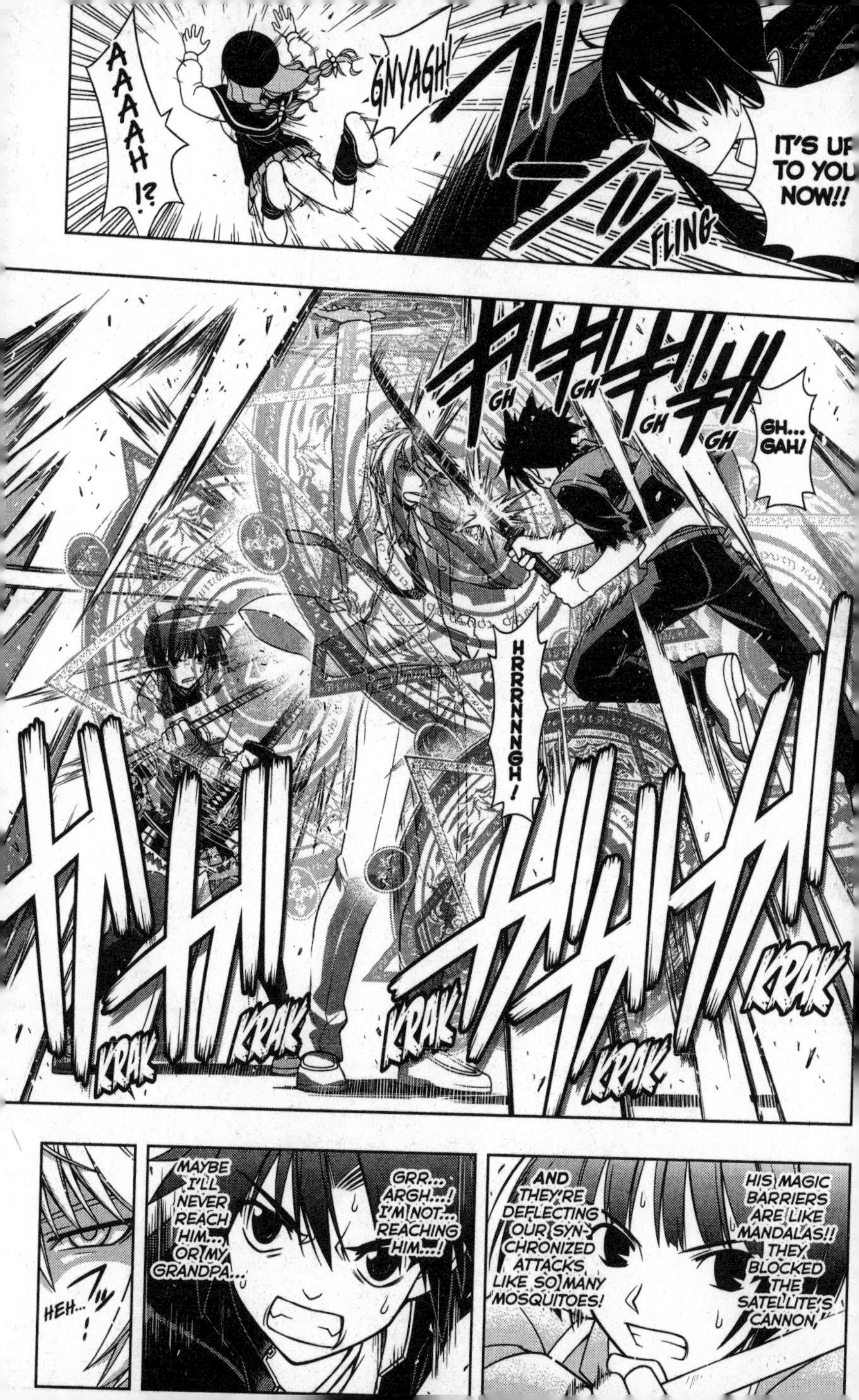
IT'S UP TO YOU NOW!!
GNYAGH!
FLING
AAAAAH!?
GH... GAH!
GH
GH
GH
GH
HRRRNNNGH!
KRAK
KRAK
KRAK
KRAK
KRAK
HIS MAGIC BARRIERS ARE LIKE MANDALAS!! THEY BLOCKED THE SATELLITE'S CANNON,
AND THEY'RE DEFLECTING OUR SYNCHRONIZED ATTACKS LIKE SO MANY MOSQUITOES!
GRR... ARGH...! I'M NOT... REACHING HIM...!
MAYBE I'LL NEVER REACH HIM... OR MY GRANDPA...
HEH...

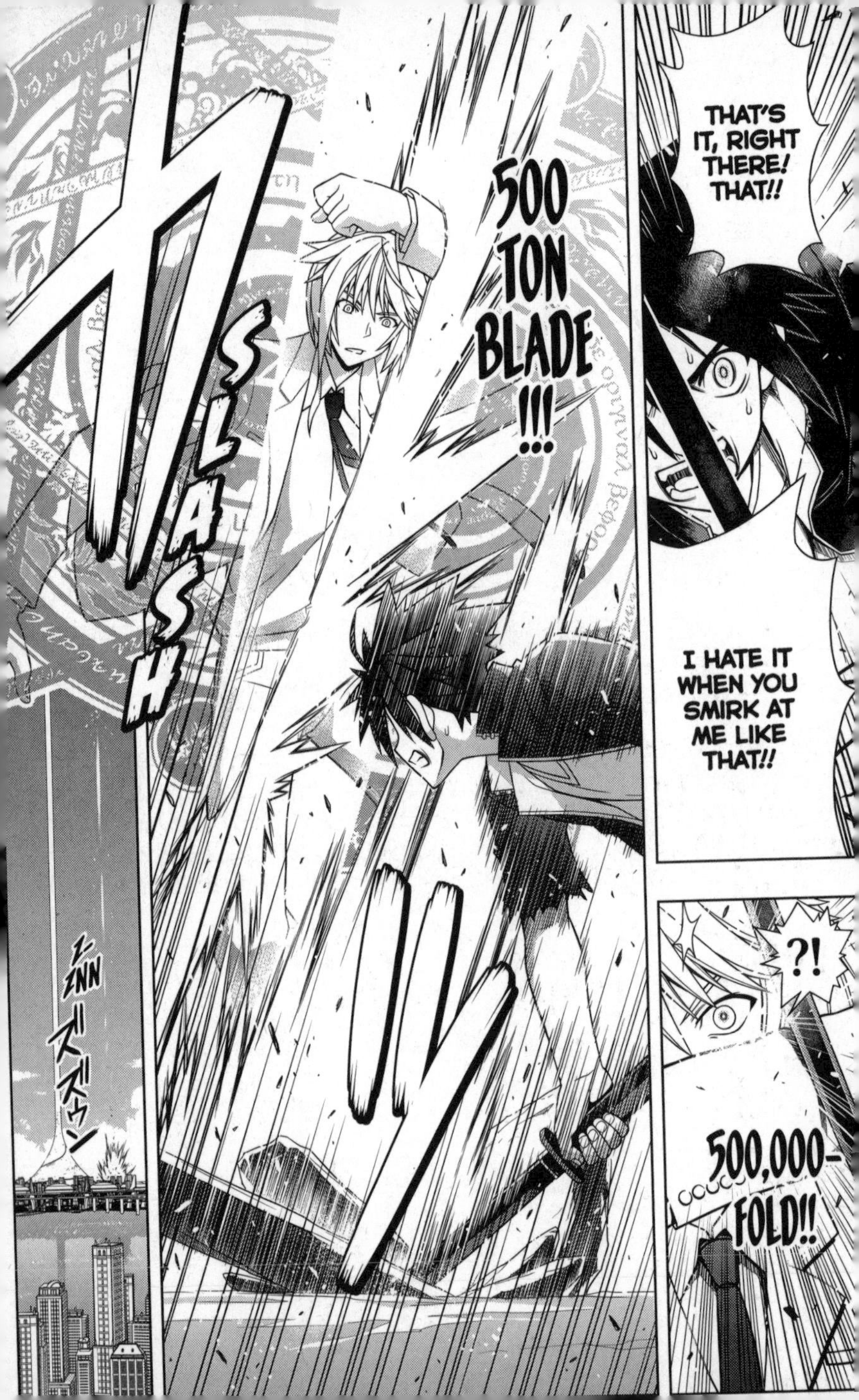
THAT'S IT, RIGHT THERE! THAT!!
I HATE IT WHEN YOU SMIRK AT ME LIKE THAT!!
?!
500,000-FOLD!!
500 TON BLADE!!!
SLASH
ZUNN
ズズウン

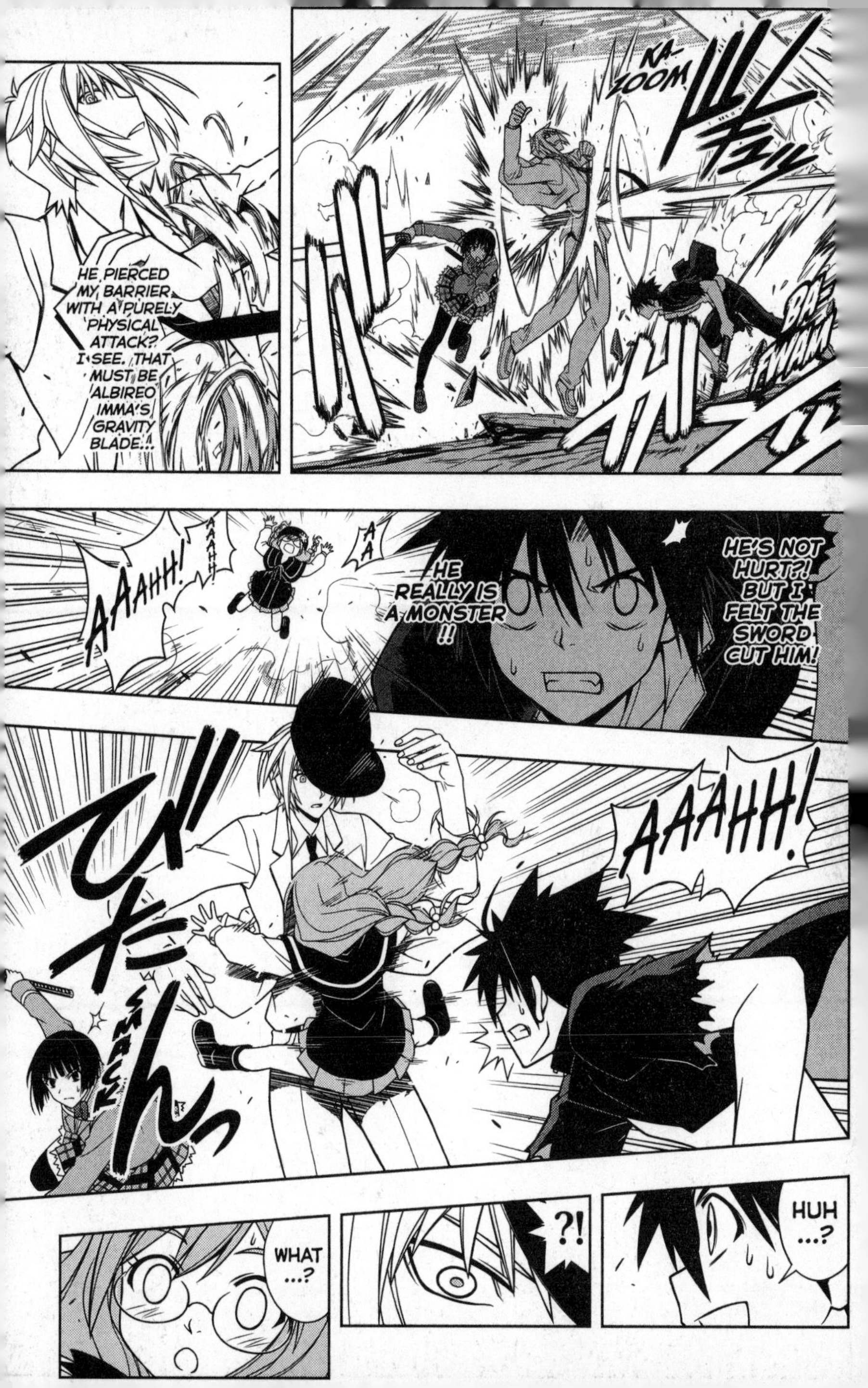
KA-ZOOM
BA-FWAM
HE PIERCED MY BARRIER WITH A PURELY PHYSICAL ATTACK? I SEE. THAT MUST BE ALBIREO IMMA'S GRAVITY BLADE...
HE'S NOT HURT?! BUT I FELT THE SWORD CUT HIM!
HE REALLY IS A MONSTER !!
AA
AAAHH!
AAAHH!
AAAHH!
SMACK
HUH ...?
?!
WHAT ...?

CHECK-MATE!

WE... WE WON!!

SLAM

BAM

!

NRGH...

BUT...

I'M SORRY!

ERGH... THEY'RE NOT GOING TO MAKE IT...!

WHAT ABOUT IKKŪ AND KURŌMARU?

CHOMP

NOW WE'VE BEAT HIM!!

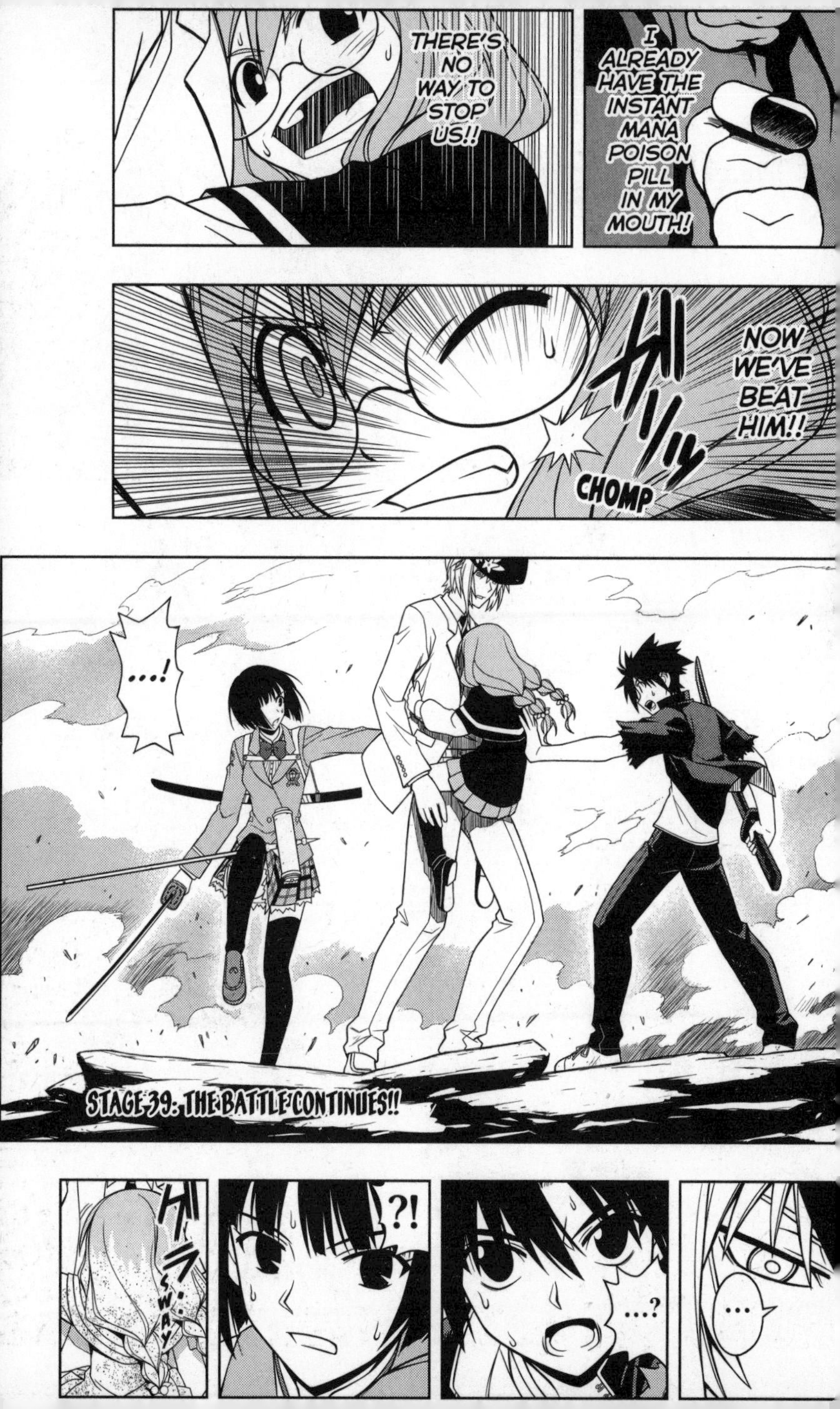
I ALREADY HAVE THE INSTANT MANA POISON PILL IN MY MOUTH!
THERE'S NO WAY TO STOP US!!
NOW WE'VE BEAT HIM!!
CHOMP
...!
STAGE 39: THE BATTLE CONTINUES!!
...
...?
?!
SWAY

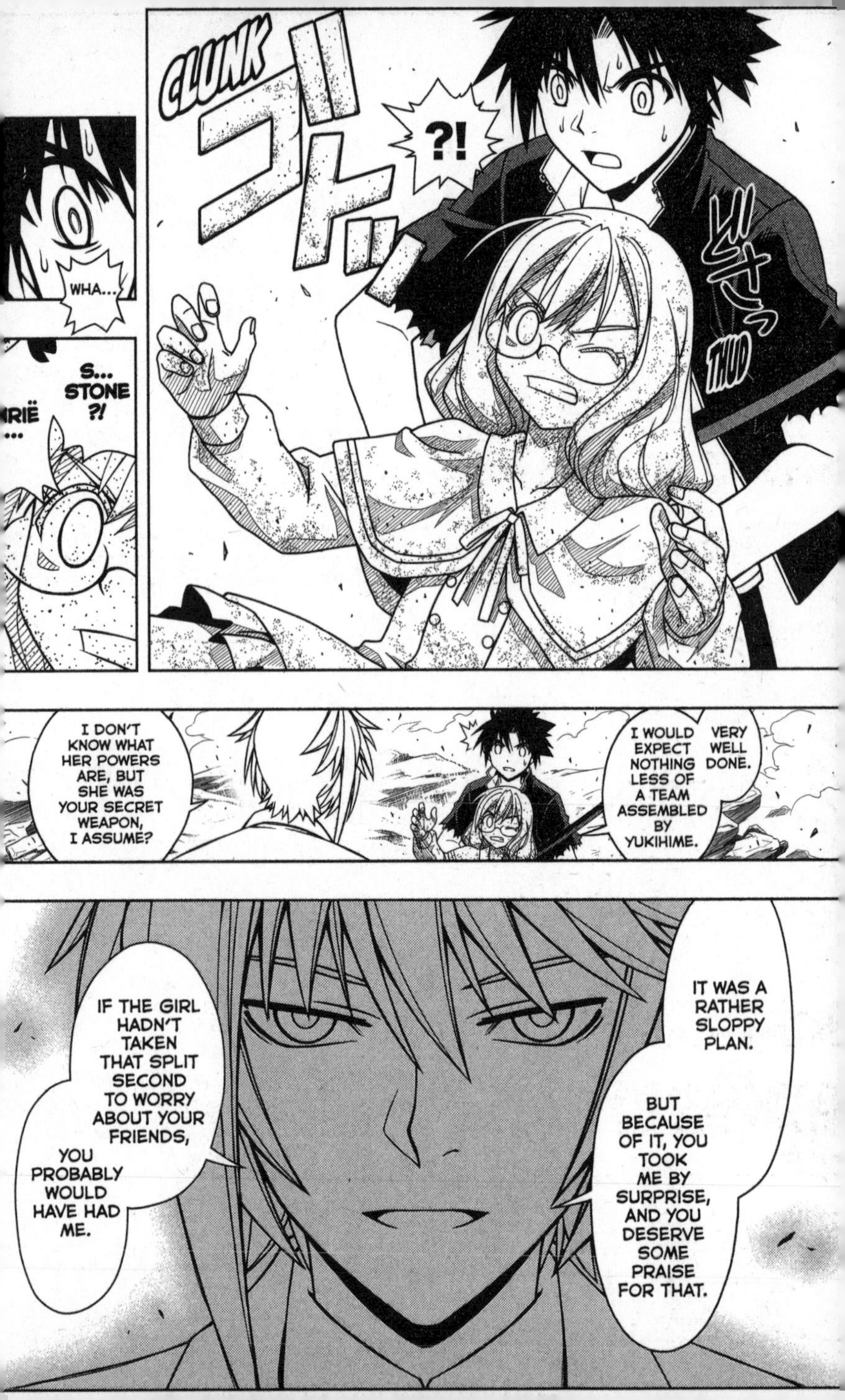
CLUNK
?!
THUD
WHA...
S... STONE ?!
VERY WELL DONE.
I WOULD EXPECT NOTHING LESS OF A TEAM ASSEMBLED BY YUKIHIME.
I DON'T KNOW WHAT HER POWERS ARE, BUT SHE WAS YOUR SECRET WEAPON, I ASSUME?
IT WAS A RATHER SLOPPY PLAN.
BUT BECAUSE OF IT, YOU TOOK ME BY SURPRISE, AND YOU DESERVE SOME PRAISE FOR THAT.
IF THE GIRL HADN'T TAKEN THAT SPLIT SECOND TO WORRY ABOUT YOUR FRIENDS,
YOU PROBABLY WOULD HAVE HAD ME.

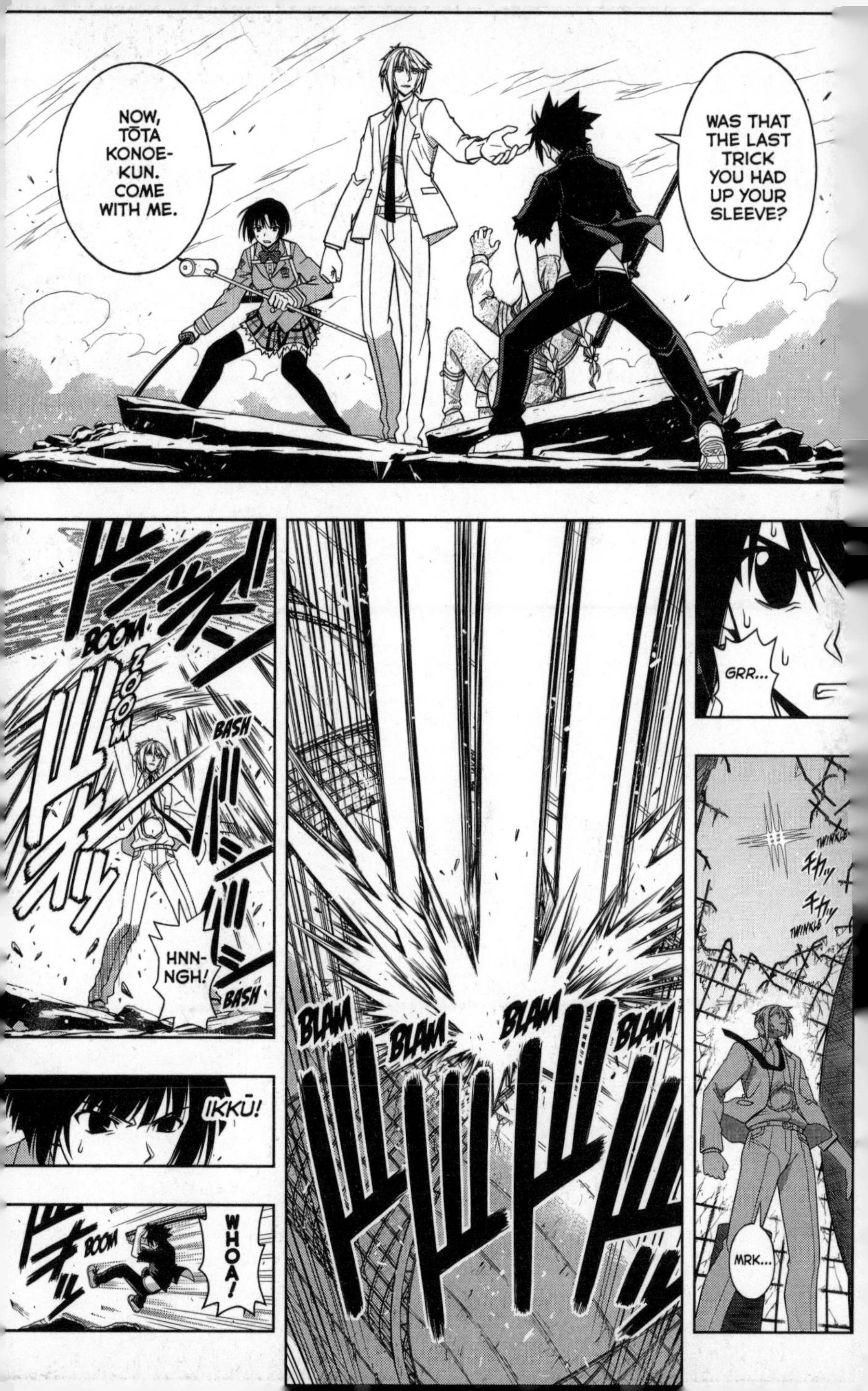
WAS THAT THE LAST TRICK YOU HAD UP YOUR SLEEVE?
NOW, TŌTA KONOE-KUN. COME WITH ME.
GRR...
TWINKLE
TWINKLE
MRK...
BLAM
BLAM
BLAM
BLAM
BOOM
ZOOM
BASH
HNN-NGH!
BASH
IKKŪ!
BOOM
WHOA!

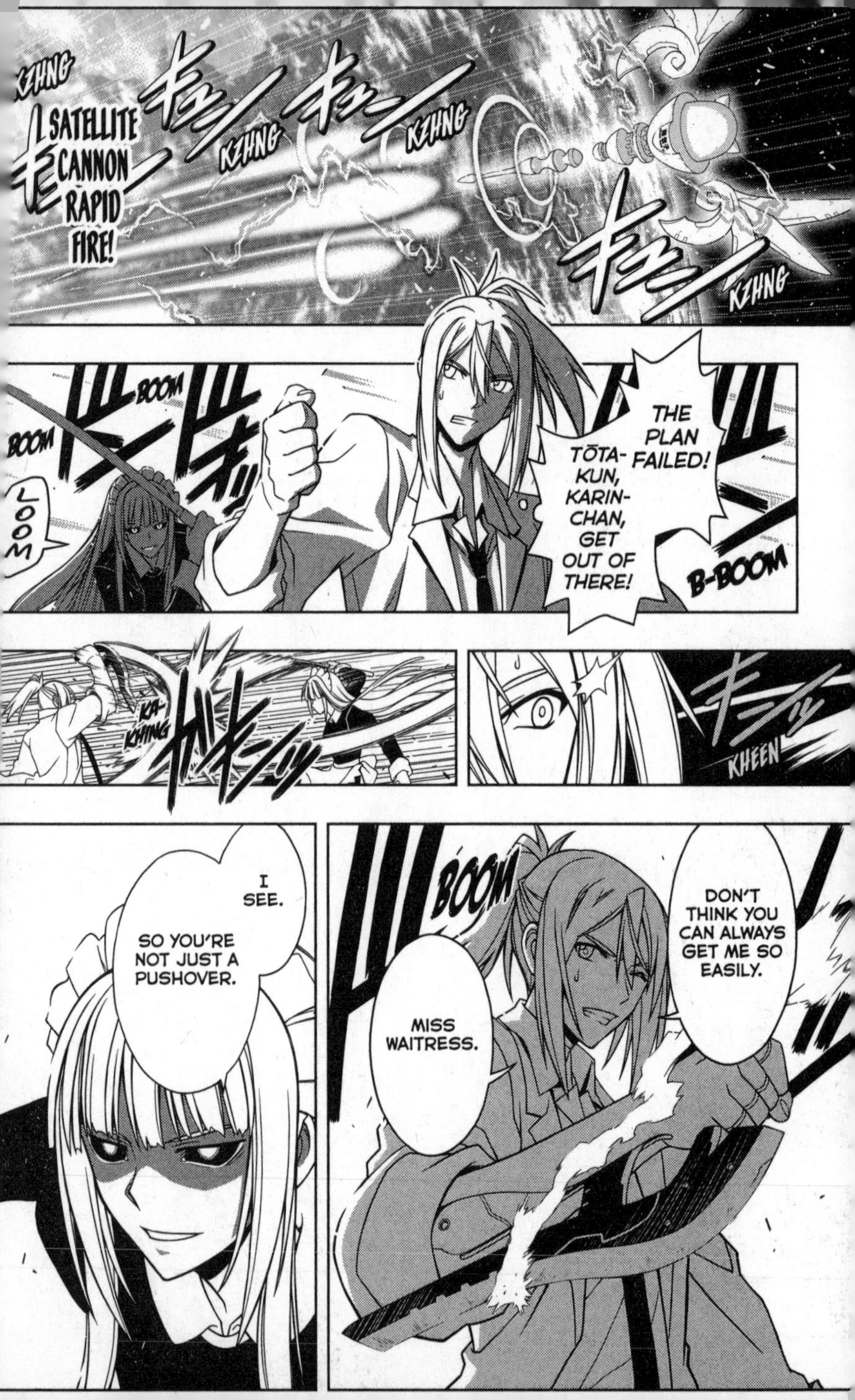
KZHNG
KZHNG
KZHNG
SATELLITE CANNON RAPID FIRE!
KZHNG
THE PLAN FAILED!
TŌTA-KUN, KARIN-CHAN, GET OUT OF THERE!
B-BOOM
BOOM
BOOM
LOOM
KHEEN
KA-KHING
DON'T THINK YOU CAN ALWAYS GET ME SO EASILY.
BOOM
MISS WAITRESS.
I SEE.
SO YOU'RE NOT JUST A PUSHOVER.

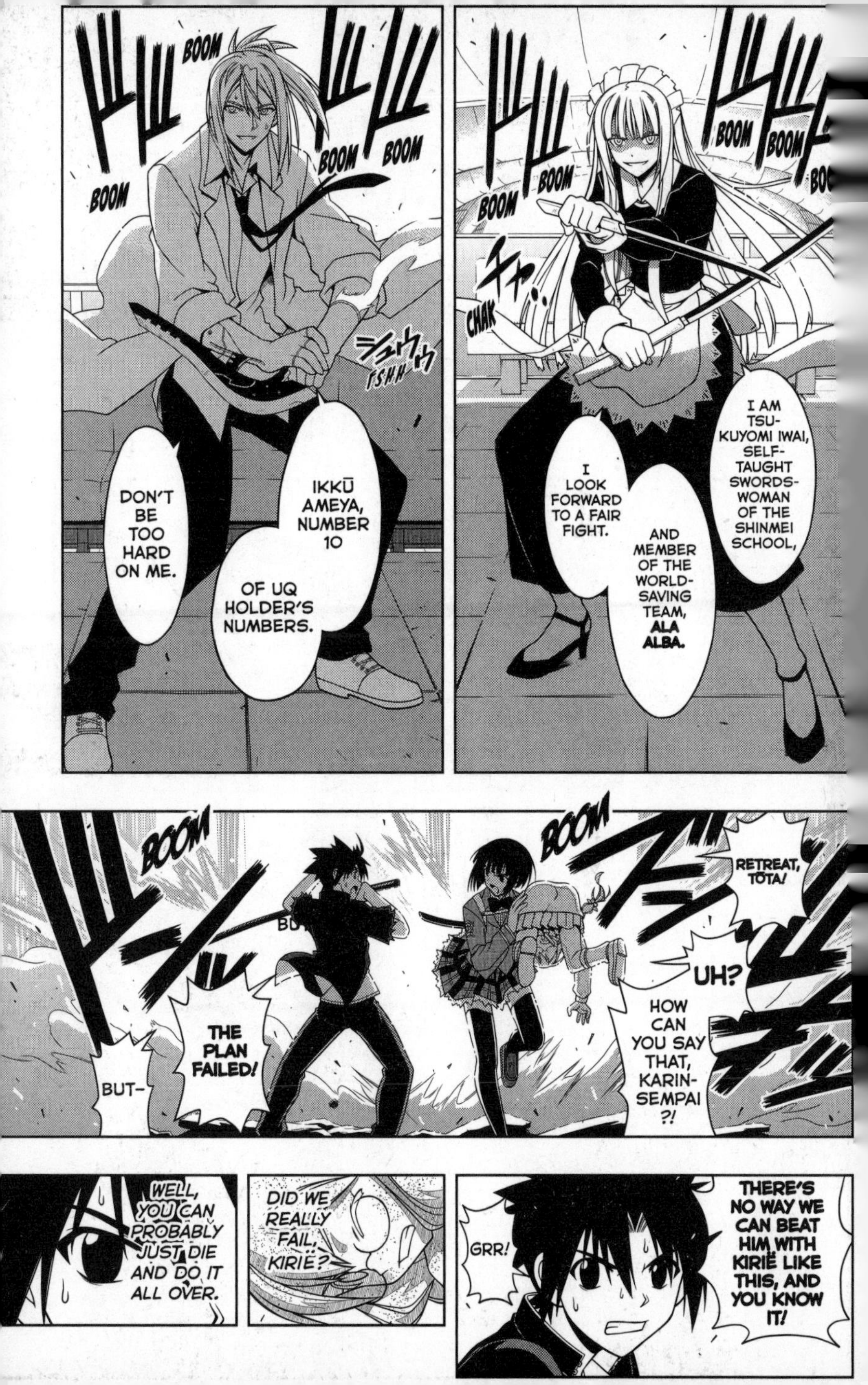
BOOM BOOM BOOM BOOM BOOM
CHAK
I AM TSUKUYOMI IWAI, SELF-TAUGHT SWORDSWOMAN OF THE SHINMEI SCHOOL,
AND MEMBER OF THE WORLD-SAVING TEAM, **ALA ALBA.**
I LOOK FORWARD TO A FAIR FIGHT.
BOOM BOOM BOOM BOOM
TSHH
IKKŪ AMEYA, NUMBER 10
OF UQ HOLDER'S NUMBERS.
DON'T BE TOO HARD ON ME.
BOOM
RETREAT, TŌTA!
UH?
HOW CAN YOU SAY THAT, KARIN-SEMPAI?!
BOOM
THE PLAN FAILED!
BUT–
THERE'S NO WAY WE CAN BEAT HIM WITH KIRIË LIKE THIS, AND YOU KNOW IT!
GRR!
DID WE REALLY FAIL, KIRIË?
WELL, YOU CAN PROBABLY JUST DIE AND DO IT ALL OVER.

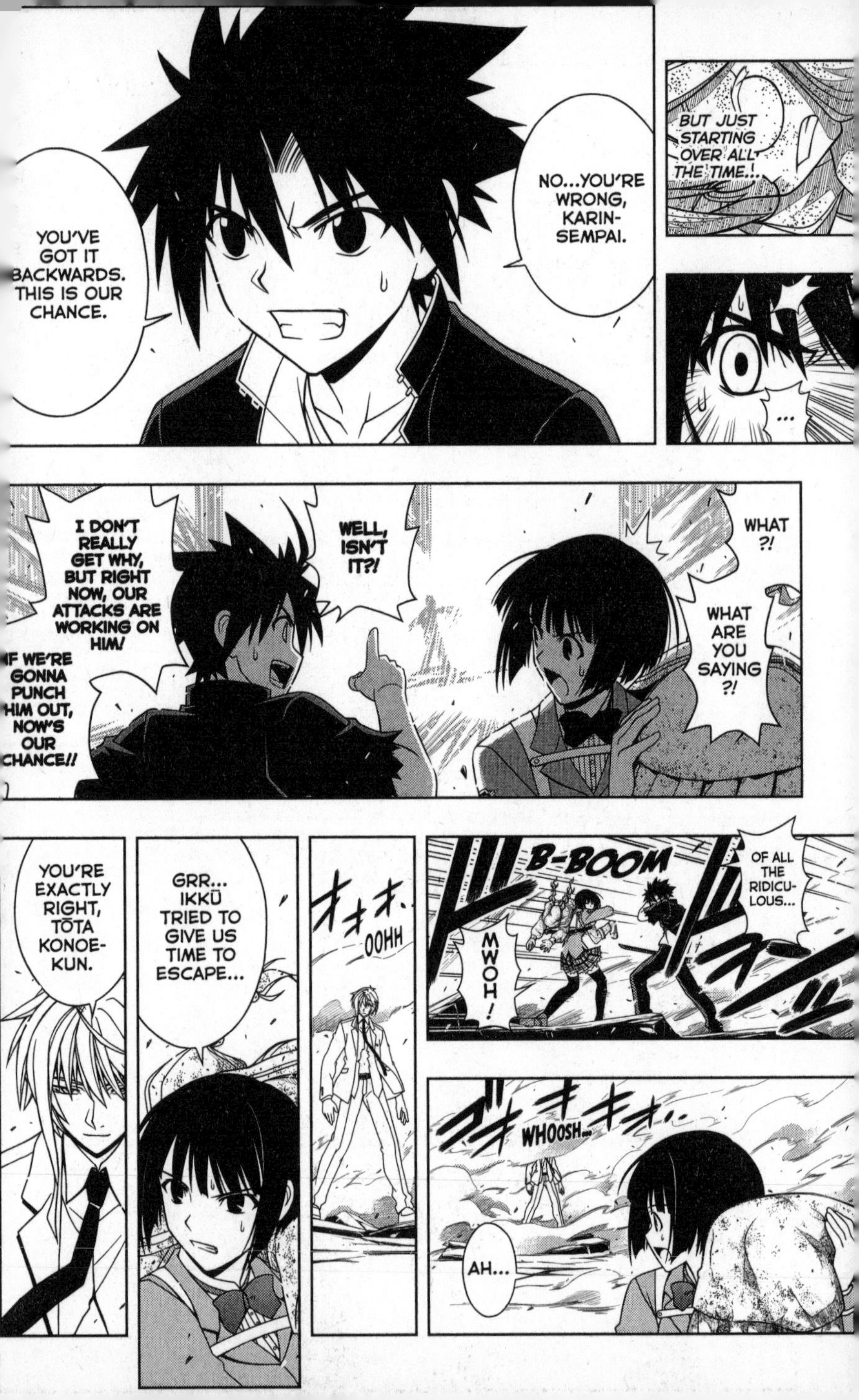

BUT JUST STARTING OVER ALL THE TIME...
...
NO...YOU'RE WRONG, KARIN-SEMPAI.
YOU'VE GOT IT BACKWARDS. THIS IS OUR CHANCE.
WHAT?!
WHAT ARE YOU SAYING?!
WELL, ISN'T IT?!
I DON'T REALLY GET WHY, BUT RIGHT NOW, OUR ATTACKS ARE WORKING ON HIM!
IF WE'RE GONNA PUNCH HIM OUT, NOW'S OUR CHANCE!!
OF ALL THE RIDICULOUS...
B-BOOM
MWOH!
WHOOSH...
AH...
OOHH
GRR... IKKŪ TRIED TO GIVE US TIME TO ESCAPE...
YOU'RE EXACTLY RIGHT, TŌTA KONOE-KUN.

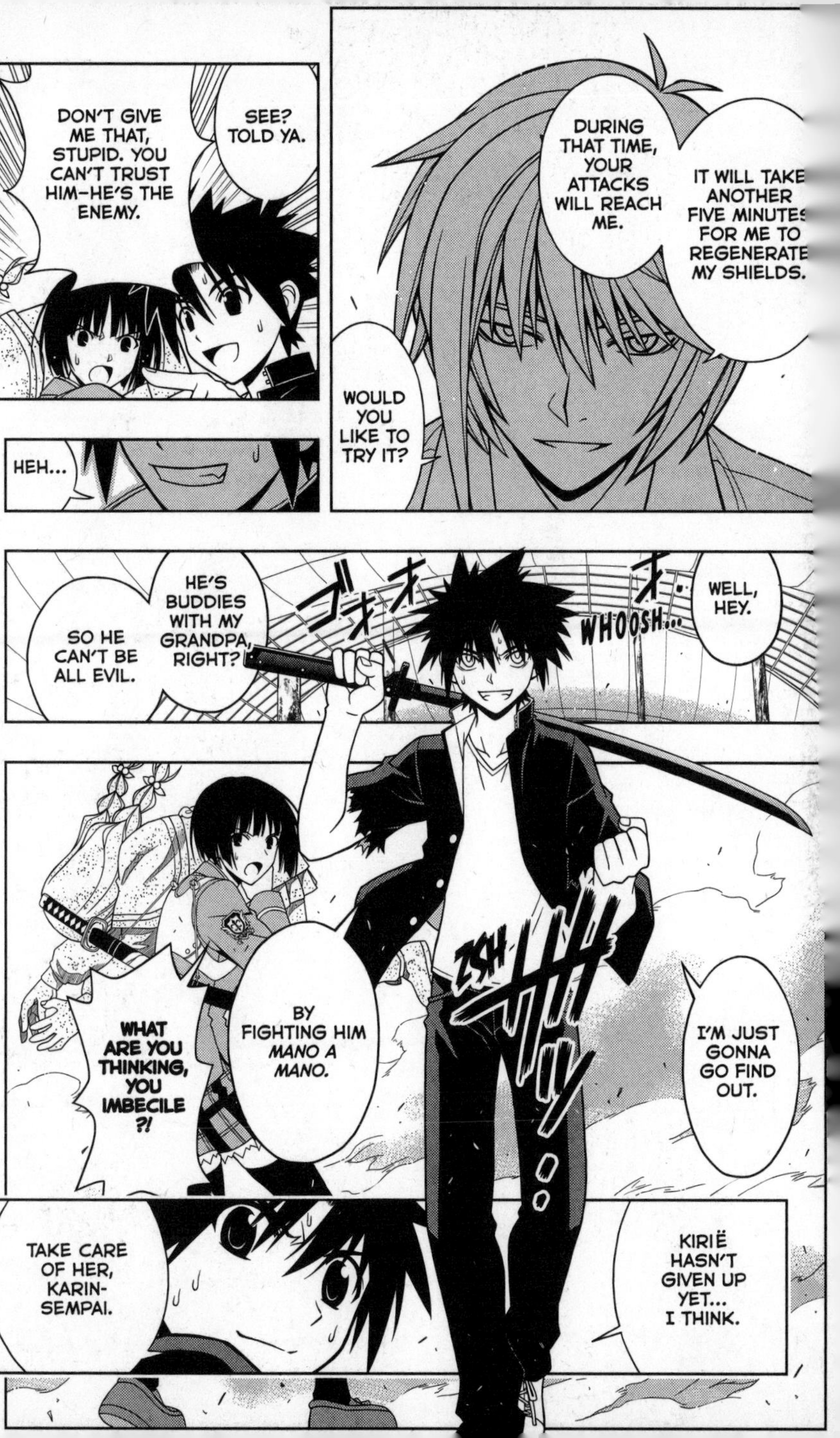
IT WILL TAKE ANOTHER FIVE MINUTES FOR ME TO REGENERATE MY SHIELDS.
DURING THAT TIME, YOUR ATTACKS WILL REACH ME.
WOULD YOU LIKE TO TRY IT?
SEE? TOLD YA.
DON'T GIVE ME THAT, STUPID. YOU CAN'T TRUST HIM–HE'S THE ENEMY.
HEH...
WELL, HEY.
WHOOSH...
HE'S BUDDIES WITH MY GRANDPA, RIGHT?
SO HE CAN'T BE ALL EVIL.
I'M JUST GONNA GO FIND OUT.
ZSH
BY FIGHTING HIM *MANO A MANO.*
WHAT ARE YOU THINKING, YOU IMBECILE?!
KIRIË HASN'T GIVEN UP YET... I THINK.
TAKE CARE OF HER, KARIN-SEMPAI.

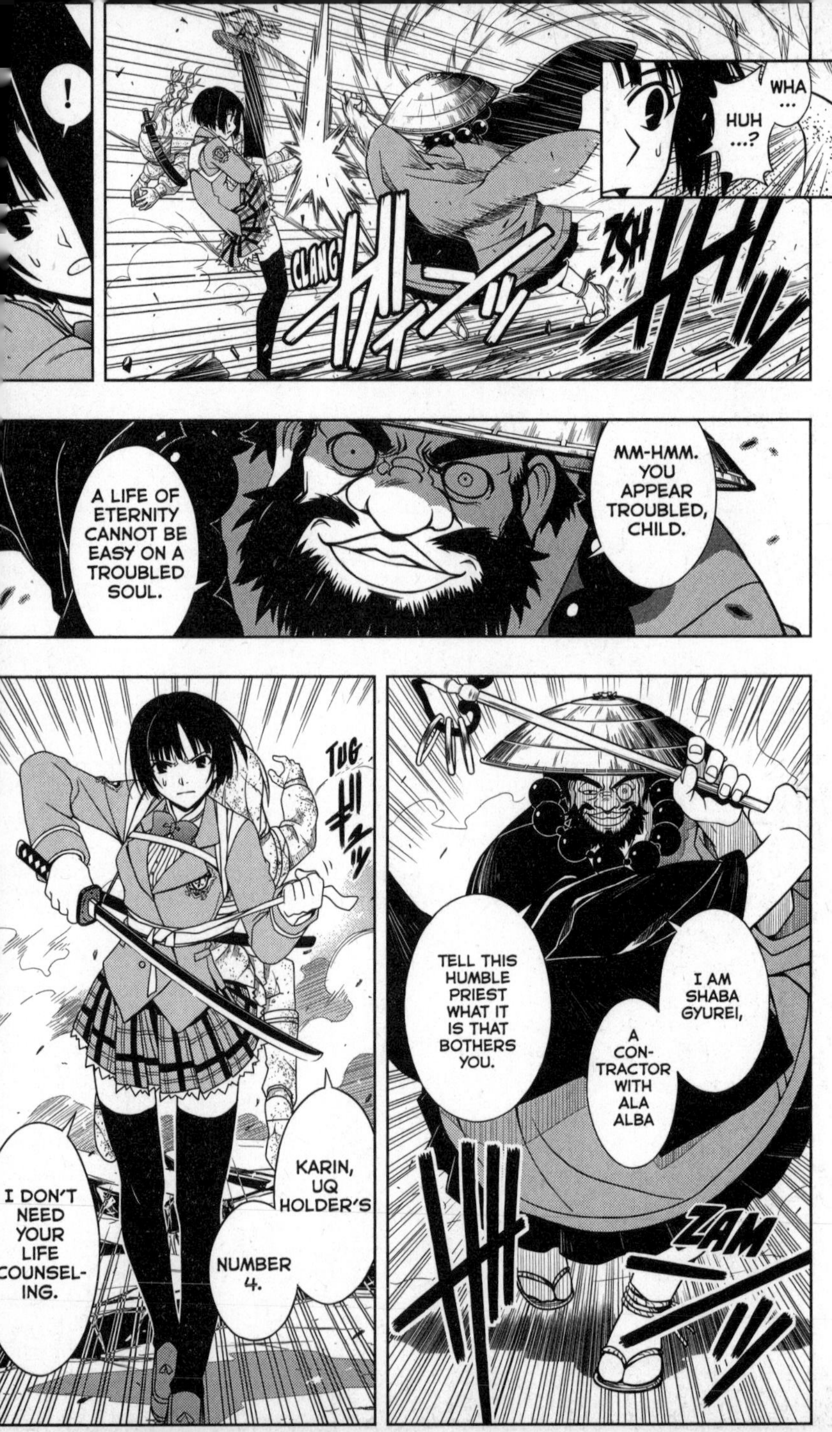
WHA...
HUH...?
ZSH
CLANG
!
MM-HMM. YOU APPEAR TROUBLED, CHILD.
A LIFE OF ETERNITY CANNOT BE EASY ON A TROUBLED SOUL.
I AM SHABA GYUREI,
A CONTRACTOR WITH ALA ALBA
TELL THIS HUMBLE PRIEST WHAT IT IS THAT BOTHERS YOU.
ZAM
TUG
KARIN, UQ HOLDER'S
NUMBER 4.
I DON'T NEED YOUR LIFE COUNSEL-ING.

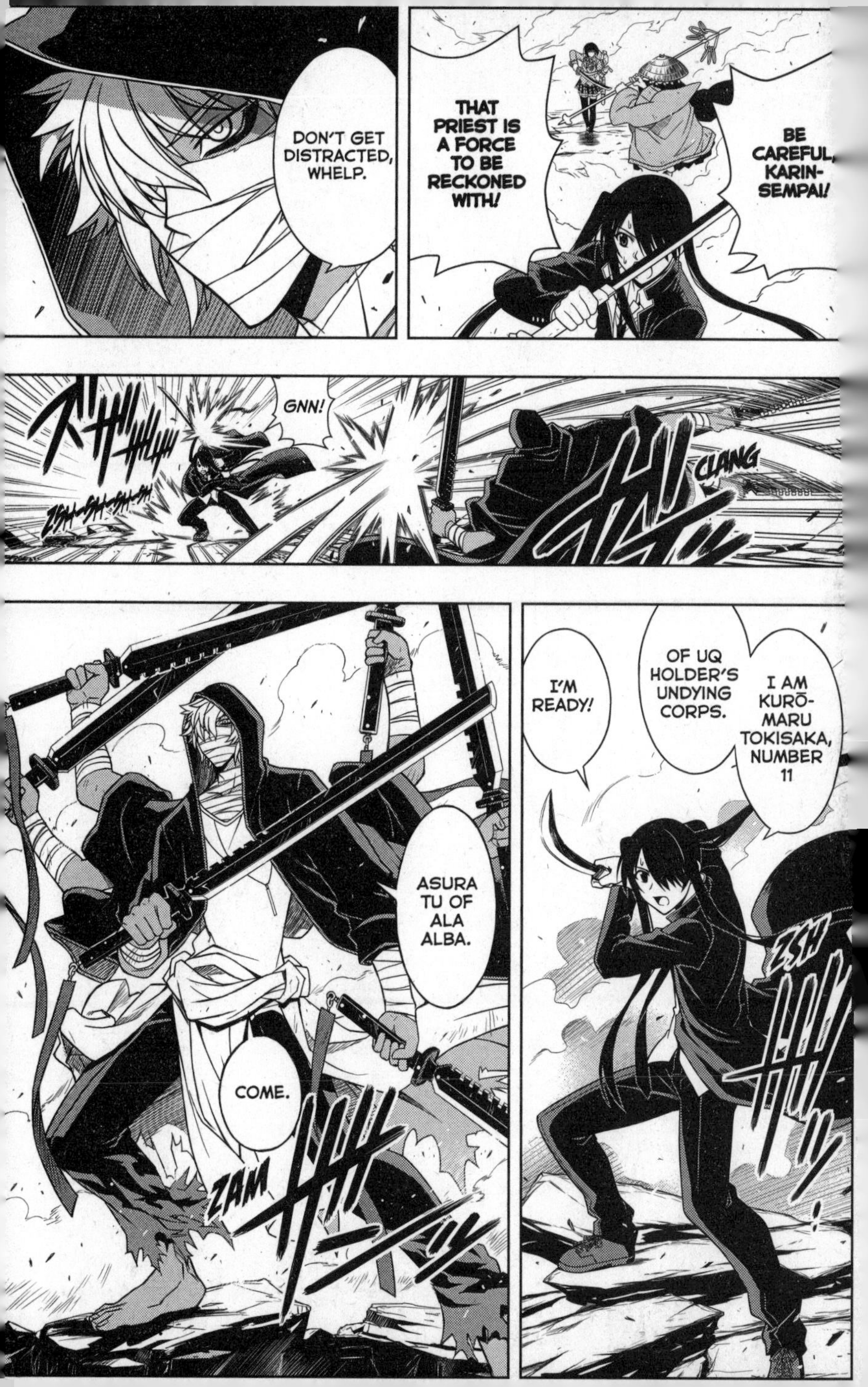
BE CAREFUL, KARIN-SEMPAI!
THAT PRIEST IS A FORCE TO BE RECKONED WITH!
DON'T GET DISTRACTED, WHELP.
CLANG
GNN!
I AM KURŌ-MARU TOKISAKA, NUMBER 11
OF UQ HOLDER'S UNDYING CORPS.
I'M READY!
ZSH
ASURA TU OF ALA ALBA.
COME.
ZAM

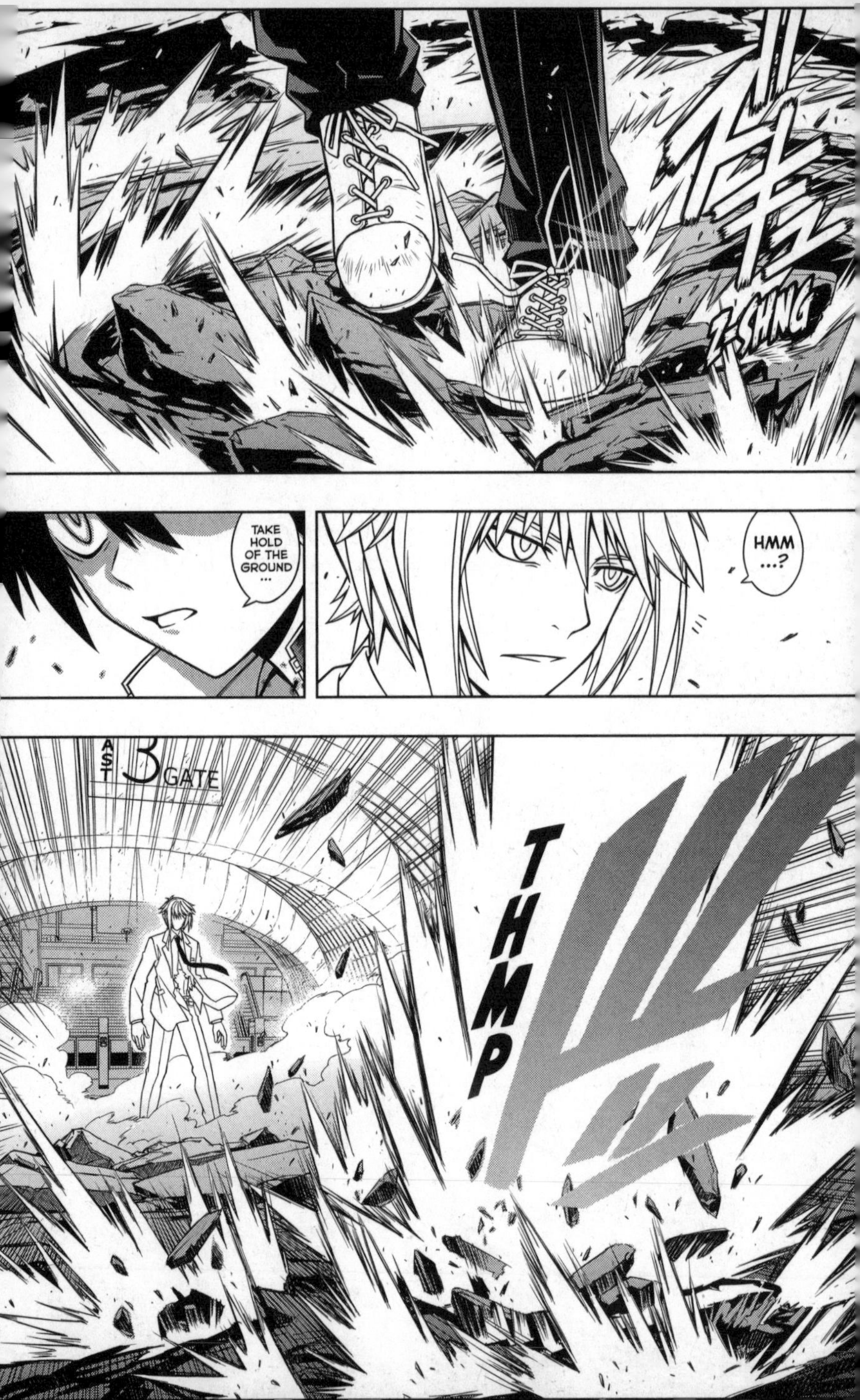
Z-SHING
HMM ...?
TAKE HOLD OF THE GROUND ...
THMP
AST 3 GATE

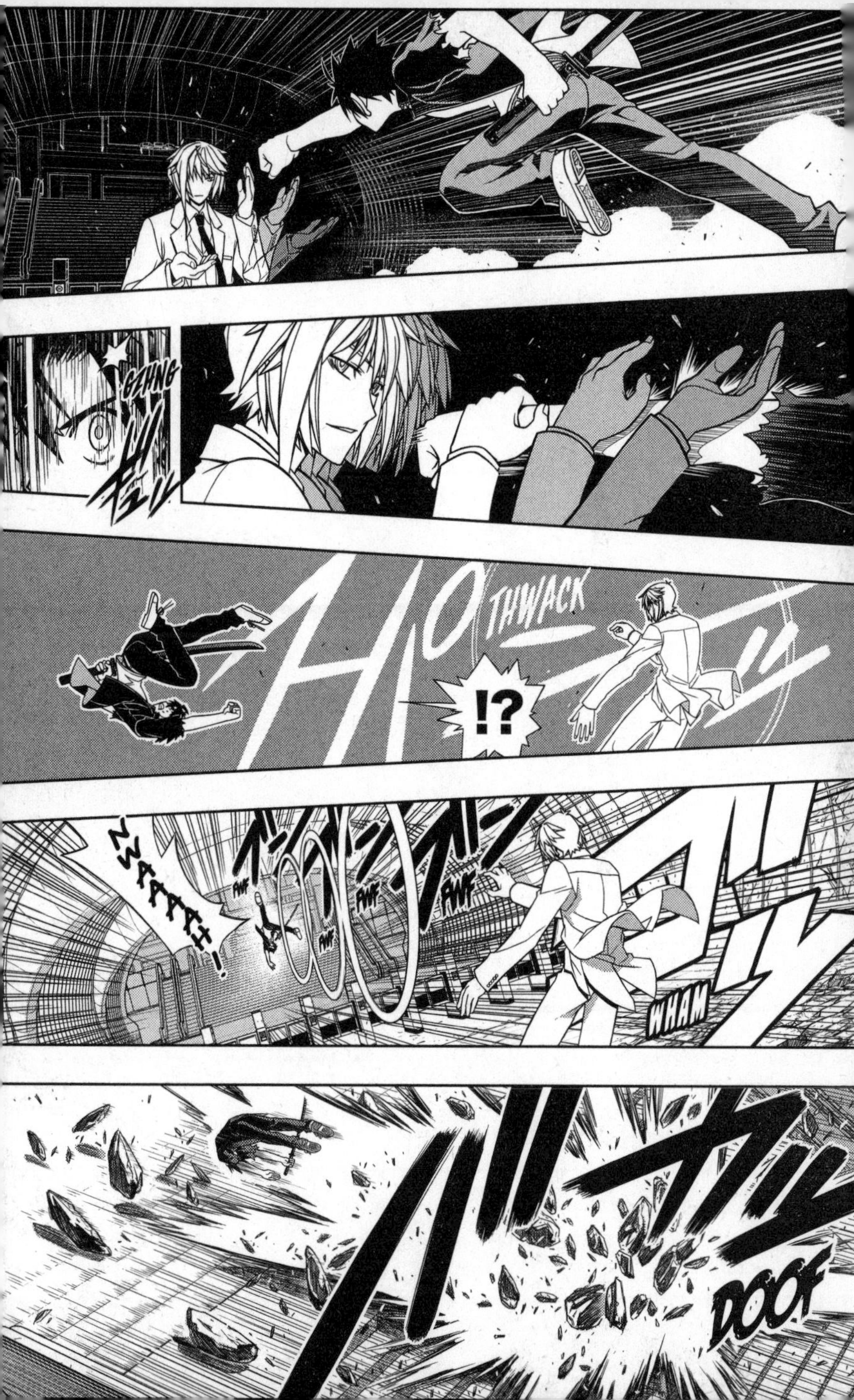
GZHNG
THWACK
!?
FWF
FWF
FWF
FWF
NWAAAAH!
WHAM
DOOF

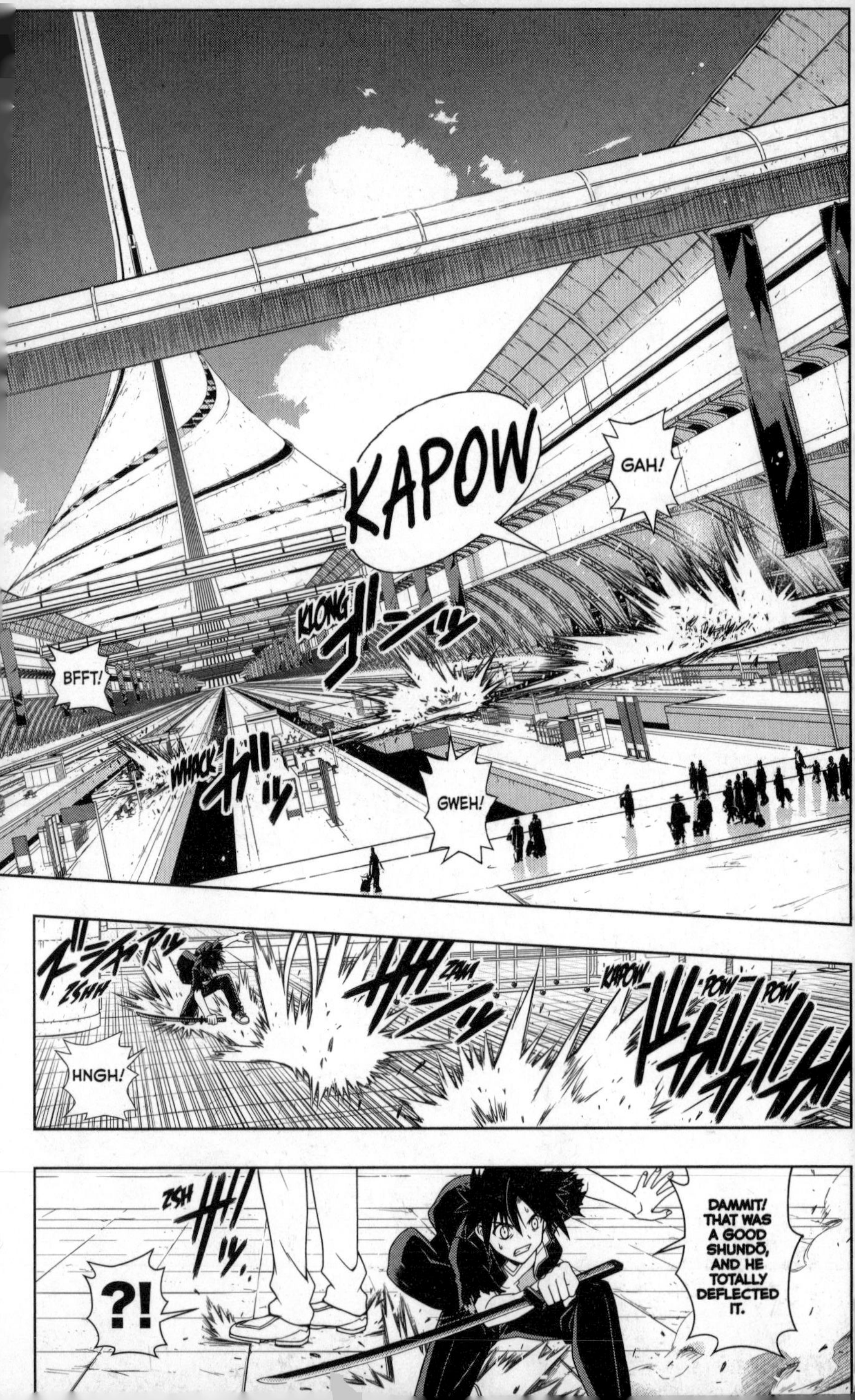
GAH!
KAPOW
KLONG
GWEH!
WHACK
BFFT!
POW
POW
KAPOW
ZAM
ZSHH
HNGH!
DAMMIT! THAT WAS A GOOD SHUNDŌ, AND HE TOTALLY DEFLECTED IT.
ZSH
?!

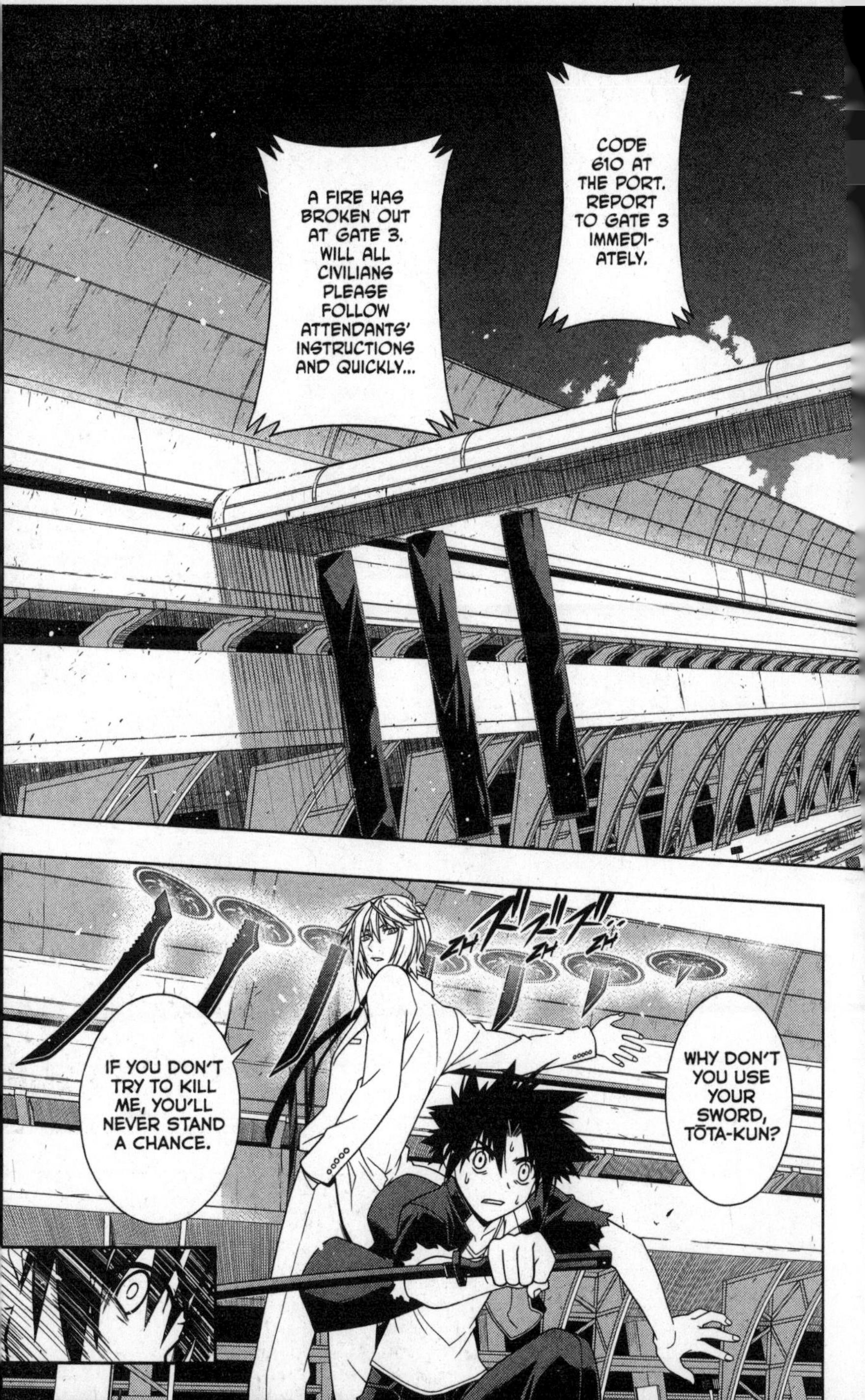
CODE 610 AT THE PORT. REPORT TO GATE 3 IMMEDI-ATELY.
A FIRE HAS BROKEN OUT AT GATE 3. WILL ALL CIVILIANS PLEASE FOLLOW ATTENDANTS' INSTRUCTIONS AND QUICKLY...
WHY DON'T YOU USE YOUR SWORD, TŌTA-KUN?
ZH ZH ZH
IF YOU DON'T TRY TO KILL ME, YOU'LL NEVER STAND A CHANCE.

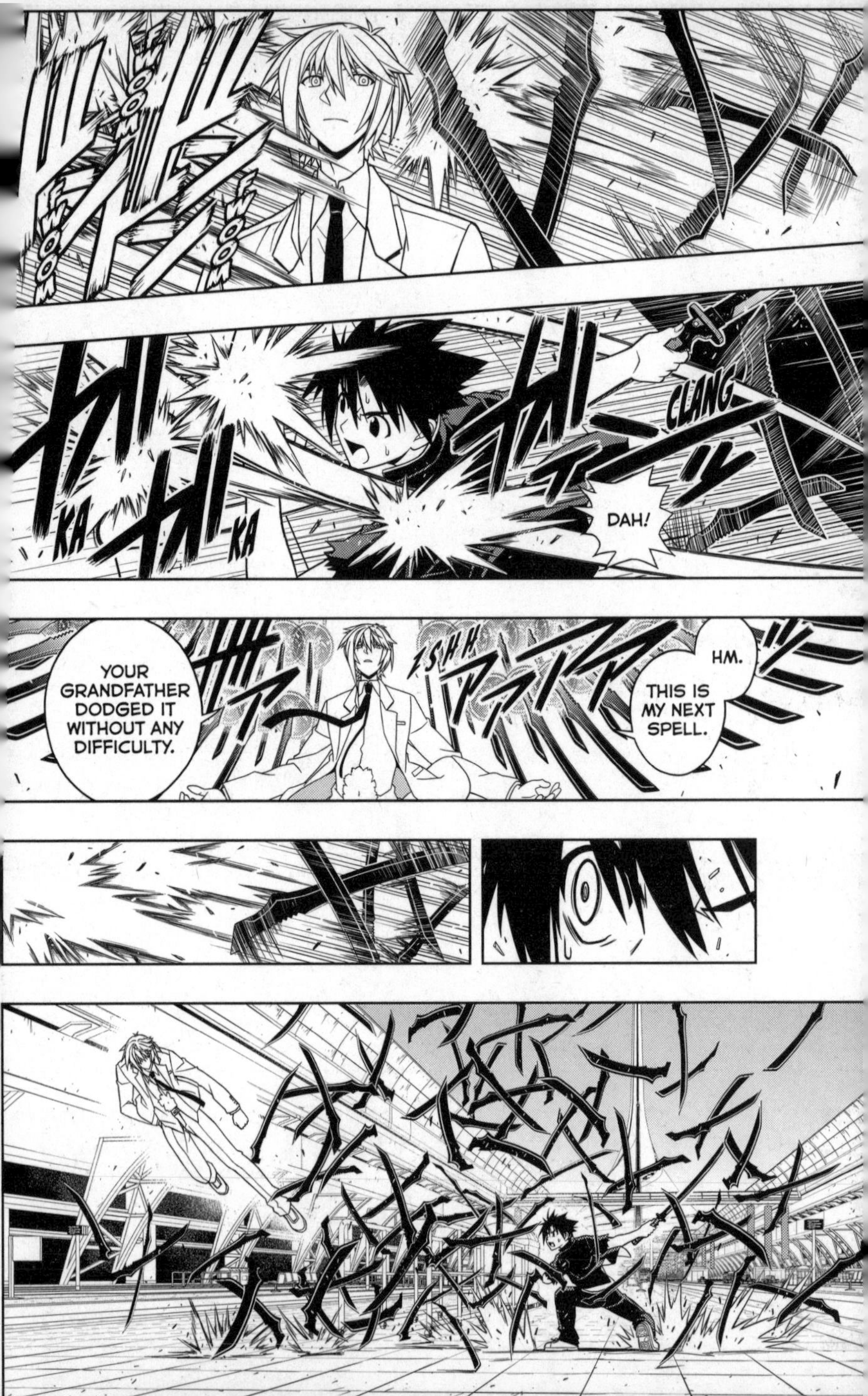
FWOOM
FWOOM
FWOOM
CLANG
DAH!
KA
KA
HM.
THIS IS MY NEXT SPELL.
YOUR GRANDFATHER DODGED IT WITHOUT ANY DIFFICULTY.

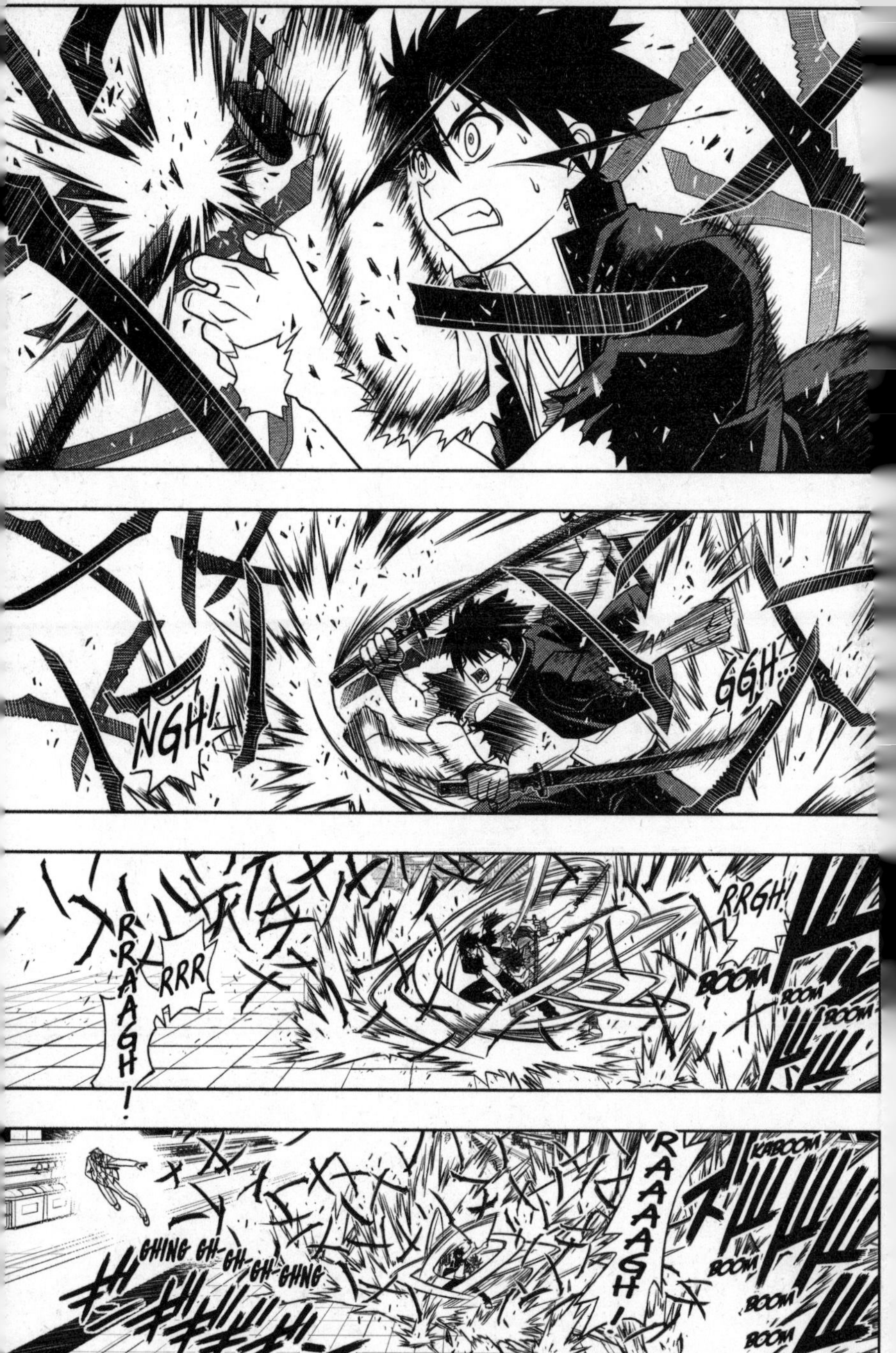
GGH...
NGH!
RRGH!
BOOM
BOOM
BOOM
RRR
RRAAGH!
KABOOM
BOOM
BOOM
BOOM
RAAAAAGH!
GHING GH-GH-GH-GHNG

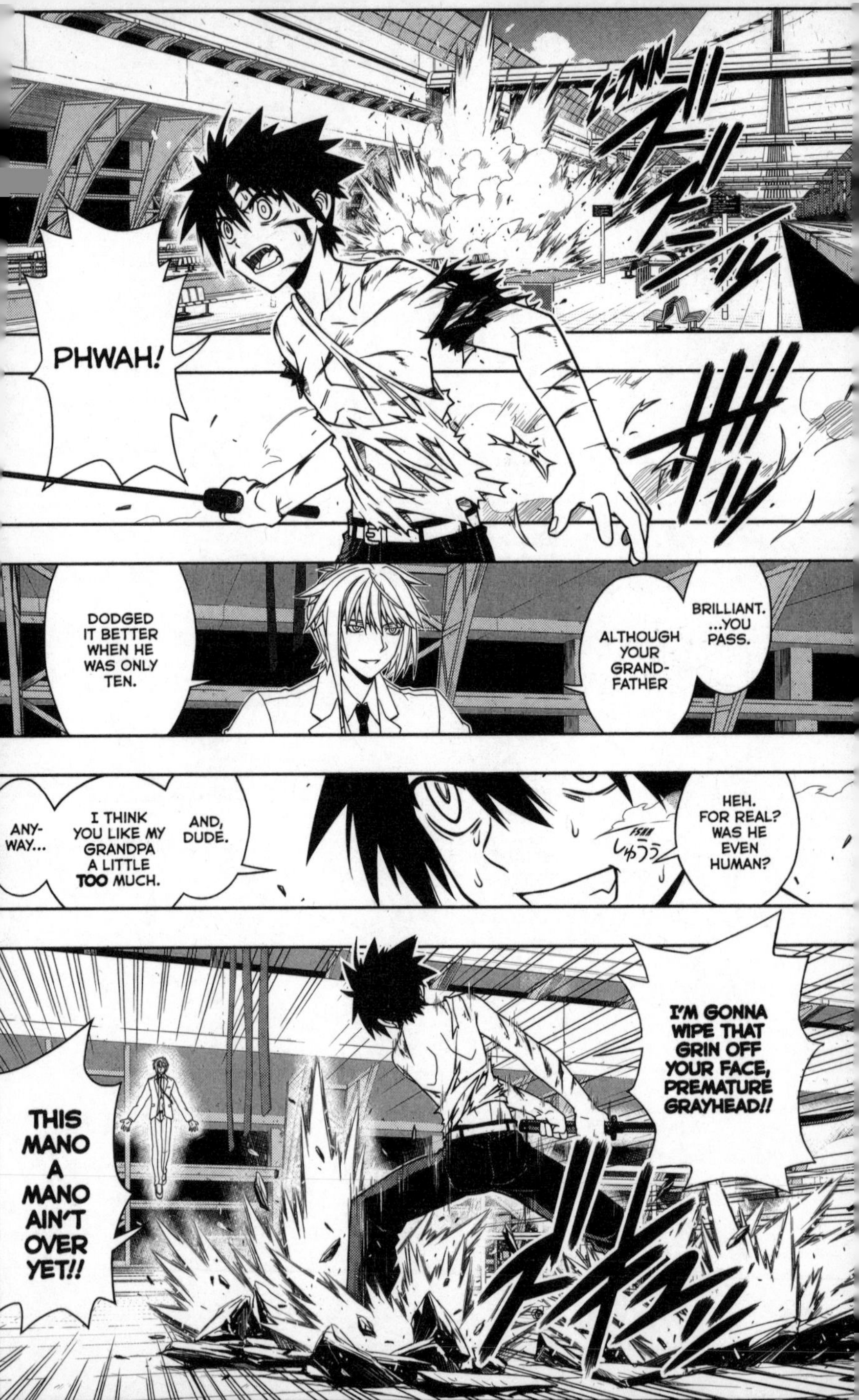
Z-ZNN
PHWAH!
BRILLIANT. ...YOU PASS.
ALTHOUGH YOUR GRANDFATHER
DODGED IT BETTER WHEN HE WAS ONLY TEN.
HEH. FOR REAL? WAS HE EVEN HUMAN?
AND, DUDE.
I THINK YOU LIKE MY GRANDPA A LITTLE TOO MUCH.
ANYWAY...
I'M GONNA WIPE THAT GRIN OFF YOUR FACE, PREMATURE GRAYHEAD!!
THIS MANO A MANO AIN'T OVER YET!!

UQ HOLDER!

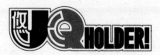

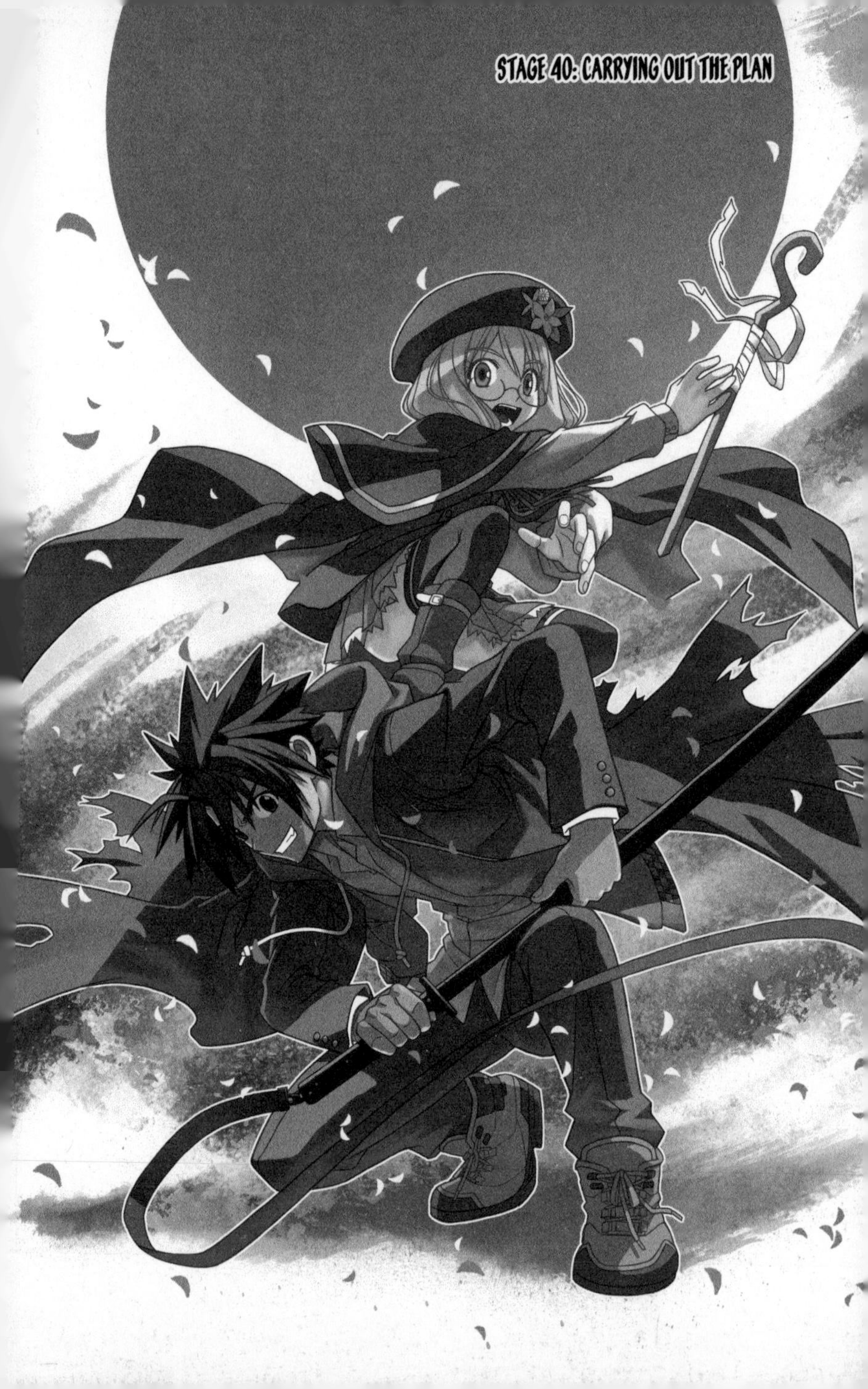
STAGE 40: CARRYING OUT THE PLAN

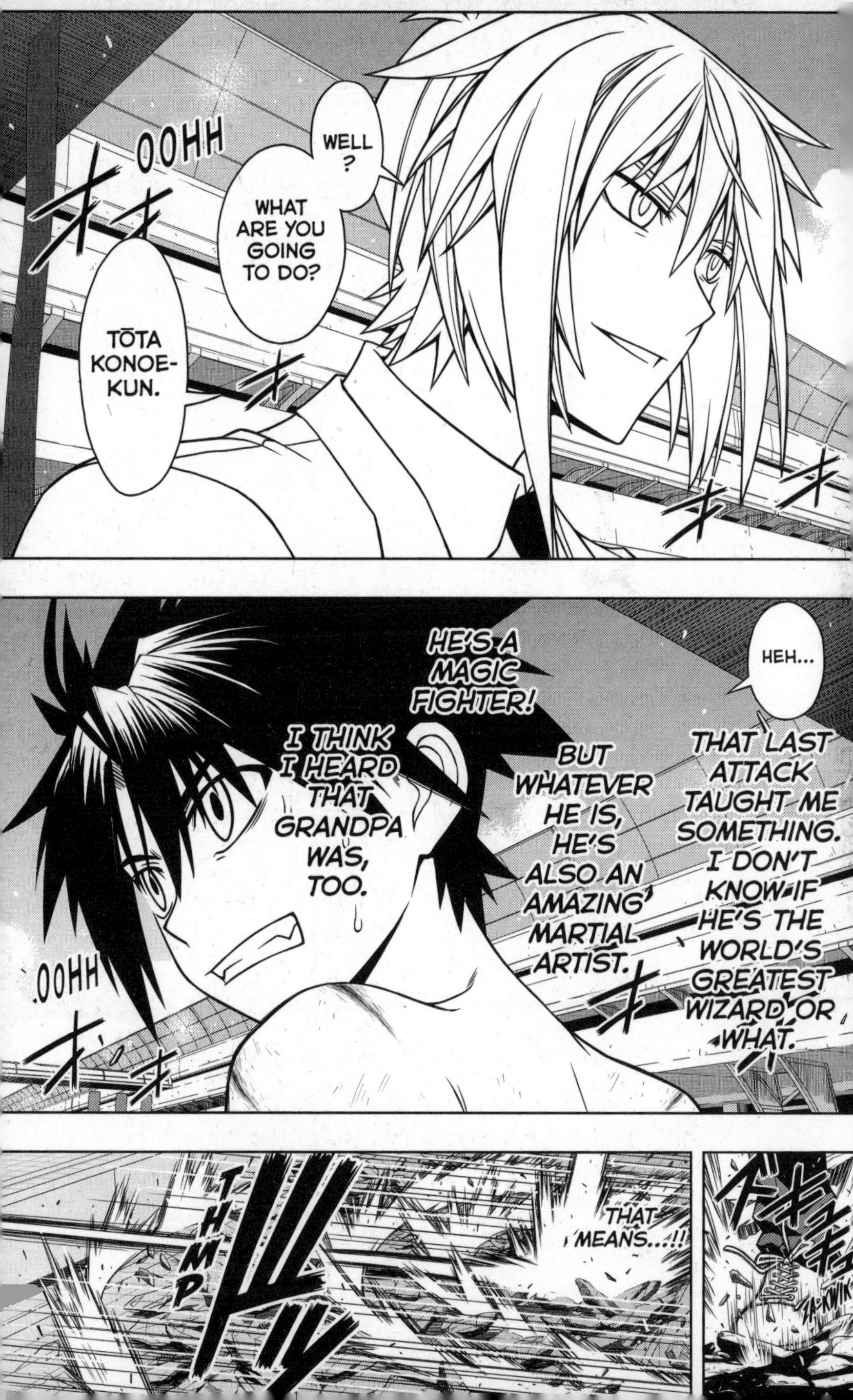
OOHH
WELL? WHAT ARE YOU GOING TO DO?
TŌTA KONOE-KUN.
HEH...
THAT LAST ATTACK TAUGHT ME SOMETHING. I DON'T KNOW IF HE'S THE WORLD'S GREATEST WIZARD OR WHAT.
BUT WHATEVER HE IS, HE'S ALSO AN AMAZING MARTIAL ARTIST.
HE'S A MAGIC FIGHTER!
I THINK I HEARD THAT GRANDPA WAS, TOO.
OOHH
ZA-KWIK
THAT MEANS...!!
THMP

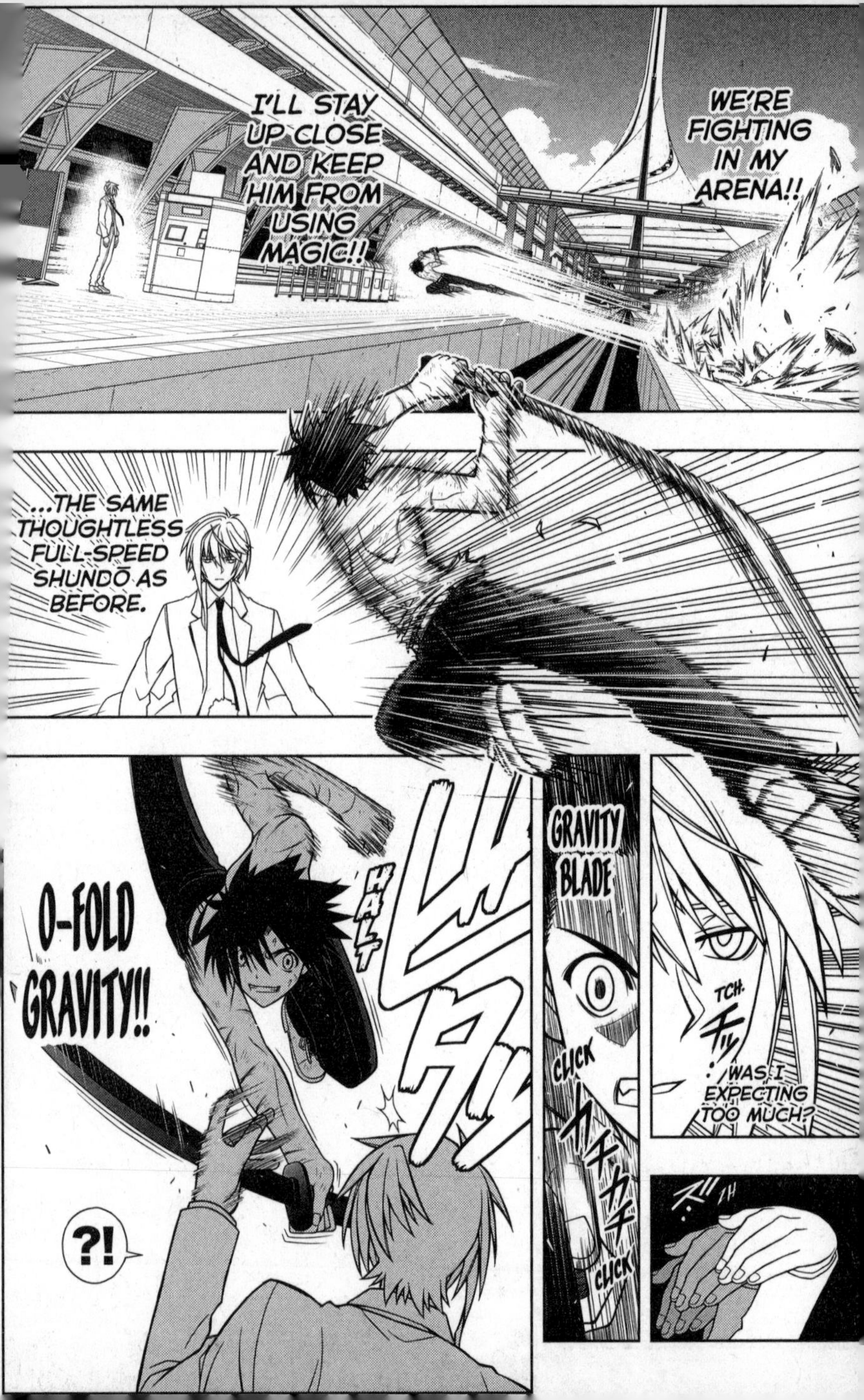

WE'RE FIGHTING IN MY ARENA!!
I'LL STAY UP CLOSE AND KEEP HIM FROM USING MAGIC!!
...THE SAME THOUGHTLESS FULL-SPEED SHUNDO AS BEFORE.
TCH.
チッ
...WAS I EXPECTING TOO MUCH?
GRAVITY BLADE
CLICK
カチ
カチ
CLICK
HALT
0-FOLD GRAVITY!!
?!

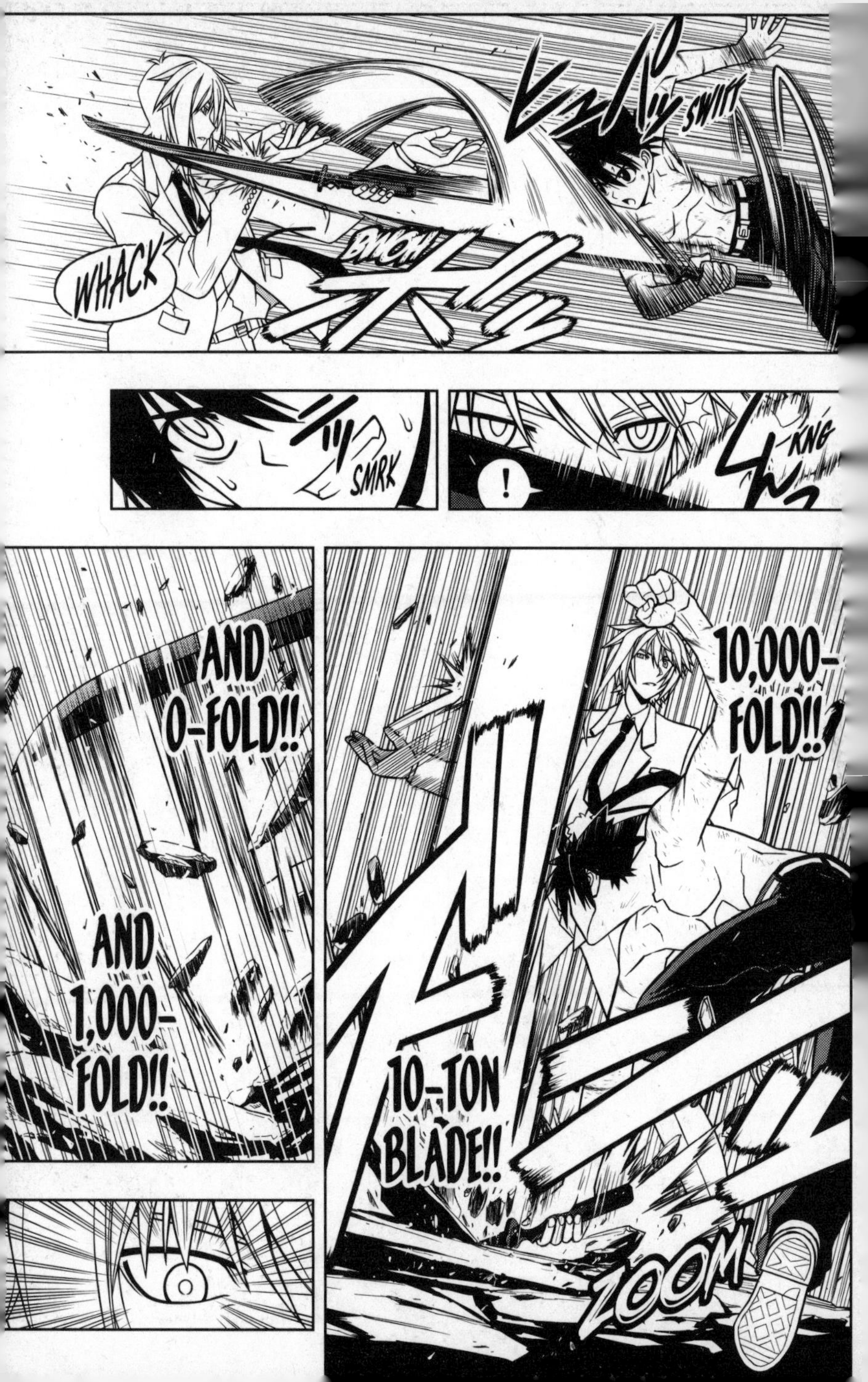
SWIFT
BWOH
WHACK
KNG
!
SMRK
10,000-FOLD!!
10-TON BLADE!!
ZOOM
AND 0-FOLD!!
AND 1,000-FOLD!!

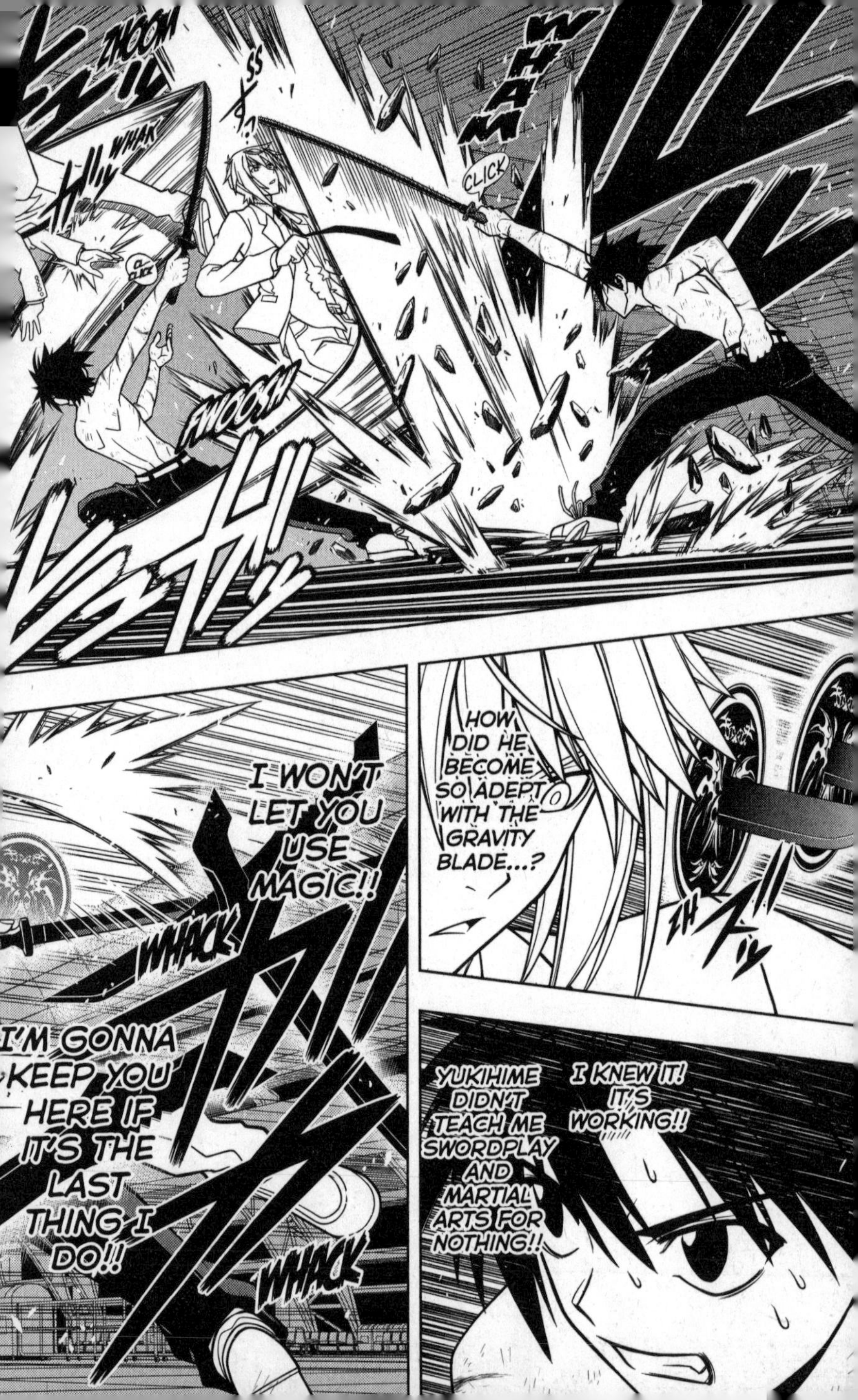
WHAM
CLICK
SS
ZHOOM
WHAK
CL CLICK
FWOOSH
HOW DID HE BECOME SO ADEPT WITH THE GRAVITY BLADE...?
I KNEW IT! IT'S WORKING!!
YUKIHIME DIDN'T TEACH ME SWORDPLAY AND MARTIAL ARTS FOR NOTHING!!
I WON'T LET YOU USE MAGIC!!
WHACK
I'M GONNA KEEP YOU HERE IF IT'S THE LAST THING I DO!!
WHACK

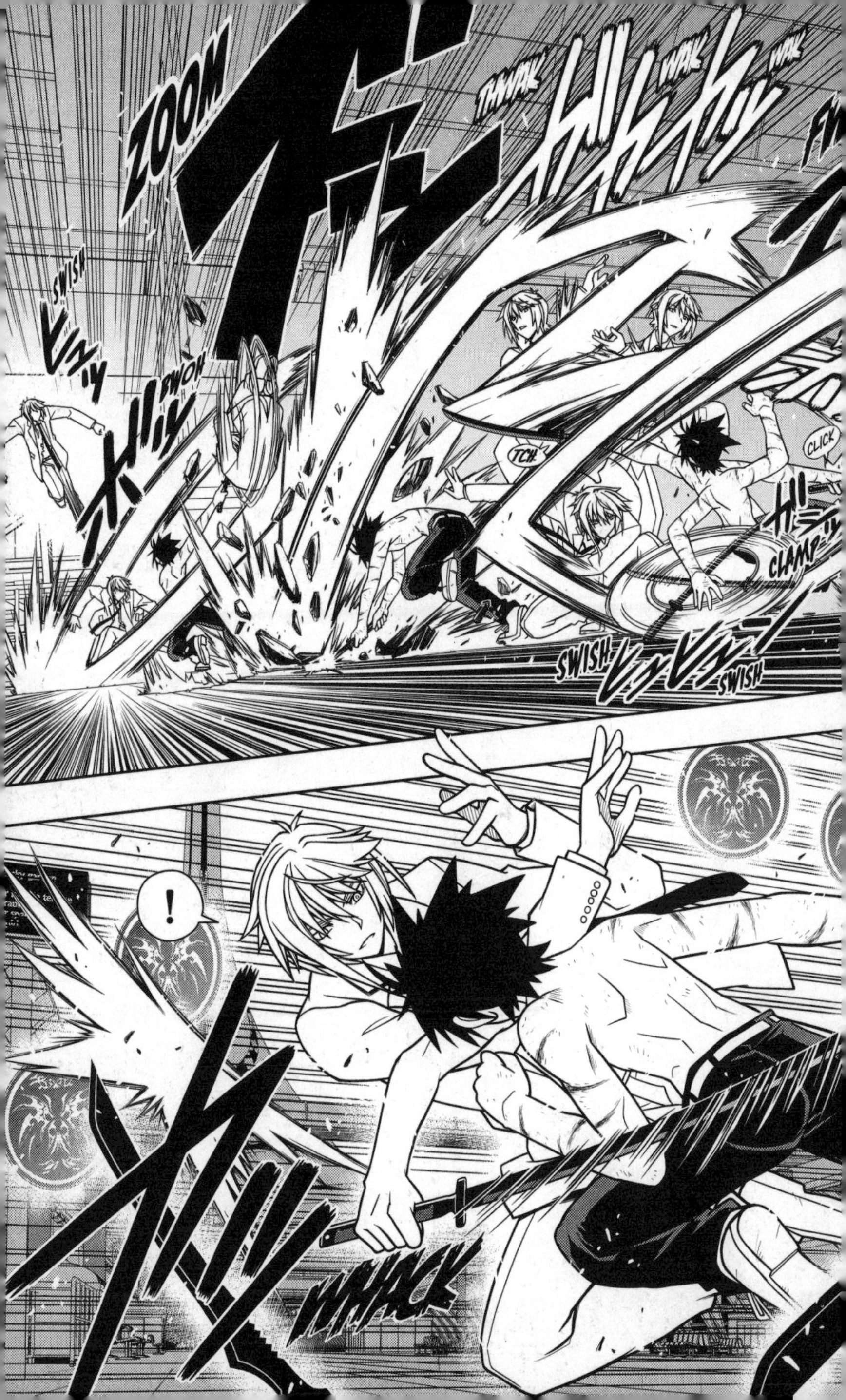
WAK
WAK
THWAK
ZOOM
SWISH
BWOH
CLICK
TCH
CLAMP
SWISH
SWISH
!
WHACK

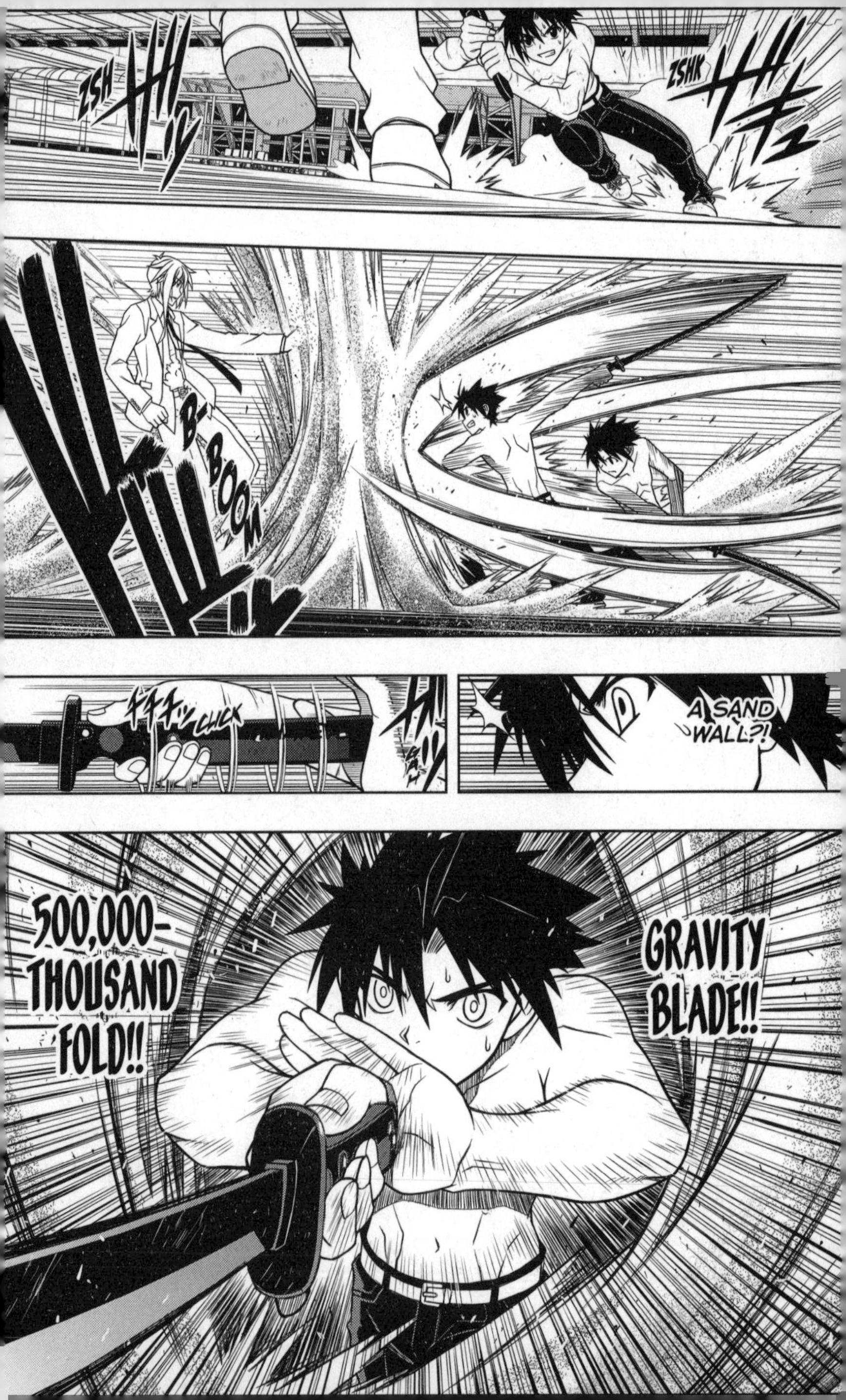
ZSHK
ZSH
B-BOOM
A SAND WALL?!
CLICK
GRAVITY BLADE!!
500,000-THOUSAND FOLD!!

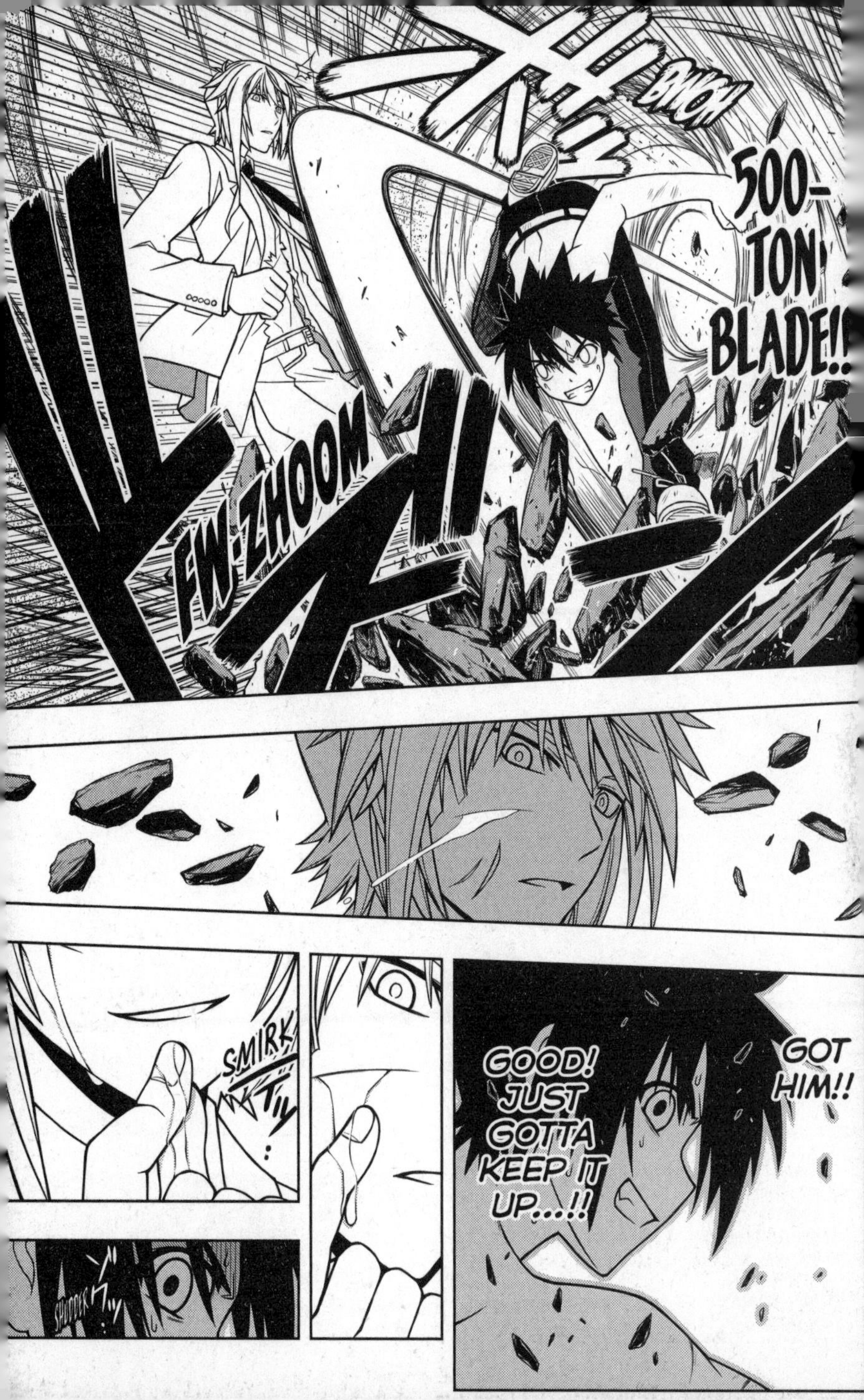
BWOCK
500-TON BLADE!!
FW-ZHOOM
GOT HIM!!
GOOD! JUST GOTTA KEEP IT UP...!!
SMIRK
SHUDDER

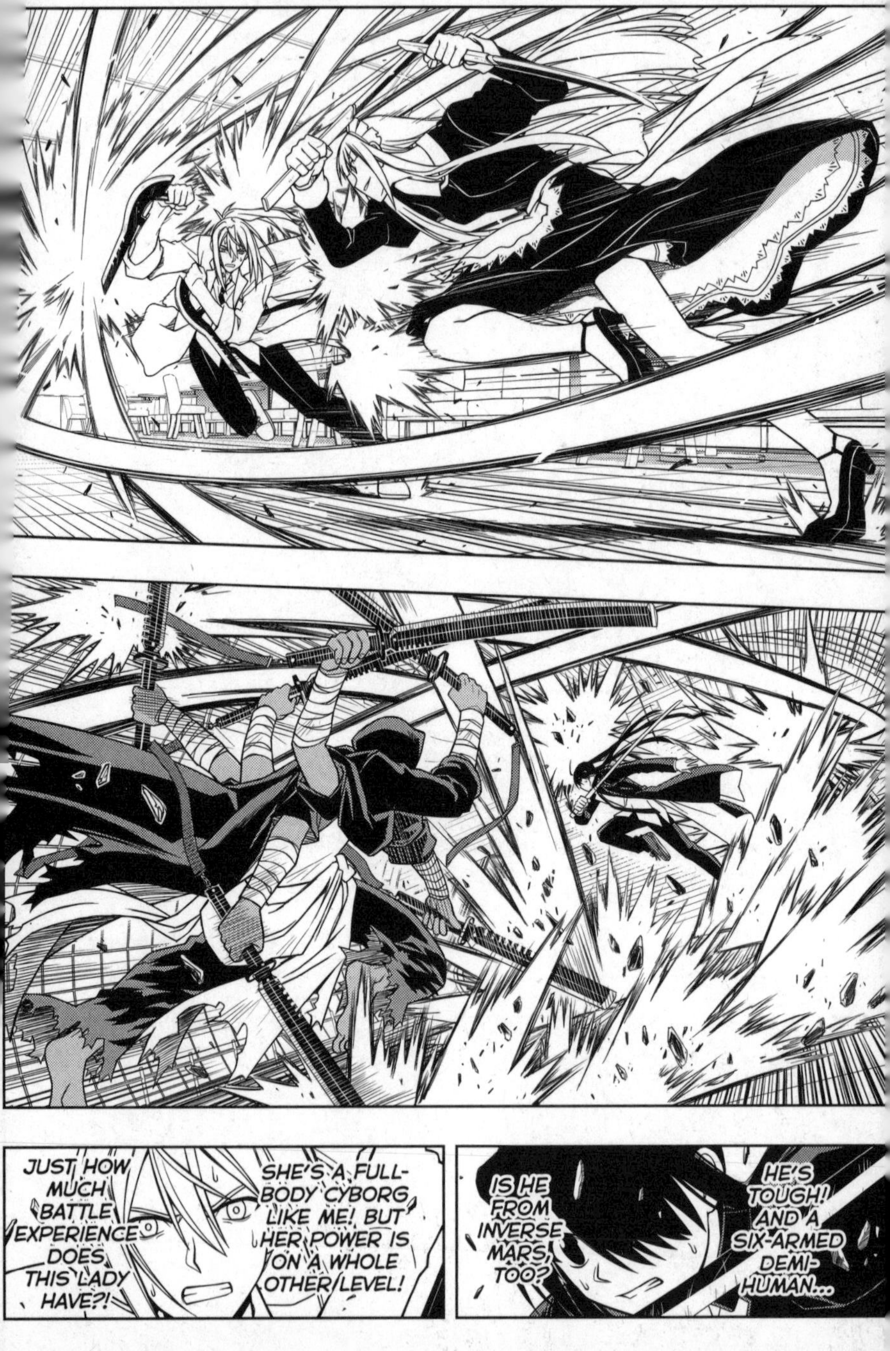
HE'S TOUGH! AND A SIX-ARMED DEMI-HUMAN...
IS HE FROM INVERSE MARS, TOO?
SHE'S A FULL-BODY CYBORG LIKE ME! BUT HER POWER IS ON A WHOLE OTHER LEVEL!
JUST HOW MUCH BATTLE EXPERIENCE DOES THIS LADY HAVE?!

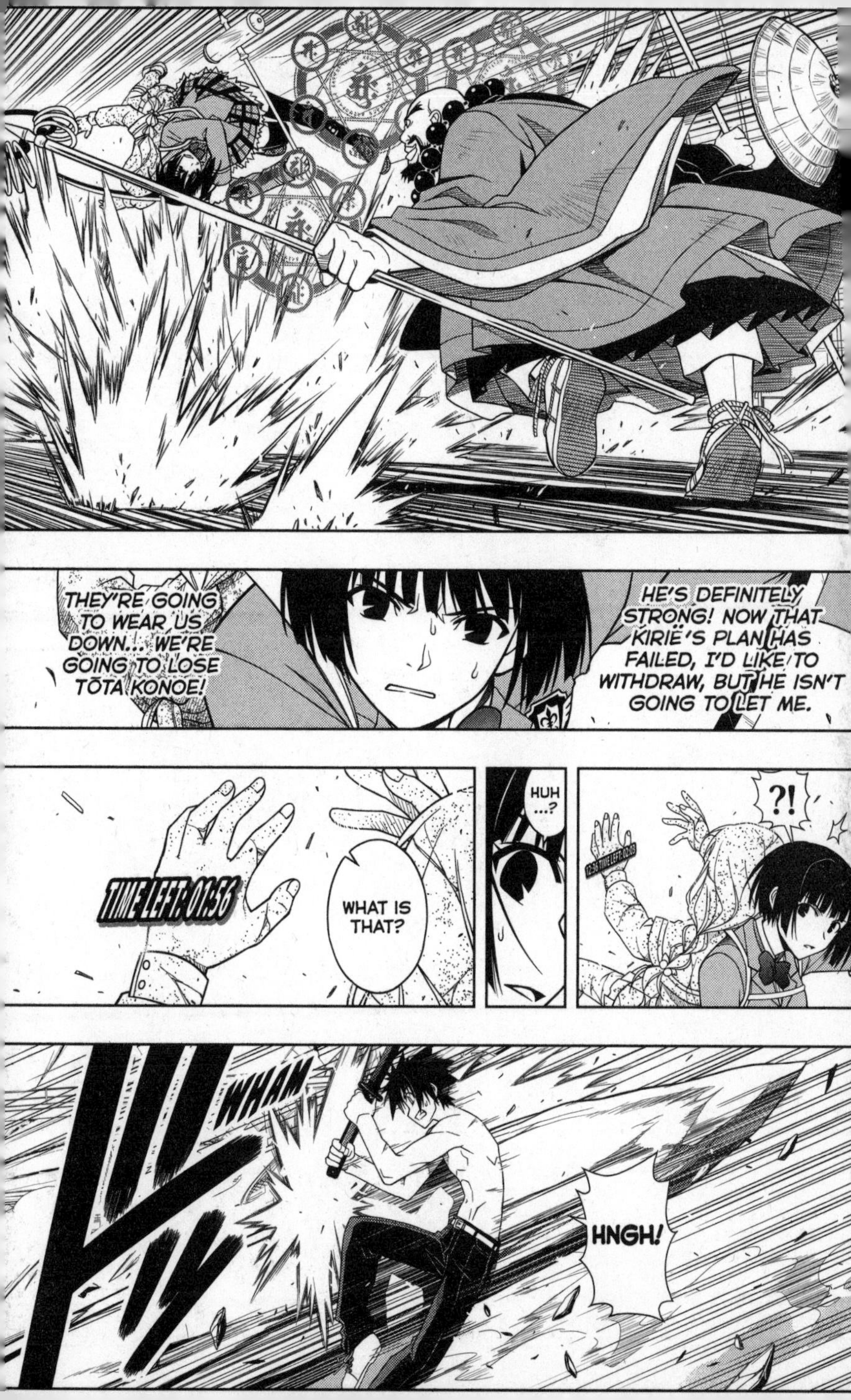
HE'S DEFINITELY STRONG! NOW THAT KIRIË'S PLAN HAS FAILED, I'D LIKE TO WITHDRAW, BUT HE ISN'T GOING TO LET ME.
THEY'RE GOING TO WEAR US DOWN... WE'RE GOING TO LOSE TŌTA KONOE!
?!
12:36 TIME LEFT: 02:03
HUH ...?
WHAT IS THAT?
TIME LEFT: 01:56
HNGH!
WHAM

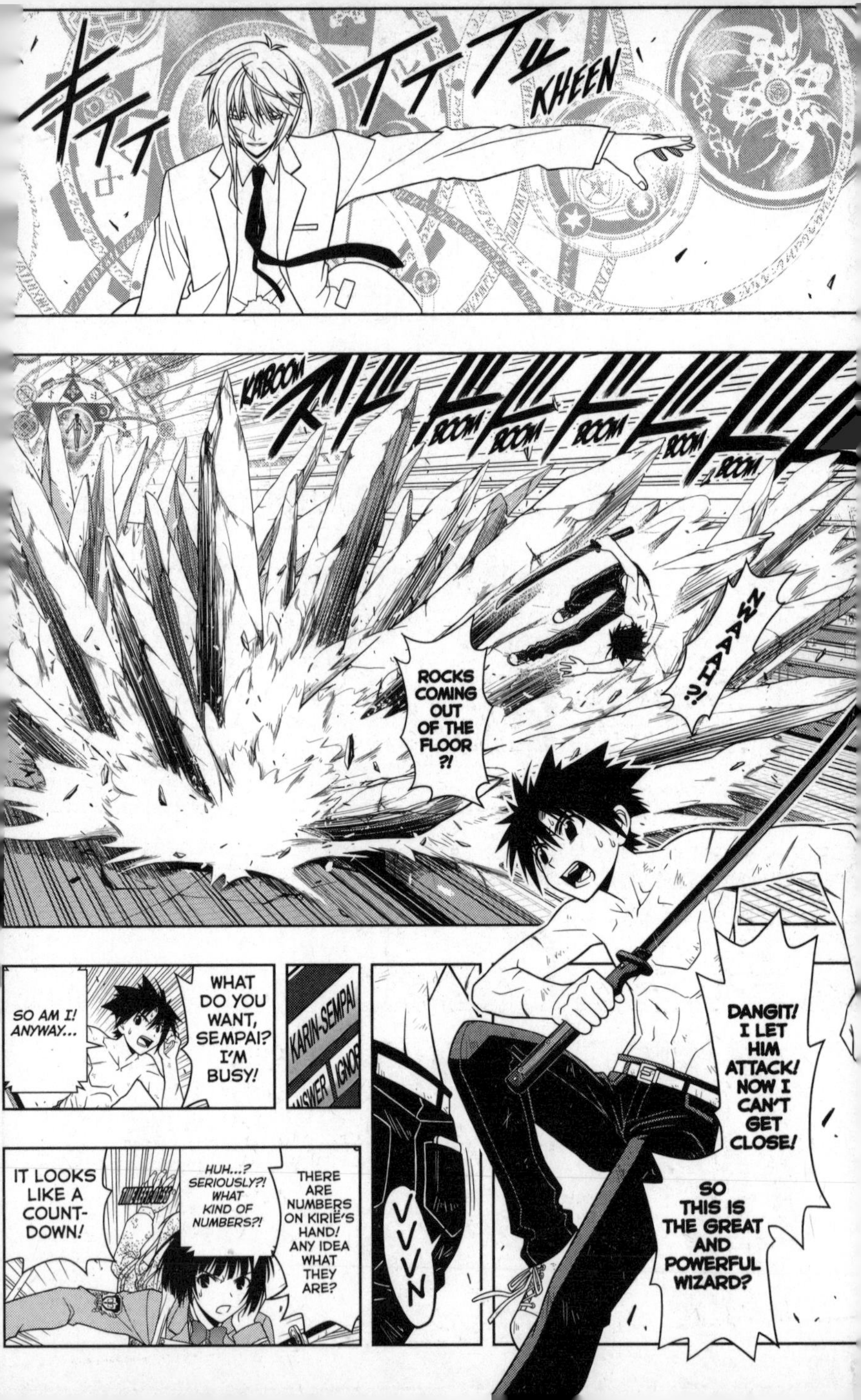
KHEEN
KABOOM
BOOM
BOOM
BOOM
BOOM
BOOM
WWAAH?!
ROCKS COMING OUT OF THE FLOOR?!
DANGIT! I LET HIM ATTACK! NOW I CAN'T GET CLOSE!
SO THIS IS THE GREAT AND POWERFUL WIZARD?
VVVN
KARIN-SEMPAI
ANSWER
IGNOR
WHAT DO YOU WANT, SEMPAI? I'M BUSY!
SO AM I! ANYWAY...
THERE ARE NUMBERS ON KIRIE'S HAND! ANY IDEA WHAT THEY ARE?
HUH...? SERIOUSLY?! WHAT KIND OF NUMBERS?!
IT LOOKS LIKE A COUNT-DOWN!

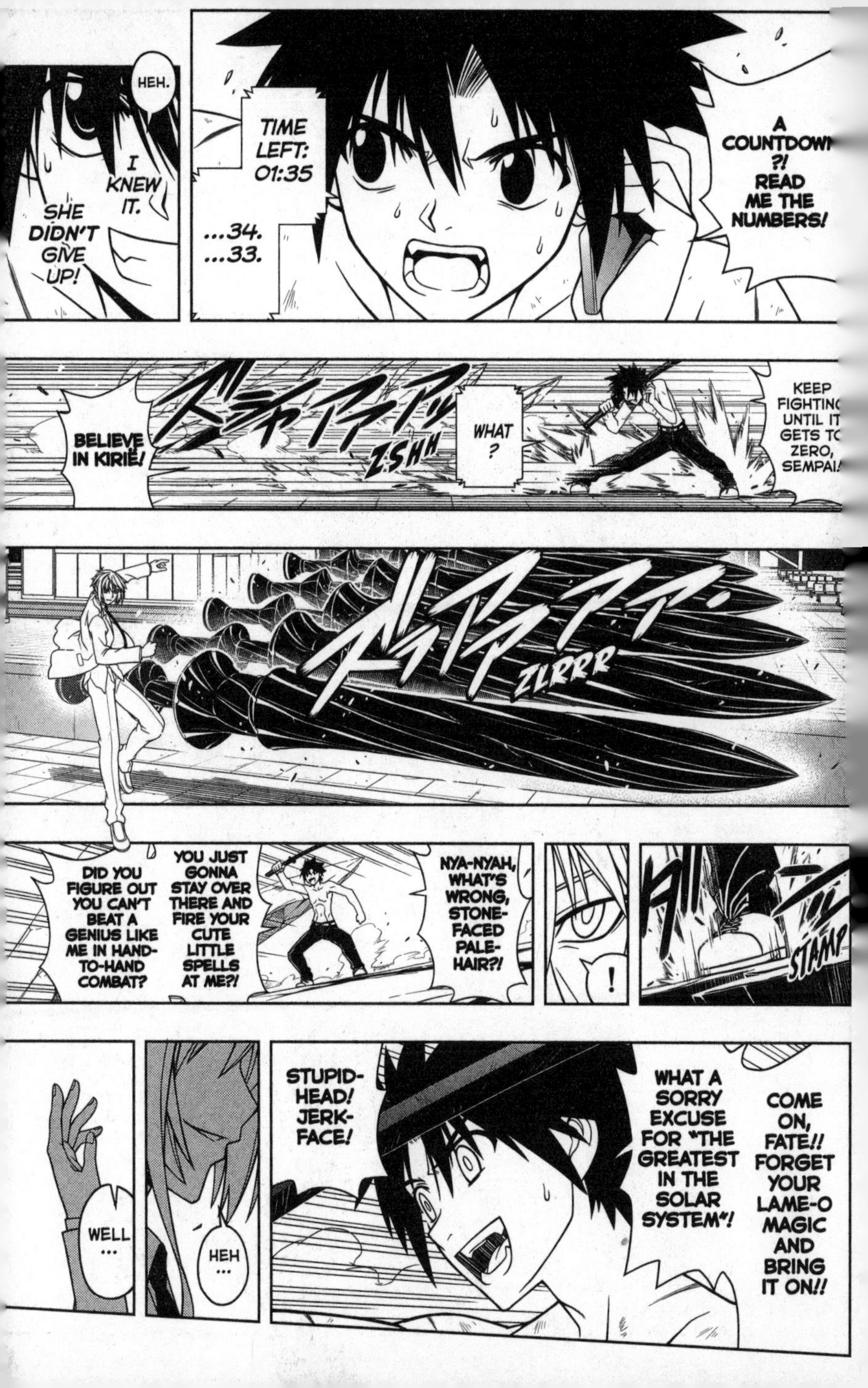
A COUNTDOWN?! READ ME THE NUMBERS!
TIME LEFT: 01:35
...34. ...33.
HEH.
I KNEW IT.
SHE DIDN'T GIVE UP!
KEEP FIGHTING UNTIL IT GETS TO ZERO, SEMPAI!
WHAT?
ZSHH
BELIEVE IN KIRIË!
ZLRRR
STAMP
!
NYA-NYAH, WHAT'S WRONG, STONE-FACED PALE-HAIR?!
YOU JUST GONNA STAY OVER THERE AND FIRE YOUR CUTE LITTLE SPELLS AT ME?!
DID YOU FIGURE OUT YOU CAN'T BEAT A GENIUS LIKE ME IN HAND-TO-HAND COMBAT?
COME ON, FATE!! FORGET YOUR LAME-O MAGIC AND BRING IT ON!!
WHAT A SORRY EXCUSE FOR "THE GREATEST IN THE SOLAR SYSTEM"!
STUPID-HEAD! JERK-FACE!
HEH ...
WELL ...

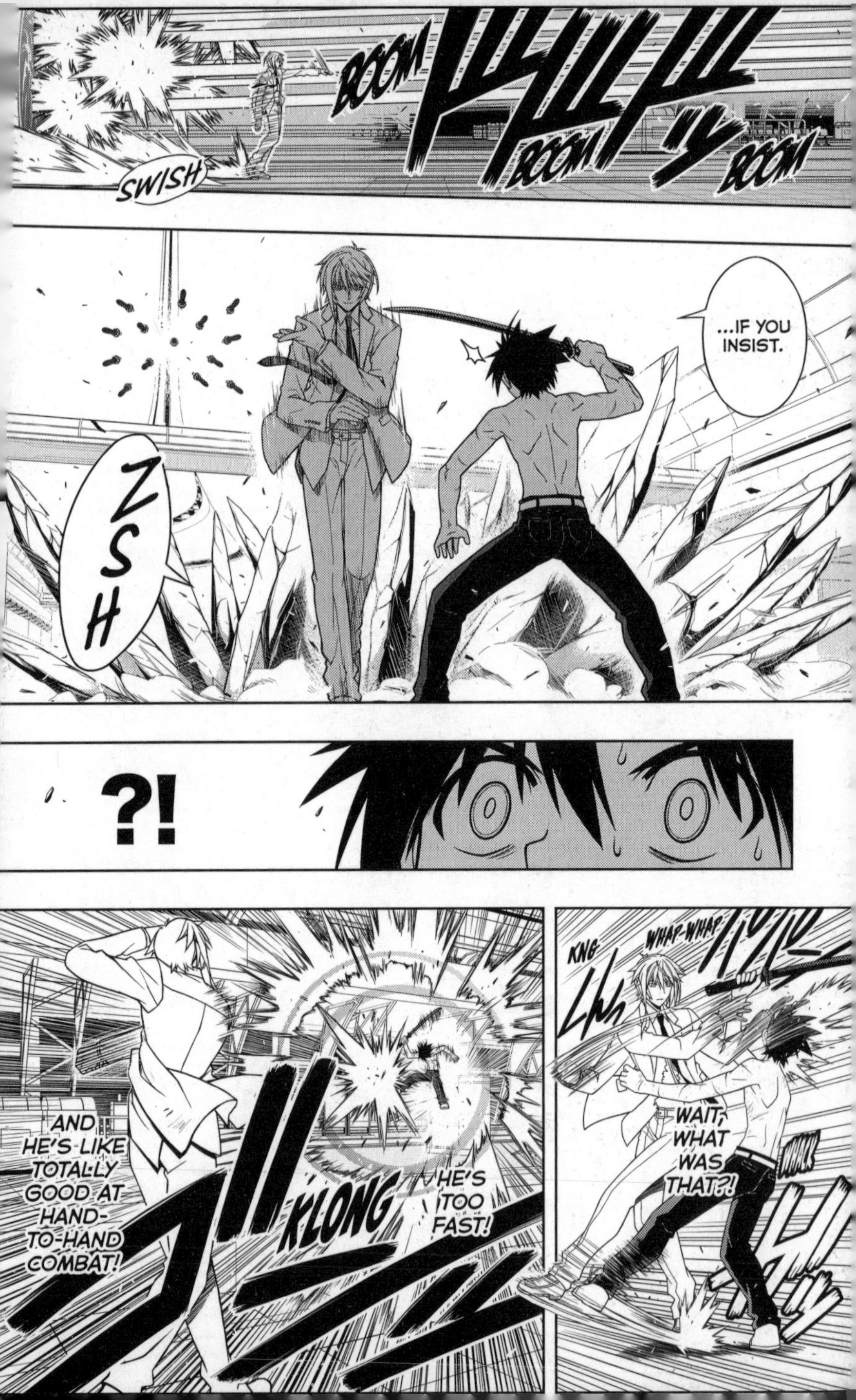
BOOM
BOOM
BOOM
BOOM
SWISH
...IF YOU INSIST.
ZSSH
?!
KNG
WHAP-WHAP
WAIT, WHAT WAS THAT?!
HE'S TOO FAST!
KLONG
AND HE'S LIKE TOTALLY GOOD AT HAND-TO-HAND COMBAT!

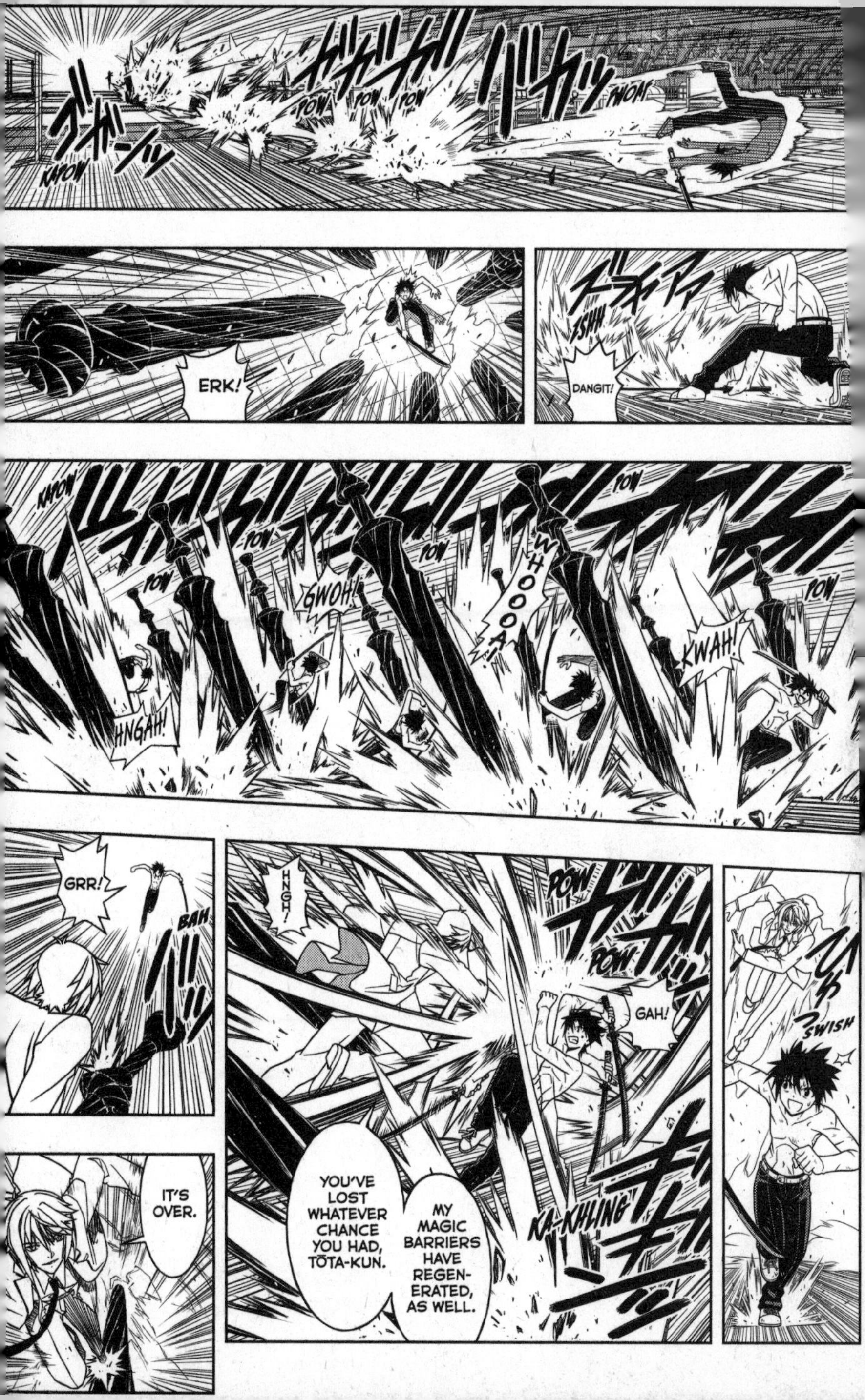
FWOAH
POW
POW
POW
KAYOW
TSHH
DANGIT!
ERK!
POW
POW
KWAH!
WHOOOOA!
POW
GWOH!
POW
POW
KAYOW
HNGAH!
SWISH
POW
POW
GAH!
HNGH!
YOU'VE LOST WHATEVER CHANCE YOU HAD, TŌTA-KUN.
MY MAGIC BARRIERS HAVE REGEN-ERATED, AS WELL.
KA-KHLING
GRR!
BAH
IT'S OVER.

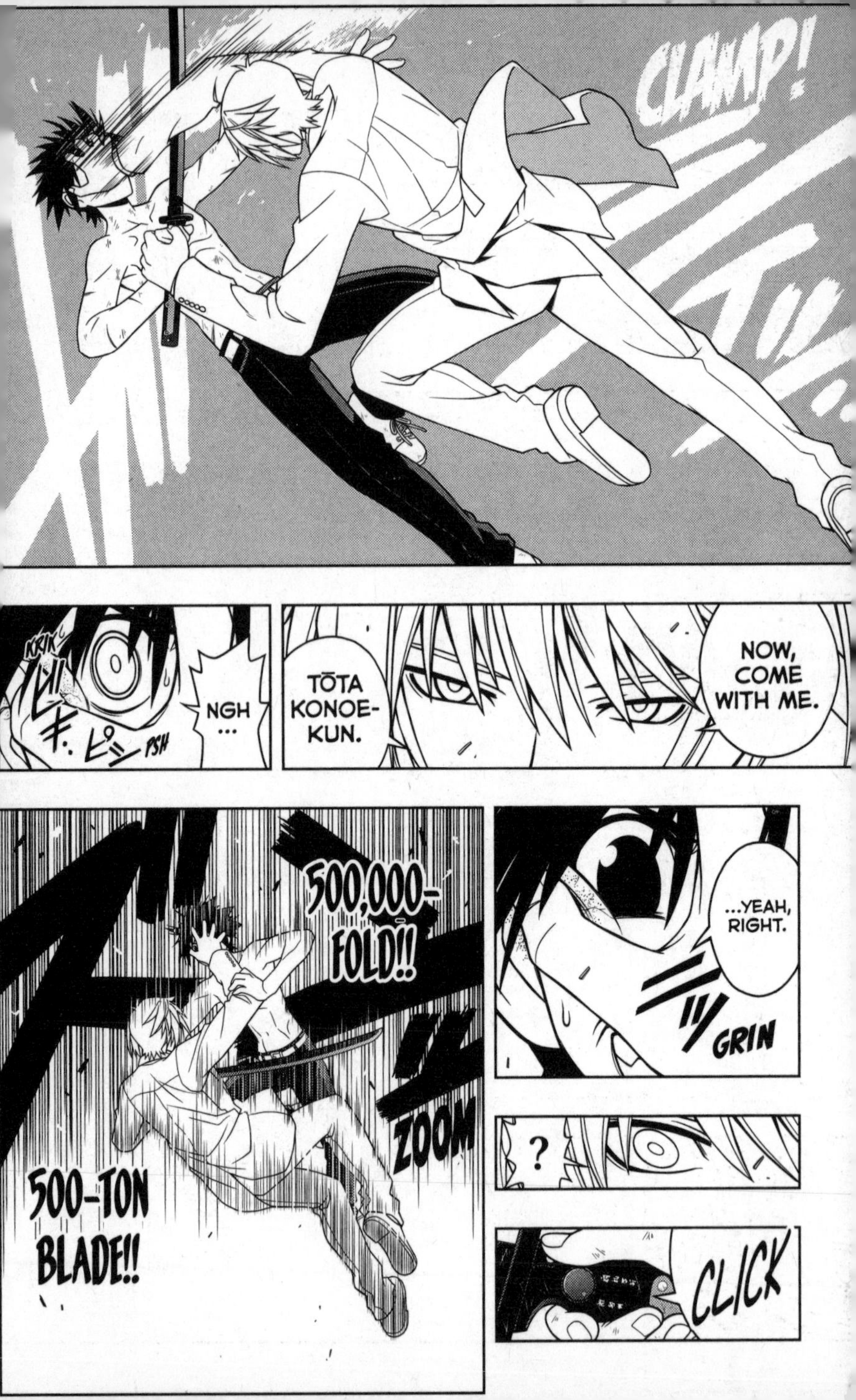
CLAMP!
NOW, COME WITH ME.
TŌTA KONOE-KUN.
KRIK
NGH...
PSH
...YEAH, RIGHT.
GRIN
?
CLICK
500,000-FOLD!!
ZOOM
500-TON BLADE!!

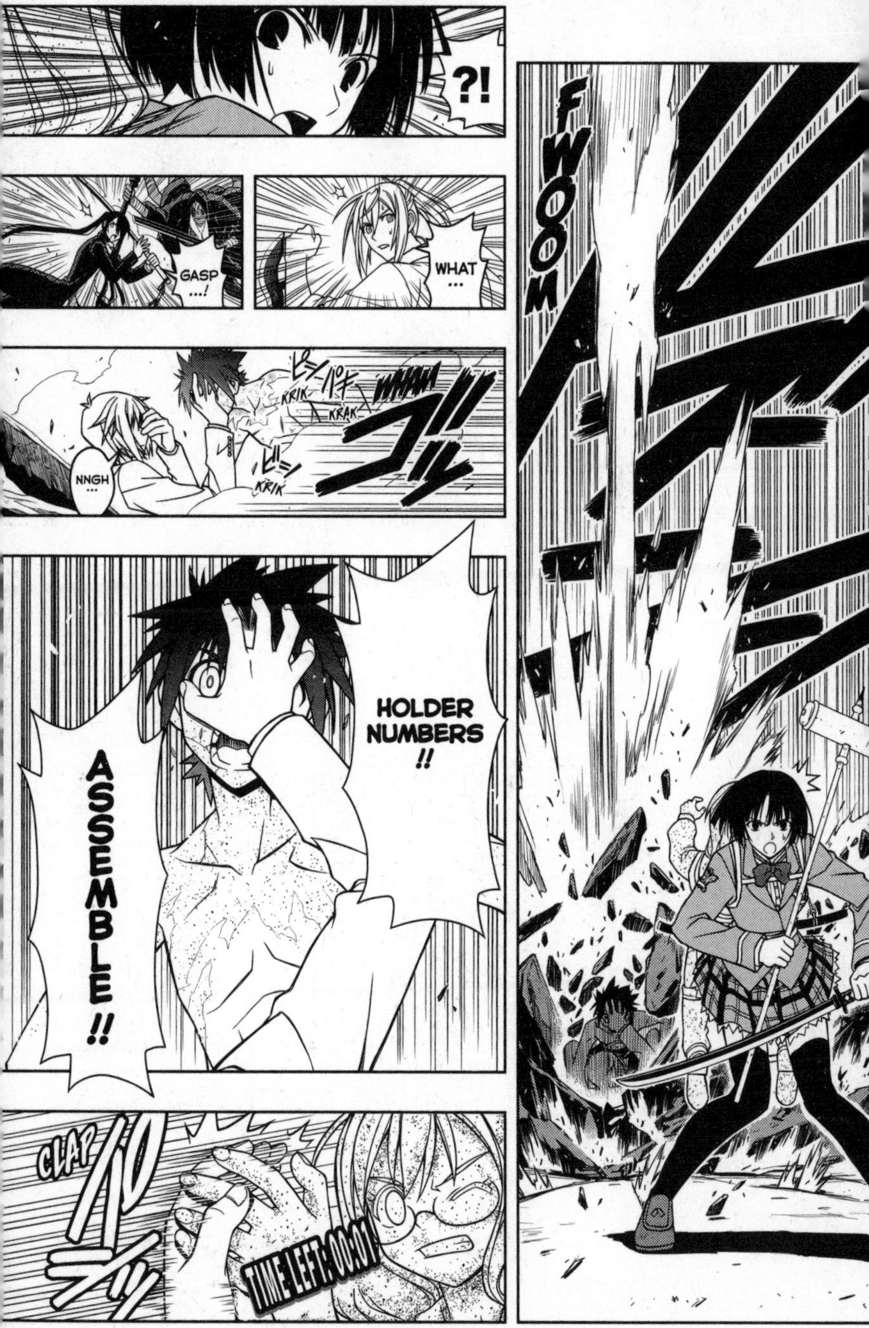
FWOOM
?!
WHAT ...
GASP ...!
KRIK
KRAK
KRIK
NNGH ...
HOLDER NUMBERS !!
ASSEMBLE !!
CLAP
TIME LEFT 00:01

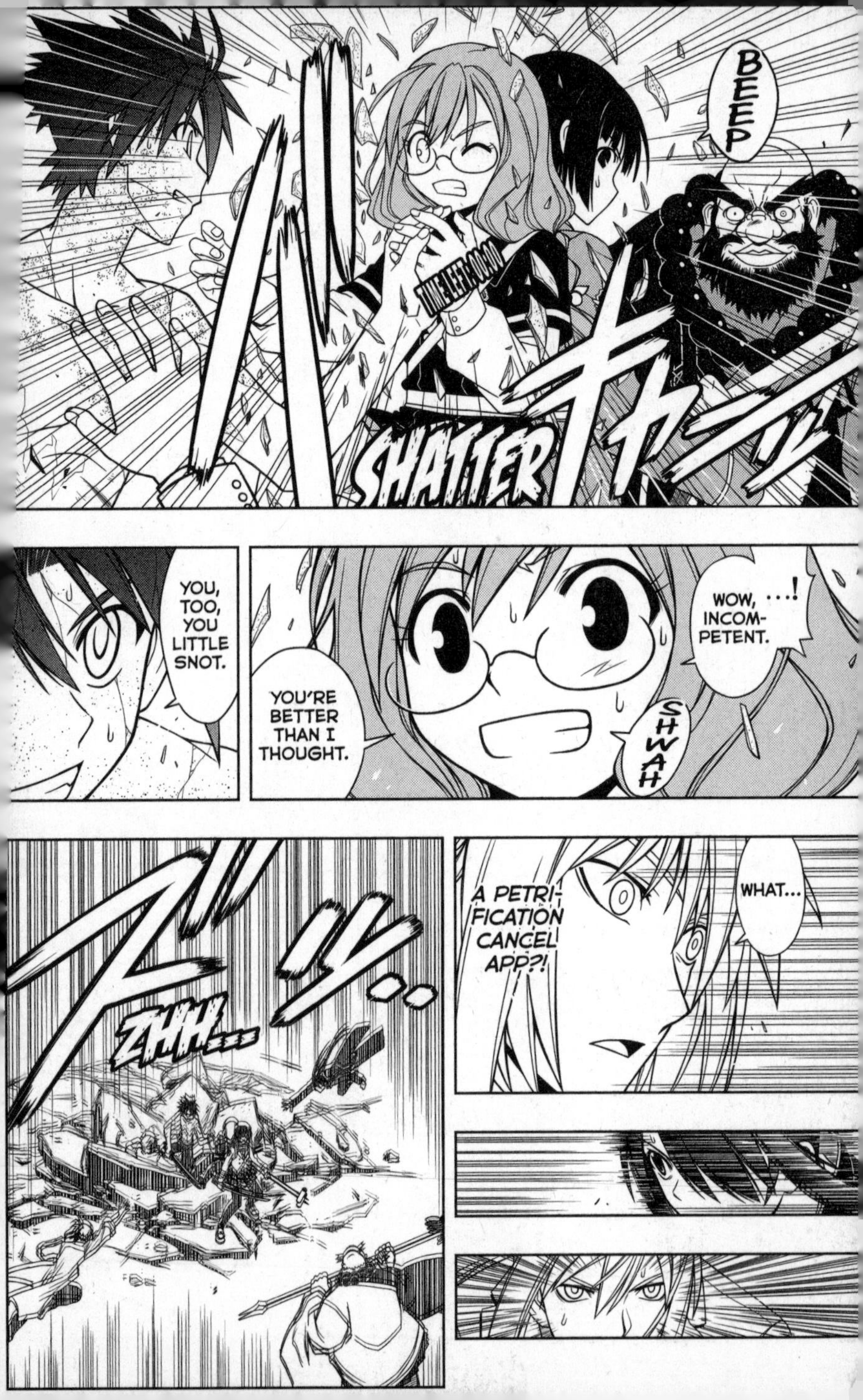
BEEP
TIME LEFT 00:00
SHATTER
...!
WOW, INCOMPETENT.
SHWAH
YOU'RE BETTER THAN I THOUGHT.
YOU, TOO, YOU LITTLE SNOT.
WHAT...
A PETRIFICATION CANCEL APP?!
ZHH...

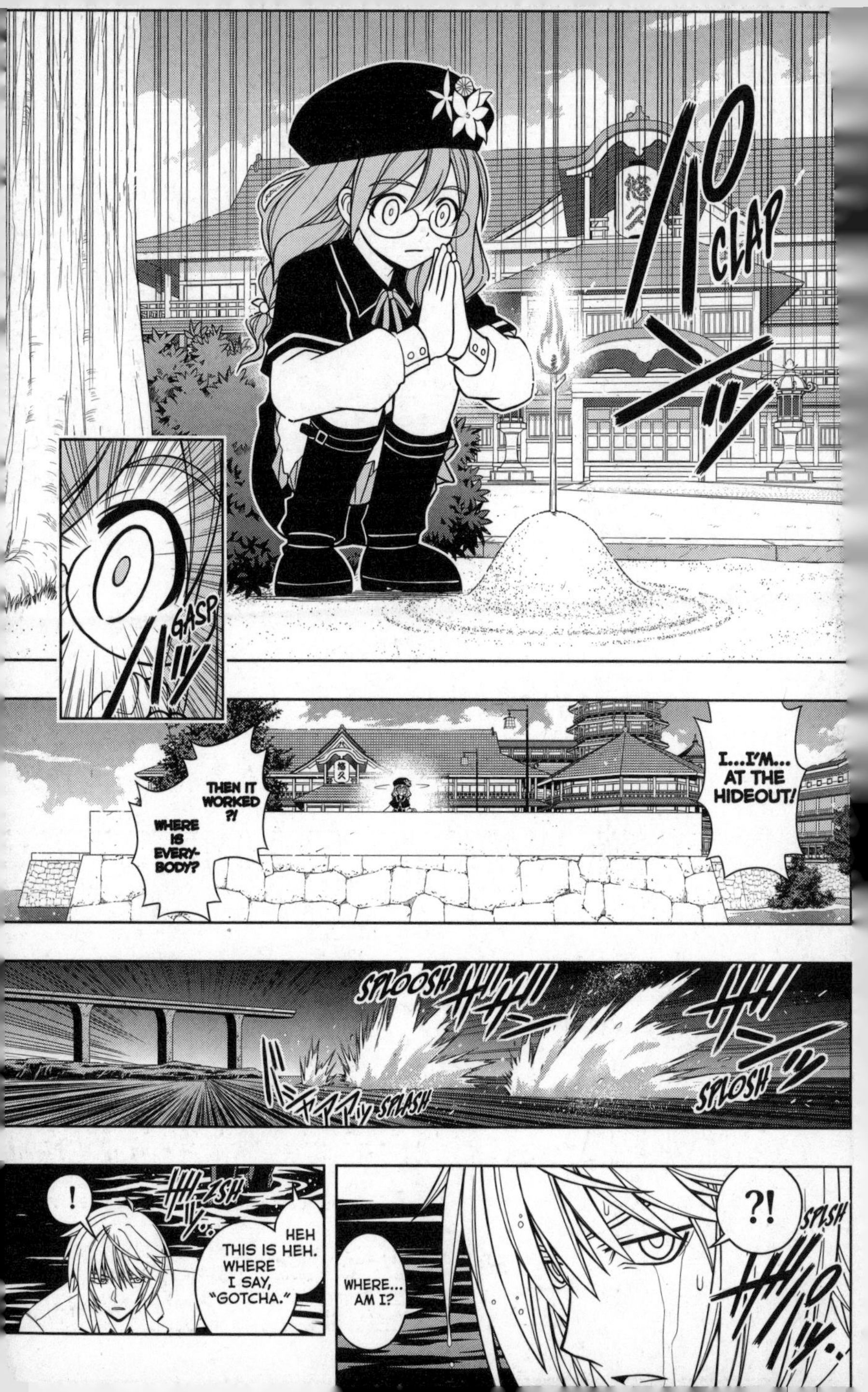
CLAP
GASP
I...I'M... AT THE HIDEOUT!
THEN IT WORKED?!
WHERE IS EVERYBODY?
SPLOSH
SPLOSH
SPLASH
?!
SPLSH
WHERE... AM I?
!
HEH HEH. THIS IS WHERE I SAY, "GOTCHA."

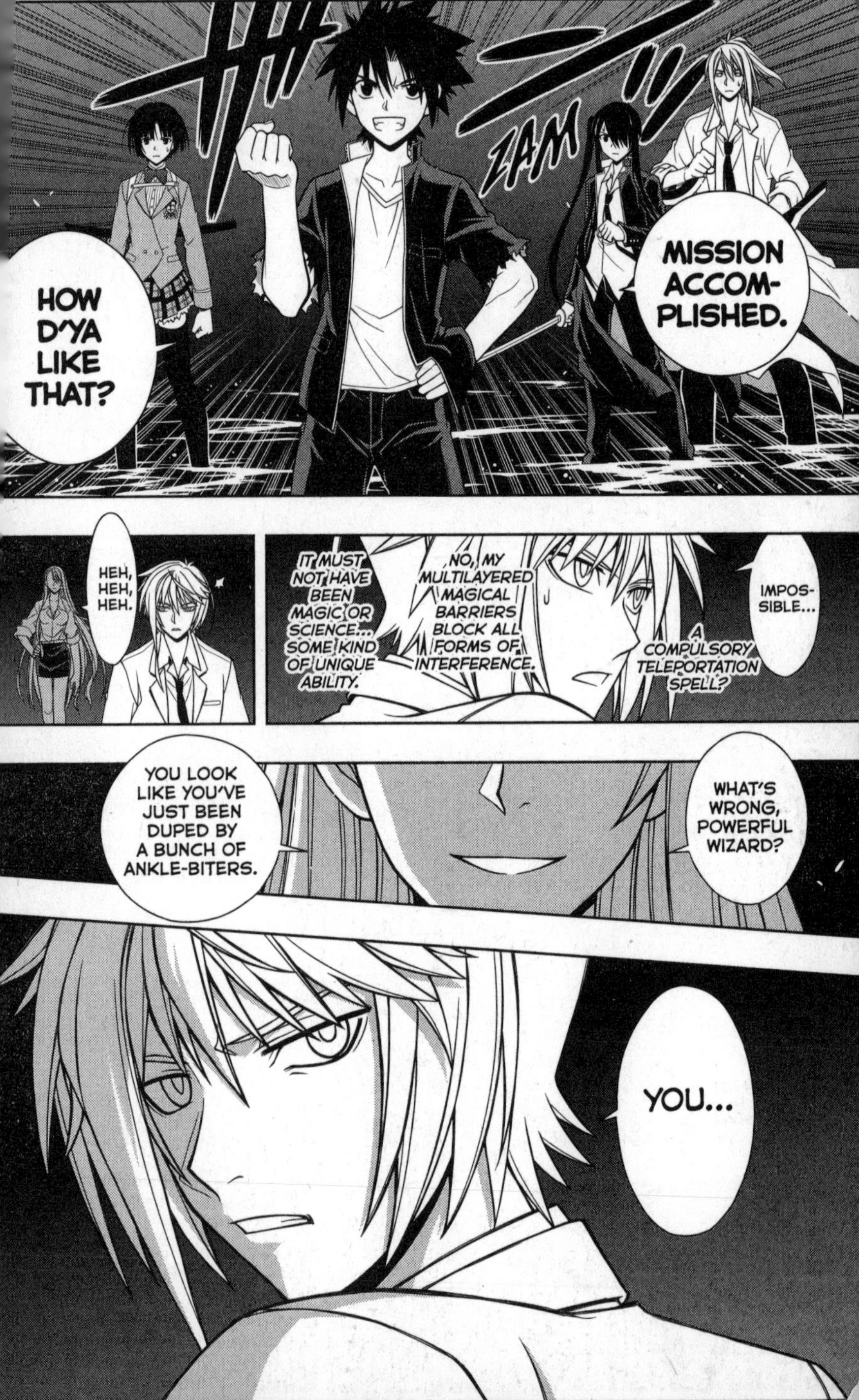
ZAM
MISSION ACCOMPLISHED.
HOW D'YA LIKE THAT?
IMPOSSIBLE...
A COMPULSORY TELEPORTATION SPELL?
NO, MY MULTILAYERED MAGICAL BARRIERS BLOCK ALL FORMS OF INTERFERENCE.
IT MUST NOT HAVE BEEN MAGIC OR SCIENCE... SOME KIND OF UNIQUE ABILITY.
HEH, HEH, HEH.
WHAT'S WRONG, POWERFUL WIZARD?
YOU LOOK LIKE YOU'VE JUST BEEN DUPED BY A BUNCH OF ANKLE-BITERS.
YOU...

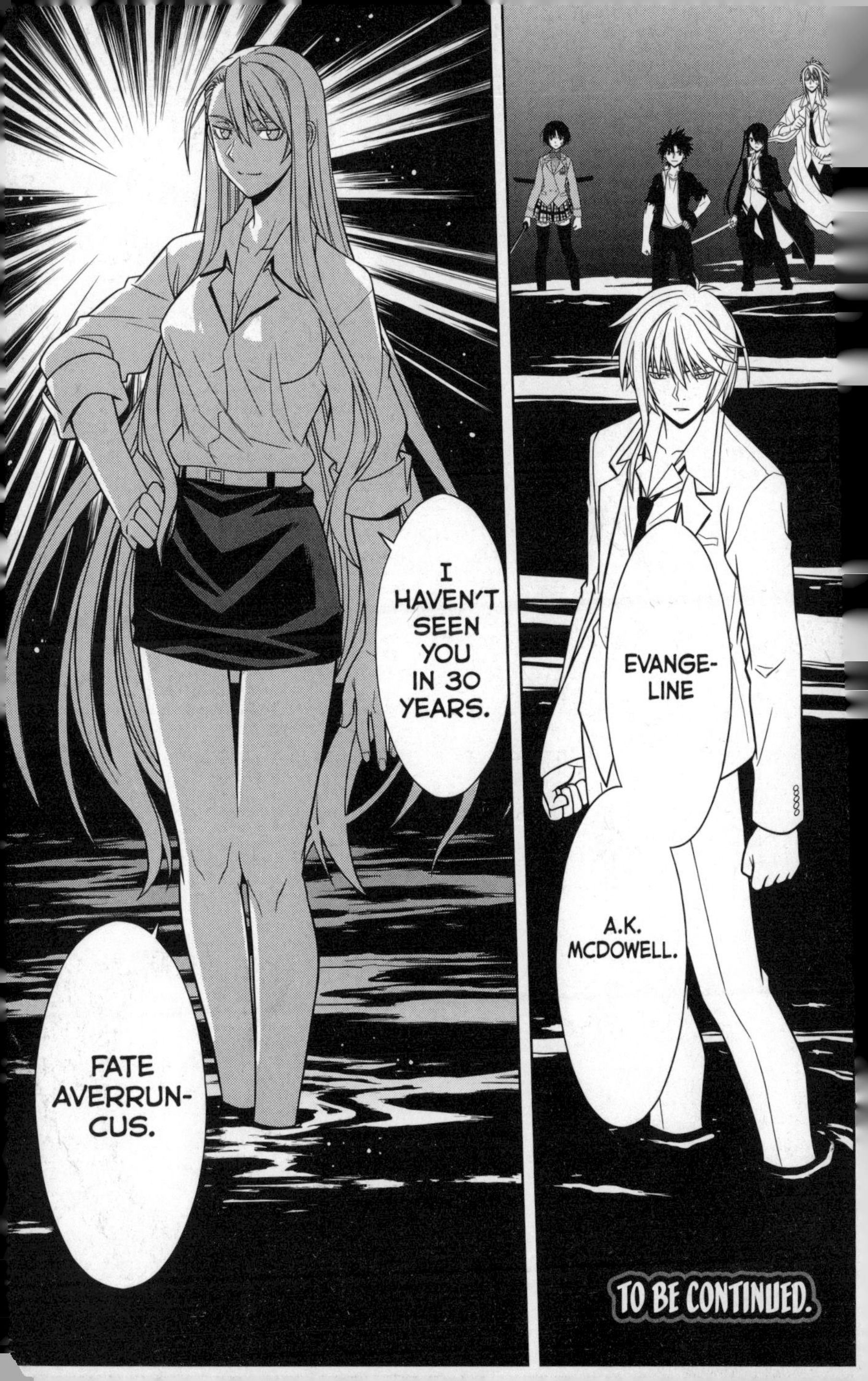
EVANGE-LINE
A.K. MCDOWELL.
I HAVEN'T SEEN YOU IN 30 YEARS.
FATE AVERRUN-CUS.
TO BE CONTINUED.

UQ HOLDER!

STAFF

Ken Akamatsu
Takashi Takemoto
Kenichi Nakamura
Keiichi Yamashita
Tohru Mitsuhashi
Susumu Kuwabara
Yuri Sasaki

Thanks to Ran Ayanaga

http://commonsphere.jp/doujin

UQ HOLDER! VOLUME 4 IS A WORK OF FICTION. NAMES, CHARACTERS, PLACES, AND INCIDENTS ARE THE PRODUCTS OF THE AUTHOR'S IMAGINATION OR ARE USED FICTITIOUSLY. ANY RESEMBLANCE TO ACTUAL EVENTS, LOCALES, OR PERSONS, LIVING OR DEAD, IS ENTIRELY COINCIDENTAL.

A KODANSHA COMICS TRADE PAPERBACK ORIGINAL

PUBLISHED IN THE UNITED STATES BY KODANSHA COMICS, AN IMPRINT OF KODANSHA USA PUBLISHING, LLC, NEW YORK.

PUBLICATION RIGHTS FOR THIS ENGLISH EDITION ARRANGED THROUGH KODANSHA LTD., TOKYO.

FIRST PUBLISHED IN JAPAN IN 2014 BY KODANSHA LTD., TOKYO.

ISBN 978-1-61262-832-5

PRINTED IN THE UNITED STATES OF AMERICA.

WWW.KODANSHACOMICS.COM

9 8 7 6 5 4 3 2 1

TRANSLATOR: ALETHEA NIBLEY AND ATHENA NIBLEY
LETTERING: JAMES DASHIELL